ISBN 978-0-483-00144-2
PIBN 10186213

This book is a reproduction of an important historical work. Forgotten Books uses
state-of-the-art technology to digitally reconstruct the work, preserving the original format
whilst repairing imperfections present in the aged copy. In rare cases, an imperfection in
the original, such as a blemish or missing page, may be replicated in our edition. We do,
however, repair the vast majority of imperfections successfully; any imperfections that
remain are intentionally left to preserve the state of such historical works.

THE WHOLE WORLD KIN:

A PIONEER EXPERIENCE AMONG REMOTE TRIBES,

AND OTHER LABORS

OF

NATHAN BROWN.

"Freedom is in the air; we inhale the gospel of a common brotherhood; the globe becomes one household, and all its members are kindred." N. BROWN, *Tokio, June 22, 1873.*

HUBBARD BROTHERS, PUBLISHERS,

PHILADELPHIA.

7516D24

A.286832

EXPLANATORY NOTE.

Packets of letters from the East India mail of fifty years ago, have furnished some pages of the accompanying record. The older dates are on thin, yellowed and crumbling square sheets, folded to form their own envelopes, which, instead of stamps, bear figures denoting enormous rates of postage. The gaps in these fast-vanishing traces are partially filled from family traditions; out of later correspondence and occasional brief diaries, an outline of the remaining years has been compiled, and a few descriptive settings of the narrative are based upon other reading, and memory. Grateful acknowledgment is here made to those who have forwarded letters for use and reference, and furnished personal recollections. Facts have also been obtained and extracts made from letters found in back volumes of the *Baptist Missionary Magazine.*

E. W. B.

PHILADELPHIA, July 15, 1890.

CONTENTS.

V.

MOULMEIN. 1833-34.

VI.

ALONG THE IRAWADI. 1834-5.

VII.

CHANGES. 1835.

VIII.

UP THE BRAHMAPUTRA. 1835-6.

XIV.

Removal to Jaipur. 1839.

XV.

Journey to Calcutta. 1840.

XVI.

In Weariness and Painfulness. 1840.

XVII.

Signs of Promise. 1841.

XVIII.

Life on Sibsagar Tank. 1841–55.

XXXVI.

SHADE AND SHEEN ON THE BLUFF. 1873–85.

XXXVII.

TRANSLATION AND PRINTING. 1873–85.

XXXVIII.

THE GOSPEL OF A COMMON BROTHERHOOD. 1873–85.

XXXIX.

THE TWILIGHT TASK. 1884–5.

XL.

THE DAWN OF A NEW YEAR. 1886.

LIST OF ILLUSTRATIONS.

Extracts, whose authorship is not indicated, are from letters or other writings of Rev. Nathan Brown.

PRONUNCIATION OF ASSAMESE VOWELS.

a, as in father.

e, as in prey.

i, as in machine.

ó, as o in chromo.

ú, as oo in poor.

ai, as in aisle.

au, as ow in now.

ONE day some seventy-five years ago, a little lad came out of the doorway of a low, unpainted farm-house in Vermont, with a sorrowful, yet determined expression on his face. He trudged along the country road alone for a considerable distance; his countenance growing more and more troubled as he proceeded, till at length overcome, apparently by fear or distress, he turned and ran home, the tears coursing down his cheeks. After being comforted and encouraged by his mother, he started out again, but was overcome and turned back as before. He had evidently undertaken some difficult or unpleasant business, but it was not given up; again he set out, furnished now with a trifling commission from his mother, to open the way for his own more serious errand. On he marched with more heart to the house of a rather remote neighbor. It was Mr. ——, an isolated, rough-mannered man, of whom the country people reported strange things; that he believed in no life apart from this green earth; that he had been heard to say he should come back as one of the birds, squirrels or cattle when done with this body; and worse than all, that the Bible was not true, and that there was no God! Filled with concern by these reports, the little boy had for some days been thinking the matter over; had become oppressed with a

(2)   (17)

sense of responsibility, and determined to visit the
atheist. His mother had noticed his seriousness, discovered his plan, and, fearing that he might encounter
harshness and profanity, had tried to dissuade him from
going, till, finding that the idea was a fixed conscientious
purpose, she had at length consented, and the child had
set out on his errand. At last the two-mile walk along
the hilly road was accomplished ; the house was reached,
and the mother's message delivered. The real object
of the visit was then disclosed by the question, "Mr.
——, *do you believe the Bible ?*" "No ; no more than
I believe in the dog's barking." Not daunted by this
blunt negative, the little missionary commenced trying
to convince the unbeliever that there is a God. "Who
the d— sent you here to tell me that?" was the angry
retort. "Nobody sent me," returned the boy, "but I
came to tell you THERE IS A GOD." He said it as he
would have told a blind man there is a sun ; and then
turned homeward, his mission accomplished, his mind
at rest.

The lad's home was on a farm not many miles from
the Massachusetts line ; his parents were Nathan and
Betsey Goldsmith Brown. They had left New Ipswich,
N. H., about a year after the birth there, on June 22,
1807, of this their first child, Nathan, to occupy a log-
cabin high up on the breezy hills of the " wilderness
town " of Whitingham, Vt. The five Brown brothers,
Josiah, Joseph, Jonas, Amos and Nathan, who removed
from New Ipswich to Whitingham between 1795 and
1810, did a good share of that " drudgery divine,"
which changed these forests into well-kept farms. Their
plows had at first encountered about equal proportions
of stone, stump and soil, but the excellent quality of the
mold, enriched by many a yearly layer of maple, beech
and birch leaves, vindicated their good judgment in se-
lecting this spot ; and muscle, "grit " and patience,

inherited from their father, Josiah Brown, overcame all obstacles. The following is part of a newspaper paragraph found pasted in a manuscript book of family records:

"Just before the revolutionary war broke out, two brothers, John and Josiah Brown, then young men, removed with their families from Concord, Mass., to New Ipswich, N. H., and settled near each other on new land situated on a high elevation called 'Flat Mountain.' They carried with them strength, energy, patriotism and strong religious faith. Here, in this new country, they felled the trees, cleared up the forests, and in due time made for themselves and families comfortable homes. They both reared large families of children, whose numerous descendants are now scattered far and wide throughout the land. John and Josiah traced their lineage back to John Brown, who came over to this country [to Plymouth] a few years after his brother Peter of the Mayflower, and settled in Duxbury, Mass. Old John Brown, the martyr, whose soul is marching on, was probably a descendant of Peter of the Mayflower. Josiah Brown married Sarah Wright, and they raised a family of twelve children, who lived to adult age, several of whom settled in Whitingham."

A characteristic incident is related of this unconquerable old man, young Nathan's grandfather. When about eighty years old he was visiting his son Nathan at Whitingham, and one day saw ten or twelve men at work near the house repairing the road where it was rendered dangerous by a very large rock, which lay partly above the surface. The neighbors had supposed it impossible to remove this obstruction, but he undertook to convince them to the contrary. He helped the men dig round the rock and place crowbars in position. All then laid hold ; the old man gave a tight grip to his own bar, and said in a voice of thunder, "*Think men*

are mice? Take right hold and turn it over. *Heave-
oh !"* The aroused spirit of Bunker Hill sent the
boulder flying from the path. Josiah Brown had, in his
younger days, seen active military service, being first
lieutenant of a company of New Ipswich minute-men at
the breaking out of the revolutionary war. On the
memorable 19th of April, 1775, he happened to be in
Lowell. Hearing the news, he at once rode home to
New Ipswich, collected his company, marched all night
and reached Acton for breakfast; did not overtake the
enemy, but went on and enlisted for eight months.
He fought in the battle of Bunker Hill, where his company (Capt. Towne's) did sharp execution, being good
marksmen and having the wind in their favor. They
were the last company to leave the field, and Lieutenant
Brown believed he fired the final shot before the retreat.

It was this same grandfather whose resolute right
hand wore the blue mitten once famous in New Ipswich
town-meetings. It became a common saying in regard
to undecided voters, that "they always waited till they
saw the blue mitten go up."

New England farms of the pioneer period were good
training-schools for the tougher fibers of character. The
farmer-boy, almost as soon as he walked at all, toddled
through the blast-blown wintry drifts to the barn to look
after his favorite horses, heifers and sheep. When large
enough to shoulder an axe, he strode to the wood-lot
with his father or brothers, his brave laugh ringing out
on a cutting icy wind; and moonlight nights found him
with his comrades shooting down the dizzy hill-slopes on
a home-made sled. As years passed, he settled into
steady hardihood. On those same slopes he learned to
plow, hoe and reap for fourteen hours a day, under a
sun whose rays struck perpendicularly the soil he trod.

Nathan Brown was one of these farmer-boys. As
soon as he was old enough to work, his father's sixty-

five acres of woodland, sugar-orchard, grain, grass, flax and potato fields gave him enough to do, and a vigorous constitution was built up, enabling him to excel in athletic exploits. In ball-playing, leaping with a pole to the eaves of a house, diving and remaining under water, his strength was equal to any of his playmates. Before his young eyes, nature presented an aspect of grand wildness. The furious primeval forces that snapped those rocky ribs and dashed the huge boulders into their places, seemed ready at any moment to wake from sleep; and there must have been a fascination to an adventurous boy in the jagged cliff, dark gorge, and especially the trout-yielding mountain brook.

Whitingham Center, now a deserted village, whose unoccupied, storm-wrecked old buildings serve only to mark its site, was in its prime during the youth of Nathan Brown. From the surrounding hills, farmers came to the village to dispose of their produce, and during the business season, its street and stores were daily a scene of lively traffic and social chat. The old meeting-house was erected by the town in 1798, for the double purpose of a place of worship and a town-house. The several denominations, Congregationalist, Universalist, Methodist and Baptist—to the latter of which the five Brown brothers belonged as did their father before them—had equal rights in the building, and used it in turn. "Seldom a Sabbath passed in the pleasant season of the year, but that from three to four hundred devout worshippers would attend meeting at the old church, then the common center of attraction for the whole town." *

The Brown brothers were active in building up a church of their own faith and order, of which Jonas and Nathan were chosen deacons. The latter was ordained to that office by council, January 8, 1817, and served the

---

* History of Whittingham, by Leonard Brown.

church as long as he continued to live in Whitingham. On the 5th of August, 1816, an interested company had assembled on the bank of a small stream near Deacon Nathan Brown's house and witnessed the baptism, on profession of his faith, of his son Nathan, then nine years old. "My first religious impressions," the latter wrote some time after, "were very early; as far back as I can remember, serious thoughts occupied my mind." He seems to have felt almost from infancy, the sharp distinctions of right and wrong. "Did I *steal* this?" the little fellow asked his mother one day, holding up a pretty stick thrown away by some carpenters at work on a neighbor's house, and was so distressed that nothing would pacify him till he had gone back and returned his treasure. When first sent to school, at about six years of age, he was taught the catechism on Saturdays, as was the custom. When he comprehended that there was a great Being who could see him, but was himself unseen, the idea overpowered him. On going home he asked his mother: "Where is God?" and immediately burst into tears, awed and afraid under the conception of an invisible, almighty Power. He took in the Bible histories with a vivid grasp, and, child-like, made them all his own. One day his mother found him patiently sitting in an apple-tree, and on inquiry found that he had heard about Zaccheus, and, like him, was waiting "to see the Lord go by." During the summer in which he was nine years old, there had been a revival of religious interest in the neighborhood. Little Nathan had attended the meetings and felt, like the Pilgrim Christian, a great burden of sinfulness weighing upon him, from which he knew not how to escape, till, one day, while reading Watts' Hymns, he came to the verse:

> "Come hither, all ye weary souls,
>   Ye heavy-laden sinners, come;
> I'll give you rest from all your toils,
>   And raise you to my heavenly home."

"I thought the promise was mine," he afterwards wrote; "I felt that I could come to Christ and give my soul into his hands. I took great comfort in reading the word of God, in singing hymns and prayer. Sometimes I felt that I wanted to lie awake all night, singing and praising God. At this time I was baptized and joined the church."

That the mother's influence was no small factor in the development of Nathan's character, may already have been inferred. Her son William writes: "She was the very soul and life of prayer-meetings. . . . My brother's spirituality, strong feeling of opposition to oppression and sympathy with the weak, I think were, in a great measure, received from the mother." An act of cruelty was sure to bring the flash to her eye and a protest to her lips, which had their source in a true feminine tenderness. "No animal could be abused without her remonstrance, heedless of the curses rained upon her by heartless drivers." The familiar lines entitled "Mother, Home and Heaven," written by her younger son,* show what this mother must have been to her boys.

"Three words fall sweetly on my soul
    As music from an angel lyre;
They bid my spirit spurn control
    And upward to its source aspire;
The sweetest sounds to mortals given,
    Are found in Mother, Home and Heaven.

---

* William Goldsmith Brown, the author of "A Hundred Years to Come," also of " Roanoke," " Before Petersburg " and other war lyrics, was born in Whittingham, Vt., March 3, 1812, and is now living at Stevens Point, in Wisconsin, the last surviving member of the family.

Dear Mother! ne'er shall I forget
　Thy brow, thine eye, thy pleasant smile!
Though in the sea of death has set
　Thy star of life, my guide awhile,
Oh, never shall thy form depart
　From the bright pictures in my heart!

And like a bird, that from the flowers,
　Wing-weary, seeks her wonted rest,
My spirit, e'en in manhood's hours,
　Turns back in childhood's Home to rest;
The cottage, garden, hill and stream
　Still linger like a pleasant dream.

And while to one engulfing grave
　By time's swift tide we're driven,
How sweet the thought that every wave
　But bears us nearer Heaven!
There we shall meet, when life is o'er,
　In that blest Home, to part no more."

The atmosphere which surrounded the happy group
of children in the Whitingham farm–house was a healthful one. While their frolics and inventions gave life to
"cottage, garden, hill and stream," they were growing
up into the mould of such homely virtues as industry,
honesty and kindness. While Nathan's father and
uncles were serving their fellow-townsmen as select-
men, school supervisors and representatives to the legis-
lature, no doubt the discussion of town affairs heard by
the growing lad aided in his education and that of his
brother and sisters, Sophia, William and Nancy. Farm
life itself, with its varied employments, was more picturesque and exciting than it can be in the present generation. First, a comfortable home must be built to
take the place of the log–cabin of the pioneers. Meantime not only the food, but the clothing of the family
was raised from the soil and manufactured at home.

Fields of flax were cultivated to supply material for the family linen, which, as well as the wool, was spun and woven at the homestead. Firm and substantial clothing was thus provided, but the children could not eat the bread of idleness. and even their beloved books must often be read by snatches. What wonder that one of the Waverley novels proved more attractive to Sophia than the spinning-wheel, and was laughingly unearthed from the heap of rolls of wool where the mother had hidden it, or that the " Scottish Chiefs" accompanied Nathan and William to the field and rendered but indifferent assistance in clearing it of rocks ? One of the pleasant memories of this home life dates still farther back and shows the two older children in the sugar-orchard, entrusted with the boiling of maple sap. Nathan built a comfortable booth of hemlock boughs for Sophia, and within it the hours passed swiftly, while the brother and sister bent over the same book undisturbed, except perhaps, by the occasional boiling over of the sap.

The district school-house stood a few rods from the homestead, and to it the sturdy older brother led the little one, the pet of the family and the school. The latter was destined by the parents for a professional life ; but it was decided that Nathan, being hearty and strong, should be a farmer, and accordingly, at a suitable age, he performed field-work during the summer months and attended school in winter. This prospective farmer, however, was sometimes discovered perched in a tree studying, when, after their "nooning," the hay-makers were summoned to the field ; and after work, at evening, his mind, like a bent bow, sprang back to the interrupted train of thought. When possible, study and labor were combined, and Nathan might be seen chopping wood with a book beside him, held open at the place with a chip. An occasional glance at the open page, and the chopping would go briskly on, while the lesson was thus committed to memory to the tune of " My Good Old Axe." It was perhaps the same axe which his poet-brother afterwards had in mind when he wrote :

" This good old axe my grandsire bought
    In by-gone days of honest toil,
When men at manual labor wrought,
    Nor feared their brawny hands to soil
By wearing homespun on their backs,
    And swinging thee, thou good old axe !"

The oxen plowing in the field must have wondered one day, when Nathan sent William off fishing and seated himself by the plow to study, on the plea that the cattle ought to have a rest ! Such oddities gave rise to consultations on the part of the father and mother, which resulted in a gradual change of plan. and the opening of less irregular, though still difficult, footpaths up the hill of science. Nathan had come quite early into possession of a greatly valued treasure by the discovery, among his father's books, of a copy of " Æsop's Fables," with the Latin and English printed in parallel columns. Afterwards, in order to advance in Latin and be introduced to the fascinating mysteries of Algebra, the lad walked daily, one winter, through the drifts to Sadauga.

He was now about fourteen ; the serious business of life had begun ; his mind was absorbed in the world of thought and discovery which opened out before him. His sister remembers that when their young companions came to visit them, Nathan, after starting his guests in some game, would withdraw to another part of the room and become so absorbed in study as to be oblivious of all that was going on around him. Once, full of mischief, the little girl crept behind and drew away the book from his hand. He remained all unconscious ; the train of thought went on undisturbed till the volume had to be consulted and was missed; then his bewildered expression, as he looked at his hands, heard the shout of laughter, and slowly came to realize the situation, was the best part of the evening's entertainment.

College began next to be thought of. An arrangement was entered into with "Priest"* Wood, a venerable, white-haired pastor in the adjoining town of Halifax, by which Nathan was to reside with that clergyman, be fitted by him for college, and in return, cut and saw wood, and do other "chores" about the premises. In addition, he guarded at night the village store, which had been recently robbed by burglars, sleeping there with pistols and a watch-dog. In the intervals of his studies at Halifax and Williamstown, the young student taught school, his first term being at Monroe, Mass., when he -was fifteen years old. Among his pupils in these early efforts there were some much older than himself; but a natural aptness and a good-humored manner won him their respect. He had already attained a man's ordinary height, and weighed 150 lbs.

He was seventeen when admitted to Williams College as sophomore. Three busy years followed. In his case, as in that of probably the majority of his fellow-students, it was necessary to economize both time and money. Alma Mater herself was, in those days, a plain, homespun young matron. The buildings were unadorned, the domestic arrangements simple. The wood-shed did duty as gymnasium, where saw-horse, saw and hatchet constituted a most effective apparatus, while pails of water brought by the pupils for household use from the spring at the foot of the hill, served well for lifting-weights. The lads were up betimes; prayers

---

* Rev. Thomas H. Wood. The Congregational minister of those days was commonly entitled " Priest; " the Baptist, " Elder."

and a part of the recitations came before breakfast, and in winter by candle-light. During the long winter vacation some of the students taught district schools in neighboring towns ; the summer term continued through July and August, and commencement took place in September.

Those were happy days. Nathan's favorite study was mathematics. With some ten or a dozen of his class, and a few of the class above, he joined in forming a mathematical club for the invention and solution of original problems. Sometimes he would study a fortnight on a problem rather than give it up, a circumstance which it is believed never occurred. In the "Mathematical Stork Society," as the club was called, his initiatory name was the " Crowbar of Mathematics," while his room-mate, Wheeler, was the "Kingfisher of Triangles ;" John Morgan, or the "Grand Stork of Intellect," of the class above, being president. The boys used to say, so it is reported, that "when a problem was proposed, the Owl of Science would come and look at the rock, the Master of Infinitesimals would dig under it, but the Crowbar would have it out in a jiffy." His brother remembers seeing him "making observations on the stars, in the vacations, with an old, disused pump-log, or at the bottom of a well. He made at that time an almanac foretelling eclipses, etc."

A singular occurrence is connected with his spring vacation of 1825. He was attending church at Whitingham, on a Sunday forenoon, when he fell into a reverie, strangely fancying that Graves—his room-mate that term—was dead, and that he was appointed to deliver his funeral oration. He had no idea that there was any truth or reality in the impression, still, it was so strong that he composed mentally some considerable portions of a eulogy which he was called to deliver on his return to college. On leaving the church he went to the post-office, as was the usual custom at Whitingham on Sunday noon, many of the church-goers living at too great a distance to come on other days, and there he found a letter, on opening which, he was astounded with the intelligence that Graves was indeed dead! On his return to Williamstown, he was appointed to deliver the funeral oration, aud actually used the materal composed that Sunday morning.

Another vacation incident is the setting out by Nathan of the rows of maples whose wide-spreading branches now shade with abundant leafage the road that passes through the old farm. Before being set out they were closely cut down on the latest scientific principles, so much so that a passing neighbor, seeing a row of unpromising stumps, and with a view, probably, to taking the conceit out of a college lad, asked: "Nathan, has thee cut off the *roots*, too?"

Except during these home vacations and intervals of teaching, the college years· were filled with close and continuous study. The examining professors had entered him sophomore against his own preference, and the shortened course was a tight strain for the farmer-boy. But his perfect physical constitution carried him through; he came abreast, in time, of his more thoroughly prepared classmates, and at the end of the course it was found that he had touched the goal ahead. "He left the lime-kilns of Vermont," some of the students said of the country lad, "washed up his face, and came down here to take the valedictory."

Mark Hopkins thus describes the graduating exercises of the old time: "Commencement was a great day for the whole vicinity. The procession, with its band of music, was formed at East College and passed through the lower hall of West College to the church on the hill. It was long. The struggle to enter the church after the procession was in, was fierce. And the church was

crowded. Back of the church was a multitude, with
numerous peddlers, and there were all sorts of shows."
The students came and went by stairs erected at an
open window at the rear of the church and near the
stage adjoining the pulpit.

The 5th of September, 1827, was a day of serious
purpose to many of the class then graduating, twenty-
four of whom were candidates for the ministry. A
sentence or two from Mr. Brown's commencement
essay, "Infidelity not Philosophy," will serve to show
its tone : " Let a man only possess the meek and childlike spirit of the gospel, and no philosophy can spoil
him. The more he sees of nature, the more he sees of
God." His valedictory message to his classmates
breathed a missionary spirit: "Let us hail the light
that is waking the nations and gladdening the church.
And when we go out from this seat of science, whether
it be our lot to plead the cause of the oppressed, to
administer the healing art, or to bear the messages of
love to sinful men, let us take the Bible in our hands,
and be that the only lamp to guide our feet."

In his baccalaureate sermon President Griffin thus
addressed the graduates :

"I long to see every class go forth in the spirit of a
Mills and a Hall, a Richards and a Robbins, determined
to make their influence felt on the other side of the
globe. Will you not, my dear pupils, carry this spirit
with you, will not every one of you say, with an eye
lifted to your dying Lord, Here am I, soul and body,
here am I, send me, if it be to the ends of the earth.
All that I am and have, *I consecrate to thee,* to promote
the salvation of the world. Oh, my dear pupils,, can
you resist the influence of this holy enthusiasm ?"

Nathan Brown's religious purpose had become con
centrated while at college, largely through the influence

of the devout president. Griffin's trumpet tones awoke answering vibrations in the younger spirit; its motive became definite, the keynote was struck. Twenty years before, Mills, Richards, Rice and Hall had "prayed American missions into existence" under the shadow of a haystack near the college grounds, and the harvest thus far had been chiefly that of the reaper Death. Ann Judson already lay under the Hopia tree at Amherst. Judson had tracked his way in blood from Ava to Oung-pen-lá. One who now decided to be a missionary faced the probability of imprisonment and death.

The keynote was self-sacrifice; the theme, the world's salvation. Catching a strain of the theme, Nathan Brown, when nineteen years of age, had written the poem entitled "The Missionary." * It was a spontaneous production, thrown off in a few hours, under the inspiration of one of Dr. Griffin's eloquent sermons, which first led the writer to contemplate a missionry life.

THE MISSIONARY.

My soul is not at rest. There comes a strange
And secret whisper to my spirit, like
A dream of night, that tells me I am on
Enchanted ground. Why live I here? The vows
Of God are on me, and I may not stop
To play with shadows, or pluck earthly flowers,
Till I my work have done and rendered up
Account. The voice of my departed Lord,
Go, TEACH ALL NATIONS, from the eastern world
Comes on the night air, and awakes my ear.

And I will go. I may not longer doubt
To give up friends and home, and idol hopes,
And every tender tie that binds my heart

---

* Afterwards published as "The Missionary's Call," and later adapted and set to music by Edward Howe, Jr. For music, see Appendix.

To thee, my country!   Why should I regard
Earth's little store of borrowed sweets?   I sure
Have had enough of sorrow in my cup
To show that never was it His design
Who placed me here, that I should live in ease
Or drink at pleasure's fountain.

    Henceforth, then,
It matters not if storm or sunshine be
My earthly lot; bitter or sweet my cup.
I only pray, God fit me for the work;
God make me holy and my spirit nerve
For the stern hour of strife!   Let me but know
There is an Arm unseen that holds me up,
An Eye that kindly watches all my path,
Till I my weary pilgrimage have done,
Let me but know I have a Friend that waits
To welcome me to glory, and I joy
To tread the dark and death-fraught wilderness.

And when I come to stretch me for the last,
In unattended agony, beneath
The cocoa's shade, or lift my dying eyes
From Afric's burning sands, it will be sweet
That I have toiled for other worlds than this;
I know I shall feel happier than to die
On softer bed.

    And if I should reach heaven;
If one that hath so deeply, darkly sinned;
If one whom ruin and revolt have held
With such a fearful grasp; if one for whom
Satan has struggled as he hath for me,
Should ever reach that blessed shore, oh how
This heart will flame with gratitude and love!
And through the ages of eternal years,
Thus saved, my spirit never shall repent
That toil and suffering once were mine below.

II

PRELIMINARY WORK—MARRIAGE.

THE missionary spirit awakened at Williams led first to a home field. A Juggernaut had been found in Vermont. Printed as a part of the commencment programme, is found a brief constitution, with the following preamble:

"WILLIAMS COLLEGE, July 9, 1827.

In view of the alarming progress of intemperance, believing it to be a national and moral evil, and that it is our duty as patriots and Christians to use our utmost exertions for its suppression, we agree to form ourselves into a society by the name of the Williams College Temperance Society."

Among the fifty-three names of undergraduates appended to the constitution, is Nathan Brown's. He had started a temperance crusade in his own town during the previous vacation; had lectured on temperance, written out a pledge, and induced many, young an old, to sign it. His earnestness was magnetic; he carried the young people along with him, and even conservative farmers became convinced that summer work in the fields might be done on the stimulus of nature's beverage alone. Mr. Brown's sister remembers that their uncle Josiah had—like all well-to-do "temperance" farmers of the time—besides barrels of cider, jugs of distilled spirits stored in his cellar. Indeed, it was hardly supposed possible to maintain a decent hospitality without these supplies. His boys, Clement, Edmund and

George, having signed the pledge, planned a raid upon these spirits, and, aided and abetted by their cousins, Nathan and William, removed and set fire to them. The father subsequently fell in with the new total abstinence movement, and lived to keep the pledge to the age of ninety.

The tenor of Mr. Brown's appeals is shown in an address delivered in 1830, before the Bennington County Temperance Society, and repeated at Whitingham :

" It is no ordinary foe that has attacked us. It is no ordinary mischief that he is doing. And by no ordinary means will he be subdued. Away with your bow and arrows when you hunt the tiger ; give him a death-blow or let him alone. There is only one remedy for intemperance. Nothing less than total abstinence will effect the cure.   ·

. . . And has *woman* nothing to do in the temperance cause? . . . Oh, if there is a being under these heavens that has a right to lift up a note of remonstrance, on the subject of intemperance, it is woman—injured and afflicted woman. Shall she stretch forth her hand to rescue the widows of India from the flames, and may she not plead in behalf of her sisters at home, whose husbands are bowing under the wheels of a heavier car than Juggernaut's, and who are themselves doomed to a more dreadful immolation than the widows of Hindustan?

. . . The conflict is between the powers of light and the powers of darkness. The struggle is yet to come. The strongholds cannot be taken, the enemy's camp will not be surrendered, till every patriot and every Christian has come up to his duty. Gird on your armor, ye that wish your country well."

At this time Mr. Brown was one of the associate principals of Bennington Seminary. On leaving college he had decided it must be his first business to pay off the debt incurred in obtaining his education. For this

prpose he tau ght, first a winter school in Sunderland
and afterwards the academy in Ipswich, Mass., for about
a year. While at Ipswich, time hanging heavily on his
hands, he made a poetic translation of the first, and part
of the second, book of the Æneid, and became so
familiar with the original as to be able to repeat from
memory the whole of the first book. Leaving Ipswich,
he took charge of a select school in Concord, N. H., for
one winter, after which, in the spring of 1829, he entered into partnership with his college classmate and
friend, Mr. James Ballard, who had established a seminary at Bennington, Vt. Here he became acquainted
with William Lloyd Garrison, then editor of the *Bennington Times.* Among other reforms, that of phonetic
spelling here engaged his attention, as appears from the
manuscript of a lecture on that subject delivered before
the Lyceum.

Two pleasant years were spent at Bennington. A
prospectus of the school, announces its aim to be
" not so much to teach the pupils what others
have thought, as to train them to think for themselves."
The course embraced many of the scientific and literary
branches pursued in colleges at that time, and included
a normal department. Bible study on Saturday evenings and on the Sabbath, was a prominent feature.
Moral training, on the New England pattern, lay at the
foundation of the work done, and the fervent religious
spirit emanating from the young principals, gave its tone
to the institution.

Mr. Ballard's sister Eliza was a teacher in the seminary, having charge of the girls' department in the new
building. James and Eliza Ballard were the youngest
of a family of eleven, and had been playmates, comrades
and confidants. Their parents, William and Elizabeth
Whitney Ballard, had in 1788, with an infant son William, removed from Lancaster, Mass., their native town,

to Charlemont, in the western part of the state ; and here, their ten other children, Mary, John, Otis, Josiah, Jonas, Jonathan, Dorothy, Charles, James and Eliza Whitney were born; the last, on the 12th of April, 1807. Captain Ballard's* farm lay in a narrow, picturesque valley, walled in by southern spurs of the Green Mountains.   Here, "near to nature's heart," Eliza grew to womanhood, years before the " resonant steam-eagles " had flown through Hoosac Mountain, twelve miles westward, and sent their far-echoing scream along the banks of the Deerfield river.   Here she hunted in spring for mayflowers, and played under the maples in summer. On autumn afternoons she gathered apples in the quiet orchard, chased her lengthening shadow over the meadows, or climbed the steep hill-side to the upland pasture, free as her native air, queen of her father's heart, and the pet of her eight brothers.   When she was about fourteen, her parents sent her to Framingham to attend the academy there, and reside meantime in the family of her brother John.   This brother, in later years, recurred with affectionate pride to little Eliza's vivacity ; and near his ninetieth year, used to confess, with a merry twinkle of the eye. that, without asking permission of the " folks at home," he sent her one winter, to dancing-school !

When Eliza returned, she was the life of the house. Many a tradition is handed down with loving appreciation, of her winsome ways.   She possessed a frank sociableness that made her "good company" in any circle, and her gayety being the warm glow of a genial spirit, won her many devoted and life-long friends.   Perhaps a fresh girlish beauty was her least noticeable gift;

---

* Captain William Ballard was a son of Deacon Josiah Ballard of Andover and later of Lancaster, descended from " husbandman William Ballard, 32 years, uxor Elizabeth Ballard, 26 years," who with two infant children were registered in London, July 17, 1635, " to be imbarqued in the '*James*,' John May, master, for New England, per certificate, &c."

yet her clear dark eyes, well-curved mouth, fair complexion, blooming cheeks, and soft brown curls, are photographed in the memory of old neighbors and friends.

Buckland, the birthplace of Mary Lyon, lies along the opposite side of the river from East Charlemont, within sound of voices. The little girl and her brothers had, no doubt, shouted to catch the echo of their voices from their father's wood-lot in Buckland, which sloped sharply to the water just in front of the house. The picturesque town of Ashfield, farther back, covers the slopes of adjacent hills. Here was Sanderson Academy, the scene of Miss Lyon's early labors, and here Eliza received some uplifting influences in the winter of 1826-7, being one of the fifty pupils who listened to Miss Lyon's daily lectures that term. Miss Ballard had already shown an aptness for teaching, and had exercised the gift in the western district of her own town during the previous autumn, and in the following spring she introduced the "monitorial system," learned of Miss Lyon, into Putney, Vt. It was a novelty in that community, and was looked upon with suspicion till the young teacher's hard earned success won approval. She wrote to her brothers Jonathan and Charles: "The first week, I wished myself a thousand times back in old Massachusetts, spinning tow, or in some other employment less exposed to criticism and observations. But I found I must gain a little more independence of mind and make them believe I am something, when indeed, you know, I am nothing. I felt myself nothing in comparison with what I found they were expecting." How she wanted a letter from home! "If some of you do not write to me pretty soon, I will not try to stay. . . . Tell James, [then at home from Williams on his last vacation,] I take it for granted he has forgotten me." She stayed, became much attached to her pupils, and gained useful experience in teaching.

In 1828, Miss Ballard went to Bennington and undertook responsible duties in her brother's seminary, having charge of the girls' department in the new building, where her bright, winsome presence—still remembered by surviving pupils—no doubt contributed much to the success of the school.

The college friendship between Mr. Brown and Mr. Ballard, based on a similarity of principles and opinions was strengthened by their joint interests at Bennington, and in the autumn of 1829, a further relation was anticipated. On the 6th of May, 1830, Nathan Brown and Eliza Ballard were married at East Charlemont. Prepared for trial, anticipating a rough path in life, the pair joined hands with a purpose to labor for the coming kingdom. The crab-apple trees by the homestead door, unexpectedly burst into bloom that day, in advance of the usual time; this happy omen, the birds singing in the May sunshine, and the bride's white robes, seemed types of the eternal gladness, and its sure triumph over the fleeting ills of life. The following are two stanzas of a hymn composed for the occasion by Mr. Brown, and sung by the choir to the tune of Greenville:

> When the waves of disappointment
>   O'er hopes brightest scenery roll,
> When the loved in death are sleeping,
>   When with anguish sinks the soul,
> Who, without a friend to share it,
>   Could drink all the bitter bowl?
>
> *   *   *
>
> And when all the strife hath ended,
>   Sorrow spent its fellest dart,
> When the ties that bind the spirit
>   To the earthly regions, part,
> Love shall warm death's icy fingers,
>   Ere he lays them on the heart.

III

THE VOWS OF GOD.

Mr. and Mrs. Brown made their wedding tour from Charlemont to Framingham in a chaise, and were accompained by their brother and sister, Mr. Jonathan and Miss Dorothy Ballard. They afterwards visited Whittingham, and then continued their work in Bennington Seminary during the remainder of the year.

Near the close of 1830, a letter from John Conant, Esq., of Brandon, led to Mr. Brown's undertaking the editorship of *The Vermont Telegraph*, a weekly religious newspaper. Writing to his wife Dec. 21st, he says :

" Here I am, at work in good earnest. A room full of newspapers, from all parts of this little world, and work enough to do. It is not yet quite certain whether I stay. I feel like a missionary. Indeed I am one. I pray that God will give me humility and strength, and devotedness to his cause."

In a few weeks, having decided to remain for the present, he went to Bennington for Mrs. Brown, and they commenced housekeeping in Brandon. The new post was a vantage-point from which the strongholds of error at home could be attacked ; the young editor found them many and strong. Slavery and secret societies were plainly discussed and openly opposed in the columns of the *Telegraph*, sometimes in face of the disapproval of cautious friends.

A wave of religious revival reached Brandon during the summer, and Mr. and Mrs. Brown found opportunity

for congenial work. Meantime the paper carried the
latest news from Burma to the villages and farm-houses
of Vermont, and did much to quicken missionary zeal.
The Missionary's Call was now for the first time published, in the *Telegraph.* Some years before, it had been
sent to the Missionary Magazine, and it is said that the
young writer made up his mind to take its acceptance
or rejection as a token from providence, whether he
ought to offer himself for the foreign field or not. It
was not accepted, yet the fire ceased not to burn within
his spirit. When appeals for reinforcement of the Burman mission reached America, Mr. and Mrs. Brown
heard as those who are listening for their Master's voice.
" What Christian," wrote the former, " can read the
late appeals from Mr. Judson, and not feel a desire to
go and stand for the help of the Lord against the
mighty ? For one, I cannot think of staying back."
He wrote to his parents in August, expressing his desire, and asking their advice.

The letter fell like a bolt on the old home in Whitingham. Deacon Brown replied :

"We received your letter, and read it with many tears
and sighs, and much anxiety about your future prosperity. We should be glad to have you spend your days
in this country, but if God has designed that you should
leave your native land, I hope we shall not be found to
fight against him, nor murmur at his dispensation, but
say, as Paul's friends said when he was determined to go
to Jerusalem, that ' when he would not be persuaded,
we ceased, saying, The will of the Lord be done.' "

An application to the Board met with a cordial response. The secretary, Dr. Bolles, visited Mr. and Mrs.
Brown at Brandon, and the result of the interview, after
careful consideration of the step, was a decision to go.

Mrs. Brown left Brandon early in November, for East Charlemont. "I long to be on our way," she wrote. "I never looked forward to anything with so much de.light before." Her husband says in one of his letters to her:

"I feel since you are gone, that the time of our departure for Burma is at hand. Delightful thought! It fills my heart with a higher joy than I have experienced before for years. Next to a crown in glory, I choose a missionary's life on earth. We have chosen it, dear sister; it is opened before us, and let us rejoice."

Before this point was reached, the cost had been counted; some, at least, of the bare realities of missionary life had been faced and examined; the veil of mystery and enchantment had been lifted, and they well knew that after the glow would come the gloom, after the exalting hour of consecration, the burden and heat of the day.

The church at Brandon were in active sympathy with their young brother, and taking him by the hand, encouraged and helped him through the ordeal of his first lay sermon, which he wrote at their request, and read before them at a Saturday meeting, November 26. The subject was the consecration of business; Zech. 14; 20, 21:

November 27. "I concluded not to *read* again. It did not seem to be preaching, nor could I enjoy my mind while delivering it. The heavens seemed brass over my head, while I appeared to be going on in my own strength. To-day Elder Merriam was to preach here, but very unexpectedly did not come, so as I had preached once, the deacons insisted on my preaching to-day, though I had not made the least preparation.

But finally I read the chapter which contains the parable of the rich man and Lazarus, and the Lord was pleased to give me freedom in speaking from it, so that although in rather a disjointed manner, yet I got along with tolerable ease, and found, when I sat down, that I had been speaking forty minutes. This afternoon they requested me to preach the same I did yesterday; so I went into the pulpit (without my sermon) and was enabled, from recollection, to preach it with more satisfaction than I did yesterday."

In January 1832, Mr. Brown resigned his connection with the Telegraph, and entered Newton Theological Seminary, where he spent a few months in hard study. Mr. Wareham Walker took his place as editor of the *Telegraph.* While at Newton he was encouraged by such brotherly words as these from Vermont pastors;

" I am delighted with the spirit which has been awakened in Vermont by the circumstance of *your* going to Burma; if you never should reach there, the appointment itself has already wrought almost infinite good."

" Such a missionary spirit was never witnessed among Baptists before." "This is a blessed day—a day in which our churches are fast coming up out of the wilderness, and girding on the armor, to fight the battles of Immanuel. You can tell brother Judson, when you meet him in far distant Burma, that the 'mountains of ice' are melting down."

On the 15th of August following, Mr. Brown was ordained at Rutland, Vt. Dr. Daniel Sharp, of Boston, preached the ordination sermon, and Rev. Leland Howard, of Windsor, Vt. gave the charge. Mrs. Brown was present, and after the ordination, was, with her husband, publicly set apart to the missionary work.

Then followed the last weeks with parents, relatives and friends, before a separation, which in those days, was like that of death. An unwonted solemnity must have attached to the sermons which Mr. Brown preached, during the summer and autumn, in the hill towns of Vermont and Massachusetts. From the dates hastily minuted on the back of these now time-stained manuscripts, it appears that he was kept busy preaching from June till the time of his sailing. His parents had the opportunity of hearing him preach several times in Whitingham. Probably October 28th was the last of these occasions. From the text, "In their mouth was found no guile," the young preacher lifted the thoughts of the assembly, many of whom were his near relatives, out of the painful present into the happy company of the "hundred and forty and four thousand," whom the seer beheld standing with the Lamb on Mount Zion.

On the 6th of November, the good-byes were said in his boyhood home. Two traces of this last day's occupations are found. One is a note written to a gifted yet skeptical friend;

"In taking leave of one with whom I have long been intimate, and whom I expect to see no more, permit me to ask three questions:

If you had as good evidence that Gen. Washington died on the 4th of July, as you have that Jesus Christ performed the miracles ascribed to him in the New Testament, would you not believe it?

If these miracles were actually performed, can you consider then anything less than the sanction of Almighty God to the doctrines which he taught?

If the doctrines which Christ taught be true, what what will be your condition after death?

Your friend and well-wisher,

NATHAN BROWN."

Whitingham, Nov. 6th, 1832."

The other is "The Farewell," addressed to his parents, of which the following is the last verse;

> My father and my mother!
>   Not again ye take this hand,
> Till, clothed with immortality,
>   We tread the spirit land.
> I shall meet you there, I shall meet you there,
>   But not to mingle tears;
> I have no farewell to bid you more,
>   For the everlasting years.

On the next day the homestead at East Charlemont was crowded with neighbors and friends, who came from near and far for the last hand-shake. In our days of European summer tours, and "Round the World" holiday trips, it requires an effort of retrospection to conceive the pathos of those farewells. It was, at that time, a serious journey from Capt. Ballard's house even to Boston; when Mrs. Brown's brother Otis, went "west" on horseback to southern Ohio, to establish himself as a physician, his ride of eight hundred miles was concealed from his mother, as it was thought five hundred was all she could bear; later, "brother Charles'" journey to New Orleans had the charms and the terrors of romance. And, now, could it be that two oceans must heap their tides and toss their foam for twenty thousand miles between parent and child, till death's less cruel flood should bring reunion? It would not bear thinking of; kindly jests, homely advice, gifts, hurried preparations, and the hum of many voices relieved the last scene. The erect, commanding figure of Mrs. Brown's white-haired father, now nearly seventy years of age, was noticeable in that company, as he greeted one and another old friend and neighbor; his keen blue eyes shining out of a face lined more with genial humor than with care. "Why, mother;" said the grand old man, "after all, it is'nt so bad as if the children were going to be *hung!*"

The same brother and sister who accompanied Mr. and Mrs. Brown on their wedding tour, now went with them again over the same road, to Boston. Their sister Sophia was also one of the company; and in the carriage with her father and mother, little Dorothy Sophia Brown, now six months old, started in a basket on her long journey to India. "I often told her," wrote her mother seven years after, to the grandparents, "how she was carried back after we were in the coach, to receive your fond parting kiss; and the crown her grandfather gave her at parting, was preserved by her as a precious keepsake.'

The missionaries were hospitably cared for in Boston at the home of Mr. William Reynolds, while greatly to their disappointment, delay after delay occurred in the sailing of the ship which was to take them to Calcutta. During this interval Mr. Brown responded to calls for missionary sermons in Boston and vicinity, and also in Providence, where, also, a farewell meeting was held. His last Sunday evening was with Dr. Sharp's church, and his text, "God reigneth over the heathen."

At length the message was brought that the *Corvo* was ready for her passengers. Mr. Brown wrote to his father and mother from the ship, December 21st:

"There are going out with us Mr. Webb and wife, and Miss Harrington, to Burma. Mr. Sampson and wife, Congregational missionaries, are bound to Bombay; he is a printer, and is to take the place of Mr. Garrett, lately deceased. This is the same ship which carried out Mr. Read and wife, Mr. Jones and wife, and the lamented Mr. and Mrs. Hervey. It is affecting to think that we are treading their steps on deck of the Corvo,

and how soon we shall tread their steps to the grave
we know not. But come death how or when it will, we
have the consolation that it will not come without the
bidding of our heavenly Father.

Saturday, December 22, 10 o'clock. There is a fine
stiff breeze, which will soon waft us to a warmer
climate."

It was a beautiful morning; Mrs. Brown said, " I
think I may count it in many respects the happiest of
my life." " Sister Dorothy " and Mr. and Mrs. Bolles
had been watching from an upper window the little boat
which carried the missionaries out to the ship, and
through a spy-glass had seen them climb the ladder to
the deck and disappear from sight. Soon after, the
anchor was raised and the vessel moved slowly eastward
out of Boston harbor.

IV

FROM BOSTON TO BURMA.

DRIVEN headlong by a wintry nor' wester, the Corvo reversed the Mayflower's course, plunged through a terrific storm, then turned south. In due time the icicles dropped from her beak, and January became June in all but name. Under an awning on deck the barefoot baby had many a frolic with kind Captain Town, formed a great and lasting friendship with Miss Harrington, and helped her papa fish for albatrosses. He, in turn, inducted her into the fearful art of standing upright, and accompanied her in dangerous and exciting expeditions across the cabin floor, trolling her along with his pencil, until at length she grew fearless enough to toddle the deck with him.

Only the usual incidents varied the monotony of the journey. "No pirates, mermaids, or sea-serpents to tell of," writes Mr. Brown, but his diary shows that these deficiencies were more than made up, by the zest with which he studied every new bird and fish, and the grand aspects of ocean. Sitting on the bowsprit one midnight he says ;

" It was pleasant to see with what majesty and ease the ship, at every succeeding wave, would dip her bosom like a swan in the yielding element ; now bringing the waters almost to my feet, and now raising me twenty or thirty feet above the billows that were dashing and foam ing beneath her bows. There was a sublimity too, in the idea of being suspended hundreds of fathoms above the solid ground, while sea monsters were gliding through the dark, still waters below, or playing among the coral caverns of the ocean's undiscovered bed."

The Corvo traversed eighty degrees of latitude; then passing Tristan, ran east near the fortieth parallel south, and a little before the southern autumnal equinox, turned northward, and having "doubled the Cape," re-entered the torrid zone, March 28th. In April, the prudent captain found it necessary to put sailors and passengers on limited allowance of water, which in the increasing heat, was sometimes a distressing deprivation.

Meantime the missionaries' hearts had been made glad by seeing some results of their labors among the sailors, two of whom, during the voyage, avowed their Christian faith, and were afterwards baptized at Calcutta.

The southwest monsoon drove them up the Bay of Bengal with comparative speed, and on April 30th, Mrs. Brown writes:

"Mrs. Webb comes running to me with joy sparkling in her eyes, and says: 'From the observation just taken, we are within twenty-two miles of the Juggernaut pagoda.' *Two o'clock.* This far-famed monument of idol worship is just in sight. *May 2nd.* Cast anchor this morning, near Kedgeree, a little above the mouth of the Hoogly. . . . A boat came to us this forenoon, manned by natives, naked except a strip of cloth about the waist. One came on board to get our news. The water to-day is as muddy as the Deerfield in a freshet. Several vessels are anchored near. An Arabian just passed."

While waiting for the tide, the Corvo drifted off into shoal water, causing a further delay. At last on the 4th of May, the hundred miles' passage from the mouth of the river to Calcutta was accomplished in eight hours, and the final anchorage made. Mr. Brown and Mr. Webb first went ashore and were cordially welcomed by the Rev. William H. Pearce, who invited the Ameri-

THE MOST SACRED TEMPLE OF JUGGERNAUT AT PURI.

can missionaries to make his house their home, while waiting for a passage to Moulmein. On their return to the Corvo, Mrs. Brown, Mrs. Webb, and Miss Harrington were lowered over the ship's side into a covered boat, took off their bonnets in order to sit upright, and were rowed by a dozen swarthy natives to shore, where they encountered a crowd of palkee-bearers and a din of voices in an unknown tongue. Each traveler being inducted into a separate, hearse-like box, they were raised by poles on the shoulders of the bearers, who trotted off with them, keeping time with a dissonant, improvised chant. Mr. Brown wrote, May 8th, to Col. and Mrs. Whitney :

"The natives have intelligent countenances, features by no means coarse, and those of them who are dressed look very well. But heathenism holds her iron hand over them, and binds them down to a dark and gloomy condition for life, and a cheerless prospect in the hour of death. Last evening I dined with Capt. Town, when I heard Mr. Hall, our supercargo, ask his servant, " What has become of my bearer, that was sick yesterday ? " " Oh, we carried him to the river because the doctor gave him over." The poor creatures, as soon as the ignorant, soothsaying doctors have prophesied that they must die, are hurried away to the river side, and left for the tide to carry off, or suffocated by stuffing their throats with mud. . . . Last Sabbath I attended the native church, where the Rev. Mr. Pearce, at whose house we reside, preaches in Bengali. Their number was small, but I never saw so attentive an assembly. Every eye was fixed upon the preacher during almost the whole sermon. Eight natives were baptized the Sabbath previous."

A Mohammedan festival just then in progress, introduced the missionaries at once to some noisy orgies.

" To Rev. J. M. Graves :—Crowds were marching through the streets with a great noise and drumming, some beating their breasts, while others were dancing before them with wooden temples on their heads, decorated with all the tinsel and finery imaginable. . . . The votaries of the False Prophet are no less cruel than the Hindus, and more bitter against Christianity. 'You are under a Christian government,' said a Mussulman the other day, to a native preacher in Mr. Pearce's

MOHAMMEDAN MOSQUE ON THE HOOGLY RIVER NEAR CALCUTTA, INDIA.

church, who was formerly a Mohammedan, 'And therefore you are out of my power; but if I had you in a Mohammedan country, and under a Mohammedan ruler, I would cut up your flesh by inches.' This is the genuine spirit of Mohammedanism."

On the 18th of May, Dr. Joshua Marshman sent a
boat down the river to bring the new missionaries to
Serampore for a visit. The trip of thirteen miles up
the Hoogly was, to the travelers, a panorama full of
life and interest. Odd-looking craft from the interior,
bringing neat wares to the city for sale ; fleets of
cargo-boats with wicker cabins and grass roofs, trans-
porting merchandise ; clumsy but comfortable budge-
rows, propelled by twelve or eighteen oars, conveying
English officers back and forth from surburban residences to the city ; rafts, junks and pinnaces ; every
conceivable form in which timber could be shaped to
float, and which could be propelled by means of poles,
oars, ropes or sails, might be seen, while canoes poled
with long bamboos by muscular Bengalis, shot in and
out among the larger vessels. Along shore, spacious
villas and gardens of indigo-planters and resident officials, with broad verandas and terraces. shaded by mango
and cocoa-nut trees, occupied the background, while
the banks were overhung by noble palms, banyans,
and betels, and down over the water's edge drooped
thickets of the graceful bamboo. In contrast, were
seen here and there, cultivated tracts of rice and sugar-
cane, and clusters of native huts, resembling New
England haystacks.

About ten miles above Calcutta, lies Barrackpore,
along a noble reach of the Hoogly. The governor-
general's residence was surrounded by a park bor-
dering the river, and on the fine smooth road, which
was shaded by enormous banyans and peepuls, his elephants might be seen at evening, and the merry voices
of English children in high airy howdahs, heard from
the boats below.

Opposite, were the neat, unpretentious buildings of the
Serampore mission. Here Mr. and Mrs. Brown spent
the last few days before leaving for Burma. They found

William Carey quite feeble, sinking slowly towards the last peaceful change, with childlike submission and confidence. "I cannot say I have any very rapturous feelings," he said to a friend during this period of decline, " but I am confident in the promises of the Lord, and wish to leave my eternal interests in his hands—to place my hands in his, as a child would in his father's, to be led where and how he may please."

The venerable Dr. Marshman was still at his work, at this time under pressure of the commercial disasters which were affecting the whole British community and fell with peculiar severity on members of the Serampore mission.

The following poem printed in a Calcutta paper, was written by Mr. Brown some years after Marshman's death, and, gives expression to the inspiration derived by the young missionaries from the pioneers of Serampore. Mr. Brown says of the circumstance which suggested the verses :—" I remember hearing from Mrs. Marshman, a description of their arrival in India, and the strong emotions of her husband on reaching Serampore on the morning of Sunday, October 13th, 1799. He left the boat, and after walking a short distance, fell upon his knees, thanking God for his mercies, and imploring his richest blessings for India."

LANDING OF MARSHMAN.

From the home of his sires, in a foreign bark,
A stranger has come o'er the waters dark,
And the gorgeous East hath met his eye,
But he passes the City of Palaces by,
For the Christian rulers its pomps that share
No welcome give to the man of prayer.

The mists were rising o'er temple and tower,
Strange birds were singing in grove and bower,

As he trod the shore, at the dawn of day,
Where the shadows unbroken, of ages, lay,
Where the flame and the car had their tribute of blood,
And its hecatombs drank the relentless flood.

And the struggle of hopes and fears untold
O'er that lone heart in its anguish rolled,
As on bended knee to the earth's green breast
He sunk, with the burden of souls oppressed;
" Oh God! for thy blessing on this dark clime,
To be poured in its fullness through coming time!"

To the mansions of mercy arose the prayer,
And God's " Amen " was recorded there;
And the cloud passed off from the weeper's mind,
Like the roll of the waves he had left behind,
And there fell on his vision the morning ray
Of a glory that never shall pass away.

And there he sleeps ; and around that sod
Dark lips are chanting the praises of God ;
From valley and mountain and distant wave
They are hymning the Lord that came to save ;
And the roses of Sharon sweetly bloom
O'er fanes that were sacred to guilt and gloom.

He is gone to his rest, but the work begun
Shall extend with the years of the rolling sun ;
And the saint from his home in the skies shall behold
Throng following throng to the Saviour's fold ;
And precious to God shall be India's shore,
When the idols it loved are remembered no more.

A storm delayed the return of the visitors to Calcutta. Mrs. Brown wrote to her parents May 21st:

" We took our leave of the family last night, purpos-
ing to take the boat this morning at four o'clock for

Calcutta, but a heavy storm of wind and rain, almost like a hurricane, renders it impossible for us to move. We have engaged our passage to Moulmein in the barque *Phenix.*—Thursday 23d : Returned to Calcutta. Great damage has been done by the storm. Many vessels are ruined or lost, and the country, at the mouth of the river, is completely inundated. 30th : Sail to-day."

It proved slow work getting down to the mouth of the Hoogly from Calcutta, the wind being strong against them. Mr. Read, the excellent pilot of the *Phenix*, remained on board six days—more than a third of the entire voyage. After he left, the unpleasant discovery was made that the captain and both mates, though managing to keep tolerably sober on land, were intemperate men at sea ; and during a gale, passengers and crew were in great danger, all three officers being for two days quite besotted. Mrs. Brown wrote January 21st :

"Last night we had a heavy gale, during which the captain came down from the deck and sat in the cabin, as stupid as a log. Munglo, the chief servant, when one of us inquired of him what occasioned the noise and disturbance on deck during the night, said, ' One master tell, pull this rope ; one master tell, other rope. They so drunk ma'am, they no agree.' When I heard Munglo's story it almost made my blood chill."

Moreover, the *Phenix* turned out to be an old timber-transport, infested with snakes, scorpions, tarantulas and centipedes. Mr. Brown writes to East Charlemont :

"GULF OF MARTABAN, June 12, 1833.

My Dear Parents: While watching by the bedside of your dear Eliza and her little daughter, I am strongly reminded of our circumstances a year ago, when I was watching beside them under a parental roof. Though through the great mercy of God, we are not now visited with dangerous sickness, yet I assure you we are by no means in a pleasant situation. We are on board a ship that is full of scorpions and all manner of venomous reptiles. This afternoon Eliza found in our cabin a centipede as large as your finger. This evening, while she was on deck, I killed a scorpion in our bed! Little Dorothy Sophia was in the bed, and I was preparing to lie down by her, when I discovered the venomous creature. I think I shall sit up most of the time, nights, to watch."

Thankful indeed must they have been, that they were near the end of the voyage. Mrs. Brown says, June 15th:

"We have at last come to anchor off the coast of Amherst, about twenty-seven miles from Moulmein. How I wish I could go on shore and visit the Hopia tree, under which sleep the ashes of that dear saint, Mrs. Judson. It is very near. We are all sadly disappointed in not having reached Moulmein to-day. I suppose we might have been there this morning, but for the carelessness of the officers, who, in consequence of neglecting to take an observation day before yesterday, ran too far south."

The *Phenix* reached Moulmein on Sunday afternoon, June 16th. A boat pushed out from the jetty towards the ship, came alongside, and received the missionaries; and in a few minutes they faced a crowd of curious natives collected by the waterside. Mrs. Brown afterwards describes them:

"Those were half-clad, who were clad at all, in filthy garments; their unwashed faces, matted hair filled with vermin, and the red saliva oozing from their mouths like blood, being stained by the betel-nut and lime which they were chewing, gave them them a forbidding, not to say horrible, appearance."

Messrs. Simons, Hancock and Judson were on the wharf. The meeting was not one of many words. This was the second answer to Judson's appeal for reinforcements ; and to the new-comers, it was the day of actual entrance on their life-work. They had long been accustomed to think and speak of Burma, as "home." "This is a happy moment to me," Mrs. Brown said to Mr. Judson, as they walked on together to Mr. Hancock's house. "It is probably a happier one to us who are here," Mr. Judson replied.

V

MOULMEIN.

SOME glimpses of life in Burma fifty years ago, may be had through the missionaries' off-hand pen-talks with the "folks at home."

"Come sister, leave your garden and flower-pots, and the beautiful scenery of your Deerfield, to stand for a few moments upon the banks of the Sal-wen, and look at our little home in idolatrous Moulmein. But I can give you no idea of it. It seems as though we were on some other planet than earth, and surround-by another race of beings. The dark yellow faces, Burmans and Talains dressed in striped and checkered cloth, of which a single piece, six or eight yards long is the whole dress which a man wears; women, some of them, dressed very decently in red, green and yellow silk, while most of them have only a single blanket wrapped about the waist, with rice bas-kets upon their heads; Mussulmans in loose white robes and turbans, and Chinese, many of whom reside here, and are the best mechanics and artists we have."

The shaven mendicant priest is seen walking in dingy yellow robe from door to door, a palm-leaf fan a yard in diameter in one hand, to screen his face from view, and an earthen dish for receiving rice and fruit, in the other; the cooly carries his bag of tools over one brown brawny shoulder, his only at-tire being a strip of cloth bound about the loins; the gaily dressed Burman woman passes on her way to the temple, with a dish of offerings on her head, her baby in a scarf on her back, and leading her older children by the hand.

These last are being trained to be good Buddhists, and will presently prostrate themselves with her, and lisp the prayers she has taught them, before a serene-faced Gautama, not without stolen glances of curiosity at the folded feet, and the mysterious, equal-fingered hands,

AGODA AT MAULMEIN, BURMA. LITTLE BELLS SUSPENDED FROM ITS SUMMIT SWING IN THE WIND.

clasped in eternal repose. Will these little worshippers some day hear of those other hands, once laid in blessing on heads like theirs?

To Rev. Dr. Baldwin,—"The pagodas here are numerous. Walking out in the jungle this afternoon, I came to an old one, the relic, no doubt, of centuries, surrounded by tall, beautiful mango-trees, I climbed to the top of it, where I presume I might have counted a dozen others in different directions upon the neighboring hills, most of them crumbling with age."

The true light shone the brighter in contrast with these surroundings. Mrs. Brown writes of the baptism of two Burmans and a Karen eighty-one years of age:

"It was one of the most affecting scenes I ever witnessed, to see this old man, who had come some distance from the wilderness, so blind and decrepit that he could not walk without assistance. openly renouncing his idolatry, and bowing to the cross of Christ. Mr. Judson, in his examination, asked him what he had been doing all his life. He said, "he had never worshiped Gautama, except once, but had spent a great deal of time and money worshipping the Nats or evil spirits, and he had obtained only poverty by it, for they had never done him any good. Since he had heard about this new religion, and believed that Christ died to save all mankind from sin, he never had anything make him feel so happy in all his life."

In the zayat or native chapel, Mr. Judson preached every Sunday in the Burman language, to an audience seated on the floor upon bamboo mats, the men on one side, the women on the other, the preacher himself sitting in a chair during his discourse. Mr. Brown wrote to his parents:

"You would be much gratified to see this veteran missionary with his band of Burman Christians around him. He appears rather young for a man of his years (forty-five) and enjoys quite good health, owing in a great measure to his regular habit of walking three or four miles every morning before breakfast. He wears no hat on these occasions, and goes with immense rapidity. His manner of administering baptism is very impressive. The candidate kneels down with the water up as high as his chin, when the administrator pronounces the baptismal formula, and placing his hand upon the head of the candidate, gently bows him beneath the stream."

E. B. July 7. "I have been to the native chapel, and enjoyed the privilege of sitting at the communion table with a company of converted Burmans. Mr. Judson administered the ordinance in so plain and simple a manner that I felt almost carried back to apostolic times. He is laboring very hard to complete the translation of the Scriptures into the Burmese language."

Of Mr. Judson's social traits she says;

"Although he was a little reserved at first, I find him to be a very pleasant, companionable man. From what was said of him in America, I expected to find him so much engaged in his labors and contemplation on religious subjects, as to have lost all relish for society. But it is not so. When he is out of his study he is as lively and social as any of us. [To D. B.] He spends an hour walking around the mission compound every evening between sunset and dark, for exercise. He frequently comes to the veranda and steals away Sophia to walk with him. I suppose she reminds him of his own little one. He calls himself 'Grandpa' to her."

The Browns were occupying the old house next to the Hancocks, which had been occupied by the Bennetts when they left for Rangoon. Besides these two buildings, there were, on the east side of the mission enclosure, (called a compound) the printing office, the zayat, and Mr. Cutter's house, where Mr. Judson boarded; sleeping and studying, however, in one end of the

zayat. Mrs. Hancock's school-house was across the
way from the Browns. In the government compound,
adjacent on the east, to that of the mission, was the
residence of the British commissioner. Some distance north was the chapel, where Mr. Simons, while
studying the language, preached on Sundays to the
English soldiers, and beyond which he resided, in a
house formerly occupied by Mr. Kincaid. Here in
the northern part of the town, was the cantonment,
and west of it ran the main road along the river. A
range of hills extending north and south, back of the
town was crowned here and there by ruinous, bat-
haunted pagodas.

In plain sight of one of these were the mission
houses. The Browns' consisted of three good sized
square rooms, partitioned with jungle reeds tied together by rattans, the walls being made of the same
material, and supplying light and ventilation through innumerable openings. These were also useful in promo-
ting the education of small Burmans outside. Mr.
Brown, looking up from his writing, often saw a
child's bright eye glued to a hole in the wall; sometimes
an entire matted head was thrust through the larger
openings called windows.

Dried palmyra leaves, tied on, answered both for
plaster and wall-paper. The teak posts on which the
structure was perched, to keep it high and dry in the
rains, served also to lift the floor out of the way of snakes.
The roof, a thick layer of grass and palm-leaves, was tied
down to the bamboo-frame-work by rattan strings. The
basket lid called a door, turned on hinges of rattan, and
was latched with rattan loops and a bamboo peg. It introduced the occupants to a springy floor, made by laying a sort of raft of whole bamboos upon the posts un-
derneath; the carpet being then manufactured on the spot,
by a row of coolies, sitting across one end of the floor,

holding in their hands lengths of bamboo cut green and split into strips, and weaving them down, moving along over the part woven, until the opposite side was reached. The windows had no glass, _{nor} venetians; the matting propped out, served for an awning. A pleasant enough dwelling, in dry weather, and in the day time! Not a board or nail had been used in constructing this building; bamboo filled the place of timber, brick and stone. The broad veranda furnished a comfortable place for the *dirgy* or native sewing-man, who sat in a shady corner, cross-legged on a mat, holding the end of his seam firmly down between his brown toes. Here, too, the venerable Ko Shway Bay used to sit, copying Dr. Judson's translation of the Old Testament for the printer. In the dining room, which opened to the veranda, it was the pleasant custom of all the missionaries of the compound to assemble, from their several houses, to hold morning worship, and to exchange greetings, returning to their own houses for breakfast.

With a few articles of furnishing brought from Calcutta, and some which Mrs. Bennett had left, Mrs. Brown commenced house-keeping in this basket, the week after her arrival. Her kitchen was a little bamboo shed several rods distant, and there the cooking was done by a Mussulman servant afterwards changed for a Burman, who also set table, washed dishes, and went to bazar. Provisions were found to be about twice as expensive as in America, and some articles enormously so. But rice was generally abundant, and the art of eating curry was soon mastered. The fruits were plantains or bananas, dates, pineapples, oranges, guavas, mangoes; all delicious.

Tables and chairs were among the Calcutta purchases, but a bedstead was lacking. Some ingenious Chinaman manufactured one of bamboo, which had only the trifling defect of being unable to stand, till it

was tied to the floor. Hence arose trouble from little
red ants, whose predatory excursions could only be interrupted by setting the legs of furniture in cups of
water. One night, waked by a stinging sensation,
Mrs. Brown found that a column of ants was marching with military precision across the bed, and her
head happening to lie in their track, was being traversed like any other Alps. In this case, however, the
Alps arose and moved off, with numbers of the invaders, who never returned to the main column, being
pursued with slaughter during the remainder of the
night. The next morning, the sufferer, pale and exhausted, related her miseries to the more experienced missionary sisters, expecting condolence, and
asking advice. " Oh," coolly remarked one of them,
" I always turn my pillow the other way, and the ants
will crawl off of their own accord!" An excellent
suggestion; for an army of ants being under exact discipline, will, in such a case, walk out of the forest, and
return to the order of march.

The unaccustomed ears of the new-comers found
other enemies of sleep in the jackals, companies of
which occasionally came·running under the house in
search of prey, setting up at short intervals a most
heart-rending yell, like that of a tortured human being. This music was alternated by the full orches-
tral performance of a troop of rats whose nests were
in the old thatch overhead, running from side to side
over the framework of the roof with such a noise that
it was difficult to believe a band of robbers had not
entered the house, supposing it unoccupied.

These were the ripples in the current of their life.
The letters of this summer are full of animation and
hope. "We are all in good health" Mrs. Brown tells
her mother, Aug. 6th. " I never enjoyed better health
than since I came to Moulmein." To brother James:

"I never in my life felt so quiet and composed, so much as if I were about the very business for which I was sent into this world, as now."

Little Sophia, merry and mischievous, ran about on the elastic floor of the veranda, playing with her dog and kids. Later, an uncaged parrot, and a monkey, were added to her list of pets. "If the gate happens to be left open," her mother reports, "she will whirl herself down the door-steps, and make her way over to her Grandpa Judson's in the twinkling of an eye." The little runaway was watched by Mee May, a young Burman girl, of whom Mrs. Brown says, "Her father was going to sell her for sixty rupees, to pay his debts, unless some one would advance the money. Mah Doke pleaded with Mr. Judson to get some of the missionaries to take her, that she might be kept under religious influence. She is good-tempered, and seems grateful that we did not let her be sold for a slave. She loves Sophia, and is faithful in looking after her. [Later;] Mee May is a very teachable and interesting girl. Oh, that she were a Christian!"

Those were bright days for Mee May. She talked Burmese to Sophia, drawing her about the compound towards evening in the cradle, now converted by a Chinaman into a wagon. But Mee May was too valuable an article of merchandise to be given up permanently by her parents, until all the money possible was made out of her. The following summer, having an opportunity of selling her in marriage to a Portuguese sailor, they attempted to starve her into submission. "You must marry the man, or pay the ransom," her grandmother threatened. "Do you not like him, Mee May?" inquired Mrs. Brown. "He is a foreigner; I do not know that I have ever seen him; I cannot love him. I will obey my parents in all other things, but I cannot obey

them in this." On being told that under the English
government, her parents could not force her to marry
against her will, she seemed quite cheered, and went
home again, as was her custom, at night; but
had no sooner entered the house, than her father
attacked at with a large bamboo club, pursued her
into the street, and beat her so that she was scarcely
able to move. Her mother followed him, and in like
manner exhausted her strength upon the poor girl, who
at length found her way back to the compound and sat
down upon Mrs. Brown's doorsteps, crying aloud. Two
of her little sisters were sent by the mother to demand her
knot of artificial hair, to be deprived of which, was to a
Burman woman a token of open disgrace. Mr. Brown
sent the children home, remonstrated with the father,
and kept Mee May under his protection.

"The next morning I took her to school as usual,"
writes Mrs. Brown, "but the father and mother came
after her, and began by demanding her hair; when she
fled home to our house, followed by her parents, who
were told by Mr. Brown that they would have their
daughter no more till the time was expired for which
they had bound her out to us. Since that time I have
not dared to send her to school, and she does not venture to leave the house at all."

This was the second affair of the kind which had
occurred in Mrs Brown's family. A child of twelve or
thirteen, in her employ, was whipped and deprived of
food by her mother, in order to compel her to marry a
man who already had a wife, because he had offered a
considerable sum of money for her.

In a country where such scenes were possible, it
must have been instructive to the native converts to
witness the solemnization of a Christian marriage. On
Sunday evening, June 23d, 1833, a quiet wedding took
place in the zayat. Mr. Simons and Miss Harrington

were married by Mr. Judson in the presence of the missionaries and a company of native Christians.

For the first year, the study of the language was the principal business of the new missionaries, and it proved a trial of patience. " I never felt so hurried before in my life," Mr. Brown wrote to his parents, "as I do to get a knowledge of this language, so that we can go up into Burma and commence our labors."

Already Judson's Testament, with the news that God so loved the world as to give his Son, had gone up as far as Ava with Kincaid, and thence came cheering reports.

E. B. July 30th, 1833. " Have just received encouraging news from Brother Kincaid, who is at the royal city of Ava, making an attempt to prepare the way for the preaching of the word throughout the empire. From what we heard last week, we feared he would be obliged to retire. But now he states that his veranda is crowded with inquirers, while the enemies, as far as he can see, appear to be sleeping. He is urgent that one of the brethren here should join him immediately. Oh, how I should delight to go if we could only speak the language. While I am writing, Mr. Brown receives the following note from Brother Judson :

'*Dear Brother :*—Another soul seems to be born into the kingdom—a stiff old Buddhist of sixty ; he heard the gospel thirteen days ago, and has been with me all the morning professing his full belief and desire to embrace the religion of Christ. This makes six hopeful inquirers on hand, most of whom have appeared since your and Brother Webb's arrival. I hope it is an earnest of many future blessings to be drawn down by your prayers.

Yours,   A. J.'

This intelligence has warmed my heart, and led me to rejoice anew that I am here to witness the power of the religion of Christ in subduing the stubborn hearts of idolators. This old man, who, only thirteen days ago first heard the gospel, is now publicly, amidst bitter opposition, avowing his full belief in it. There is joy in heaven, my friends, and shall not we rejoice?

CHRISTIAN KAREN GIRLS.

Sabbath P. M., August 25.   Mr. Brown has gone up the river a few miles to a neighboring village, with Brothers Cutter and Hancock, to distribute tracts. We went to the zayat this morning to hear Mr. Judson preach to the natives ; I begin to understand *words* but could not connect them enough to make out a single sentence.

Tuesday, September 3d. Mr. Judson is quite ill. I went in to see him last evening; he sat wrapped up in his arm chair and looked as pleasant and patient as if nothing was the matter. 8th. Attended the baptism of six Karen girls from Miss Cummings' school, at Chummera, and three Burmans. 9th. Went into the school this morning with Sister Hancock, and felt so embarrassed for want of the language, that it made me quite sad. Mrs. Hancock tried to comfort me by saying that she could not speak a word when she commenced, and that a white face had a great influence over the children, though you do not speak a word.

I rejoice that there is a door opened for me to be doing a little for the heathen. By such small beginnings I hope, by and by, if the Lord spares my life and health, to be able to go about from house to house, reading and explaining the Scriptures, and in that way winning some poor heathen women to Christ. October 2d. My forenoons are mostly occupied in school; the afternoon is devoted to study, the evening to sewing, mending, preparing the school children's work, teaching Mee May to read, etc."

Fridays were given to the women's prayer meetings, which she thus describes to her father and mother Brown :

"They commence in the morning, and are coming in little companies during the day. Although I can understand but little, the Spirit of the Lord seems to hover over us, and I usually find it a precious season. I have now a most interesting group before me, two women and two little girls, Mee Pa and Mee Hla; the latter are members of the school, who have lately been baptized. There are now upwards of fifty pupils in the school, fourteen of them Karens, from Chummera, where Miss Cummings is stationed."

A year later Mrs. Brown had come to feel quite at home with the little Burman girls, being able to explain to them their Scripture lessons, and it was a "feast" to her to see "their black eyes shine" with intelligence as she told them of Eve's paradise, her temptation and fall.

"When you pray for me," she writes, "do not forget the heathen girls under my care. We give them each a suit of clothes to wear on the Sabbath. These I keep in a chest, and they all come early Sabbath morning, with smiling faces, washed clean, to dress. Immediately after worship, they come into the house, and we have a Sabbath-school. The first exercise is for each one to tell all of the sermon she can remember. After that, Mr. Brown prays in Burman, and reads some portion of Scripture, then asks questions, and explains the lessson to them."

Eight or ten of Mrs. Brown's day-pupils were women. One is entered as having "come with her husband from the jungle, to learn about Jesus Christ's religion." The school register of the summer and autumn of '34 has escaped the ravages of time and white-ants. It shows one pupil's name dropped from the roll because "*her mother has sold her* to pay a debt of sixty rupees;" another is dismissed because "*her mother has sold her for a slave.*"

A letter from Rangoon in the fall of '33, seemed to render it desirable that one of the Moulmein missionaries should remove thither. A meeting of the mission was called, and Mr. Brown offered to go. The step being decided upon, preparations were begun for the removal. Before the time for leaving came, however, another letter was received, which reversed the decision, and the Browns remained for the time being, at Moulmein.

E. B., Oct. 24. "Seven years to-day, since Mrs. Judson died and was buried under the hopia-tree at Amherst Have just been walking with Mr. Judson and talking about her, and the other missionaries who have died in Burma. He says Mrs. Judson's sufferings are but faintly described in her memoirs; that she was so very brief, he has sometimes felt it his duty to write a narrative himself, The hopia-tree, he says, is so named from Prof. Hope, a celebrated botanist of Liverpool. One of the same species shades our house. It is large, somewhat resembling the elm in shape. The graves of the missionaries are scattered here and there. In the shade of this house, is a little monument under which rests Judson Wade, one of Mrs. Boardman's children. A few rods distant, is the grave of the first Mrs. Kincaid and her little one. The English soldiers have built a monument, and placed an enclosure around it."

November brought the first news from home. Eleven months had passed; other missionaries had received letters, but by some mischance there had been none for the Browns.

E. to D. B., Nov. 25. "Early this morning, Mrs. Simons sent me a chit [note] stating that she had heard there was an arrival from Calcutta. I went over to our old house, where we all meet for morning worship, with my heart all in a flutter. But no one had heard anything. Mr. Hancock and Mr. Webb immediately set off for the ship, and before noon I was presented with the thousand times welcome box from home! . . . It is the *little* things that I want you to be most particular in writing— such as will let me right into your thoughts and actions. Only let me know what makes you joyful, and what makes you sad, and you will always find a heart to sympathize with you. If you had been much *more* particular in your journal I should have liked it better. . . .

Oh why do you talk so extravagantly about missionaries,
as if they were mere spirits? Do you think a voyage
across the sea has changed our natures altogether?
. . . We are prone to go astray, and should be
looked upon as a company of poor sinners, who are in
need of your prayers."

Sister Dorothy's home journal brought a pleasing
surprise in the news of the engagement of Mr. Brown's
sister Sophia to Mrs. Brown's brother Jonathan. A later
letter announced their marriage at Whitingham on the
23rd of May, 1833. Their family life, thus closely connected with that of their missionary brother and sister,
extended unbroken for many years in the town of Charlemont, four miles west of Capt. Ballard's.

The home-friends had written repeatedly, but mails
were infrequent. Ships appear to have left Boston
for Calcutta only about once in six months, and to have
had no fixed dates of sailing. Mr. Brown, unable to sail
the first of July, 1832, had been obliged to wait till
December for the next opportunity, and just before
leaving, he wrote to his parents, asking them to send
letters "by the ships that go out to Calcutta in the
spring!" Besides, communication between Calcutta
and Moulmein was liable to be interrupted; delays and
losses of precious letters occurred, followed by anxieties
and heartaches on both sides of the water. The fate of
the "Young Rover," a vessel carrying treasures to Calcutta, and on which Mrs. Brown's letters of the summer
of '34 were burned, was a terribly tragic one. When
fairly out at sea, the crew combined to get possession
of a lac and a half of rupees ($70,000) which they knew
to be on board. They confined the captain in the cabin,
killed the mate, and after stabbing and drowning several
persons who refused to connive, ran the vessel ashore,

and set her on fire, burning the captain and a boy alive in the cabin. Arrested through the report of the cook, who escaped and swam ashore, the bandits bought off the Burman officials with part of the booty, and went their way, to be again arrested however, and sent to Calcutta for trial.

The winter was one of hard study of the language. "I have strong apprehensions," Mrs. Brown writes again to Sister Dorothy, "that your brother Nathan is committing suicide studying Burman palm-leaves.* Were it not for his little Sophia, I do not know but his case would be hopeless."

Though he lived only about two years in Burma, Mr. Brown always retained a strong affection for and memory of the language, so much so that he was able on his return after eighteen years' absence, to preach in Burmese, and translate a number of hymns. Says Dr. Jameson, of Bassein, in the Missionary Magazine, 1886: "He lived in Burma long enough, and learned the Burmese language well enough, to write several of the best hymns in the language. They are mostly translations of favorite English hymns, such as 'Guide me, O thou great Jehovah,' 'The day is past and gone,' 'Who are these in bright array?' 'There is a happy land.' I doubt if there will ever be a hymn-book published for Burman Christians that will not contain several of Nathan Brown's hymns, which are great favorites with the native Christians, as the English originals are with English speaking Christians."

Judson's great labor, the translation of the entire Bible into Burmese, was completed Jan. 31st. In the spring, his trip to Tavoy, and unannounced marriage, caused a ripple of pleasant excitement in the little mission circle

---

*Burman books, written with a style, upon leaves of the palmyra palm cut into oblong sheets, and strung through the center on a cord.

of Moulmein, and added a strong, devoted spirit to its
working force.

Among the valued friendships formed by Mrs. Brown
in Burma, was one with Sarah Cummings, our first
maiden missionary on the field. In the spring of 1834,
Miss Cummings came down from Chummera, and dur-
her fortnight's stay at Moulmein, made her home with
the Browns. Alone at her station sixty miles from a
white settlement, surrounded by wild beasts and a pes-
tilential climate, this brave woman literally gave herself a living sacrifice. Repeatedly prostrated by jungle
fever, caused by " exhalations from the putrified sub-
stances which cover the whole region," and frequentlⱪ
obliged to escape to Moulmein for her life, she as repeatedly re-ascended the Salwen to Chummera with her
natives, " who in all my travels," she says, " are my only
companions." On she pressed, sometimes through
torrents of tropic rain, to her home in the tiger-haunted
jungle, because the Karens lived there ; untaught, unhappy women, and wailing children there, needed the
helping hand of a friend. " Let him who is in love with
hardship, danger and death, follow me," said Garibaldi.
Sarah Cummings had heard such a message from the
Captain of her salvation. Her frail cottage was so near
the jungle, that at night she sometimes heard the steal-
thy footsteps of tigers roaming under neighboring
houses for prey, and once she was startled by the out-
cry of her people, approached by a tiger while returning
from evening worship. Crocodiles infested the river.
Occasionally the natives succeeded in killing the fierce
creatures ; once Miss Cummings saw one which had
been caught, " break loose, and dart with exceeding
swiftness and force, into the bushes."

None of these things moved her heroic purpose. She
seems to have made as little of her perils and sufferings
as of her labors. She had written to Mrs. Brown, on

recovery from an illness, " The day glides sweetly over my head, and softly and silently my nights pass away. As to loneliness, I have not known the feeling since my return." And to her home-friends, at the close of her first year of missionary life ; " I have encountered no great hardships. . . . Crosses, self-denials, sufferings, trials, none I have to mention, worthy of the name. The evils I anticipated have not been realized, and *a year, happier than has been the past, have I never seen.*"

One day in July, 1834, she called the Karen children about her, with their parents, to say farewell, and they saw that she was struck again with that deadly fever Another hasty trip down the river to Mrs. Brown's house, a prompt summons to the kind English physician, every means of restoration tried—in vain ! A few days later, Mr. Brown wrote home, " Her precious life, like a jewel dropped into the ocean, is gone !" Thus died Sarah Cummings, August 3rd, 1834, aged thirty-nine ; nineteen months after landing in Burma. Brief as were her labors, Karen converts were the result of them, and the church at large derives a deeper inspiration of divine life from such a death, while

> " Our souls, with glad surprise,
> To higher levels rise."

Mr. Brown to Dr. Bolles, August 4, 1834.

" Does any one ask, what has that precious life accomplished ? As her Burman teacher, whose conversion had taken place through her instrumentality, was standing by her bedside a few moments before her death, I said to him, ' Of what use *now* is it, that the female teacher came to Burma ?' Looking up with an appearance of some surprise, he answered, ' By her coming, many Burmans have become disciples.' But when I asked him, ' If Miss Cummings had not come to Burma, would *Moung Shway-Goon* have become a disciple ?' it was only by sobs and bursting tears that he could express the emotions of a soul that felt itself just escaped from misery and hell. Oh, thought I, if Christians in America could witness the eloquence of this poor Burman's gratitude, how would they long to lie in that saint's place, and die, with but even one such trophy of redeeming grace beside their bed! Surely the consolation of having been instrumental of such conversions, must sweeten death. It sweetened hers : it sweetened her life—her toils in the lonely wilderness—and as she welcomes those converts one after another to the blessed world, it will sweeten to her the joys of heaven. At the close of the day she was followed to the grave by a numerous company from the English and native churches, and there we committed her mortal remains to their kindred dust, in the sure and happy hope of a resurrection through Jesus.

> ' There rest, blest saint, till from his throne
> The morning break.' "

VI

HAVING a favorable opportunity, in the fall of 1834, to go up the Irawadi river, Mr. Brown, in compliance with a resolution of the mission, made the tour to Ava and back, distributing scriptures in the villages and making acquaintance with the inhabitants. He set out from Moulmein, October 24th, in company with Mr. Cutter. Five days' sail in the schooner *Susan* brought them to Rangoon, at the time of one of the three great festivals. Pilgrims from all parts of Burma had come to pay their devotions and present offerings at the famous Shway Dagong, or Golden Pagoda. This imposing pyramid of brick and stone, once covered entirely with gold leaf, towers three hundred feet above the eminence on which it stands, and is the most prominent object in Rangoon. Its octagonal base is encircled by many smaller pagodas of similar form. The peculiar sanctity and glory of the shrine consists in eight hairs of Gautama, which the priests assure the people are there preserved.

Some memorable chapters of missionary history are associated with Shway Dagong. When the British men-of-war entered the Irawadi in 1824, every person in Rangoon who wore a hat was taken prisoner by the Burmese government, with orders that they were to be executed the instant the British fired the first shot. Among these prisoners were the American missionaries Wade and Hough. They were bound ready for execution, when the thunder of the fleet so terrified both keepers and officials that they fled. A panic-stricken mob drove Mr. Wade before them to the great pagoda, where he was confined in a close vault. He was found there the next day and released from his chains by the British soldiers.

It was here, on the slope in front of the pagoda that the Vintons and Kincaids ministered to sick and starving refugees during the second Burman war. Five thousand Karens had fled from their burning villages and encamped around Rangoon; Christians had been tortured, crucified, literally cut in pieces alive; the fugitives were almost dead from starvation, exposure and disease. The missionaries filled two deserted monasteries with the sick, and cared for others under the trees on the slope. On the arrival of Mrs. Vinton, a hospital for cases of small-pox was built close to their own house, "so that they could the better care for the patients who needed them most."

Mr. Brown, standing at the base of the pagoda, could look down on one side upon a landscape gemmed with lakes, and green with palms and tamarinds; on another upon the city; and on still another, upon the Rangoon river, one of the mouths of the Irawadi, now alive with native boats from the interior. On the festival days he went about among the thousands gathered to offer homage to the sacred relics, distributing printed leaves which contained the story of Jesus Christ.

"The people snatched for them eagerly, and it was with difficulty that we could distribute, owing to the multitude that crowded around us. Saturday morning, it being the Burman Sabbath, and second day of the festival, we went up to the great Shway Dagong pagoda, where we found the Woongee [Burman magistrate] and other principal officers engaged in witnessing an exhibition of boxing. Thousands were thronging around to catch a view of the spectacle; some mounted on temporary stagings, while others covered the old pagodas and banyan trees, all gazing with eager interest, and cheering at every fresh onset of the combatants. As we passed by the great pagoda on our return, we found a man standing with a dish of silver before him, which the people had presented that morning as offerings. He was beating a small gong, or metal drum, and crying, 'Who wants to go to nigban for five rupees? Only five rupees, and you go to nigban!' Sabbath morning, the last of the festival, we took a small boat and visited all the large boats in the river."

A group of Karen inquirers came to Rangoon, while Mr. Brown was there, fourteen of them desiring baptism. They were from Maubee, a village north of Rangoon, where several converts from Moulmein—three of them young lads from Mrs. Hancock's school—had been telling the good news, praying and reading aloud the solitary tract in their language.

Before daylight, Monday, November 17th, the journey up the river was begun in a small boat, with a cargo of tracts and gospels. Three native assistants, Moung Doot, Moung Shway Thah, a Christian youth from Moulmein, and the preacher Ko San Lone, accompanied the expedition; the latter to go as far as Thayet, and then return to Rangoon, to continue his work there. A canoe was taken along so that, divided into two parties, the missionary company could visit both sides of the river at once.

Finding the people eager to receive the tracts, Mr. Brown seems to have thrown himself at once into the work of distributing, reading and explaining the scriptures, walking in the sun sometimes nearly all day, in order to lose no opportunity. As a consequence, Sun-

day, the 23d, found him, just above Danu̯byu, nearly ill
from the exposure, and a lesson of prudence was learned.
He had found many thrifty and industrious Karens on
both sides of the river, and some men who could read
Burman, took books to read to their neighbors.   One
company who were harvesting their rice, having obtained
a book, immediately left their work and ran home to get
one of their neighbors to read it.

Every opportunity was embraced, the assistants sometimes taking advantage of funerals occurring in the
towns they visited, to preach to the crowds gathered on
such occasions.   At Henzadá, Ko San Lone found the
devil, he said, preventing the people from receiving the
books by means of his agents going through the streets.
At the village of Shwaygyen a new boat was just being
launched, propitiatory offerings of plantains and water
having first been made to the nats or tutelary demons,
one of whom, the missionaries were assured, certainly
came down to inhale the odor of the fruit, for the pot of
water was seen to shake!   After the launch was over,
San Lone drew a quiet little circle around him and
preached till eight o'clock.

San Lone's adversary grew more and more active as
the party ascended the river.   In one village an unusual
inability to read pervaded the population, which being
privately translated, meant *fear of the governor.*   The
interesting old town of Kanaung was reached December
2d.   This place was one great orchard, two or three
miles in extent, of mango and tamarind trees, and it
contained numerous ancient pagodas.   Crowds gathered
to hear the preacher's arguments.   At Myanaung, the
government officials were forbidden to take any Christian writings, and the people were much afraid.

At Kyanghen, matters were still worse.   The missionaries went through the principal streets with their
precious burden, as was their custom, but scarcely

an individual dared openly to receive a book. They heard on every hand the discouraging reply, "We do not want ; we do not want."

"Do not take it," said one woman to her husband, who, bolder than the rest, had accepted a book from San Lone. "Do not take it; you know what an affair the governor's son made of it last year." "What matter ?" he answered ; "*may I not find out who is my God?*"

Shwaydaung was a beautiful village, embowered in a garden of tall trees, many of which were loaded with fruit. Here the foreigners were more favorably received, even the governor and his suite accepting tracts and books. One man offered to exchange a Burman book which he had copied with great care, for the Life of Christ.

On the 8th of December, Mr. Brown reached the ancient city of Prome. It being a heathen worship day, he went at once to the pagoda of Shway Sandau or the Sacred Hair. Here the intelligent head priest acknowledged the inefficacy of idol worship. The missionaries quietly passed among the throngs with their tracts in their bands, which nearly two hundred people asked for and received. It was the same city from which four ·years before Judson had been driven after spending himself in her streets, preaching the gospel. A similar hostility was manifested now. About three o'clock that afternoon, while Mr. Brown and his companions were at work distributing, a herald was sent through the streets with beat of drum, prohibiting the people under penalties of the law, from receiving any of "the foreigners' white books."

"After the order was issued we of course desisted, but many afterwards came to the boat and received books. Ko San Lone has been preaching nearly all day in various parts of the city, and has found many who appear serious. Several spoke very feelingly of Mr. Judson's preaching here, and his being ordered away by the government. His doctrine they said, was good, and they believed the religion to be true, but alas, they dared not now read the books, or even have them in their posession. We think, on the whole, we have not distributed two hundred tracts anywhere to better advantage than at Prome, and we have no doubt they will receive an attentive perusal, though perhaps it will be in some secret corner, or at the dead of night."

December 12th was a day of encouragement at Thayet, where the rulers appeared friendly. Inquirers were here found, the fruit of previous distribution, and the missionaries were called into several houses to read and talk about their religion. At a funeral they proclaimed the good news of everlasting life, and on their return that way later in the day, found the assembly still undispersed and listening to one of their number reading out of the Epistles.

At Engya, after what must have been a very busy and fatiguing day, conversation was kept up till late at night, around the boatmen's camp-fire, whose red reflection, mingled with the pale moonlight, shone on an unwonted scene—a group of half-clad Burmans squatted around the fire, doubtless eager disputants, asking " How can these things be?" The white faced young foreigner was trying in a broken way to tell them of sin, its consequences, and of a purer and greater light than Buddha.

It was full moon when the party reached Menyua, the next evening, and hence another great worship day, a month since they gave tracts at Shway Dagong. After having visited the villages below, they came up to Menyua just as the sun was sinking behind the mountains ; and above the spires of the eastern pagodas slowly appeared the round, great moon, throwing its silver sparkle on the ripples around the boat. A sound of rude music was heard in the distance; it grew more distinct and more harsh, as they approached.

Mr. Brown betook himself to the shore, went up into the village, and found the people assembled to witness a play, which appeared to be acted with all the spirit and vivacity that would characterize a theatrical exhibition in more enlightened lands. There was no opportunity that night, to give the bread of life, so much needed, but the next morning a hundred tracts were distributed in that village. At Myengún, eighteen miles above, many were given the next evening by moon-light.

Numerous ruined pagodas, but few inhabitants, had been found the day before, in Taung-gwen, the town of the *Mountain Curve.* Many of the names of villages were oddly significant. Nearly all the villagers of *The Fierce Crocodile* had gone down to witness the play at Menyua. At Yuabuleh or *Pearl Village*, some distance back from the river, a good distribution was made. Among the village names appears *One Mango Tree*, to which place the boatmen were actually driven back by mosquitoes one evening, declaring they could not work the boat, and must wait till morning. Another place was *"Not Salt Enough !"* The following sound like sum-mer-resorts : Bird Lake, Around the Banyan, Banyan Foot, Pleasant Air Shore, Mango Grove, Flower Basket, Teak Mountain, Beautiful Shore, Brilliant Stone, Golden Pauk Tree, White Elephant Island. Less attractive are The Great Whirlpool, and Dark Sky. But who could ever be induced to live in " A Hundred White-ant Hills ?"

To return to the travelers ; a little after sunrise, December 19th, they found a company of Shan traders, who had erected a temporary market opposite Yuathaya. Some of these men being able to read Burman, took books, which would be carried to a region then unvisited. Large quantities of curious petrifactions of logs and stumps about Wetmasút attracted the travelers' attention. At Yenan-ghyaung (Petroleum Creek) the missionaries visited a hundred and fifty oil-boats, giving a book to each captain who desired it.

"22. Saw, off at a considerable distance, on the eastern side, the ruins of the old town of S'haleh. We went out to visit the place. It bears the marks of having anciently been very populous, and the remains of numerous old pagodas are scattered around for many miles. Saw a stone inscription near one of the more recent pagodas, bearing the [Burman] date 417, that is 780 years ago.

"23. Went over to S'henbyú-gyún and distributed one hundred tracts and books. Many of the people refused. Here we received a letter from Brother Kincaid, stating new difficulties with the government, [he having been summoned before the authorities and ordered to leave Ava,] and advising us, in the present critical state of things, to come up with as little noise as possible, and not give any more books.

27. Left the boat just as the sun was rising above the spires of old Púgan, and went out to examine the ruins of this once magnificent city. In every direction, as far as the eye can reach, pagodas, bearing the marks of former greatness, are scattered over the site of this ancient capital. Found here many inscriptions on stone, most of them dated between six and seven hundred years ago. The largest temples are all built in the ancient style, not round and solid, but opening in large high galleries inside. One of them, Shyen Ananda, is still kept in repair, and contains four colossal figures of Gautama, in a standing position, and richly gilt. The body of the edifice is a huge structure of a pyramidal

form, 175 feet square, with a wing of 50 feet by 90, projecting from each of the four sides. There are four or
five other temples of the same size. They are immense
piles, and cover upwards of an acre each. We sung, as
we walked through the echoing halls,

'Jesus shall reign.'

He will reign; long after our voices shall be hushed in
silence ; long after these images shall have crumbled on
their pedestals. When the grass shall be grown over
the spot where stood these stately temples, then shall
there be a kingdom established here that must flourish,
with undecaying vigor,

' Till moons shall wax and wane no more.' "

On the 6th of January, 1835, Mr. Brown reached Ava,
the terminus of the trip, called by the Burmans Enwa,
(Outlet of the Lake) or briefly, Awa, (The Outlet), from
a small lake anciently situated here, but which is now
filled up. This city, the scene of Judson's heroic endeavor and tragic suffering, was a point of intense interest to all friends of missions, as the door to the inner
strongholds of Buddhism, and Kincaid was determined
to hold the door open by main force. In his own words,
a year before, "Let us have time to make a fair trial,
and I trust it will tell upon this people through all coming time." He had now been here a year and a half,
preaching with his native assistants to throngs of inquirers, in zayats, on verandas, and in the shadow of
heathen temples ; fearless under the threats of one of
the most cruel despotisms ever known. Repeatedly
had he been forbidden by the ministers of government
to continue his work, but he held on, till inquirers became converts, and converts, brave witnesses for Christ
by baptism in the waters of the Irawadi, at a time when
the act exposed them to the risk of speedy martyrdom.
" Are you ready to suffer for the name of Christ ?" was

the question asked of the venerable Ko Gway, when he requested baptism. "I know there is danger, he replied," " *but I must be on the side of the Eternal God.*" A little Christian church was organized, and Burmans already worshipped Jesus on the very spot where Judson was tied with cords, and dragged to the death-prison.

Just two months before Mr. Brown reached Ava, Mr. Kincaid was summoned one morning at an early hour to the palace. "The manner in which I was called," he writes, "indicated that a fearful storm was gathering, and in this I was not deceived." On arriving at court, he saw the " black book" brought out and was compelled to listen to a list of charges, the substance of which was that he was a setter forth of strange gods, and that his object in the city was "to bring into contempt and destroy the religion which has been revered for ages," and was told by a Woongee that he "must promise to give no more books, and not go about preaching."

" I cannot make such a promise," answered the missionary.

" You must promise."

" I fear God more than earthly kings, and cannot promise ; if you cut off my arms, and then my head, I dare not promise."

They then said he " was not fit to live in the empire, and must be sent off," their rage venting itself on his landlord, who was threatened with being burned alive for renting a house to this pestilent foreigner. Mr. Kincaid adds, "If I can judge from the temper and language of this morning, the government is determined to proceed to extremities. . . . I feel distressed for this little flock, gathered from among the heathen. Precious souls, they have entered a kingdom against which the world has waged an unceasing war, but if they are faith ful to the end, the boon of eternal life is theirs. O, God, restrain the wrath of the heathen. Save thine own heritage, and have mercy on this great city."

Notwithstanding his bold refusal to desist from preaching the gospel, Mr. Kincaid was allowed to go back to his house. An order was issued for him to leave the empire immediately, but was afterwards recalled. Spies were placed over him, and officers appointed to seize every person that should venture into the house, but through his many friends about the court, he was able to guard against surprise. In less than two weeks he had the privilege of baptizing "one of Cæsar's household"–a young man who was in almost constant attendance on the king, and whose sister was a maid of honor in the palace. The stability and fortitude of the native brethren in those perilous times, greatly endeared them to him, and encouraged his heart. They even shared his heroism, manifesting an anxiety to diffuse abroad the knowledge of the true God. "For some days before the brethren (Brown and Cutter) arrived, and during their stay," he wrote, January 27th, "I did very little for fear of arousing the government." This course had the desired effect; the storm blew over. He adds, "It does not appear to be duty to remain inactive longer;" and he accordingly sent out his preachers again, and resumed the giving of books, to Burmans, Mohammedans, Brahmans and Chinese.

Two years later, this missionary pathfinder went up the Irawadi three hundred and fifty miles farther, to Mogaung, with a view of pushing on if possible, to Assam and China, but found it impracticable at that time to penetrate so far, as the natives would not accompany him, and he was forced to turn his boat down the river. Meantime civil war had broken out in Burma, bands of robbers ranged at will; the missionary was captured, sentenced to death, wonderfully

delivered ; re-captured, suffered the most cruel hardships, escaped from his sleeping guard almost naked
and famished ; wandered for days alone in the wilderness ; was mourned as dead ; and finally, almost by
miracle, re-appeared in Ava, to find a new king in
power.

Mr. Brown remained nearly three weeks at the capital, but there is scarcely any record of what he did
or saw there. The government seems to have exercised
no active hostility during the visit, as his movements
were unhampered, and a casual reference appears in
one of his letters, to an interview which he had with
Prince Mekara. Much that a Burman missionary ought
to know, was to be learned in this populous walled
city, with its inner town of palaces and pagodas, in
glittering contrast to the surrounding swarm of miserable hovels, in which the masses of the people lived.
With these defrauded, oppressed masses, he daily gained
a deeper sympathy.

" The people of Burma are absolute slaves—with the
exception of one man, their monarch. No man dare
say " *I*" in his presence ; the only expression for the
first personal pronoun, which would be allowed in the
mouth of even the highest official, is *your royal slave.*
The same style must be used by the common people
when addressing any of their rulers. No officer is
allowed a salary ; of course he lives by extorting from
those who are under him, whatever he thinks fit. This
wretched system, together with the immense sums ex-
pended for erecting pagodas and supporting the priesthood, completely impoverishes the country. Their
cities, even "Golden Ava" herself, are but vast collec-
tions of mere hovels. True, there are gilded palaces
and pagodas ; and upon the stream are royal boats,
whose oars, covered with gold, are flashing in the morn-

ing sun, but for purposes of comfortable residence, we find nothing in Burma that can compare with any of our snug Green Mountain villages. The inhabitants of this country are not allowed, even in the cities, to build themselves substantial houses of brick, or in any way to rise above the common degradation by sur_ rounding themselves with the comforts and conven_ iences of life, lest they should be regarded as aspiring to the privileges of rank."*

Mr. Brown visited Amarapoora and Sagaing, former capitals. At the latter, a solitary, neglected grave was found. It was that of Dr. Price, Judson's fellow_ prisoner in 1824, who, after the close of the war re_ turned to Ava, and died there, February 14th, 1828. The missionaries now had a stone erected with inscrip_ tion.

"Jan. 24, 1835. Having all our things on board, together with the printing-press, we prepared to take leave of our dear brother and sister Kincaid, and the little band of disciples. Farewell to the golden city! May the Lord have mercy upon the thoughtless thou_ sands that tread thy streets, and bring them into the light and liberty of the glorious gospel.

We take with us from Ava, one of the young disciples, Moung Oo Daung, who we think will prove a valuable assistant in the mission. His father was the Waw-mhú, or officer of the Royal Palanquin, under the old king, and was one of the first whom brother Kincaid baptized.

29. Sa-lé. The people were very eager for tracts. The boat was some distance from the bank, and they came wading through the water for books till after dark."

---

*Letter to Vermont Baptist Convention, March 10th, 1835.

At Yatt'haung Mr. Brown had the pleasure of baptizing an earnest and intelligent young convert, the son of a Buddhist preacher. Both father and son had requested baptism.

"They both appeared very well on examination, and there seemed to be no reason why their baptism should be deferred. We told them we were satisfied with them, and that we would immediately repair to the river for the purpose of administering the ordinance. We accordingly started on. But the old man's heart failed him at the trial, and he declared that his fear of the rulers was so great that he dared not go forward. The son was unmoved. He said he was indeed afraid, but he must be baptized; he would confess his Lord, and though they should throw him into prison, or sever his head from his body, he could never deny that he was his disciple. So the young man was baptized. His name is T'hunaung. We gave him a copy of the New Testament for his directory, and left him, like a sheep in the wilderness, not knowing that we shall ever see him again in this world, but hoping and believing that we shall find him safe at last in his heavenly Father's home."

This solitary Christian, converted through the Bible alone, remained steadfast. Mr. Brown heard nothing of him for more than twenty years, when a letter from Mr. Kincaid mentioned that he was then a preacher of the gospel. The same letter stated that a great interest in the Christian religion was manifested in all the regions from Prome to Ava, the fruit of Bibles and tracts circulated years before.

Rangoon was reached on the 10th of February, and Moulmein on the 20th. A few days later, persecution broke out in Rangoon, and San Lone, who since his return had been preaching there, was called to attest his faith by suffering. The cloud burst unexpectedly; Mr.

Howard and his native assistants were laboring unmolested until the morning of the 25th of February, when San Lone was summmoned from the veranda, where he was preaching, to appear before a government official— the same one who had before broken up Mr. Kincaid's school, and whipped the teachers. San Lone was imprisoned and loaded with irons, but said that "he was very happy during all his imprisonment, that though his feet and neck were hurt with irons, he did not think of his pain, nor was he afraid to be in the hands of his persecutors. . . . When he considered what a God he had to serve, he could not fear man, and therefore he exhorted all to repent, and believe in the Lord Jesus Christ." Like Paul and Silas, while fastened with fetters, he prayed and sang praises to God, and the prisoners heard him. Meantime outside, the common question on the street was, "When is that Christian to be executed?" for the rulers, in order to intimidate the frequenters of Mr. Howard's veranda, and also with a view to obtaining money for San Lone's release, proclaimed their intention to kill him.

Through the efforts of the missionary and others, and the payment of about three hundred rupees, San Lone was at length released, with the threat that if he should ever attempt to preach or distribute tracts again, he would be immediately executed. A few months later, he was taken ill of a fever, soon after his return from a journey into the jungle, and died, August 5th, 1835, never having fully recovered from the effects of his imprisonment.

Mr. Brown said of San Lone's qualities as a preacher, that he was remarkable for his prudence and gentleness in discussion with the advocates of idolatry, never provoking or triumphing over them, but winning his way to their hearts by kind words. He literally gave up all, in love and loyalty to his Master, having once been in good circumstances, but on his release he was entirely destitute. When hard pressed to renounce Christ, and told that he would be put to death unless he would worship the image of Buddha, he refused to purchase release at such a price, and declared that he could never renounce the religion of Jesus, or worship as God, a being whom he did not believe to be such.

So lived and died San Lone, like many other Burman and Karen Christians who have with unrecorded heroism borne cruel persecution, have sealed their faith with blood, and joined the noble army of martyrs.

SACRED GARDENS ATTACH

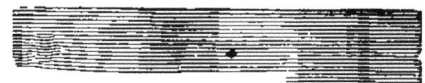

UDDHIST TEMPLE.

VII

CHANGES.

EARLY in December, the ship *Cashmere* had brought eleven new missionaries to Moulmein with Mr. and Mrs. Wade. Of these, the Deans had already gone on to Singapore en route for Siam, the Wades and Miss Gardner to Tenasserim, the Howards to Rangoon, the Vintons up the Salwen to Miss Cummings' station at Chummera, and the Comstocks to Arakan, while the Osgoods remained at Moulmein.

Before Mr. Brown went to Ava, it had been decided that he should on his return, begin a much needed work at Obo, at the junction of the Ataran with the Salwen, about two miles from the mission compound. On the 25th of March he entered this field, and wrote a few days later :

"We are now situated in the north part of the town of Moulmein, with a population of ten or twelve thousand around us, who know not their right hand from their left. I have begun to hold meetings in my blundering way, for although I have been here nearly two years, I am by no means master of the language."

Native visitors soon began to come to him, and besides talking with these, it was his practice to go daily into the streets to spend two or three hours in religious conversation wherever he could find a listener. Some were interested, but ancestral Buddhism flowed in their veins; it was a part of themselves; Christianity was only an entertaining foreign curiosity. A solid barricade against the missionary's appeals was the calm, invariable reply, "It is the religion of my ancestors." Meantime some European women from the neighboring cantonment came to see Mrs. Brown.

E. B. April 21. "Have just had a little prayer-meeting with three of the soldiers' wives from the patchery [barracks]. They are very ignorant of the gospel. Only one of them knows how to read, but they seem anxious to learn the way of life. They requested the favor of coming in every Tuesday morning and spending an hour with me in prayer and religious conversation.

May 5. I have had a delightful interview this morning with the three women from the patchery. All of of them expressed a hope that they had passed from death unto life. Their feelings were very tender, and truly a new light seemed to have beamed in upon their minds. I trust they are not deceived.

July 26. It is a time of considerable religious inquiry among the soldiers. Many are serious and several have asked for baptism. I trust the good seed sown by Mr. Simons and others has not been altogether in vain.

Sabbath evening. Aug. 2. Mr. Brown went at 5 o'clock this afternoon to administer the ordinance of baptism to five candidates for the English church.* Three of them are women from the patchery near, whom I have before mentioned. One of them came in to tell me her feelings, this morning. To use her own expression, 'Once I was all for fine dress, but now I want to spend my life serving the Lord," Mr. Bennett's journal adds, that "in the evening Mr. Brown preached to a very large and attentive audience, a discourse peculiarly adapted to the state of his hearers."

---

*A church of Europeans, connected with the Baptist mission.

Mrs. Brown describes a Burman funeral procession which passed her veranda May 12th, on its way to the neighboring burning ground. "The coffin was decorated with net, tinsel and paper of the most fanciful colors. The top was of an oval form, the whole ten or twelve feet high, placed upon a sort of bier made of bamboos, and was borne upon the shoulders of some twenty or thirty men. They went dancing, crowding, pushing and hallooing through the street in the most ridiculous manner, stopping every few minutes, and swinging and whirling the coffin in every direction. A large procession of people followed, in a little more orderly manner. After the procession, walked twenty or thirty priests, all dressed in their yellow cloth; next and last were the friends of the mourners carrying the meritorious offerings for the priests, consisting of pineapples, plantains, cocoanuts, sugar-cane etc. They all passed on to the burning-ground, and seated themselves in the zayats built for such occasions, while a few of the men cut the wood, piled it, and prepared for the burning of the body. The assembly gathered around, and seated themselves upon the ground. The body was then placed upon the wood and the fire kindled. While it was burning, the priests (as I learned from our teacher) preached to the people and relatives, telling them how great cause they had for rejoicing, since the meritorious deeds of their friend in this life had secured for him a state of exalted blessedness, which he had now entered. When the discourse was finished they all arose, the relatives advanced towards the body, made most boisterous, affected lamentations, smiting upon their breasts and crying, "A-meh, a-meh!" (alas, alas,) and retired wailing as they went through the street. Two or three remained to watch the body until it was consumed."

Her entry of July 17th notes the birth of their second child:

"On opening my journal this morning, I find that a long time has elapsed since the last date. Many changes have taken place in our circumstances and prospects within the last two months. On the morning of the 7th of June, we were made the joyful parents of a little son. We have given to our little one the name of his grandfather, William Ballard."

On the 8th of June, an important meeting of the mission was held. It had long been a cherished hope of the Board at home, as well as of missionaries in Burma, to introduce the gospel among the Shans—an interesting family of tribes inhabiting unexplored regions to the north and east—and through them it was expected by inland routes to reach China, whose seaports were at that time sealed against foreigners. A proposal was now made by the Rev. W. H. Pearce of the English Baptist mission in Calcutta, and several other friends of missions in Bengal, that the American Baptists should commence a work among these people in Assam, this country having become a part of the British dominions at the close of the Burman war. The proposal was the result of a communication received by Mr. C. E. (afterwards Sir Charles) Trevelyan, one of the secretaries of the East India government, from Major Jenkins, Commissioner-general of Assam, inviting missionaries to come to that province, and promising them protection and assistance. The invitation was accepted, and Mr. Brown was set apart to the work, to be accompanied by a printer with a press. Burma had been his appointed field, and two years of precious time had been spent in acquiring the Burman language ; but the voice of providence now seemed to call to regions still beyond, and he cheerfully took the torch his brethren placed in his hand, and set his face to go down into the new mine. He at once began the study of the Shan language under the instruction of two Shans, one from Zimmai (Chien_gmai) in Laos, and one from the region above Ava. Before embarking in August, he had made out a voca_bulary of two or three thousand words. June 11th Dr. Judson wrote home :

" Brother Brown embraced the proposal with instant enthusiasm, not merely because of the above advantages; for Assam presents a splendid opening for missionary efforts, and Brother Brown is excellently well qualified to take the lead in that great and important mission. My heart leaps for joy and glows with gratitude and praise to God, when I think of Brother Jones at Bankok, in the southern extremity of the continent, and Brother Brown at Sudiya in Assam, on the frontiers of China— immensely distant points—and of all the intervening stations, Ava, Rangoon, Kyouk Phyoo, Moulmein and Tavoy, and the churches and schools which are spring- ing up in every station, and throughout the Karen wild- erness. Happy lot, to live in these days ! O happy lot, to be allowed to bear a part in the glorious work of bringing an apostate world to the feet of Jesus."*

Passage for the little family of four, was engaged on the *Cashmere Merchant*, bound for Calcutta, and they left their home at Obo on Wednesday, August 5th. All things seemed ready for their departure on the follow- ing Monday, when, on Saturday, at Mrs. Osgood's, their infant son was taken ill. No apprehension was felt till Sunday evening, when, soon after Mr. Brown came in from the English chapel where he had been preaching, sudden alarming symptoms were developed ; the father

---

*Wayland's Life of Judson.

and mother exclaimed together, "Little William is dying!"

The missionaries all came in; and though the case was hopeless, Dr. Richardson remained during the night. After many alternations of convulsions and exhaustion, at seven o'clock the next morning the baby died.

"We were all ready to embark on Saturday; [Mr. Brown wrote from Calcutta to his parents,] the vessel started from her moorings Sabbath day, and we were expecting to go on board early Monday morning, carrying with us our two dear children. But God had ordained otherwise, and before we set sail, we were called to deposit our darling in the silent dust. . . . Little William's sufferings appeared to be very great. He seemed to be struggling with death all night; and there was no time when we thought he could possibly hold out much longer. There were often intermissions of one or two minutes in his breathing, when we thought he was dead, but life kept returning, till about seven o'clock, when having waited a long time for the breath to return again, we at length found that it was all over, and the little beautiful marble face began rapidly to grow cold and stiff. The funeral was attended about twelve o'clock, and the body buried beside the grave of our lamented Sister Cummings. The remarks of Mr. Judson at the funeral consoled our hearts with the reflection that it was for our good, and the good of our dear child, that God had taken him away. We feel that we needed the affliction. Oh, may it be sanctified to us, and may we be led by it to live more soberly, righteously, and godly in this present evil world."

E. B. "Mr. Judson gave us a short but comforting exhortation. He well knew how to appreciate our feelings, for he has passed through similar scenes. After the services, we, together with a few English soldiers and

Burman Christians, followed his remains to his little grave. At five o'clock the same day we took leave of our friends in Moulmein with sorrowing hearts, and together with Brother and Sister Cutter and the little one we carried there with us, we embarked for Bengal."

The wounds made in the mother's heart within those twenty-four hours, first by the sudden piercing certainty of what must befall, then by the night of agony, by the death in the early morning, by the mid-day burial, by the tearing away at evening from that from which her heart would not unclasp itself, left scars that never were effaced. Sustained, but not benumbed, she knew, through all her gentle endurance, what the mothers of Bethlehem felt. Her friends in Calcutta missed the bloom upon her youthful face of two years before. So pale, thin and altered was she, it seemed as if she were ten years older.

Copied by Mrs. Brown's hand years later, in her album, are two inscriptions; one of them from "Baby Willie's monument at Moulmein, British Burma." At the bottom of the page, a spray of leaves is delicately stitched with scarlet thread, and protected by a fragment of a letter from a missionary friend, dated Feb. 17, 1868, which says: "I send the leaves from the little grave in Moulmein. It is kept in beautiful order, and the inscription is as fresh as if put in yesterday. We shall keep a watch over the precious spot for you, and should any repairs be needed you may rest assured that they will be at once attended to." On the opposite page, copied evidently at the same time, is the epitaph of Mrs. Sarah B. Judson, who was with her on that trying 10th of August, and whose own death and burial at St. Helena occurred under somewhat similar circumstances, thus recorded by Dr. Judson: "1845, Sept. 1. Mrs. J. died at 3 A. M. ; was buried at 6 P. M., and we sailed from St. Helena in the evening."

One of Mrs. Judson's letters to Mrs. Brown, dated Oct. 30th, 1835, closes thus : " Not long since, we walked to the spot where your dear William sleeps, and thought and spoke of you. Ah! we both know how to sympathize with yourself and your dear husband on this subject. I hope Sophia is a good girl. Kiss her for me, and tell her that Uncle and Aunt Judson will always remember her."

Contrary winds prolonged the passage to Calcutta, especially towards its close. All one day the ship lay at anchor under a high wind and sea, in momentary danger of being wrecked on the shoals. Again they had to anchor and wait for a favorable wind, off Saugur, an island covered with thick jungle, and infested with tigers. At length the winding channels were threaded, and they made their slow way between the rice-fields and villages of the Hoogly, up to the city.

The party were cordially welcomed by Mr. and Mrs. Pearce, whose house was their home during some busy weeks, till boats could be prepared for the long journey. The missions of Chitpore and Serampore were again visited. At the latter, the venerable William Carey had died since their last visit, but they found Dr. and Mrs. Marshman "as well and active as ever." Here Mr. Brown formed a friendship with Rev. Mr. Mack, a professor in the Serampore College, of whom he speaks as "a man of sterling talents and extended views."

While delayed in Calcutta, Mr. Brown preached often in English, delivered a lecture on the Burman cosmogony, continued his study of the Shan language, and matured his plans of work. He here met Capt. Pemberton, an English officer who had traveled extensively in Shanland, and obtained from him a copy of an interesting old Shan manuscript purporting to be an abstract of the history of that people from the first century to their subjection by the Burman conqueror Alompra, and as

cribing to the ancient Shans a powerful empire, called
the Kingdom of Pong, said to have embraced the ter-
ritory south of Tibet, and having its capital at Mogaung, about half way between Ava and Sudiya.*
However this may be, it is agreeed by explorers and
students that the Shan or Tai race was once widely
spread; and Mr. Brown was deeply interested to find
that the languages of Farther India are closely related
to each other, pointing unmistakably to a common origin,
and hoped this fact would lead to their unification, and
thus to the more rapid spread of Christianity. With
this in view, he commenced compiling a comparative
vocabulary of those languages, which he afterwards
extended to others.

The plan for printing the languages of India in Roman
characters, being intimately connected with the proposed work of establishing a chain of associated mission stations among the scattered Shan tribes, engaged
much of his attention while at Calcutta. In connection with this work, Mr, Brown formed a cordial and
lasting friendship with Mr. Trevelyan, and found him
"a warm friend to missions and to general education."

"Thirty-five years ago,"—wrote Mr. Brown in 1867—
"Sir Charles Trevelyan and Rev. William H. Pearce, in
concert with other scholars and missionaries, conceived
the plan of substituting Roman for native characters
in printing the languages of India. Prof. Max Müller,
of Oxford University, now published his 'Missionary
Alphabet,' bringing the various plans which missionaries had used or suggested, into an orderly and complete system."

---

*Pronounced Sud′-ee-ah.

The practical benefits of romanizing have been tested by various missionary societies; the Scriptures, either entire or in part, are now printed in the uniform letters of our own English, for at least one hundred and twenty different languages and dialects of the globe.

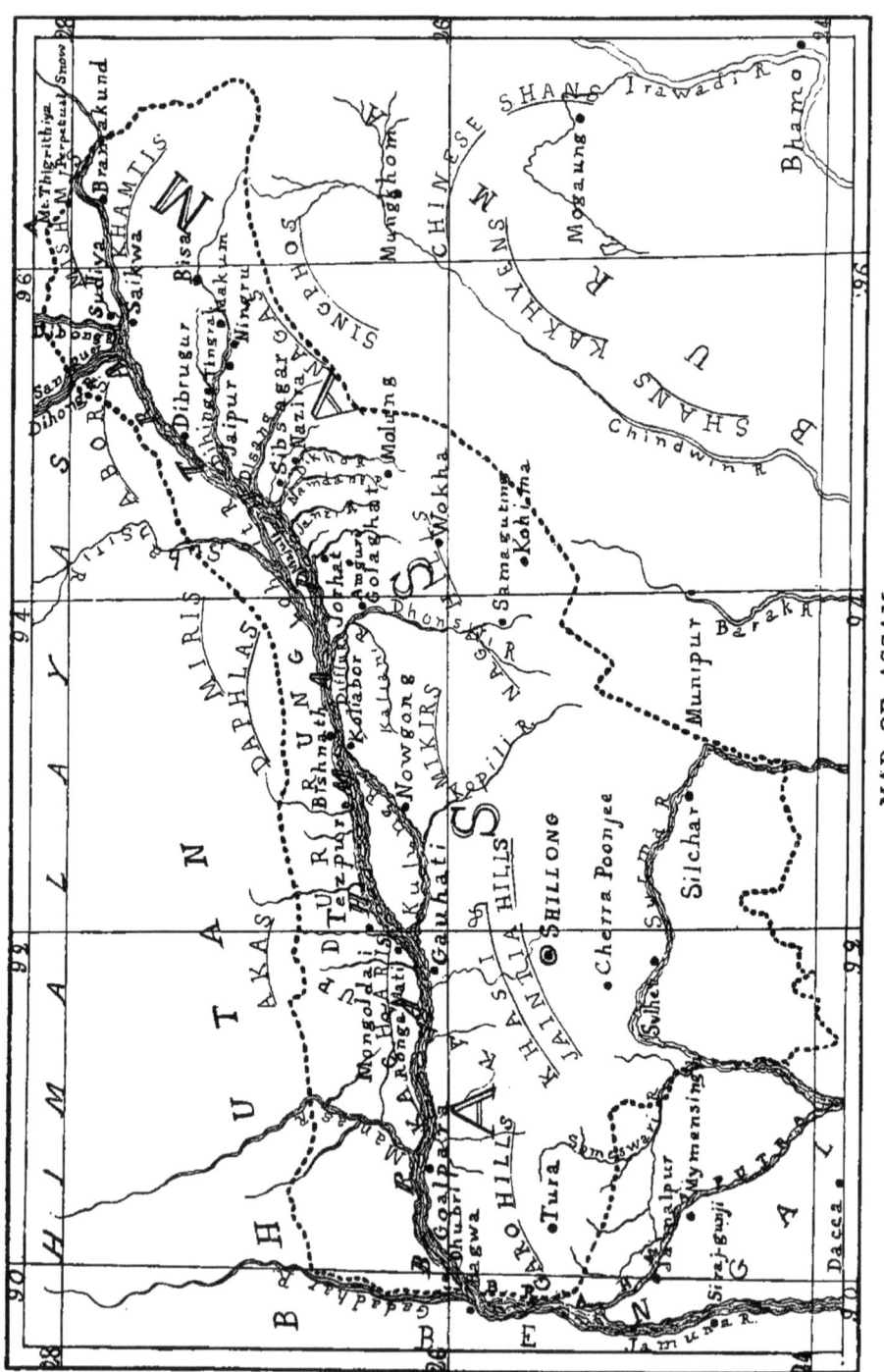

MAP OF ASSAM.

VIII.

UP THE BRAHMAPUTRA.

FROM Calcutta, the missionaries were obliged to provide their own means of conveyance to their station
eight hundred miles inland. These consisted of native
boats, dragged most of the way against a strong current,
by means of a rope attached to the mast. Some necessary articles for the journey and a Crusoe-life at its
termination, were carried along. In a sketch, by Mrs.
Brown, written for the young readers of "The Sunbeam,"
she thus destribes the rude craft in common use on the
river at the time :

"Occasionally Bengali merchants from Calcutta sent
up goods, which they bartered with the Assamese and
surrounding tribes, for the ivory obtained by killing
wild elephants, and the horns of buffaloes and rhinoceros
found in the country. The boats sent up by the merchants were very small, only some five or six feet in
width, and twenty or thirty in length, fitted up with a
kind of canopy for a roof, made of split bamboos and
palm leaves, which afforded protection from sun and rain.
The bottom was covered with coarse matting of bamboo ; the sides, partitions, door, windows and blinds all
being manufactured of the same material. The height
of the center was barely sufficient for an adult to stand.
These boats were manned by a manji or captain, with
six or eight men under him, who walked in a foot-path
along the bank of the river, pulling the boat after them
by means of ropes, somewhat as the canal boats of our

own country are drawn by horses. As no hotels or
market places were to be found on the way, it was necessary for the travelers ascending the river, to furnish
themselves in Calcutta with provisions and all other
accommodations which they might require for a journey
of at least four months. We learned that the current
of the Brahmaputra was in many places fearfully strong,
and that the bed of the river, like our own Mississippi,
was full of snags and sawyers which had been torn from
the banks by the strength of the current. Occasionally
rumors reached us, of the dense and terrible jungles we
should have to pass through, where roamed the wild
elephants, buffaloes and tigers of the country ; that the
boats would be moored at night to sandbars or small
islands of sand, formed by the changing current of the
stream, which were the daily resort of these wild beasts,
and that crocodiles and other monsters swarmed in many
parts of the river."

But youthful zeal, engaged in a good cause, sanctioned
by the great commission, was not easily dampened.
The call for missionaries to carry light to the people of
Assam, who were emphatically sitting in darkness and
in the region and shadow of death, had fallen upon their
hearts with such irresistible power, that in Mrs. Brown's
words, "We took it as a call from heaven for us to go."
Hence obstacles and dangers counted for nothing.

> "Through floods and flames, if Jesus lead,
>   I'll follow where he goes ;
> Hinder me not, shall be my cry,
>   Though earth and hell oppose."

A great purpose might well be needed, and a sure
confidence in God their defence, to give the missionary
pioneers courage and strength to push their lonely way

so far out beyond the safeguards of civilization, among savages skilled in barbarous warfare, and who looked upon a white face as that of a tyrant and an enemy.

But the more cruel, ignorant and dangerous they were, the greater the reason for the work just undertaken. Mr. Brown wrote to Dr. Judson from Calcutta, Sept. 8th, "We find there has been some disturbance at Sudiya, by disaffected tribes, but we apprehend nothing serious. What is before us, however, is only known to him who directs all things. To him we commend ourselves, and the poor heathen amongst whom we are to labor."

To another friend : "We hope soon to be able to penetrate amongst the Shans in the interior of the country, and also among the other native tribes, which are very numerous. These inhabit the ranges of the Himalaya mountains around Sudiya, and open a glorious field for missionary labor. There are the Singphos, the Miris, the Mishmis, the Abors, the Nagas and other savage tribes, some of whom are in a state very similar to the Karens, and have no written language or books. Here is the spot for missionaries to go in, and sow the seed of life."

The little company left Calcutta, Nov. 20, 1835, in three boats, one for each of the missionary families, and one to serve as a common floating kitchen and store-room. At meal time, when the exigencies of travel permitted, the latter was expected to come up alongside with supplies. Mrs Brown found her boat separated into two cabins by a partition of matting lined with coarse white cloth, of which the forward one was her apartment, while the rear room belonged to the boatmen, and there the latter cooked, ate and slept, always mooring at night by the river bank, or to a stake driven into a sandbar. Just when they would be "due" at Sudiya was a subject as to which the boatmen were profoundly ignorant, not to say indifferent. The journey

took all winter. Half a day was sometimes spent pushing
and pulling a boat off the sands which the changing
current had heaped in unsuspected parts of the channel.
When tracking became difficult, a stout bamboo stake was
driven into the bed of the river some distance in advance,
the tracking-rope was thrown around it and brought
back, then hauled in, thus drawing the boat on. This
mode of progress, called by the natives "gooning," was
not without its perils, both laughable and serious. The
boat was often tipped over, to the point of danger, and
then the natives would set up a hallooing which added
greatly to little Sophia's fright.

A detention of a week or more had been caused by
the shallow water encountered in passing into the Ganges. Of the intricacies of the delta Mr. Brown says:

"We first proceeded up the Hoogly into the Ganges,
thence down the main stream of the Ganges to the
point of its intersection with the Brahmaputra some
distance above Dacca. The Ganges and Brahmaputra
each diverge into numerous small streams as they approach the ocean; these meeting and crossing each
other in every direction, form a labyrinth of rivers,
called by the name of Sunderbunds. Boats pass from
the Ganges to the Brahmaputra at different points; the
nearer the passage is to the ocean, the more complicated
is the maze in which they are involved."

The remaining notes of the voyage are from Mrs.
Brown's home-journal.

"December 7th. Had a very difficult passage to-day
on account of the rapids. Sent a note to the daroga
[native superintendent of village] to send us fifty men
to help push the boats along, but they found it impossible, the water being only a foot and a half deep.

ANNUAL BOAT-FESTIVAL OF GANESHA, ON THE GANGES.

Feared we should be obliged to return to Calcutta. Concluded to get additional boats, take out our baggage and press forward."

The hinderance was finally overcome by dragging the boats over the sands nearly empty, and once in the deep waters of the Ganges, December 11th, after a week spent in going two miles, the little party must have drawn a long breath of relief. Here the crew "struck" for an offering to the holy river.

"When we entered the Bara Gunga (Great or Main Ganges) the men all insisted upon our giving a rupee to each boat for them to make an offering to the waters. One fellow, who speaks a few words of broken English, said, 'Master no give, boat no going; boat all break, boat all stop, all sit down.' We tried to laugh at them for their folly, and told them to try it, and if the boat stopped, to *let it stop*. The head man of the cook-boat is a stiff old Mussulman. Yet every night and morning he bathes his boat in the sacred waters of this river, to secure good luck for the day."

Within, the family settled down for seventeen literally "dragging" weeks. Sophia capered about as only she could, in such quarters. Through her mother's letters we can almost see the group in the mat-partitioned room. A call from an English officer at a government post sometimes proved embarrasing. Could he stoop low enough to escape the thatch and wedge his way through the crevices of furniture to a chair vacated for him by his host? A hearty laugh must have conduced to good-fellowship, and the sight of a friendly, though stranger, white face in the wilderness, was in itself a treat. But when they were well up the Brahmaputra, stations and visitors grew fewer and farther between. For an every-day picture, we see Sophia in the red cloak which her

Aunt Dorothy made for her in Boston before they set
sail, reading in the " Easy Lessons " sent her by Uncle
James, or ' scribbling on her slate, trying to make Burman letters," her mother writing, " muffled in a blanket," and the father hard at work on his Shan vocabulary ; both frequently interrupted by their chatterbox
with her "rhymes " and questions.   One of the latter
may bear repeating here.   Having been puzzled, no
doubt, by the multiplicity of strange languages of which
she was constantly hearing, on one occasion, when told
by her father that the Saviour loves little children and
calls them to come to him, she looked up and asked,
"Papa, does he tell it to them in English?"

Palm-leaves and woven bamboo proved insufficient to
protect the travelers from sudden tempests.   A violent
rain one night at Jamalpúr, beating in through their
wicker walls, waked and drenched them at the same
moment.

The Brahmaputra, or " Son of Brahm " is a majestic
flood, carrying the snows of the Himálayas* two thousand miles to the ocean through a channel from one to
three miles wide.   The natives consider the circular
basin called Brahmakúnd or Brahma's Well, in the extreme northeast of Assam, to be its sacred source.
Above the Brahmakúnd, rise stupendous heights of
perpetual snow, whose avalanches dash into untrodden
ravines, then melting into icy torrents, tear up and
sweep along the rocks that oppose their progress ; entering the valley at last by a series of cascades.   The
impetus gained makes the Brahmaputra, like the Ganges,
a current of tremendous power.

Much of our voyagers' course lay between banks
covered with dense jungle, composed of reed-like grass,
ten or twelve feet high, the domain of the wild elephant,

---

*Him-álay-a ; Sanscrit *him*, snow, *alaya*, abode.

buffalo and deer, as well as of tigers, leopards, wild hogs and jackals. They passed by forests, the home of peacocks and parrots, in whose thickets deadly serpents had their undisturbed haunts. In the level valleys, the river had made for itself borders of drifting sand—a comfortable couch for the boa-constrictor's long siesta after a solid meal. Here too, the crocodile loved to bask in the sunshine, returning to the water at night. At some points, where these aborigines had retreated before man, a clearing disclosed to the travelers a village, with groves of cocoa and betel, and fields of flax, mustard, indigo and rice—welcome signs of human occupation.

A SOLID MEAL.*

E. B. "Tuesday evening, January 5th, 1836. We all had quite a fright yesterday. Our boats were caught in a current so strong, that the men could not manage them. For several minutes we went round and round, as though we were in a whirlpool. . . . But we were at length borne down to a place of safety, and the boatmen by crossing over, got along without farther difficulty.

9. Yesterday we met Captain Charlton from Sudiya on his way to Calcutta for treatment of the wounds re-

*The boa-constrictor's dinner of raw venison was interrupted at this point by a shot from an English officer in Assam. He afterwards made this exact drawing of the situation.

ceived in the late battle with the Singphos. He gave us a very interesting account of the people. He thinks it would be unsafe for a person to go among them without arms, as they do not hesitate to take human life. They seem to be perfect savages, entirely in the state of nature, having no books, and are even without a written character to express their own language."

These people, inhabiting the south-eastern border hills which separate Assam from Burma, are called Singphos on the Assam side, and Ka-khyens or Ka-chins in Burma. They are an athletic race, above the ordinary standard in height, and for several generations were the terror of the Assamese, whom they were in the habit of capturing and enslaving. The captives often escaped, and when the British authorities refused to restore the fugitives, the irritated Singphos sometimes rebelled. A single British officer is said to have received and released from the Singphos 5,000 Assamese captured by them for slaves.

"Their language," Mr. Brown remarked after some intercourse with them, "possesses little affinity to any of the neighboring dialects. They have no regular and settled religious system, like the Shans, exhibiting few or no traces of Buddhism, though they possess some rude and general ideas of religion. They told Mr. Kincaid that they had a tradition that they once had books, but lost them. All their traditions are handed down in songs. Their dead are not burned, but buried with becoming solemnity."

E. B. "Jan. 15. Stopped yesterday at Goalpara, a military station, and most delightful place. Capt. Davidson came on board and invited us all to dine with him. A little before snnset, we walked up to his house, delightfully situated in one of the most elevated parts of the town. Snowy mountains were to be seen from his door. He has sent us from his garden, an apple, a plum and a peach tree in pots, to plant after we arrive at Sudiya."

At Goalpara Mr. Brown found a Shan teacher in waiting, sent down from Gauhati by Major Jenkins. Of this place, Bishop Wilson writes fourteen years later; "Its brilliant verdure, its hanging woods, the background of dim mountains, the tranquil river, smooth as a lake, quite enchanted us."

A hundred miles further east was Gauhati, the prin-cipal town in the province, interesting as being one of the ancient capitals of the Ahom dynasty, and contain-ing ruins of old fortifications. Three shrines in the vicinity are visited by thousands of Hindu and Buddhist pilgrims.

"The entrances to the [ancient] city were by guarded passes on either bank of the river. The ruins of the gateways of some of these passes are still to be seen, and the remains of the extensive fortifications may to this day be traced for miles in the mounds and ditches that now serve only to mark the ancient citadel. . . . Its brick, its mortar, its earthenware, constitute in some places a large proportion of the soil. Numerous carved stones and beautifully finished slabs, the remains of once noted temples, are constantly found beneath the surface of the ground ; its spacious tanks, the work of tens of thousands, the pride of its princes, and the won-der of the present day, are now choked up in the weeds and jungles, or altogether effaced by a false, though lux-urient soil, that floats on the stagnant waters concealed beneath."*

*Robinson's "Account of Assam."

These relics, as well as references in ancient records, show Gauhati to have been formerly one of the chief cities of India. It is beautifully situated, being encircled by densely wooded hills except where the Brahmaputra makes its way. "Several of the hills," says Mrs. Brown, "are tipped with huge old brick temples, residences of Hindu priests and nuns, and the resort of devotees to the Hindu faith." In the center of the river, opposite the station, which is on the eastern bank, stands a little rocky island called Umanond. According to the Hindu legends this island was formed by the god Siva out of the dust with which he had marked his forehead. It is a picturesque object, clothed as it is with trees, and crowned with a large temple, and is the resort of great numbers of wild peacocks and monkeys, which are all considered sacred by the priests. One old monkey of immense size was, for several years after the country came into possession of the English, maintained by the government on a pension of twenty rupees per month.

At Gauhati the missionaries were refreshed by letters from Burma and America. Here too, Sophia had a notable experience, her first elephant ride. One of Major Jenkins' elephants came to the wharf, knelt down and kept quite still while her papa carried her up a ladder to a cushion on his back. The great gentle creature then raised himself, (not minding at all that cruel mahout on his neck, with an iron spike!) walked off, and showed them the wonders of the town.

Above Gauhati, the river banks are rocky, and the current became so increasingly rapid, as sometimes to drag the boat backwards, and force the crew to run back with it. Tezpúr [Tez-poor] was reached, however, without accident, on Febrary 6th. Capt. Mathie called, and afterwards sent down palkees and elephants to take the party up to his house, where they had the pleasure of meeting Dr. McLeod, the physician stationed at

Bishnath. Near Tezpur are gigantic ruins of temples of Siva, silent witnesses of a long past civilization and magnificence. Ruined gateways aud outworks connecting the encircling hills show the ancient fortress to have been twenty miles in circumference. Here are also the ruins of the palace of Ban Raja. A mile west of the town is a swamp, the legendary scene of a contest between Krishna and the Raja, whence the ancient name, Sonitpúr, meaning Field of Blood.

E. B. " Feb. 15, Monday. We left Bishnath on Saturday, but having a strong head wind and considerable rain, did not get on far. This morning we started on, but the bank was lined with formidable rocks, and the current being very strong, the men in attempting to pull us along broke our rope, and we were driven back to within a few rods of the place we left on Saturday, before we could stop. We were very much alarmed, for had the boat hit the sharp points of the rocks while going with such force, it must have been dashed to pieces. . . . We sent back to Major White, who very kindly provided us with another rope. Our cook came in a canoe, and brought us our breakfast about noon.

19. Yesterday we had a most splendid view of the Himalaya mountains, covered with snow. We have had a fine favorable wind, and have been going rapidly under sail, all day. I suppose we have come as far as they could have pulled us with a rope, in four or five days.

20. I have this morning again to record the mercy of God in protecting us through a season of danger. Last night about midnight arose the most terrible tempest of wind and rain that I ever witnessed. The water was in great commotion. Our boats were fastened to the shore with ropes, but the wind beat upon

them with such violence, we feared the ropes would give way, and we should be sent helpless upon the dashing waves.

Feb. 29. We were detained three days last week, having got out of fowls, (our principal article of food) and were obliged to send to Jorhat', a village eight miles inland, to the Raja, for a supply sufficient to last us during the remainder of the journey. Fowls, ducks and geese are found wild in the woods of this country in abundance, and are very easily domesticated.

Lieut. Miller overtook us at Jorhat'. He is in a small boat, with a great number of men to draw it, and will reach Sudiya in half the time that it will take us to go. His wound was in the shoulder ; he has now nearly recovered, so that he will again enter upon his official duties at Sudiya. It is feared that Capt. Charlton will never recover. It has been very warm and pleasant to-day. We all sat out in the front of the boat a long time this afternoon and talked of home, and friends and days gone by.

March 2. Met Drs. Wallich, McLelland and Griffiths from Calcutta, who have been in Sudiya for several months, employed by the English government, searching for the tea-plant.* They find it growing wild in abundance at Sudiya and and the region about, and by proper cultivation it can probably be brought to as

---

Thea Assamica, the indigenous tea plant of Assam, is thought by botanists to be the original parent species, from which the varieties cultivated elsewhere are derived. The English government commenced its cultivation at Jaipúr in 1835, and in 1836, the year of the founding of the mission, the first pound of Assam tea was sent to London. Later the Assam Tea Company was organized, and it reports in 1886, an annual export of tea amounting to thirty millions of rupees. Assam tea is valued for its superior aromatic and medicinal qualities.

great perfection as in China. Mr. C. A. Bruce from Sudiya was with them.

March 12. Herds of wild elephants and buffaloes are howling around us by night, but they do us no harm. We hope, if prospered, to reach Sudiya in eight or ten days. The house Capt. Charlton left is vacated, and we can occupy it until we get ours built.

March 23. Arrived at Sudiya, all in good health."

IX

PIONEER LIFE.

Having been transferred from their own boat to a smaller one, Sophia and her mother reached Sudiya a few hours in advance of the rest of the party, and Mrs. Brown, full of courage and hope, stepped from the boat to the landing. The step was the first in a toilsome course, which extended through years of hardship and suffering, leading not seldom into experiences of anguish and scenes of terror. Had she turned from the prospect before her, and persuaded her husband to seek some less exposed and more promising field, it might have been considered only the natural dictate of prudence. But there is a martyr-spirit which transcends mere self-seeking prudence; its laws and allegiance being those of another kingdom. Quietly and with purpose of heart, she went on; she could not do otherwise. Nathan and Eliza Brown may truly be said to have gone "bound in the spirit, unto Assam, not knowing the things that should befall them there."

The station of Sudiya, situated in one of nature's mountain coliseums, lies near the borders of Tibet in sight of the white domes of the Himálayas. From among the northeastern hills, Sudiya Peak lifts its turret-shaped crags, and to its right is grand, rugged Thigrithiya, whose triple peak looks down upon a wall of snow-mantled mountains, and the rounded ridge and lower ranges which in their turn overlook the Pass of Brahmakúnd. In the east, the lofty natural lighthouse called Beacon, after the sun has set, holds his fire on its summit visible more than a hundred miles, and before sunrise, catches the first ray from the under world. Southeast of Beacon, the Di- hing' River winds through its deep basin, and beyond, the Naga Hills continue the circular wall, through whose further gate the Brahmaputra issues. Sweeping to the right, around the low southwestern curve, the eye rests on Reging', the mountain home of untamed Abors, [Ah'-bors] and conical Regam', twin guardians of the northwestern gate, through which the Sanpú, the real Brahmaputra, here called Dihong', brings its flood a thou- sand miles from farther Tibet. Beyond the opening, dis- tant Himalayas show their snows in a clear air. The out- lying domes and towers of this many-gabled, and ice- tiled "roof of the world" recede before the vision, and leave at the exact north point, a pass, through which the Dibong' rushes to join its kindred torrents.

The lower, nearer spurs of the mountains are thickly wooded to the base, and the valley also, at that time, was for the most part, a dense tangled forest-jungle of caoutchouc, bamboo and palms, inhabited by tigers, bears, buffaloes, wild elephants and rhinoceros. Here and there in the depths of the forests, and the fast- nesses of the mountains, the exploring missionary could find a clearing, containing a native village. Following eastward in the track of returning Mishmi traders, he might reach the homes of that industrious tribe on the hills skirting the river valley. Inhabit- ing the northwestern hills were the fierce Abors, the terror of the Assamese, a colony of whom having lately come down to settle, Mr. Brown became parti- cularly anxious to have evangelized. Southward in the valley of the Buri-Dihing', were the Singphos; be- yond them the Nagas, and southward still, the main body of Shans, an outlying tribe of whom called Kham- tis, lived in the vicinity of Sudiya.

The early history of Assam, would contain records of incursions upon its fertile soil by warlike tribes from beyond its mountain barriers. Prominent among these invading tribes, were those of the Shan or Tai family, a branch of which, called Ahoms, crossed the mountains north of Burma, early in the thirteenth century. By degrees, they possessed themselves of the valley of the Brahmaputra, naming it after themselves, Ahom or Ahám, the "Peerless," (afterwards softened to Assám) and so assimilating themselves to the Hindu inhabitants in language, customs and religion, as to be regarded, not as aliens, but as a new caste of Hindus. Extending its sway over the lower provinces, the Ahom dynasty came into collision in the seventeenth century with the Mohammedan invaders from Bengal, successfully resisting them. A Mohammedan writer says of the Ahoms, against whom Aurungzeb sent an army, "They were enterprising, well-armed and always prepared for battle. Moreover they had lofty forts, numerously garrisoned, and plentifully provided with warlike stores, and the approach to them was opposed by thick and dangerous jungles, and broad and boisterous rivers." A century later the country became the prey of revolutions, and was for a time under the heel of a cruel Burman despotism, from which it was released by annexation to the British empire in 1826. Meantime upper Assam had been subject to incursions by other branches of the Shan race, among whom were the energetic Khamtis, who pushed on as far as Sudiya, and for a time ruled that part of the country. When the Burman rule was replaced by the British, the Khamti chief was allowed to retain his authority under the Raja Purunder Singh; but the misrule of the latter led the British government, after a few years. to take the administration into its own hands. The Khamtis resisted, by attacks and massacres; and the British troops severely punished the ma-

rauders, scouring the jungles in search of the ring-
leaders. From 1834 to 1840 was a period of excitement,
suspicion and defiance on the part of the hill-tribes, and
of panic among the unwarlike Assamese of the valley.

KHAMTI MAN AND WOMAN.

It was precisely at this unpropitious time that the
first missionaries arrived. The people to whom they
had been sent, were these very Khamtis. They were
not a numerous tribe; Mr. Brown wrote to Dr. Bolles,
not long after he commenced his labors for them;

" There are perhaps 1500 or 2000 Khamtis at Sudiya, and as many more in three or four other places between here and the Patkoi hills, separating us from the Burman territories; but the great body of Shans around Mogaung' and Bhamo' are not at present directly accessible to missionaries; though we hope they soon will be.."

Going out soon after his arrival, in company with an English officer, to visit the surrounding villages, he had discovered to his surprise and disappointment, that the only Shans within reach were a few scattered Khamti hamlets, and that the main body of the people for whom he had been preparing to labor, and from whose Christianization important results had been expected, lived " beyond the mountains !"   Even there they were reduced in numbers.   When Mr. Kincaid visited Mogaung in February 1837, he was informed by several elderly Shans who held office under the governor, that two-thirds of their people had disappeared from the provinces in the thirty years just past, having perished in deadly feuds with the Ka-khyens or Singphos, and been wasted by famine, massacre, devastation and oppression; hundreds of villages having been reduced to utter desolation.

The course to be pursued admitted of no question. Here, on this spot, was his field.   Hither he had been sent, and here he would labor for the heathen—of whatever race or name—who peopled this valley. Accordingly, he commenced work for both Khamtis and Assamese.   "This region," he tells his parents, " providentially opened before us; and after long and tedious journeys, we have at length arrived upon the ground where we shall no doubt spend the remainder of our days."   Moreover although too high expectations in some respects, had been raised, his faith in the mission to Assam remained unshaken; he believed it to be "one of the most important and encouraging fields in all the East."

The people immediately around the missionaries, were the valley Assamese; hence still another tongue must at once be learned. It was a written language, but without dictionary or grammar, and there was no interpreter. Pointing to an object, Mr. and Mrs. Brown would catch the name from the lips of a native, and write the sounds in Roman letters, enlarging their vocabulary of nouns day by day, and quickly picking up verbs and modifiers with the imperative momentary necessity of using them.

Almost every conceivable obstacle lay in the way of the new enterprise. Though under the British flag, the pioneers were in a hostile country, exposed to the attacks of savages. Having no permanent shelter for themselves or the inquirers they should gather about them, they must first turn their hands to the building of a school-house, next to dwellings for their families, and every detail must be taught to laborers to whom the whole operation was a foreign novelty; who had no tools, and with whom there was no intelligible means of communication. Men must be sent into the forests to cut timber for posts, but where is the axe? This useful article not having been included in the missionary's outfit, Yankee ingenuity is taxed to provide a substitute.

Here were pieces of iron; fragments of wood could be gathered, heaped and charred, and the softened metal at length beaten out and ground into something that would cut down trees, and shape them into the required posts. These the natives afterwards transported by hand to the building spot, the use of oxen for that purpose being unknown. The posts being firmly planted five or six feet deep, and standing several feet high, a floor of bamboos was laid on them as in Burma, reed walls were tied, and afterwards plastered with a composition of which mud was the principal ingredient. Lime for whitewash was the next necessity.   Luckily the missionary " came from the lime-kilns of Vermont," and was able to put into practice his observations there. He taught the coolies how to made a kiln and burn lime.

All this was at the expense of precious time, while a world of work of another kind was widening out daily before him, and the needs of the surrounding savages pressed sorely in on his spirit.   But it was a struggle for physical existence amid hostile surroundings; the fever-breeding rains in summer, and the chilling winds of winter lay in wait for the lives most dear to him.   In this inland climate, both summer's heat and winter's cold were greater than in the same latitude by the sea shore.   In October, Mrs. Brown wrote; " The weather is now delightful;" but when winter came, a fire in the house was necessary for the family health and comfort. There was not a stove in the district, probably not in the province of Assam.   For lack of better appliances, during the first cold season, a box filled with earth, held the fire in the children's living room, and the room held the smoke.   Before the second winter's cold came on, Mr. Brown found a bed of clay, molded it with the help of the natives, constructed a brick-kiln, and when the bricks were baked, laid the chimney with his own hands.   But the mud mortar seemed a treacherous dependence; what if the bricks should tumble about the children's heads in the next gale or earthquake?   The amateur mason came into the house tired out, bespattered, and almost discouraged.   He had lost faith in his chimney.   The hopeful wife encouraged him to go on and complete the experiment.   "If we fail," she argued, " others who follow, will have the benefit of our experience.   We were pioneers here, and we must be pioneers in everything that is done for the present.' She soon heard him singing at his work,

> " When we've been there ten thousand years,
>   Bright shining as the sun,
> We've no less days to sing God's praise,
>   Then when we first begun."

The chimney was a success ; and during that second winter, the father had the satisfaction of seeing his family comfortable by the fireside. A box of glass and other useful building articles were sent out by Mrs. Brown's brothers, and she wrote to her brother Josiah, May '38, " The window glass adds greatly to our comfort. Nathan with his own hands made some sashes last winter, and we have now one glass window in each room."

During the first rainy season the pioneers suffered from lack of nourishing food, being shut out from sources of supply in an isolated region. They were often obliged to send off two or three days' journey, for provisions, and made nearly all their purchases with salt, as the natives had little knowledge of or use for money. Even rice, the staff of life, was scarce.

"The poor natives," says Mrs. Brown, "are so improvident that they never lay up a store beforehand, so that they usually have a time of suffering at this season every year. There is no baker in the place, so that we get no bread. We brought with us a barrel of American flour from Calcutta, but it is mouldy, and will not make *bread.* We hope in a year or so to get a garden started, and raise vegetables of our own. I never felt so grateful for food as now. Being a little short gives us all an excellent appetite.

Our privations are no greater than we had reason to expect on first coming to a new and so remote a station, where there have never been more than two or three English residents at a time. If we can preserve our health, and ere long be the means of elevating some of the poor heathen around us, from this dreadful misery and darkness, we shall through eternity have cause for rejoicing that the Lord sent us here.

We are all of us picking up the Assamese language quite fast. Our cook and all in our employ are Assamese. A little slave-girl, who had run away from her cruel master, came to me the other day, and begged for a home. I felt the want of a little girl to do many things for me, and she seemed such an object of pity, I took her, and shall keep her as long as she is a good girl and wishes to stay with me. Her name is Loubúri."

N. B., May 19. "To day, a young priest, sixteen or eighteen years of age, came of his own accord, and offered to lay aside his sacred garments, if we would receive him as a scholar, and teach him English. Finding him to be an intelligent lad, we agreed without hesitation to receive him. The next day, he laid aside his yellow cloth, which procures for every priest the homage of his fellow-man, and to be styled "Phúra"—that is God, or Lord—and put on the common dress of the country. Several brethren in Windsor, Vt., have offered the money necessary to support two native scholars, and we have concluded to take this young priest for one of them. We call him Elijah Hutchinson. He is an orphan."

From the treasurer's account it appears that Elijah was afterwards employed by the mission as a school-teacher.

On the 7th of June, 1836, a few half-frightened, wholly unclad young savages squatted on the matting at Mrs.

Brown's feet in the just finished bamboo school-house. A gleam of intense curiosity mingled with suspicion, might be detected in the furtive glances with which they watched her movements, the most timid crouching by the door, or edging towards a window, alert and ready like startled deer to leap out at any moment and fly back to their native jungle. Who this strange white creature might be, and what she could want of *them*, must have been study enough for one day. By degrees Mrs. Brown gained the confidence of the little boys, and Mrs. Cutter of the girls ; and began to give them such instruction as was possible with only ten weeks practice in the language. On the 19th, Mr. Brown had finished a small romanized Assamese and Khamti spelling-book for their use.

"For the last six months we have had a native school in operation. During the latter portion of the time, the school has been carried on by Brother and Sister Cutter. The scholars have made surprisingly rapid progress, considering the time that has been devoted to them. They can now read in their own language with ease, and the class in English have made such advances as to be able to read simple sentences with general correctness."

"They appear to be bright, intelligent boys," Mrs Brown reports. "and very anxious to learn."

When the mission families removed from Capt. Charlton's house at cantonments to the banks of the Kuril, a mile distant, another school-house was put up, in which she taught the village girls.

"I have just been out," she wrote to a friend, June 17, 1837, "to oversee the men who are to-day finishing off a school-house. I hope to commence a school for girls next Monday. Pray, my dear friend, that the Lord may bless and prosper me in this work. Mrs. Cutter has the boys' school which I commenced last year. It numbers about forty scholars, and they are all getting on finely. She has advanced one of the boys to be a teacher, so that they have been able to continue the school, although they have both been ill."

Later in this year other schools were established in neighboring villages, and the wild jungle boys who at first would fly from a white face as they would from a tiger, were persuaded in numbers to come in.

The following words of encouragement to the struggling mission, came from Dr. Judson :

"I am glad to hear that you are beginning to print the language in the Roman letters. This is what I should do in such a country as yours, however injudicious I think it to attempt to do so in such a country as Burma. . . . I am glad to hear also that you are getting up schools. In your situation, schools and elementary works, ought, I think, to engross almost your whole attention. I hope that you will soon see schools flourishing around you in every direction."

And to Mr. Brown:

"The tomb over your little William is finished. . . . We sometimes walk out to the burial ground, and recall the past. Tell Sophia that I shall always remember her, though I suppose she will forget me. . . .

Your letters are full of interest. You have a hard field to cultivate ; but it will, in time, yield a rich harvest. We are going on as usual. A few baptizings now and then. Hard at work revising and reading proof-sheets. Have been printing a second edition of the Life of Christ, 15,000, preparatory to a thorough revision of the New Testament, which we intend soon to print in an edition of ten or fifteen thousand. I wish

you would kindly send me any corrections that have occurred to you. . . . I have many things to say, but
my letter is called for by Bro. Hancock, who is just
going off to Bengal.

With affectionate regards to Sister Brown,

Your Brother,

A. JUDSON."

N. B., May 11. "Yesterday we received a large packet
of letters overland from Ava! This is the first direct
communication, I believe, that Europeans have ever had,
through the Shan and Singpho country. Capt. Hannay,
who brought the letters, left Ava in November with one
thousand men, but he did not come farther than Mungkhom, having accomplished the chief object for which he
was sent up, namely, to seize the Daphla Gam [Chief of
of the Daphlas] in hopes thereby to settle the disturbances among the Singphos. Capt. Hannay sent on, however, a company of twenty Burmese and Singphos, who
have been forty days coming from Mungkhom to this
place. They represent the route as very difficult. Many
of the intervening tribes of Nagas were fighting, which
rendered it unsafe to pass through, and so they were
obliged to travel out of their way. Much of the distance
they had to cut their track through almost impenetrable
jungles.

Between Ava and Mungkhom the people are chiefly
Shans and Singphos. At Mogaung, a Burmese governor is stationed. Capt. Hannay was several times inquired of for tracts, which shows that there would be a
wide field for distribution in that quarter. Had considerable conversation with the Burmans who came
over, and gave them tracts and scriptures, which they
were glad to receive. Promised to give them one or
two entire copies of the New Testament on their return
from Gauhati, which place they are to visit, before they

return to Ava. They are going there by order of the
Burmese government for the purpose of searching out
ten or fifteen hundred Burmese subjects who are said to
be residing in Assam.

May 23. Had the satisfaction to learn that Mr. ——
has abandoned the sale of ardent spirits. He has been
induced to take this step in consequence of reading the
Seventh Report of the American Temperance Society,
a masterly document, and one which ought to be in the
hands of every officer in India. It has often been the
practice hitherto to secure the good will of the native
chieftains, by making them large presents of ardent
spirits, thus encouraging a habit which produces the
same ruinous effects on these poor people, that it does
upon the American Indians. The greatest curse of this
country, at present, is opium. A large portion of the
inhabitants are completely besotted by it. It carries
off immense numbers to an untimely grave."

A melancholy case came under Mr. Brown's observation about a fortnight later, in the person of one of his
workmen, who had been a confirmed opium eater, and
died, reduced to a mere skeleton, after a protracted illness,
during which medicines han no effect. While trying to
relieve the sufferer's physical and spiritual wants, the
missionary found that he was conscious " even from the
faint light of nature," of his low estate. He had no
hope of happiness beyond the grave, said that he had
been a great sinner, and must now endure whatever
punishment God should inflict upon him. Doubtless
Mr. Brown told him, however imperfectly, of the blood
shed for the remission of sins ; but his journal entry expresses only his painful inability to " communicate to
his mind, in proper and perspicuous terms, the love and
mercy of a Saviour, even towards the vilest of sinners."

"Not one of his old acquaintances or companions would deign to help or regard him in the least, during his sickness; not one could be found to attend upon him in his last moments, or close his dying eyes, and it was with the utmost difficulty I could obtain persons to bury him. They said it would injure their caste. Truly 'the dark places of the earth are full of the habitations of cruelty.' This poor laborer was treated no worse than thousands of others, who have in like manner, been deserted by their friends in the hour of sickness and death. What aggravates the sufferings of the people is their poverty and improvidence—scarcely ever do they lay up anything against the approach of sickness or old age, and consequently are left, at the time of their greatest distress, without the means to procure even the necessaries of life."

In sending out articles for this station, our friends could select nothing which would be more acceptable or useful than a good *box of medicines.*"

Mr. Brown found a piteous state of physical destitution among the Assamese. He wrote home suggesting that a missionary farmer should come out to teach the natives husbandry, that they might learn how to supply their own wants, and acquire habits of industry, thrift and temperance.

"In order to do anything effectually, the business should not be done by missionary laborers, but by some lay brother sent out expressly for the purpose. Such a person would not need any support from the Board after the first year or two, as the establishment would necessarily bring in considerable profits. The soil around Sudiya is inferior to none in the world. and produces all the tropical fruits, and would produce nearly if not quite, all those of the temperate regions. There would be a good sale for everything raised, and other missionaries, having such a market to go to, would not be necessitated, as now, to spend a great portion of their time in procuring the necessaries of life."

With so much around them to draw out sympathy, the toilers needed to be sometimes themselves reinforced by words of cheer. Mrs. Brown writes to her home-friends :

June 19, Monday. "A dawk [mail] boat came in yesterday, and brought to our great joy, a large packet of letters from America, via Moulmein. I sat up until nearly twelve o'clock last night reading them, and went to bed to dream of friends and home, and joys departed never to return. Just for a moment fancy yourselves in the heart of Asia, far removed from every trace of civilization, education, or Christianity, surrounded by heathen who are given to lying, theft, opium-smoking, "idolatry, witchcraft, hatred, variance, emulation, wrath, strife," to everything wicked, rude and unlovely, who are without any conception of the object for which you came among them, and you can perhaps form some idea of the situation, and imagine the joy that gladdens our hearts when a packet of letters come to hand from our beloved America, from our dear friends who feel for us, sympathize with us in all our trials, pray for us, and often speak encouraging words to urge us onward in the path of duty. Often when nearly discouraged, and ready to faint, have I received new life to press onward, by means of your kind letters."

On the 8th of September, 1836, the vacant place in the household was filled by the birth of a second son, who was named after both his grandfathers, Nathan Ballard Brown.

E. B., Dec. 31. " I had quite forgotten that this was the last day of the year, until we had assembled for evening worship, when the sudden recollection led me to reflect upon the mercy of God towards us as a family during the past year. He has carried us through perils upon the waters, through perils in the wilderness, and restored us repeatedly from dangerous illness. " Bless the Lord, O my soul, and all that is within me, bless His holy name."

X

PERILS IN THE WILDERNESS.

THE martyr missionary, Winfrid, of Germany, is said to have prayed in the eighth century :

" O merciful God, who willest all men to be saved,
And to come to the knowledge of the truth,
Have mercy upon the Assamese,
Hindus and Mohammedans,
And all the inhabitants of Assam.'

Such a prayer went up daily from the thatched cabin of the Sudiya pioneers.

A year's observation of the character, habits, and religious ideas of the Assamese tribes, only strengthened Mr. Brown's conviction of the importance of the field.

"We ought to have one missionary for every distinct language spoken here, which are at least five, besides several other Naga dialects a little farther to the South. . . . There is another tribe which I hope will not be forgotten in sending out further missionaries, namely the Mishmis, living on the hills to the north-east. . . . Two or three days ago I saw a company of them, consisting of thirty three men, all armed with spears and marching along in Indian file, just come down from the mountains for the purpose of selling their trinkets. I should not have had the least fear in accompanying them back, provided I had understood their language. A thorough acquaintance with the native tongues is a *sine qua non* in traveling amongst these rude tribes."

"There are so many fields of labor here,' he' adds, "that a missionary is at a loss which to enter." He had already recommended Nowgong to the consideration of the board, as a desirable post of occupation, and Gauhati as a center of operations for the Christianization of the Garos.

The next year, in view of the fact that the English Baptist missionaries were about to vacate Gauhati, Mr. Brown made another appeal for the Nagas, Khasias, Mikirs and others, and said of Assam in general:

"We know of no more inviting field in the missionary world—no field where we could with so much satisfaction labor and die in this precious cause. But the solitary efforts of the few now on the ground, are but a drop in the ocean—they are swallowed up and lost amid the wide-spread desolation and darkness, and unless the field is speedily supplied with more laborers, we fear the cause will languish, while heathenism continues to spread and strengthen itself for years to come. May God in mercy look upon us and send us help, and bring salvation to this benighted and long neglected land."

Meantime he himself went on with his work for the Assamese and Khamtis, having prepared in January, 1837, a tract consisting of the parables of Christ, which was put into immediate use as a text-book in the schools, the pupils daily committing to memory lessons from the parables. The Sermon on the Mount and a catechism followed in the spring.

In February the missionaries removed from canton·ments to a native village, a mile above, on the north bank of the Kuril. This location gave them easy access

by boat to most of the surrounding villages.   Imperfectly
sheltered as they had been, both during the rainy and
the cold seasons, they had already suffered considerably
from fevers, but thus far the well had been able to look
after the sick.   In May, Mr. and Mrs. Brown were both
attacked at the same time, after some days and nights of
anxious watching over their infant child, ill of the fever
The condition of the family, with no physician or nurse
and it would seem, very insufficient if any domestic.
attendance, was distressing.   Mr. and Mrs. Cutter were
also ill at the same time.   Little Nathan, only just past
the crisis of the fever, wailed unattended, till at last the
sick mother, unable longer to listen to his cries or witness the acute distress of the father, who was alarmingly
ill, with great effort left her bed for the store-room to
find something for their relief, and twice fell fainting to
the floor.   At length friendly help came: an apothecary
arrived with leeches and medicine; the kind Bruces "did
all they could for our comfort," and sent two of their own
servants.

About this time the news that new missionaries were
on the way, was received with "great joy," and some
trembling.

"It is a bad season of the year. to come up the river,
on account of the heavy rains and strong currents, which
make navigation ·extremely difficult during the months
of July and August.   May our brethren be preserved
from every danger!"

On the 26th of April, Messrs. Thomas and Bronson
had started from Calcutta.   The first part of the journey
was prosperous, but after passing Goalpara, their progress was retarded by the rapid current, a head wind and
almost impenetrable jungle, through which, unable longer
to row against the stream, the oarsmen were obliged to

break their path, in order to tow the boat. Above Tezpúr some of them fell ill and the others became almost disheartened. At Bishnath, June 17th, nine more men and three canoes were hired, and new ropes provided. Later Mr. Bronson says :

"After slowly progressing a few days, we were detained by a tremendous current, against which our boatmen declared themselves unable to advance. The rain fell in torrents, rendering our situation very distressing. Here I was taken ill of the deadly jungle fever, owing no doubt to fatigue and exposure to the exhalations of the dense jungle about us. In this state of things it was proposed that Brother Thomas take a small boat and hasten with all possible speed to Sudiya, to obtain medical assistance, and more men to assist in pulling our boats up the river. After much deliberation this plan was agreed upon."

On the 1st of July, accordingly, Mr. Thomas entered a light canoe with four natives, who rowed rapidly up towards Sudiya.

On his way he met two small boats containing four men sent down by the Sudiya missionaries with ropes to aid in pulling up the budgerow ; but he still pushed on to obtain the needed medicines for Mr. Bronson. On Friday morning, July 7th, he had taken an early start, the three canoes moving in line near the bank, all making good headway against the current. They were near Saikwa, within an hour of Sudiya ; his field of labor was in sight, when two trees, from whose roots the earth had been washed by the swollen stream, were jarred, lost balance and fell with a crash across the middle boat, in which Mr. Thomas sat, instantly sinking it, the larger one felling the missionary with a bolt of death. There was one movement of the hand, one bubbling breath, and

the spirit escaped to everlasting life. His oarsmen
sprang out, but either afraid or unable to remove the tree,
between which and the sunken boat the body was
wedged, left it under the wash of the swift current.

That morning the missionaries at Sudiya were reading
letters just received from Burma, giving the intelligence
that the friends at Ava were safe. Looking up, they
were startled by the unexpected re-appearance of three
of the boatmen whom they had sent down to the assistance of the travelers. The men seemed speechless with
horror or fear, but at length the details of the accident
(except the name of the victim, which they did not
know), were elicited from them. Mr. Brown was ill;
Mr. Cutter quickly secured a boat and men, took spades,
hoes, axes and blankets, and hastened to the fatal spot.
The current having washed for some time against the
fallen tree, had changed its position and that of the canoe, and the body was soon lifted out of the water and
conveyed to the station, where on the following afternoon the English officers, Mr. Bruce and the missionaries
committed it to the grave; Mr. Brown conducting the
funeral services. Though still very feeble, he started
the next day down the river to assist the remaining missionaries, learning from a letter in Mr. Thomas' trunk,
of the dangerous illness of Mr. Bronson. The following
is Mr. Brown's own account of this journey:

'Reached at two o'clock the mouths of the Dihong
and Dibong rivers, whose tumultuous currents bore me
on with the greatest rapidity. Stopped about six o'clock
amidst a great number of islands. Almost despaired of
finding the missionaries, on account of the numerous
channels. Had a hasty supper cooked upon the sand,
and lay down for the night in my little canoe, but felt
very uncomfortable, owing to the cold and wet, as we
had heavy rains.

Tuesday. Started early this morning, and soon left behind us the labyrinth of islands which had so perplexed us yesterday. Came into the open stream near the mouth of the Dibru river, and about eleven o'clock I had the unspeakable happiness of meeting some boatmen who gave information that the missionaries' budgerow was three or four hours below. Found them in the greatest distress ; their boats moored beside a low, unhealthy jungle, where they had been stopping for several days, the boatmen refusing to proceed any further against the current ; and to add to their afflictions, they were out of provisions, while Brother Bronson lay extremely reduced by a very severe attack of jungle fever. As soon as they heard that a white man was coming, their feelings overpowered them, and they immediately sunk upon the couch in tears. I entered the room, but the emotions with which we met were too strong for utterance, and we all sat down and wept together.

After consultation, we concluded to leave the large boats and hasten on in small canoes to Sudiya, with all possible speed. We were surrounded by an unhealthy atmosphere, which it was necessary for us to escape from as soon as possible. We accordingly hastened to cover with mats, and fit up as well as we could, two small canoes, each about a cubit wide, which I had brought down with me. Brother Bronson and I entered one of them, and the two sisters the other, and thus we commenced our uncomfortable journey, while the rain poured down in torrents. Though very inconvenient for traveling, these light boats are the safest which can be used in coming up the river at this season of the year. We started on Wednesday morning, and reached the mouth of the Dibru river about eight o'clock in the evening. Felt the need of a good supper, but could not obtain it, and were obliged to content ourselves with a hasty meal cooked with difficulty upon the wet sand. Brother Bron-

son is in a very low state, and we fear the journey will
be more than he is able to bear, especially since we can
procure no food suitable for a sick person.

13. Thursday. To-day a kind providence has favored us with a fair day, and we passed rapidly up the
quiet waters of the Dibru, avoiding the great river, where
the current is very dangerous.

15. Saturday. To-day we have been struggling
with the currents of the great river. Passed many
dangerous places, where the trees had fallen in from the
bank and obstructed the passage, while others were continually falling, as the stream carried away the earth from
their roots. Many of these spots exactly resembled the
place where Brother Thomas was killed, and our journey
was on this account clothed with additional terror,
Passed into another small stream at evening, the Keruá,
which will bring us out nearly opposite to Sudiya.

17. Reached Sudiya at six o'clock this evening. Although our situation since leaving the budgerow, has
been very unpleasant, yet we all feel our health rather
improved than otherwise.

Brother Cutter started off for the purpose of bringing
up the budgerow and the baggage boat. He succeeded
in starting the boatmen on, and we had at length the
pleasure of seeing the boats arrive in safety before our
doors, with all the baggage, among which were the new
printing and standing presses sent out for this station.
These have arrived most opportunely, as we stood in
great need of them."

Mr. Bronson says :

"The coming of Brother Brown was to us like that of
an angel of mercy. He brought us many little comforts,
which we very much needed, and what was more welcome
than all, the means of leaving the dismal jungle in

which we had so long been detained. We immediately prepared to leave the boats, and on the following morning set out in two dingees for Sudiya. These boats are only large trees, hollowed. I filled my half of one, as I lay on a small mattress. . . . . The spot where my dear brother closed his mortal career is to me one of mournful interest. One end of the boat still lies under the pressure of the tree that fell upon him. The other end rises considerably above the water, as if to point out the spot to the passing traveler, and tell the mournful tale."

The following stanzas are from Mr. Brown's " Lines on the Death of Rev. Jacob Thomas," which were published at the time in the *Calcutta Christian Observer*:

* * * * *

Alas ! the shore thine eye beholds, thy feet shall never
 tread :
Yon lofty tree a summons hath, to bear thee to the
 dead !
The dwellers in that valley ne'er shall hear thy warning
 voice,
Nor the wild sons of yonder hills at thy approach
 rejoice.

And thou that lovedst him, child of sunshine ! now for
 grace to rise,
And fix thy hopes for comfort high beyond the fading
 skies ;
To thee the loved returneth not ; he treads the spirit-
 shore ;
The eye that kindly beamed on thee—it beams on earth
 no more.

Gloom hung over the mission all through that summer. It is not strange that at times a shadow fell even upon Mrs. Brown's cheerful spirit, deepened by anxiety concerning home-friends, from whom, by some mischance, almost no news reached her during that sad year. She writes to her sister, September 24th:

"You will no doubt have heard long before this reaches you of the distressing situation in which our new missionary friends reached us. . . . The body of Brother Thomas was rescued, brought here and buried. Mr. Brown got two or three canoes and a large number of men and went down the river as fast as possible to find the remainder of the company and bring them away. He succeeded in getting them all here alive, after having passed through seasons of suffering too great to be described. Mr. and Mrs. Bronson have since lived in our family. He gained strength very fast after landing, but has had two or three slight attacks since. Mrs. Bronson, having overdone taking care of her sick husband, has been ill ever since her arrival, and much of the time we have thought her dangerously so. Dear child, she has had a hard introduction into the missionary life.

. . . Oh, sister, I dare not express all I feel. I sometimes have an unconquerable desire to see my friends once more before I die. But the Lord has been gracious to me; I should be very ungrateful to speak of trials and sufferings without at the same time acknowledging the goodness of the kind Hand that has so often given me support, and at times such sweet peace and consolation. As much as I desire to see you once more, I have no settled wish to give up laboring in the missionary field and return. No, it is my happiness to be here so long as I can in any way help forward the blessed cause. The souls of the poor heathen are as

precious to me as ever. It is but little that I am able
to do for them, but that little will help to prepare the way
for others who may follow me. I pray to be contented in
this situation, knowing that those who sow and those
that reap are alike accepted of the Lord, if they only
labor in His spirit.

October 18th. Mrs. Bronson is still very ill indeed ; I
cannot possibly find time to write. I have been obliged
to dismiss my school for a few weeks. . . . Pray
don't forget me. If you cease to write me often, I cannot
promise you that it will not break my heart. I shall try
to write a letter to brother Jonathan and sister Sophia
very soon."

With the cold dry season, a good degree of health, to
which a settled home must have contributed much, returned to all the members of the mission families ; the
work progressed accordingly, and hope revived. Mr.
Bronson entirely recovered, and commenced the study
of the Singpho language. Mr. Brown wrote to his
parents :

" We are a happy band ; and as we are beginning to
gain familiarity with the language we feel encouraged.
We have two very flourishing schools, and are printing
tracts and books for them as fast as we can get them
prepared. I read a portion of the Scripture with explanations in the Assamese language every evening at
the school-house, and close with a prayer. Quite a
number of Assamese are generally present. Eliza and
I both feel much more settled in missionary work now
than we have ever done before. It is a field that we
have long fixed our hearts upon, and it becomes every
day more interesting to us. Oh, that we may see the
work of the Lord commence here and witness the out-
pouring of the Holy Spirit upon this valley of dry bones.

I long to get a better knowledge of the language so that I can preach freely."

Mrs. Brown to Mrs. Lyman, February 2d, 1838:

" Our little son has for the last two months improved astonishingly; he can now almost walk alone, speaks a few words, (Assamese) and is as lively and happy as a bird. . . . Oh, what would I not give could I speak as freely in Assamese as in English? . . . There is a good number of scholars in the schools now, and we trust they are gradually gaining a little light. Mr. Brown is at work night and day translating the Scriptures and preparing books for the schools in the Shan and Assamese languages."

XI.

OF SUCH IS THE KINGDOM OF HEAVEN.

A STAINED scrap of paper appears to be the post script of a letter written at Sudiya one Saturday night in March, 1838, and through it as a lens, a pioneer "interior" may be seen. The belated Assamese fisherman or Khamti chief, poling his canoe homeward up one of the branches of the great river, might easily detect through the darkness, at one point, a few thatched roofs higher than his countrymen's huts. If he leaps ashore, curious to see more, he will find a garden-path leading up from the waterside to one of those dwellings. Within are lights and voices. Through that strange, transparent place in the wall, he may see a white-faced woman, unlike any in the hill or valley tribes. What can she be doing with her pointed quill, covering a bit of—is it white cloth or bark—with rows of odd black marks? She raises her head, smiling, and looks through a wide-open door into another room, where firelight from the hearth glances on bamboo rafters, and lights up a hanging basket, which is slowly swaying to and fro with the weight of a sleeping infant. Sleeping too, close by the fire, are the baby's pet dogs, Spring and Sancho, and his cat. Yonder, in a child's cot, shine a pair of bright eyes, from under a crown of flaxen curls, whose owner's lively prattle will soon be drowned in dreams. At a table sits the father, also plying a quill, while on the floor, a Khamti lad is engraving a picture on lead, under his instructions.

It was a peaceful, happy time. The mother writing that postscript, felt the comfort of one who has her family in health and safety about her.

The father writes by a later mail ·

"Our two little ones are playing around us in all the sprightliness of childhood, happy as the day is long. Eliza has been remarkably well this season, and we hope that we have both become so inured to the climate that we shall be exempt from those fevers that are so common to new comers.

We have been in constant expectation of a Burman war, but it has held off so long that it is rather doubtful whether it will take place just at present. We have had another Singpho disturbance here this summer, the result of which has been twenty or thirty killed amongst the people belonging to the English, and perhaps half as many on the other side, and the troops have burned several Singpho villages with their rice-fields.

Eliza has been translating Worcester's Primer, of which I shall send you a copy in a few days.

The pictures were engraved by a young Khamti belonging to our school. I have taught him to cut drawings in lead; the bulls, horse, duck and peacock were cut by me, all the rest, or nearly all, by the Khamti, without any assistance."

This pupil, whose name was Yong, seems to have given signs of talent, for the cuts are said, in the annual report of the Board for 1839, to be "executed with remarkable precision and delicacy."

"The Bronsons, who have been with us the past year, have now gone to form a new station at Jaipúr.* We

*Pronounced Jai poor'; (ai as in aisle.)

have daily evening worship in Assamese at the school-house, and every Sunday we go out to sit in a zayat on the great road, to talk to the people who come along. We cannot discover any interest in religious things among the people generally. All they know about religion is their caste, which, if they rigidly keep, they think they are very holy. Such a perfect destitution of all religious principles, although they profess to believe in a God, I never saw in any people."

Little Sophia gives some further particulars of the Sudiya life, outdoors and in, to one of her Charlemont aunts, under date Feb. 2, 1838:

" I have pieced most of the calicoes you sent me, into blocks. And I thank you for them. . . Mr. Miller and Dr. Pingault have gone up with a number of sepoys to fight with the Singphos. We don't know but they will attack us here. If they do, we will go down into cantonment, or get into a boat and go to Calcutta, or some place where they don't fight. . . . I suppose you have heard King William is dead, and that Princess Victoria has become Queen of England. The idea of being under the government of a lady must seem rather strange to you."

She had written to her grandmother the year before, that " we have a new house, and we have got it white-washed ;" that "we have a nice garden ; we have peas and beans, and carrots, spearmint and lemons, corn growing up, and peaches and mango trees and plum trees;" that " Mr. Vesey shot a tiger one day," and that "Mr. Miller has got a lame arm—the Singphos shot him," that "the heathen people are very foolish, they have a great image under a tree, and Shensan told me to say salam to it, but I think I will not do so any more, for the Bible says I must not worship an image, but must worship God," and that "I shall be five years old next month, and then it will be my birthday, and then Mamma will make a cake for me."

Among her other correspondents, whose letters she carefully preserved, were "Aunt Simons" (her quondam friend, Miss Harrington of the Corvo), now living in Ava, and "Uncle Simons;" who kindly gave her the latest news of their little people. From the house in Obo, where she and brother Willie used to be, she received pleasant accounts of two little missionary girls who lived in Moulmein. And there were letters from Mrs. Bruce and Aunt Bronson in Jaipur; from the latter she finds out all about her "wee baby sister," Mary Bronson, whom Aunt Bronson had carried off from Sudiya. A child so sociable and affectionate as Sophia could not but feel keenly the repeated partings from her playmates; she had grieved sadly in Moulmein at saying good-bye to the missionary children who came and went; and now in Assam her little friends still had a sad way of leaving her. "Nathan and I are the only white children in Sudiya now," she writes to Aunt Dorothy.

A complete set of the publications of the American Sunday School Union which had been sent to the mission, proved a great boon to this lonely little girl. Among her papers is found a manuscript catalogue of a part of this library, made out by herself. She loved the "pretty story-books;" they were her constant companions.

Her parents found ways of supplying her with the outdoor recreation so natural and necessary to childhood. There was a healthful amount of play in the day-time; the garden had its lilies and jessamines to be looked after ; there were sunset walks with mamma and papa, sometimes varied by the babas* being put into the baby-carriage and drawn by the latter ; and in hot weather there were pleasant evening excursions down the Kuril in the dingee. How refreshing was the change from sultry heat to delicious coolness, as soon as the point was turned, and the boat entered the great river ! " Papa " himself was full of fun and jollity, enjoying the play-time just as well as if he had not seen thirty years instead of six. If only baby Nathan would grow up faster ! She tries to interest him in her books, but he prefers a hammer.

A little letter to Uncle Simons, September 26, '38, tells him, " I do love my dear brother Nathan very much," and that he is two years old, and can say *"Moi America manuh,"* (I am an American man.) She adds regretfully that " Nathan cannot talk *well*," and at that word the letter sudddenly stops.

An hour or two later, the motherly little sister was taken with jungle-fever. On the 28th the disease assumed an alarming form, and medicines ceased to have effect. She became insensible ; and on Saturday morning, the fever ceased, from having run its course, and was succeeded by the mortal coldness. A little past noon that day, September 29, 1838,—"while we stood watching, a solemn stillness settled over her features— the golden bowl was broken—the gentle spirit had passed away !"

Her death was almost as sudden as that of little William. The mother's piteous cry was, " How can I give thee up, my child ? my child ! " but she also said, " I trust I do sometimes feel a quiet resignation to the divine will." Mr. Brown wrote to Captain and Mrs. Ballard :

---

*A term applied by the natives to European children.

Sudiya, October 2d, 1838.

My Dear Parents: How true it is, that in the midst of life we are in death! Had you been called to select, from the three who left you six years ago, the one that should first be called away, would you have taken the little blooming flower that was reposing in all the fresh- ness of health upon her mother's breast? Yet so it is, she is taken, and we are left. The dear little child has finished her race. Her sorrows are ended.

. . . There had evidently been a great change in the dear child's mind within the last three months, such a change as nothing but the Spirit of God could produce. I believe she has been happy in the idea of death, and in fact, has at times had a strong desire to depart and be with Christ. About a month before she died, she was very sick with a fever, and seemed to be perfectly reconciled to the idea of death, if it should please God to call her away. This was very different from what she used to be, as she was always very much terrified and distressed at the thought of death.

The next day after our little daughter died we had another born, which we call Eliza Whitney. May the Lord bless you, dear parents, and abundantly fit you for the solemn change through which you must ere long be called to pass. Eliza sends her best love,

Your affectionate son, N. BROWN.

The following is from the little memoir of Dorothy Sophia, written by her father :

"Our kind friends, Captain* and Mrs. Hannay, came and assisted in the preparation for her burial. Her remains were enclosed in a rude coffin, covered with

---

*Captain, afterwards Colonel Samuel Hannay, of the British army, form- erly stationed at Ava, and later at Jaipúr, was at this time second in com mand of Upper Assam, and had removed, during the summer of 1838, to Sudiya.

white cloth, and the same evening, just as the moon was rising above the eastern mountains, we followed her to her lonely grave. On the morning of the next day, the young people and other natives who were acquainted with Dorothy Sophia, assembled at the house, where her father addressed them from those precious words which had been so great a comfort to her : ' Suffer little children, and forbid them not, to come unto me ; for of such is the kingdom of heaven.' He also read to them portions of her journal, with which they were greatly affected, especially those passages in which she expressed such strong desires for their conversion. "

In the following May, Mr. Brown built a small brick monument over the grave, and set in it a slab of black marble prepared in Calcutta, with an inscription in English and Assamese.

E. to D. and S. B. November 4th, 1838. " Yes, our dear child has gone. Her place is everywhere vacant ; we no more hear the sweet prattle of her voice, or the joyous sound of her footsteps as she came bounding over the walks to meet and greet us on our return ; her place at board and hearth there is none to fill. At the family altar, her Bible lies untouched ; from her place of secret retirement no more is heard the voice of prayer and praise. Her little brother, too, ever made glad by her presence, goes moaning all the day, but yet too young to realize what a blessing he has lost.

Her death took place under most trying circumstances. Mr. and Mrs. Cutter, our dear friends, and only missionary associates, had left us for Calcutta only a week before, in the hope of obtaining such medical assistance as would benefit her declining health ; and the idea of being left without a female friend, and with no doctor in the place, with very little hope of ever meeting dear Mrs. Cutter again, did quite overcome me."

Alluding to her little daughter's conversion, the mother continues :

"We have been called upon to mourn for one of the most interesting and affectionate of children. . . . She had gained a great conquest over her naturally irritable temper, and was patient, obedient, kind and lovely in her ways. . . . There was a marked and decided change in her whole conduct. She seemed rapidly to grow in grace, and in the knowledge of the Lord. . . . I have known her to go alone several times in a day to pray for help to overcome particular temptations. Only a few days before her last illness she sat by me sewing ; she had a needle too small for her thread ; she worked a long time trying to thread it ; at last I observed a frown upon her brow, which betrayed impatience. I said, 'Sophia, I am afraid you did not ask God for patience this morning.' She said, 'Mamma, I will go and ask him now,' and immediately went alone to pray. She came back to her work with a calm and peaceful countenance, and soon remarked, 'My work don't trouble me now ; I feel patient.'" .

Before this, little Sophia had found much difficulty in overcoming her faults. Finding her alone one evening, in tears and sobbing because she had done wrong and had broken her good resolutions, her father said, "Can you not, my dear child, cast your soul upon Christ, with all your sins, and believe that He will pardon them all, as He says He will ? And can you not give yourself to Him to be His obedient child, and do just as He wants you as long as you live, and through all eternity ? " She replied, " Yes, papa, I think I will."

The father used to often take his little daughter in his arms and sing to her. Her favorite hymn was one with the chorus :

"In Jesus' arms there yet is room."

It was a grief to her that she could not join him, never having been able to learn. But when her mother told her that in heaven every one would have a voice to sing, she was quite satisfied. Once, after singing the hymn in which the line occurs :

" Sweetest of all names is Jesus,"

in order to find how much she understood, her father asked, "What is the sweetest of names ? " The little one quickly replied, "*Jesus* is the sweetest of names, and the Bible is the best of books."

One evening they were walking together on the veranda, talking about the stars which were shining above the mountain peaks in all the glory of a cloudless summer night. Her papa had explained that the twinkling points were worlds, containing millions upon millions of celestial inhabitants, each cared for by the same loving, protecting power as the inhabitants of earth. To test her comprehension and faith, he asked, "Are you not afraid, Sophia, that the Lord Jesus, with so many worlds to take care of, will forget such a little girl as you, and such a sinner too ? " She paused a moment, then replied, with peculiar emphasis, "*No papa, I do not think He will forget me.*"

Sophia was much concerned at the misery and degradation of the people about her. "I want the heathen should become Christians," she wrote in her little journal, "because then they won't quarrel and steal and lie." "I have formed a plan of having a school of Assamese children when I grow up, if mamma lets me, and I live. I want they should learn about Jesus, very much, now while it is not too late."

From memoir : "One evening while her father was reproving the *mali*, or native gardener and his son for theft, and telling them of the consequences of their evil ways, she listened with great interest, and· was heard praying for them after she had retired to her room.   The next day she asked her mother to pray for them, and said, "Mamma, if we pray for them, and teach them better, perhaps they will become Christians sometime."

And now the little missionary, at the age of six years, had gone home, to be with brother Willie and Aunt Cummings ; for that brave woman had found time among her many labors, for a tender, playful comrade-ship with Sophia, calling out the latter's honest and af-fectionate tribute, " *I love Aunt Cum-im.*"

Among the words of sympathy received by the parents were the following from Dr. Judson :

"Moulmein, Nov. 25, 1838.

Dear Brother Brown: Your letter, giving an account of Sophia's death, we lately received, and Mrs. J. and myself wept over it, and truly our hearts bled with yours.   All things considered, it appears to be the severest loss that has ever been occasioned by the death of any child belonging to the mission.   We think of you alone at Sudiya—the Cutters absent—the Bronsons removed—and on the back of all the rest, your darling eldest one, that you brought with you to the country, who had accompanied you in all your wanderings, and had grown up to be the dearest society you knew, next

to one another, so affectionate, so intelligent, daily de-
veloping some new loveliness, must be torn away from
your longing gaze and your fond embrace. The savor
of piety she has left behind is truly consoling. You
must assuage your sorrows by the consideration that
she is now resting in the bosom of the Saviour, safe,
safe beyond all the ills of life, all the evils of sin, all the
terrors of future wrath.

> 'Now, like a dew-drop shrined
> Within a crystal stone,
> Thou'rt safe in heaven, my dove,
> Safe with the source of love,
> The everlasting One.'

You have been privileged to rear a tender nestling,
a young immortal, a native of the earth, but an heir of
the skies. Grieve not that Jesus has plumed her un-
fledged wing for a premature flight, and taught her
early to sing the songs of paradise.

I hope, my dear brother, you will not fail to prepare
a little memoir, both in English and the native language. The extracts contained in my letter, and in
another you wrote to Mrs. Simons, which I have seen,
indicate that there are materials for a most interesting
account.

*   *

May God train up our children for heaven, and it is
enough. However they fare in this world, and whether
they live longer or shorter, O, may their souls be
saved, must be our daily, hourly prayer.

Mrs. J. sends love to yourself and dear sister. Let
us pray for one another, that we may be resigned to the
will of God, whatever befalls; and that the heavy afflic-

tions we may respectively be called to sustain, be blessed to our sanctification and greater usefulness.

Yours, ever affectionately,

A. JUDSON."

Thus, like a bird fleeing from approaching storms to a kindlier sky, little Dorothy—"God's gift"—took her homeward flight.

> "Oh, well it is forever,
>   Oh, well for evermore!
>   Her nest hung in no forest
>   Of all this death-doomed shore."

XII

MAKING ACQUAINTANCES.

MR. BROWN had built a shed or namghor beside the village road, in which, on Sundays, and fre quently during the week, he now began to talk about the new religion to companies of Assamese fishermen, Mishmi traders, and savages from the neighboring hills.

"April 29, 1838. To-day, had a good number of people at the zayat ; among others an old, fat, good-natured Assamese priest, who avowed that as to religion, it was of more concern to him how he should be comfortably clothed and have his stomach filled, than what should become of his soul. This is doubtless the real feeling of most of them, though few would be so frank as to acknowledge it. This man's doctrine did not appear to excite the least surprise in the minds of the bystanders, though they acknowledged that it was far more noble to attend to the concerns of the soul than those of the body, and even the old priest himself seemed at last rather ashamed of his principles. As he could read, we offered to supply him with some religious books, but he refused, saying he had learned one religion, and how could he throw that away and learn another ?

June 1, Friday. Commenced occupying the new zayat, which we have put up on the road leading to Bozál Village.

September 24. Have heard the news of the Jorhat Raja being deposed by the English government, on account of his oppression of the people, and his delinquency in paying the government revenues. The whole country is now directly under the control of English officers.

October 3. An eclipse of the moon this evening, nearly total. Such an event is generally looked upon by the natives as ominous of some calamity. They have no idea of the manner in which it is produced. They suppose a demon, called Ráhú, is eating the moon, and in order to frighten him away they all fall to screaming and beating their tom-toms. The mode of calculating eclipses is not unknown to the learned Brahmans of India, though the knowledge is confined to very few.

4th. Had a visit to-day from the Bisa Gám, a Singpho chief, whose village is one or two day's journey up the river. He appeared very favorable to the idea of our making books in the language of the Singphos. He is quite intelligent, reads and speaks both Burmese and Shan fluently. Gave him the Burman Digest and Shan Catechism, also a few medicines, which he asked for.

8th. Recommenced the schools left by Brother and Sister Cutter. We have now three, one in the village of Duisong, one at Bozal, and one in our own compound. The latter is reduced to a small number, owing to the division of the school; the children of the native inhabitants remaining with us, and the children of the sepoys being removed to form a school at the cantonments, which will be taught by Mrs. Hannay.

23d, Sunday. Heard of the sudden death of the Sudiya Khówá, the Khamti chief, who formerly had rule over all this district. Went out to his house this morning and found a number of Assamese and Khamtis assembled to lament his death. He was generally very much beloved by the people, and although his office was long since taken away, yet the natives have always continued to call him the Rája. His son,

a bright little boy, has attended our school for several
months past. He is the sole inheritor of his father's
estate, and probably will be a person of much influence
among his tribe. Found among the company several
persons who could read, and gave away six Khamti
Catechisms.

Many of the natives say Sudiya Khowa died of sorcery
(daini khále), the way in which they generally account for
any sudden and violent disease, which resists the power
of medicine. Some of them attribute the death of my
daughter to the same cause. They imagine there are
two kinds of sorcerers, *daini* and *bhutia*,* the former
found only among the Khamtis, the latter among the
Ahoms, or Assamese. The former are cannibals,
feeding on the flesh of living persons, and are regarded
as far the most terrible A person who is a *daini*, is
able to assume any form he pleases, though he sometimes attacks his victim in his own proper person. He
cuts open the body and takes away such portions of the
flesh as are suitable to be eaten, then fills up the vacancy
with dirt, grass or other materials, healing the wounds
so as not to show the slightest scar."

"We had a bigoted old Hindu in our employ for several
years as gardener, [Mrs. Brown wrote after her return
from India], who had long been ailing, and was emaciated nearly to a skeleton. He came to the house one
day, his limbs trembling, his face distorted, his body
bent over with pain, and clinching his hands in his breast,
said he had a *daini* in him and should soon die—he was
nearly consumed—there was nothing left of him but
straw! He died about a year after with delirium trem-
ens. The *daini* was opium."

---

* Pronounced *dye-nee* and *bhoo'-tee-a*

In case of severe sickness the Assamese send for a priest to propitiate the demon. If the case becomes alarming, a *Medhi* or medicine man is resorted to. "So great," says Mrs. Brown, "is their faith in the power of this mysterious personage, that he often effects a cure in cases of very severe illness"

A woman-servant being attacked with cholera, refused medicine and insisted on being taken to her own house and sending at once for the Medhi, to charm out the bhútia which had taken possession of her. Accompanying her to her hut, Mrs. Brown witnessed a remarkable scene :

"Before he arrived she was in a state of collapse. With her eyes fixed and her teeth set, she was to all appearance dying. The Medhi, who looked more like a demon than a human being, seated himself on the ground beside her, drew out from his wallet some roots and herbs, of which he prepared a decoction, and pressed a few drops between her teeth with a spoon. Then dipping the branch of a sacred tree into the liquid, he commenced waving it over her, repeating in a hurried jabbering manner, muntras [incantations] from the sacred shasters, gesticulating with head and hands at the same time.

In a very few minutes the muscles of his patient began to relax; her eyes closed, and in less than an hour he had put her into a quiet sleep. When she awoke, after a few hours, she reported herself well, and in three days was again at the house at work."

Another Assamese fakir or medicine man, here introduced, is playing a guitar on his back for penance. The long nails of his fingers and toes hang down below the arm and coil about the foot. The praying beads are around his neck; the wand of peacock's feathers used for charming away disease, with his bamboo crook and bag containing his earthly all, are by his side. His clothes and person are never washed. He smears his face and hands with a mixture of red clay and white ashes every morning, sits by the wayside during the day, and creeps into a cave in the rock at night.

The belief in dainis and bhútias was not confined to the lower and more ignorant castes. On one occasion at Sibsagar, a Christian Brahman widow stated with all gravity at a prayer and conference meeting of the church, that she had been at a witch's house, peeped through the cracks, and saw the witch feeding the young bhútias !

AN ASSAMESE FAKIR.

The Browns now stood alone at their truly desolate post. They had said good-bye to friends and associates, one after another, until all were gone. The infrequent mail-boat was their only remaining connection with the civilized world, and they must have watched for it as Crusoe did for the ship. When it came and brought no letters, Mrs. Brown got out her old ones, read them over and choked back the tears. Her husband felt " like a man on a treadmill, or at the pump of a sinking ship."

Early in the spring, Mr. Bronson had made an ex
ploring tour into the Singpho and Nága districts, and
stationing himself at Jaipúr as a central point, commenced the mission to the Nágas in March, 1838.   In
January, '39, taking a rubber tent and an interpreter, he
climbed the mountains in search of their remoter villages,
sometimes making his dangerous way through picturesque cañons, along a narrow path overlooking craggy
cliffs far below.   On a mountain summit, he found a
large village, embowered in trees, where he was hospitably entertained, and so gained the good will of the
aged chief that he sent two of his sons to teach the
white stranger their language.   These foresters did not
worship idols, but made offerings to evil spirits, of whom
they lived in fear.   They had " no priests, no houses of
worship, and no favorite creed."   The day before the
missionary left, nearly all the villagers visited him, and
requested him to read to them the books he had prepared.   " So eager were some of them to hear," writes
Mr. Bronson, "that they remained until nearly midnight, when I dismissed them."

Receiving news that hostile forces were advancing
upon Jaipúr, Mr. Bronson returned January 29th to provide for the safety of his family, and writes:

" We had but just seated ourselves at dinner, when
several persons came rushing into the house, half breathless from fatigue and fright, saying that the Khamtis
and Singphos had attacked Sudiya, and that another
party of the enemy intended to attack us at Jaipúr, and
drive every white man from the country.   As we had
no stockade, or means of defense aside from a detach-
ment of forty Sepoys, we felt that our situation was peculiarly dangerous."

XIII.

PERILS BY THE HEATHEN.

Not only were Burma and the neighboring provinces in a turbulent condition, but the cloud in the northwest had now taken to itself definite shape. Suspicions, intrigues and negotiations had at last culminated in a declaration of war against Dost Mohammed, soon to be followed by the entrance into Afghanistan of that army, whose extinction amid its blood-stained snows, is one of the most sickening chapters of history. Every remote station of the British possessions felt the fever-pulse of war.

N. to W. G. B. November 11, 1838. " We are likely soon to be surrounded by wars and commotions. The tocsin has already sounded in the north of India, and an English army of twenty or thirty thousand strong is advancing towards the heights of Kabúl. The Russians are at the bottom of it—stirring up the native tribes of Persia and Kabúl to make war upon the English, and furnishing them with arms and money. In addition to this we are every day expecting open war with Burma, in which case another English army will be collected for that quarter, in fact is, in a great measure collected already on the Tenasserim coast, in expectation of the event. Amid all these commotions we are safe ; if God be for us, who can be against us ? In him is our only strength and safety. Pray for us, that our faith fail not."

To parents: " The days of the Burman empire, I expect, are numbered. The cries of the poor Christian Karens who are chained down to work upon the temples of Gautama have gone up into the ears of the Most High, and call for retribution upon that wicked government, which has so long persecuted the people of God."

The same letters recorded with thankfulness the providential averting of a personal calamity heavier than could, at that time, have been borne. Anxious to revisit the spot where all that was mortal of little Dorothy Sophia had been laid, Mrs. Brown was intending, on the evening of the third of November, to walk with her husband to the mission burying-ground ; but found herself too ill to do so, not having yet recovered her strength from an attack of fever on October 28th.

" As the event proved, it was a great mercy she was not permitted to go. I went out alone, just as the shades of night began to render objects scarcely visible, and as I came near the grave, I discovered, instead of a single mound, two large ridges of newly thrown up earth. On advancing nearer, what was my horror to behold the earth entirely thrown out from the grave, and the coffin exposed to full view ! The coffin had been opened, probably in the preceding night, with the expectation of finding silver or other valuable articles, which the natives supposed we had buried with the child."

The almost distracted father ran home through the gathering darkness for a lamp, returned with a native to the grave, and descending into it, found the body undisturbed.

" Although I had six or eight coolies living with me, who have been employed in making repairs on our house, it was with difficulty I could find any to help throw back the earth into the grave. When I asked them to assist, they all refused, except two old friends that have been long with me, and for whom I shall always entertain a partic- ular affection. By their assistance the grave was again covered."

Soon after Sophia's death, her father wrote out the brief story of her life, and it was issued by the Publica- tion and Tract Societies of Philadelphia and London, under the title "The Missionary's Daughter, a Memoir of D. Sophia Brown, who died in Assam." Of the four months immediately following, there is but little record to be found. Mr. Brown prepared a large amount of matter for the press, and about a dozen children came to his wife for instruction. From Mrs. Hannay's letters, it appears that rumors continued rife, of war with Burma and Nepaul. In those troublous days, the two ladies found consolation in a growing friendship. Since that 29th of September, when Mrs. Hannay came up from cantonments to the mission house; quietly took in hand to do what was to be done, helping the mother dress her dead child for its last bed; and so far as a pitiful woman might, dulled the cruel edge of misery, while Captain Hannay was with his own hands making the coffin; there had been a bond between them which continued while life lasted. Captain and Mrs. Hannay sometimes walked up at evening and joined in family worship with the missionaries, till these peaceful scenes were broken up by midnight massacre.

It was about three o'clock on Monday morning, Janu- ary 28th, that Mr. and Mrs. Brown were suddenly roused out of quiet sleep by the dreadful yell and war-cry of savages. Startled, and uncertain, at first, as to what it might mean, Mr. Brown sprang to the window and found that the sound came from the direction of the stockade.

The noise increased, and soon the sky was red with the light of the burning village. The crack of musketry was next heard, followed by the roar of guns. Hastily dressing, the family prepared for flight.

E. B. to parents : "In a few minutes the whole of cantonments and numerous buildings round about, appeared to be in flames. We knew not but a party of the enemy were lurking about our house to massacre us and set our house on fire, and where to betake ourselves for safety and protection we knew not. At first we thought we would hide ourselves in the woods, but after a moment's further consideration, and lifting up our fervent ejaculations to God for direction and deliverance, we caught a few warm articles of clothing, a canister of biscuits, and with our two infant children we ran to the bank of the Kuril."

They reached the waterside just in time to detect a frightened cooly absconding with their boat. A loud word might betray them to an enemy crouching behind them in the darkness, but the risk must be run, and Mr. Brown was obliged to call out with urgency and emphasis before he succeeded in getting his canoe brought back. Wife and babies were then hastily and silently placed in it, and it was pushed out into the middle of the stream. Here he found himself without serviceable oars, and waded back to the shore in the dark after them, going down frequently as deep as the armpits into the water. The Khamti ayah (infant's nurse) had remonstrated with the cooly, who sat meantime shivering with fear and cold; "Why do you let the Sahib * go back ? He will be murdered, but they would not touch *you*." Unable to start the man, the brave

---

* *Sahib*, (pron. Sáhb) a foreigner; *Nem-sahib*, a foreign lady.

ayah left the boat herself, and followed Mr. Brown to
the house, where she gathered a quantity of warm clothing, and hastily tying up the bundle, balanced it on her
head and waded out into the stream. The faithful
creature struggled hard to keep her footing under the
heavy burden, disregarding her master's repeated per-
emptory orders to throw it away, and at last succeeded
in getting it and herself to the boat safely.

N. to W. G. B: "I took with me, besides a few biscuits, the memoir of Dorothy Sophia which I had just
finished, and which I dared not leave in the house, as I
expected every moment to see it in flames. Dear little
child! she has been taken from the evil to come. While
the noise of war and "garments rolled in blood" cast a
dreadful gloom over this devoted place, her peaceful
ashes were sleeping in quiet beneath the lowly sod, and
the roses were blooming fresh and sweet over her hallowed grave."

Mr. Brown kept the boat nearly opposite to the house
till after the firing was over, and then, rowing softly lest
the sound should betray them, proceeded down the river.
They approached the stockade; all was now silent there;
the sound of the war-whoop as well as the noise of musketry and artillery had ceased. Uncertain whether the
British troops or the savages had gained the victory,
they decided not to land, and falling in with a group of
fishing-boats, remained with them till daylight. They
were every moment expecting attack from victorious or
retreating savages, "not knowing," Mrs. Brown's letter
continues, "but that a company of Khamtis or Abors
were lying in wait to rush upon and massacre us, or take
us for slaves, which to us would have been more to be
dreaded."

A canoe loaded with savages, rushed hurrying by, just after they had taken refuge with the fishing-boats, and had the white-faces been caught alone on the river, the family would probably have been massacred. The worst was now to be anticipated; they knew not but that their English friends were butchered; if they themselves escaped, they might be forced to flee down the Brahmaputra in that frail canoe, without provisions. Completely encircled by danger as they were, and unable to take further steps for their own safety, they could still wait and pray, "like Daniel in the lion's den." The trembling mother gathered her sleeping babes to her breast, scarcely daring to breathe a word to her husband, and the time wore on till morning. "We endeavored by prayer," she says, "to commit ourselves into the hands of our covenant-keeping God, and to quietly and resignedly await his dispensations towards us. The night was dark; and the time we spent in this awful state of suspense, was dismal in the extreme."

At last a faint light began to streak the east, and to make visible the mountain peaks; a chillier breeze ruffled the water, and the fugitives strained their eyes and ears to catch some sign from the stockade. The dawn grew to daylight, and they heard a sound that was not the scream of savages. A soft, clear, rippling note; it was the English bugle!

E. B.: "This was the most joyful sound I ever heard, being a sign to us that our troops were yet in possession of the stockade, to which we then made our way as fast as possible for protection. I was carried on the back of one of the boatmen, from a long sand-bank in the middle of the stream, to the opposite shore. The mangled bodies of the slain, the groans of the dying, weltering in pools of blood, the cries of the widows and fatherless, were heart-rending beyond description. . . . I was obliged to turn away my eyes from these terrible sights, but I saw enough to haunt my imagination by night and by day for a long time. The last and worst sight of all was that of the *heads* of the Khamtis brought in by the hair by the sepoys, and laid in a row, to see if any of them could be recognized. Among them was the head of a venerable chief, the Ronua Gobain, whom we well knew. He had several times called upon us at our house, professing to make friendly visits, and had taken our tracts home with him to read."

The fugitives were joyfully received at the fort ; Mrs. Brown took off her cloak and wrapped it around Mrs. Hannay, who had, on the alarm, without an instant's warning, fled barefoot in her night-dress, from her house to the fort, a distance of a quarter of a mile, and was now protected from the cold by a strip of coarse native cloth. The missionaries. seated at length within the stockade, amidst a crowd of sepoys and wailing women and children, all of whom had been burned out of house and home, and were almost destitute of clothing, learned from the surviving officers the following particulars of what had happened, which Mr. Brown communicated to Dr. Bolles :

"Sudiya, Feb. 8, 1839. Through the kind care of our heavenly Father, we have been preserved through a scene of great danger and distress ; and how great should be our thankfulness for all his benefits to us. On the morning of the 28th of January, about three or four o'clock, this station was attacked by the Khamtis. They took the place completely by surprise, and after cutting down the sentries, at the first onset made themselves mas-ters of the stockade and magazine. At the same instant, four or five bands attacked the place in different direc-tions, firing the houses and murdering indiscriminately all whom they met—men, women and children. Nearly the whole village and cantonments were soon in flames. Capt. and Mrs. Hannay, Lieut. Marshall, and the apothecary Mr. Pingault and wife, were roused from their beds by the Khamti war-cry, and on coming out found themselves surrounded by the enemy. They however all succeeded in reaching the stockade in safety. This they found already in the hands of the enemy, but with the assistance of the sepoys the officers succeeded in a few minutes in dislodging them. Having now gained possession of the magazine, which contained the ammunition, they commenced a heavy fire of musketry, and the slaughter immediately became general. At length the artillery began its tremendous roar, and after a few minutes' resistance the enemy fled in all directions. The contest lasted about fifteen or twenty minutes. Col. White, the commanding officer, on first hearing the alarm, rushed out of his house, and was making his way to the magazine, but was met and sur-rounded by a party of the enemy, who overpowered and killed him on the spot. The loss of sepoys, killed and wounded, was thirty-four ; but, including women and children, with the Assamese who were killed and wounded during the action, the number cannot have been less than one hundred. Thirty Khamtis were left dead on the field ; and it is supposed the number of wounded was very large. Among the killed were some of the principal Khamti chiefs and others of distinc-tion."

The savages had no fire arms ; their weapons were battle axes, knives, and long, light spears, the points of the latter poisoned with aconite and of deadly effect. Colonel White's body was found pierced by thirteen spear wounds.

"While I am writing, the trees are clouded with flocks of vultures which have collected from all quarters to feast upon the slain. The bodies which were found the next day were buried or thrown into the river, but many remained undiscovered, and there are doubtless many lying dead in the jungles that no one knows of. We now remain at cantonments, and are every day expecting another attack; but the fort is very strong, and would be able to resist a large force. We have concluded to remain where we are, as it appears to be the safest spot we can find. In God is our only help. We feel great anxiety for our friends at Jaipúr, who are also expecting an attack. May the Lord preserve them and us."

The missionaries at Jaipúr had been in much danger, but the attack apprehended at that point did not take place. A feeling of profound gratitude pervades the letters of February. Alluding to their disappointment three years before, in not being able to secure the piece of ground near cantonments which they had selected and cleared for the mission buildings, Mrs. Brown says:

"We have always felt rather insecure, and had more or less fear that some of the rude tribes around might come upon us in the night and plunder and burn our houses and perhaps destroy our lives. . . . That spot, which we always considered so unsafe, has now proved the very means of our safety. The houses, since built on the ground near cantonments, which we selected for our own when we first came to Sudiya, were on the night of the attack burned to the ground. . . . Had we escaped with our lives, which it is by no means probable would have been the case, our furniture, clothing, houses and printing establishment, all would have been lost. How much greater reason have we to speak of the goodness and mercy of God, than to murmur and complain."

N. B.   " The enemy passed through the village where we were, killing several of the inhabitants, and why they did not set fire to our houses, I am at a loss to know. It may have been from personal friendship on the part of the chiefs, with several of whom we were well acquainted, or it might have been because they had not time, on their return from the attack."

To Mr. Josiah Ballard :   " It is reported that the Khamti chiefs gave orders not to have us killed.   Some of them have been very friendly to us heretofore, and I do not think they wished to take our lives, though they would doubtless have carried off all our property, if they had succeeded in gaining the victory at Sudiya.   Poor creatures ! They have bitterly paid for their temerity. It is supposed that about two hundred of them have been killed and wounded, and the rest are now wandering about without house or home or provisions to eat, except what they obtain by begging from others."

On the afternoon previous to the massacre, it being Sunday, Mr. Brown was on his way to a neighboring village to preach, but was met more than once by natives who tried to dissuade him from going further, urging that it was too late ; he had better not go.   At first he paid no attention to the remonstrance and went on his way as usual, but on its third repetition he decided to return home.   Yet no suspicion of the real truth crossed his mind, and the family went to sleep that night with no special alarm.   Possibly a friendly chief had taken this means to prevent the necessity of capturing him, which would no doubt have been done if he had come near enough to learn their plans.

During the days which followed the attack, there was much to be done at cantonments for those who had suffered more than the missionaries. The flames had destroyed almost every building, with the clothing and all the possessions of the English officers, a serious matter in midwinter, distant as they were from supplies. One dilapidated house remained, it was Captain Charlton's bungalow, the same in which the Browns had lived during their first year at Sudiya. This house was now in such a state of decay that during the rains, plants came growing up through the floor. "I suppose the soil has some instinctive knowledge of my passion for flowers," Mrs. Hannay writes in July, "as there are not a few botanical specimens springing up in every corner of the house, even under the dining table!"

This building the Browns now occupied in company with Capt. and Mrs. Hannay, as it was not considered advisable for them to reside at present out of cantonments. One end of the building was at the same time used as a jail for the confinement of prisoners. As soon as practicable, Mr. Brown went up to his house and brought down the furniture and goods, including the box of warm clothing received from America two days before the attack, which was now invaluable to themselves and their suffering friends. He also brought down the printing press and other mission property to the stockade for safe keeping, putting up a small building for their protection, to which, later, he also moved his family.

The Charlton house was only a few rods from the gate of the stockade, and at night the families went within the barriers for protection, sleeping on the ground in tents, dressed in their day clothing, so as to be ready at any moment to spring to their feet at the sentry's warning shot. One of the chiefs, called the Toa Gobain, who also was well known to Mr. Brown, was found to have escaped; it was surmised that his might have been the party which went up the Kuril just after the Browns came down.

"We hear that he has collected his forces again," Mrs. Brown wrote, Feb. 24th, "and we are expecting every night that he will make another attack. Capt. Hannay has stregthened the stockade so that he thinks all of us who are inside will be perfectly safe."

Alarms were not uncommon. She thus describes one which had occurred the night before:

"Just as we had all lain down to sleep, one of the out-sentries fired a musket. This gave instant alarm. In a moment the officers and sepoys were all at their posts and ready for an attack. The sentry that fired is positive that he saw four of the enemy approaching, but as soon as he fired they all ran back into the jungle. It is most likely that they were spies, coming to see if the sentries were all asleep as they were when they made the first attack; but finding them on the watch, they took alarm from hearing the musket fired, and did not venture again."

On the subject of defense Mr. Brown writes, February 5th:

"I cannot think that when I lie down and take in my two little ones by my side, that I am acting contrary to the gospel, by putting my sword and double-barreled gun under my pillow, nor could I in conscience hesitate to use them, if pushed to the last extremity."

And a year later, from Jaipúr: "Very few nights have I slept without my gun well loaded at my head, and my pistol under my pillow. Do you wonder at my thus arming myself with the weapons of death against my fellow men? I have only to say that I never did believe the Bible inculcates the doctrine of non-resistance to the murderous assassin who would butcher the unoffending and helpless, and if my mind ever wavered, it has been fully set at rest by the situations in which I have been placed. I could never stand still and see my dear wife and helpless babes cut up by the savage knife, as they most assuredly would be, should they fall into the hands of these monsters, who delight in slaughtering women and children as much as in killing an armed enemy."

Another danger, not mentioned in the letters till it was over, was the prevalance of small-pox among the prisioners in their house. In April, they left the bungalow, and moved into the little low hut of their own, in which the press and printing materials were stored. Mrs. Brown says of a visit on the 7th of March, to her neat house up the river:

"I walked up to our old mission premises with my husband this morning before breakfast. Our three deserted houses, our printing office and school-houses, our beautiful, flourishing gardens, all left to ruin, without any hope of ever occupying them again in safety, made me feel sad beyond expression."

It was still supposed by some, that the turbulent tribes were in collusion with the Burmese; and news of open war with Burma, was expected by every mail. Through and beyond this apprehension, their faith and hope saw the opening prospects which have gladdened us fifty years later:

"Should the English come into possession of the whole of the Burman empire, and the region between this and Burma, it will open new and glorious fields for missions."

With the heat of April and May, the sickness in the crowded cantonments increased. A persistent dreadful odor, and the virulent small-pox, " made the place as deadly as if it had been infested with the plague."

"Little Nathan, was brought almost to death's door by the same kind of fever with which Dorothy Sophia died. After his fever left him, he could not raise his head for more than three weeks, and now, six weeks after, he cannot go alone, or stand on his feet."

Meantime, the Assamese population of Sudiya and vicinity finding themselves continually subject to the raids of small parties of Khamtis, were daily fleeing in terror from the region. Fields and villages were deserted ; and the dispersion went on to such an extent, that the missionaries' work was taken out of their hands. Finally even the Khamtis themselves were scattered by the British troops.

To Dr. Bolles, March 29, 1839. " Since the attack on Sudiya, the country has been in a state of continual commotion. The Khamtis, Singphos and Mishmis combined, have been plundering and carrying off the peaceable inhabitants, while the troops of the government have been scouring the country in various directions in search of the enemy, and several sharp engagements have taken place in which the Khamtis and Singphos have met with considerable loss. . . . Our prospects for the present are quite blasted ; many of the inhabitants have fled ; and the Khamtis, amongst whom we were particularly desirous of laboring, are entirely dispersed. Still we trust that these disturbances will be overruled for good ; and as soon as quiet is restored, we hope the inhabitants may return to their homes as before."

This latter hope gradually died out, and in May, Mr. Brown was forced to the conclusion that he must let go his hold, and seek another post. Jaipúr was decided upon as the most eligible center of operations, as it was expected that there would be an influx of population through tea-cultivation; and there was also hope of access thence to the Khamtis, Singphos and Nagas. The decision to remove was not reached without a pang of disappointment, and much unsettling of former plans. Sudiya was depopulated, and afterwards, for a time, overgrown with jungle and effaced from the map. Many years later, it was regarrisoned, and is now again a frontier post.

XIV.

PRINTING-PRESS, type and paper were conveyed from the barracks to the boat, scattered household goods were gathered and packed ; the old home and a little flower-decked grave revisited. It was hard for the mother-heart to leave that "dear, sacred spot forsaken by every civilized being," but there was a comfort in taking up Sophia's plants from the home garden bed, to be carried to Jaipúr ; and as if conscious they had a mission to perform, these silent comforters conveyed to the sorrowing parents a "monition of the unseen."

"Since being *transplanted*, [Mrs. Brown wrote, a month after reaching Jaipúr,] they bud and blossom with a beauty and fragrance far exceeding what they ever did in their native soil. I have a kind of white lily, very fragrant, of which Sophia was particularly fond, but could seldom get more than one or two blossoms at a time. Now that it has been brought here, the stalks are filled with whole circles of blossoms. The stem I have on my table has been plucked five days, and has daily put forth new blossoms. Is it not a most striking emblem of our departed child ?"

On the 12th of May the boats pushed off from Sudiya landing, and another chapter of life was begun. Twelve days down the Brahmaputra and up the Búri-Dihing, brought them to Jaipúr, a new village on the high river bank, where they were hospitably received at the house of Mr. Bruce. The three mission families were now together for a time, Mr. and Mrs. Cutter having returned to Sudiya in April, bringing with them from Calcutta fonts of Bengali and Shan type, and they now accompanied the Browns to Jaipúr. Mrs. Brown, exhausted by heat and fatigue, succumbed again to fever, falling insensible from her chair the second morning after their arrival. Some weeks of illness followed. She wrote to Mrs. Hannay on her rceovery :

"Dear, kind, good Mrs. Bruce took care of me and of my sick children through it all. . . . We are now living in your beautiful octagon, with the addition of a hall in front. I have not yet been able to look about much, but my dear husband is perfectly delighted with the place, or will be, when it is cleared of jungle sufficiently to make it healthy. These hills, which he has visited with Mr. Bruce, animate his spirits like a visit to his own native mountains.

. . . The press has been set up, and the first sheet in Naga printed ! Mr. Brown has again commenced daily evening worship with the natives. With the servants, coolies, etc., he sometimes has quite a congregation of us all. It makes us all quite happy to commence again our missionary work. We earnestly hope we may ere long see some of the fruit of our labors. Were we all in health, I think we should form a most happy circle."

The inhabitants of Upper Assam, having been harried by months of predatory warfare, and suffering consequent famine, fell easy victims to the cholera which was now making sure and rapid progress upward from he lower districts.   It reached Jaipúr about the middle of July.

Mrs. Brown to Mrs Tucker.* Jaipúr, August 4: " Many of the poor natives are dying around us with cholera.   Some of them are taken apparently in perfect health, and are dead within six hours.   E—'s nurse [the Khamti ayah, who was with the family on the night of the massacre,] whom we brought around with us from Sudiya, has fallen a victim to that awful disease. .   .   .   There are many hills near Jaipúr which we have not much doubt would be healthful places of residence.   Mr. Bruce has been at the expense of clearing away, cutting a road and erecting two or three temporary buildings on the hill nearest to us, which he has kindly given to us to occupy.   We have only to go up the river about half a mile, cross over, and we immediately commence to ascend.   I have been up twice with both the children, and stayed three days and two nights. We all returned much improved in health.   .   .   . It is very difficult for us just now to get comfortable food, for there is almost a famine around us, owing to so many of the rice-fields having been burned in the war.   There was no doctor at the station, so we missionaries all used what little skill and knowledge of medicine we possessed, to afford relief to the poor dying natives.   .   .   .   Mrs. Bruce, Mrs. Bronson and myself each had marked symptoms of the disease, but the preventive measures, by the blessing of God, averted a serious attack.   We felt however that it was our duty to leave the place for a season.   The Lord had prepared us a place of resort ; we fled, as from a fearful enemy, to our unfinished houses on the hill.   It set in for a

---

* " Sister Dorothy " had married, in 1837, Mr. Edward Tucker, of Heath, Mass.

very rainy time, and our dwellings being open, we a
took cold."

It was here that the family lived for a short time in a
tree, a rude flooring being laid on the horizontal branches, the interlaced branches above making a roof, and the
ladder being drawn up at night.

Some weeks later Mrs. Brown was very ill of fever in
a rough open cabin of one room on the hill. Her husband was, as was often the case, her physician and nurse.
His treatment proved successful, and the rain having
now ceased, the mountain air was favorable to convales-
cence.

F. B. "Mr. Brown has about a dozen coolies engaged clearing our bill, which is a short distance from
this, with only a little ravine between. I can hear the
axe beating, and the trees falling now, while I sit writing. I enjoy a most extensive and delightful prospect
from my little veranda here. Before me is a steep
precipice, and from that, gentle descents and steep prec-
ipices succeed each other, to the borders of the beautiful Búri-Dihing. Jaipúr village is stretched along its
shore on the opposite bank. From that, in our front
view, is spread out one vast plain, as far as the eye can
reach. This plain is thickly wooded with large and
stately trees, covered with perpetual verdure; except
here and there an open field of cultivated rice. In
the far distant horizon, are the Naga mountains.
We have in all, such a variety of scenery as is seldom
enjoyed in any part of India, and nowhere in the plains.
I could sit and gaze upon it with untiring delight, were
it not that such a beautiful country is left to run to
waste, and the few spots here and there, that are inhabited, are the home of a people who know not God,
nor the gospel of his son Jesus Christ.

'On these mountains let me labor,
In these deserts let me tell
How He died, the blessed Saviour,
To redeem a world from hell.'"

Mrs. Brown fainted while writing ; a week later the family returned to the village, and were taken by the Bronsons to their house, their former dwelling being removed to make way for a new road. Here the letter was finished :

" October 15. The rumors of war are again thick around us, and we fear we may have to go through another siege here before long, similar to what we did at Sudiya. Oh, may the Lord prepare us for all that He has prepared for us. We sometimes feel almost discouraged, we meet with so many interruptions in our missionary work in this unsettled country. We beg your prayers that we may have divine support under all our trials. I am too weak to add more, so once more, dear, dear sister, farewell. Our united love to all our relations and friends."

During the summer, robbers had a second time opened Dorothy Sophia's grave, destroying the monument. In the following letter are found some details of this and other occurrences :

" Jaipúr, August 4th, 1839.

My Dear Mrs. Hannay:—Although it is the Sabbath, I cannot let the dawk go off without dropping you a line to thank you for giving us so full an account of the breaking open of the graves,* and especially Captain Hannay for his kindness in looking after them and filling

---

* Mr. Thomas' was opened at the same time.

them up again after they had been left by the inhuman
wretches who dug them open. Nidhi says, Captain
Hannay told him to fill up the child's grave with the
bricks that were scattered around, and this I am very
glad of, as I do not care about having the monument re-
built, since it might provoke them to dig the grave open
again. The stone I think we shall keep at Jaipúr, and
if Captain Hannay has an opportunity we shall be
much obliged by his sending it.

I hope you will thank Mr. Dalton for us, for his
beautiful verses on the little child. They are very appropriate indeed. . . . . The cholera is doing dreadful
work among us, considering how small a population we
have. For the last ten days there have been more or
less deaths every day. It seems to be mostly confined
to the coolies ; some of the Assamese and Dewania
[Singpho-Assamese] Sepoys have been carried off, but
none of the Bengalis. Mr. Bronson has lost his little
Singpho boy, Gami, and we have lost the old Khamti
ayah, *Joni.* You doubtless recollect her. Mr. Bruce
has lost several coolies, and *all* Soron's family, except
the old man himself, who is absent, and one of the
youngest children. His wife died first, then two of the
younger daughters, and last of all, Jogoti. It is certainly
a most melancholy event, their being all swept off together by this dreadful scourge.

For the last few days I have been upon the Deu Hal
Porbot, the bill you so often spoke of, where with Mrs.
Brown and the children I intend to remain for the
present. Little Nathan was quite ill when we took him
up, but he immediately revived, and is now comfortable.
I think the mountain air will give him strength. We
are now down spending the Sabbath here. Mr. Masters
arrived yesterday. The Bruces will be off, we expect,
to-morrow, for Calcutta. We are very glad indeed to
hear that you are coming to visit Jaipúr in the cold

weather.   Mrs. Brown unites with me in kind love and
regards to yourself and Captain Hannay, and believe
me ever

Your sincere friend,

NATHAN BROWN.

In the autumn the missionaries suffered from inter-
mittent fever in a tenacious form.   Both were often
sick at the same time, and letters ceased to be written.
Yet in the intermissions something was accomplished.
Mr. Brown made some progress in Scripture translation,
issued several new tracts, and maintained the daily
evening worship in Assamese, with Bible exposition, for
the coolies.   A catechism and book of phrases in Singpho and Naga, prepared by Mr. Bronson, were printed.
Mrs. Bronson's school had been scattered by the war,
but in the fall she recommenced with a pleasant little
company of fifteen or twenty pupils.

After having been nearly a year without a settled
abiding place, the Browns moved in November into two
bamboo rooms, around which, by degrees, they built
two or three more, and again enjoyed a home of their
own.   But the patter of Nathan's feet was not heard in
it, as in the old home on the Kúril.   The active little
fellow, now in his fourth year, sat in an unnatural quiet;
he had not once stood unsupported since that sickness
of April, in the crowded, filthy stockade at Sudiya.
His mother had been hoping almost against hope that
when the cold season should come, all would be right.
Over and over again she had supported his body with
her hands, encouraging him to walk as he did before,
but in vain, and now the apprehension had become a
certainty, that her boy was a cripple.   Under this shadow
the father and mother closed the year.

XV.

JOURNEY TO CALCUTTA.

SOON after, while sitting opposite to Nathan one day at table, his father noticed with alarm, a very peculiar hollow appearance of the right eye, indicating a disorder far more serious than even his lameness. A few days later he became blind in that eye, and, to save if possible, the other, it was decided to take him at once to Calcutta for treatment. A letter from his mother to "Sister Sophia" furnishes some of the incidents of this journey:

"The idea of leaving our missionary work so soon, after having lost nearly the whole of the previous year, made my poor husband feel almost broken-hearted and discouraged. I therefore summoned all my resolution, and told him that if he was willing to remain at home and pursue his missionary labors without me, I would, God helping me, undertake the long and hazardous journey alone."

For a woman to decide to go eight hundred miles in a canoe, through a region infested by wild beasts and bands of robbers, must indeed have required resolution, and reliance on a more than human protection.

"We wept together and prayed together," she adds; and at last, the father, committing his wife and helpless infants to divine protection, decided that duty demanded his remaining at work. On the 10th of February Mrs. Brown took two covered canoes, one for the cooking, baggage and servants, and one—the hollowed trunk of a sam-tree—for herself and children, and started on her journey, a far more formidable one than an ocean voyage, even at that time, would have been. It was winter, and enfeebled as she already was, the exposure to damp winds drawing through the boat and sweeping the sandbanks where she took her meals, soon laid her up with rheumatism and fever. Lying rolled in blankets in the bottom of her canoe, without any of the comforts so necessary to the sick, her perseverance must have had a severe test.

"One night in particular, I felt very ill, and thought I should die alone, without a friend to minister to my wants, or pray for me! But the Lord forsook me not. He graciously heard my own feeble supplications and relieved me of my pains."

To N. B.—"I have had no trouble whatever with men or servants. All are as attentive to my wants as I could wish. They all behave far better than I expected; every one appears happy and contented. The goat and myself are the only ones who wear a long face. I feel a great deal of sympathy for the poor old creature— she appears so much as I feel. I have not heard her speak a word, or utter one complaint, but she is evidently "down in the mouth," because you have deprived her of her little ones and separated her from all her friends. Her appetite is all gone, and when I see her standing over the dainties which I send her from my table without touching them, I can fancy just how the poor old creature feels." [To S. B.] "You would have been amused could you have looked upon us sometimes at breakfast or dinner. Our table was a mat spread down upon the sand. We had another to seat ourselves upon according to Eastern native custom. Our only canopy was the clear blue sky, with sometimes its lovely pale moon. Around me the nine boatmen formed three or four other parties, cooking and eating at the same time. Seeing them with so many less comforts than I enjoyed, made me constantly contented with my fare which I can assure you was none of the best. In damp weather it was rather inconvenient to be without a shelter, for a sudden gust of wind would sometimes fill all our dishes with sand, and thus render our food less palatable than before. But those of us who have passed through the war have learned to put up with any fare, and now we seldom think of mentioning so trifling a circumstance.

Almost every night I saw where we stopped, an abundance of wild elephants' and buffaloes' tracks, and now and then we passed some of these formidable beasts which had come to the water to drink. But none ever ventured to harm or disturb us. I felt more afraid of the alligators, with which the river in some places seemed filled, than of wild beasts. Often we saw hundreds of them stretched several yards out of the water basking in the sun."

One evening the boatmen ran into a cove, and fastened, as usual, to stakes driven into the sand. Seeing fires burning on the opposite shore, they congratulated themselves on their good fortune in having lighted upon a safe retreat. They gathered driftwood for their fires, and Mrs. Brown and the ayah had taken the children ashore, when a fierce hiss sounded from the water. Through the fast gathering twilight they saw the head of a crocodile reaching up from the black surface of the creek, then another and another—there was a shoal of them! Evidently the cove and creek were their own

hereditary fishing domain, and poaching on their premises was to be visited with the severest penalties.
Driven from the opposite sho re by the camp-fires, they
had come over in force to avenge themselves on the
later intruders.

Manji and men looked at each other and whispered
"*Ghorial!*" (gavial or crocodile) then at the Memsahib
and babas; and began with much volubility to assure
her that the *ghorial* in this particular locality were *tame
ones* ! But the Mem had eyes and ears, and mindful of
the highly rhetorical and imaginative structure of the
Assamese mind, failed to be reassured.

" They were continually raising their fearful heads
some feet above water, and hissing and spouting in the
most frightful manner. It was dark, and too late for us
to seek a more quiet spot for the night, I felt alarmed,
and did not know what to do. I told the boatmen that
they had done very wrong in bringing me to that place
to stop for the night. for I was afraid to go down into
the boat to sleep. My head-man assured me over and
over, that there was not the least occasion for fear ;· he
had never heard of their attempting to hurt any one ;
and that to satisfy me that the men were not afraid, they
would all sleep on the boats. ·They had before usually
slept on shore. My servants and all the other boatmen
joined him, saying, "*Bhoi na koribi, Memsahib ;*—there
is no fear, don't be afraid, madam." On their assurance,
I ventured into the boat, hoping that my unwelcome
companions would soon become quiet, and, like the rest
of the world, go to sleep. But in this I was disappoint-
cd, for they kept the water in constant commotion, and
continued their murmuring hisses all night."

At length a rap from a long flexile tail shook the
canoe ; it was repeated, again and ágain. The edge of the

canoe was only a few inches from the water, the splash-
ing was now fearful, and Mrs. Brown could hear and
feel the horrible, slimy monsters moving under and
around her. It was quite possible that with its powerful
snout, one of the reptiles might push through the wicker
wall. Were her children to be sacrificed, like the Hindu mothers,' to these demons of the river? It was now
about eleven o'clock.

"I ordered the boatmen to get up and take off the
cover of our boat, and make a shelter for me and the
children on shore, for I would not risk myself there any
longer. My orders were promptly obeyed, not a man
remaining on the boat after I left it. The noise of the
reptiles, and the fear of wild beasts on shore, prevented
my sleeping. In the morning, I found we had not bet-
tered our condition much by returning to the shore, for
the opposite bank was covered with semi-circular roads,
several rods in circumference, showing that the crocodiles were by no means entirely confined to the water,
but doubtless the fires which the boatmen kept burning
all night, prevented their venturing near us."

At the first hint of daylight, the little camp was in
motion ; the manji could not hurry the men fast enough.
Bed and bedding were thrown hurriedly into the boat,
the cover hastily attached, the men's cooking utensils
gathered up together without much respect to caste,
the stakes pulled out, and the setting-poles used vigorously yet noiselessly till the great river was reached
again. Once in the open stream, the men's tongues
were loosed, and the Memsahib heard the following remarks, made in an undertone ;

" *Bhoi nalage na ?*" (Were you not afraid?)

" *Iman bhoi agoi ketiau no korilu.*" (I never was
so much afraid before in my life).

On reaching Gauhati, Mrs. Brown was surprised to learn that it was Sunday, Feb. 23rd, instead of Saturday, as she had supposed. "I somehow lost a day," she wrote, "when I was sick on my boat with a fever," She found that the commissioner, having heard that she was on her way down in a canoe, had detained for her use a large boat of his own, which he was about sending to Calcutta for supplies ; and she was glad to leave her sam-tree for somewhat more roomy quarters.

One afternoon in March, as she lay ill and lonely, listening to the rush of the current beneath her and the tread of the boatmen as they moved back and forth with their poles, she heard the manji shouting to a boat coming up from below : "Where are you going, and who are your passengers ?"

" I am taking a Padré Sahib* to Jaipúr," was the reply.

Could it be the new missionary that was shortly expected ? It must be. She almost involuntarily cried out, " Tell him to stop, I wish to speak to him," and the next instant was ready to recall the words, fearing it might be a mistake. A glance through the window reassured her. " So easy is it to recognize our country-men, that the moment my eye was fixed upon him through my little window, I well knew that he was an American. We did not meet as strangers, but as soon as I learned his name, we felt acquainted."

Mrs. Brown's new friends were the Rev. Cyrus Barker, with his wife, and the devoted Rhoda Bronson, destined to join her brother on the Naga hills.

" We concluded to stop our boats for the remainder of the day, and at evening I felt so much cheered and refreshed by their presence and conversation, that I was able to go on to their boat and take tea with them."

---

*Foreign clergyman.   Pronounced Pah'-drey Sahb.

The next morning she saw them resume their journey up the river, while she went on her way alone.

The extension of the Tea Company's operations gave Assam an important export, and led to the advance of civilization into the wildernes. In 1840, the venturesome tiger, creeping to the jungle's edge, and thirsty elephant tramping the sedges and sand, were startled by a portentous sound—a prolonged whistle—unlike the voice of beast or bird, and fled back into the forests, affrighted by a glimpse of a monster stalking up the great water, with vapory breath and whirling feet.

To the foreign residents it was a welcome sight, reducing the long distance to Calcutta, and hastening the home mails. The overland mail to Europe, established a few years later, was an unspeakable blessing.

"It was a beautiful sight, [Mrs. Brown wrote after meeting two steamers] and it encouraged me to hope that Assam is now coming under a state of cultivation and improvement which will enable us ere long to realize as flourishing a field for missionary labor as ever we anticipated." To parents, "I have met more than a hundred large boats loaded with Chinese tea-makers and workmen to cut and clear away the jungle in the vicinity of Jaipúr." To N. B. "Well done! Hurrah for Assam! We have just passed ten large boats overloaded with coolies going to Rungpúr [near Sibsagar.] The shore was quite black with men, women and children; besides, the boats appeared to be full of heads."

To J. and S. B. "Arrived at Kulna yesterday before noon and have been stopping here since, to get a wooden anchor made for our boat. The tide sets up as far as this, and we shall go the remainder of the way only with the flowing of the tide, whether it be by night or by day.

We have now to pass through what is called the "Sunder-bunds," rendered fearful to me by the many alarming stories which I have heard of tigers jumping on to boats, and accidents from terrific gales. But the Lord who has protected me hitherto—shall I not trust him still? Good night, dearest brother and sister; I have been scribbling all the afternoon, and it is now làte in the evening, and I am tired and sleepy. You must pardon all blunders, for I have written in great haste, also the miserable chirography, for I have broken my knife and cannot mend my pen. I hope to be in Calcutta in four or five days when, if I am spared, I will add another sheet and shall send it in a box of presents which I am about to forward to you and other dear friends.

　　　From your ever affectionate sister,

　　　　　　　　　ELIZA W. BROWN."

While in her canoe, despite cramped quarters and ill-ness, Mrs. Brown had succeeded in finishing for the schools her arithmetic in Assamese, and sent the manu-script back from Gowhati, to be printed. The following, to her husband, narrates some of the remaining inci-dents of the journey:

　　　"SUNDERBUNDS, Thursday, 26th March.

. . . Last night the tide turned about dark, and we loosed our boat, although the black clouds and constant flashes of lightning foretold an approaching storm. We have no moon now until towards morning. The night was very dark, the clouds gathered and thickened near us, and suddenly a fearful wind arose, which almost in-stantly drove our boat upon a reef of sand. Every one seemed nearly petrified with terror, for our boat, while in this situation, with the fierce wind driving upon her, was in constant danger of being upset. The boatmen called upon their gods for help and refused to obey the serang's [pilot's] orders to get out and pry the boat off with poles."

An indescribable scene of confusion ensued in the darkness, while the boat was in momentary danger of being dashed to pieces under the furious wind and water.

"Poor little —— [an English child sent in Mrs. Brown's charge to school in Serampore], sat close beside me, very much frightened. He kept saying, 'Oh, dear, Mrs. Brown, the boat is breaking—what shall we do?' I told him we could not do anything but pray to God, and he would take care of us, and he kept quiet as a lamb, until all were safe. Nathan did not awake to know anything of our danger. At length the serang sprang into the water up to his neck and four of the men followed him. They succeeded in bracing their poles against the boat so as to prevent her upsetting, until the fierceness of the storm was over, which lasted, I should think, about half an hour."

The perils of the night were not yet over. The storm having passed, they pushed out once more, ran into the first creek and moored for the night. A boat went by. "You are in very bad place," said a suppressed voice; "this jungle is full of robbers."

Mrs. Brown looked around upon the panic-stricken men and down at her crippled, sleeping boy. A supernatural strength seemed to nerve her arm. Taking up one of his crutches for a weapon, she said, "Let them come if they dare; I will knock down, with this, all that come near me."

Her words had a remarkable effect; every man rallied, caught a knife or a club and resolved to fight for his life, if molested. Soon they were all talking or laughing, silently but merrily, and the Memsahib heard the words,

"Let them come if they dare," frequently repeated, as an inspiriting battle-cry.   After a time, a guard was set to watch during the remainder of the night, the rest of the men, with their weapons beside them, sank quietly to sleep, and sunrise found all safe.   A week later the spires and domes of the " city of palaces " were in sight ; the fifty days' journey was ended, and the boat slipping down with the morning ebb-tide, March 31st was, after the usual delays, moored at the ghaut.

XVI.

THEN came three hours in a palkee under the burning sun, with repeated halts of the bewildered bearers, and inquiries for " Padre Pearce Sahib's, Circular Road ;" met at last by the moanful answer, " *Moril;*" dead !

" I was shocked, but having so recently met our missionary friends, the Barkers, and heard that the Pearces were all well, and waiting to receive me into their family, I did not—I could not—believe that it was true, until I arrived at the door."

The family was broken up.   Seated in the deserted, silent house, Mrs. Brown learned from Mr. Thomas that the hospitable friend of other days fell a victim to cholera six days before, after an illness of twenty-four hours."*

A temporary home was found with another friend, and the sick child's case at once entrusted to the most skillful medical care obtainable.   For four and a half

---

* William Hopkins Pearce, for many years a laborious missionary in Calcutta, was the son of the Rev. Samuel Pearce of Birmingham, England, the friend of Henry Martyn. " Dear Brother Pearce," Mr. Brown wrote, "was one of a thousand—so gentle, so heavenly—he shone like a bright and beautiful star amidst the jarring, wrangling and confusion of the world. Let us endeavor to copy more closely his example of love, meekness, gentleness, patience."

months, through the heat of a Calcutta summer, the mother nursed her suffering boy under a prolonged and painful course of treatment, herself at times seriously ill through fatigue and distress of mind.

Later in the season, her own health improved ; she found strength to carry her load, and friends who lightened it. Among these friends were the missionaries of the Scotch Kirk. The sympathy and kindness of Dr. Charles and Dr. Mackay when she was for many weeks living alone among strangers, were never forgotten. She gives this picture of Dr. Duff, May 24th :

" I have just.returned from church, since which Dr. and Mrs. Duff called. . . . . When they rose to go, he spoke again upon the importance of living by faith, and in that way, he said, we could enjoy heaven in this world. His eyes sparkled, his whole soul seemed to enter into every word, and it seemed as if he must soon be on the wing to enjoy that of which he was now evidently having a rich foretaste."

Across the river lay the superb Botanical Gardens, and there was an occasional release for the little sufferer from the city's sickening heat, when kind Dr. Wallich's bolio was sent to row him and his mamma and little sister, over the Hoogly to Garden Reach to spend a whole day in the shadow of the great banyans and palms. There, carried safe and high on bearer's shoulder, he could reach the cool green leaves, and hear the plash of oars in the river below.

On the 15th of June the physicians gave up hope, and notified the mother.

E. to N. B.— " I received this note [from the doctor] two or three days ago, but have had no heart to take up my pen to communicate the heart-rending intelligence to you before, although my mind was partially prepared to take the dear child back without much improvement."

All that medical skill could suggest was at last done ; and the alleviation of the little patient's sufferings was now the object to work for. It being impossible to undertake the journey up the river alone under present circumstances, Mrs. Brown sent for her husband, and almost sinking under her sorrows, awaited his arrival. Captain Hannay had already written to his agents to place at her disposal for the return voyage, his budgerow, a large cabin-boat, which was at Calcutta being repaired, and to have it manned by a competent crew.

Mr. Brown started down, June 26th, himself in greatly shaken·health. Soon after his family left, he had gone eight days' journey through forest-jungle to Sudiya, with the intention of removing his little daughter's remains to Jaipúr. The sun was in eclipse as he and Capt. Hannay approached the spot ; nature seemed overspread by an unnatural gloom, which added to the shock upon his tensely strung feelings, as he beheld with unspeakable dismay that the grave had, for the third time, been opened !

To E. B., March 4.—" Nothing remained except the bones, and a few locks of her sweet flaxen hair. While I was down in the grave, searching for the bones, there was a violent shock of an earthquake. Does not this strikingly verify your dream? About three-quarters of an hour afterwards, we had another severe shock. The first took place about noon."

The dream alluded to is mentioned in a letter from Mrs. Brown to Mrs. Hannay from Jaipúr, in 1839.

" I dreamed, a week or two after we arrived here, that we were walking towards the grave in company with yourself and Captain Hannay. When we came near, Mr. Brown suddenly advanced before us ; I turned to you and said, "The grave is again open." Immediately a voice like thunder came forth from the grave. Captain Hannay said " Stop ; there are persons in there." Mr. Brown came running towards us, and said, "Don't say that—it is the voice of God !" Here I became so agitated that I awoke, and found it was in the midst of a thunderstorm."

Mr. Brown says: " The scene was almost an exact resemblance of what I saw in one of my dreams last fall." Previous to the first disturbance of the grave, he notes " repeated dreams, both by Eliza and myself, that our daughter's remains were being disturbed."

Captain Hannay supplied Mr. Brown with elephants for the return journey, and on the 9th of March he was again at Jaipúr. There, on Thursday, March 12th, Mr. Thomas' remains were re-interred in Mr. Bronson's compound. The other little bleached bones were not again committed to earth in Assam. They were placed in a small strong box and kept in the house, until Mrs. Brown's return to America, when she took them with her, and they were deposited in the family burial-plot at East Charlemont.

On the 13th of March, Mr. and Mrs. Bronson left Jaipúr for the Naga Hills ; almost immediately after, Mr. Brown was taken quite ill, and on Sunday was obliged to recall his appointment for service at his house. When a friendly face came in at noon, he burst into tears. In a few days he resumed his usual duties, but it must have been by great effort of will, for on the 21st, he writes, " Of late I sleep but little, and eat but little, and find that I need but little." About this time it was noticed that his hair was whitening somewhat, though he was not yet thirty-three years of age.

The " horror of great darkness " through which he had passed at Sudiya ; his daily and nightly anxiety for his absent family ; the knowledge that child and mother were suffering where he could not help them ; and the apprehension of a greater grief to come, led him to write :

" My heart is broken, sunk and sorrowful ; but through the loving kindness of my Saviour, I enjoy a good degree of spiritual comfort, although I am so unfaithful to Him. Since I have received your letters describing your troubles, I have been very down-hearted and distressed. . . . . But we must ever keep in mind for our encouragement, that

" The sharper and severer
    The storms of life we meet,
The sooner and the nearer
    Is heaven's eternal seat."

May 8.—Whenever you do decide, let me know the precise day you are to start, if possible, and if Providence enables me, I shall meet you at Gauhati, unless you should come in the steamer, in which case I had better wait till you reach the Dikho Múkh.*

Brother Bronson came down yesterday and staid with me last nignt. He will start to-day to meet the Barkers.

And now, my dearest beloved, once more farewell. Cry a tear upon the dear little white cheeks of your sweet babies for their far-away lonely papa. It almost breaks my heart to think of them. You are having a hard time, that I know full well, but I hope God will give you strength, and enable you to overcome every difficulty, and stand, under every trial. Give my kind love to all.

---

*Múkh; mouth ; Dikho Múkh, mouth of the Dikho river.

Sabbath eve, May 17.   Although it is half past eleven, I cannot go to bed without answering your sweet but melancholy letter of April 17, which I have received to-day. . . . . If necessary, I will start down immediately, and bring you and the little darlings home to papa's house. . . . . The Barkers are with me now.   Brother Bronson and his sister intend to start to-morrow for the Naga Hills.

June 8.—We had better suffer and die together, than be thus wandering about, unbefriended, harassed in mind and body, and feeling almost that we would rather die than live.   If the little darling gets help, however, it will be some reward for all our sorrows, and will enable us to prize the blessings of home, if we should ever enjoy them again.   I don't think I shall ever be willing to send any of the children home, so long as we both live.   No, we will have no more attachments away from home than we can possibly help, lest by and by we should feel so strong a desire to go ourselves, that we could not overcome it." .

A friend in Burma wrote to him :

"Your present trial seems almost as hard to endure as Abraham's, when God said to him, 'Take now thy son, thine only son, whom thou lovest, &c. Oh, may you have Abraham's faith ! We feel for you more than words can express. . . . . It must be one of the severest of trials, to see a child doomed to waste under an incurable disease; to hear about in one's heart a wound which must ever deepen, till the cold grave closes over the delight of your eyes.   When for a short time the mind is engrossed in other concerns, and forgets its sorrows, how painful to return to the dear object of its unceasing anxiety, and to wake up in the night, and find a load at your heart which nothing can remove ; this is sorrow, indeed, this is trouble ! "

N. to E. B. June 26: "I am on my way to meet you!
The load that rested on my spirits is relieved, and I now
look forward to the time of meeting you, with some degree of hope. . . . . We received letters from the
Bronsons just before I left. Rhoda and little Mary had
been very sick of fever, but were better. I got away
about ten or eleven o'clock this morning, and hope to
reach the new station at Tingrai this evening. . . . .
If I can meet you once more, it will make amends for
all my sorrows."

On the 18th of July, he reached Calcutta. Mrs.
Brown kept up till after his arrival, but before they could
start for home, she fell ill of a dangerous fever, followed
by pleurisy. As soon as she had rallied sufficiently to
be moved, the little family started home in Captain
Hannay's budgerow. They spent a Sabbath at Serampore. Mrs. Brown was carried up to the house for a
visit with Mrs. Marshman, and heard from her own lips
the circumstances of her husband's death three years
before. It was at this time that Mrs. Marshman related
the incident which suggested to Mr. Brown the lines entitled "The Landing of Marshman."

Mrs. Brown improved during the journey, and leaving
Gauhati, cheered and invigorated by a few days' visit
with the Robinsons, began to be herself again. Above
that station, while passing through the jungles, far from
villages or help of any kind, her husband was taken with
jungle fever. He became greatly reduced, and had
barely recovered on their arrival at Jaipúr, after some
further detention, on the 12th of December.

They found that death had visited the mission. Miss
Rhoda Bronson, after seven months on the field, was
called to her heavenly home on the 7th of December,
1840. She was devoting herself to the stndy of the
Naga language, in the hope of teaching the wild chil-

dren of the forests the way of life, when a violent attack of fever removed her from her work.   No regret embittered her parting hours.   She felt that her offering was accepted, and in perfect peace passed on to the better life.   Among her last words were, " With me all is well. I have no fear of death.   Tell my friends in America that I do not regret having come to this country."

The four months' voyage had made no material change in Nathan's condition, and it was not till January that he ceased to " creep about the floor, and amuse himself and his sister with his playthings, and ride out with her in his little hand-carriage, mornings and evenings." There was then a month of severe suffering, which the little fellow, now in his fifth year, bore with manly patience.   His mother writes :

" It was his delight to have me sit by him, put my arms around him and sing hymns.   He would keep himself quiet for hours in that way, without uttering one groan.   .   .   .   It appeared to distress him more to see me weep, than all his bodily sufferings.   He would burst out crying himself, stretch out his little arms to clasp my neck and say, ' Dear, sweet, darling mamma, don't you cry ; I feel a little better now.   If you cry, I cry.   Sing, mamma sing !   Because I go to heaven, don't you cry ; you and papa come pretty soon.'   He seldom uttered the least complaint.   If we asked whether his eye was painful, he would say, 'A little ; *so much,'* measuring about half an inch on his finger.

He learned to speak English beautifully on our way home, and we had the delightful privilege of teaching him something about God and heaven, a good deal of which, he was able, before his death, to understand. On February 3rd, he said, ' I can't stay any longer ; I want God should take me away to heaven.' "

His interest in all the affairs of the house, however, continued up to the last twenty-four hours.   Exhaustion supervened at length, and the patient little sufferer was cured of his sicknesses on the 11th of February, 1841.

On the 12th, "after a very comforting sermon by Bro. Bronson, from the precious words of Saint Paul, 'For our light affliction, which is but for a moment, worketh out for us a far more exceeding and eternal weight of glory,' the burial took place in the garden. The ground was then carefully restored to its former appearance, all traces of the grave being obliterated, lest it should be disturbed. No stone was ever raised; no one but the father could find the exact spot; and he only by its relative position to the neighboring trees.

But in the shadow of the mother's native hills, where the Deerfield hushes its waters to lake-like stillness, the following record has been engraved on a family monument near the little cdurch :

" DIED IN THE EAST INDIES.

At Maulmain, Aug. 10, 1835,
WILLIAM BALLARD,
Æ. 2 mos. 3 ds.

At Sadiya, Sept. 29, 1838,
DOROTHY SOPHIA,
Æ. 6 yrs. 4 mos. 23 ds.

At Jaipúr, Feb. 11th, 1841,
NATHAN BALLARD,
Æ. 4 yrs. 5 mos. 3 ds.

Children of
REV. NATHAN AND ELIZA W. BROWN.

' Their graves are severed far and wide,
By mount and stream and sea.' "

XVII.

SIGNS OF PROMISE.

A TRACT entitled "The True Refuge," written in Bengali, by William H. Pearce, and now translated into Assamese by Mr. Brown, arrested attention, and awakened considerable inquiry among the natives. As fast as this could be issued, Mr. Brown went about distributing it to such Assamese as could read, having now ready also for the Khamtis, besides their catechism, the History of the Creation and of the Deluge. The Gospel of Matthew was finished early in June, and other tracts, entitled "The Crucifixion," "The Way of Life," and "A Religious Address" were already in circulation, the two latter, translated by Mr. Bronson.

That no time might be lost, Mr. Brown took his books and writing to a zayat which he had put up here at Jaipúr as before at Sudiya. The sight of the foreign teacher at work upon his strange new shasters, drew in the passers-by, to look, examine, question and dispute. And an hour before sunset, it was his daily custom to read and explain the scriptures to a company of Assamese.

Five years had now passed since the first missionary effort was put forth in Upper Assam, and not one heathen had renounced his idols. But there were signs of promise ; it was worth something to have created discussion, to have awakened even hostile attention. And at length one small grain of the seed planted under most difficult circumstances, and watered with tears, sprang up.

Among the wondering, half-frightened boys whom Mrs. Brown and Mrs. Cutter gathered into the first schools at Sudiya, there was a clever little fellow called Nidhi. He made remarkable progress in his Assamese studies, and afterwards gained a good knowledge of English, continuing with the missionaries as long as they remained at Sudiya, and following them to Jaipúr as printer's apprentice. He was now fourteen years old; intelligent, capable and studious. One evening at Jaipúr, while reading alone, he came to a "little simple prayer" in English. It touched his heart; he felt himself a sinner needing a Saviour. During that night, he was repeatedly heard sobbing, and trying to pray to the Christian's God. Mrs. Brown writes:

"The next day, Sabbath, after morning worship, he spent with us. His sorrow for sin seemed to increase, and he refused to eat. . . . Monday he came to see us again, but with Pilgrim's load still upon his back. Mr. Brown took him alone, and spent some time with him in conversation and prayer. On his way home he found relief. . . . Since that time he has been on his way rejoicing. He constantly expresses a decided wish to learn and obey all the Saviour's commands. . . . Even the natives themselves, who know him, say it must be the work of God which has effected such a change upon Nidhi, for man's power could not have done it. . . . Our teacher, a Brahman, appears to be inquiring. He has been a great reviler, but his mouth seems completely stopped since Nidhi's* baptism. There are several other boys in the printing office who have knowledge enough of our Scriptures to lead them to em-

---

* After his conversion, this first convert took the name of Levi Farwell, an officer of the missionary board, and was commonly called Nidhi (pronounced Needy) Levi.

brace the truth, if their hearts could only be touched by
the Spirit of God."

On the 13th of June, a company of natives and Europeans gathered to witness the baptism, which was administered by Mr. Bronson.   Mr. Brown was ill, and
barely able to give a short address and offer a prayer, in
Assamese.   He had been confining himself of late very
closely to translation, Mrs. Brown copying and correcting
proofs to hasten on the press-work.   During May a
severe cold settled on his lungs, and at length a seated
pain in the chest convinced him that he must accede to
the advice of friends and seek medical aid ; accordingly
he set out, June 23d, for Sibsa'gar,* to consult Dr. Furnell.   Mrs. Brown remained behind at work upon translations of school-books.

"Sibsa'gar, July 6.   Found myself benefited by the
trip on the water, and since I arrived here, I have received
the kindest attention from Dr. Furnell.   Have concluded
to start again to-morrow, and go down as far as Jorhat
for the purpose of examining the country and distributing a few tracts."

He found the Tea Company's station at the mouth of
the Dikho, three feet under water, and the Brahmaputra
still rising.   It was pitiful to see the poor natives driven
from their huts, huddling in groups, with their cows and
goats, on the bund road—an embankment and highway
constructed by the old rajas—and now the only ground
above water.   There they were making drift-wood fires,
cooking rice in metal pots, and waiting for the flood to
abate.

The Sahib's canoe now sped swiftly down the turhu-
lent Brahmaputra, swollen to a width of several miles.

* Pronounced Seeb-saw'-gar.

The boat rocked as if out at sea, and there was "water, water everywhere." At length, after ascending a branch stream, called Kokela, for a few miles, the boatmen left the channel and steered out over the rice fields. In some places islands of jungle stood above water and the few trees were crowded with flocks of homeless birds. Startled deer rushed through the flooded jungle-grass, pursued by natives in boats, with spears and bows. When night came, the men poled the canoe into a fruit garden, and moored it to one of the trees. Here they were somewhat protected over night from the wind. On the 9th they reached the large town of Jorhát, the former capital and still the residence of the ex-raja Purunder Singh. Mr. Brown distributed here about a hundred tracts and books among the Assamese inhabitants, numbers of whom he found able to read. The place, however, had been rather on the decline since the removal of the seat of government to Sibsagar, two years before. Some houses were found deserted, and the roads were almost impassable from being cut up by water-courses, and overgrown with jungle.

From Jorhat Mr. Brown took the straight line for Sibsagar, as the water was now high enough to admit of a boat going in almost any direction. After passing over several rice meadows, the channel of the Tiok, a small, unwholesome stream, formed his course for many miles. That day he saw but few villages, and those were inundated. At night the boatmen had great difficulty in finding a spot of ground large enough to make a fire upon. Entering the Janzi river on the 12th, he reached, a little before dark, a cluster of villages that were not under water, and succeeded in gaining the attention of several groups of people. The next day he struck across country for the Namdang, a southern affluent of the Dikho, and the boatmen were unfortunate enough to get into some meadows of stagnant water which was

intolerably offensive and poisonous. Hastening on, a
refreshing contrast was found in a fresh cool breeze from
the Gouri-sagar, one of the numerous artificial reservoirs
of the country, so named from the goddess Gouri or
Dúrga, the wife of Siva.

" One of the largest tanks in Assam, dug in 1724 by,
the Raja Seeb Singh. This was the scene of an action
between the Company's troops and the Burmese in 1825
in which the latter were defeated and shortly after ex-
pelled from the country. The Assamese have the
greatest dread of the Burmese name from a remembrance
of the atrocities perpetrated by them during their short
rule in Assam. They are strongly attached to their
present rulers, regarding the Company as their deliver-
ers from the Burmese yoke.

Reached the stone bridge just above the junction of
the Namdang with the Dikho, about 3 o'clock, (July 13th.)
Found here a large village of Dooms or fishermen, and
spoke for about an hour to an interesting congregation."

He reached Sibsagar the next day, and there heard of
the death of Mrs. Hannay. On leaving Saikwa the previous year, Captain Hannay had stationed the troops at
Sibsagar, whence Mrs. Hannay, in feeble health, had
been taken to Gauhati, in the vain hope of restoration.
She died there on the 4th of July, 1841. A package of
her letters to Mrs. Brown, carefully filed and laid away
under the inscription : "*The love where death his seal
has set,*" still remains, the witness to a faithful friendship.

On the 19th Mr. Brown started on his return to Jaipúr, going first to Dibrugur, where he was hospitably
entertained by Captain Vetch, and distributed a large
number of tracts.

" This station is beautifully situated at the mouth of the
Dibru river, and although quite new, already contains a

considerable population. It is one of the best locations for a missionary in Upper Assam, and had it been a European station at the time of our leaving Sudiya, we should, no doubt, have selected it in preference to Jaipúr. At that time, however, it was under the authority of the raja who governed Motok, and the Jorhat district being in an unsettled state, Jaipúr was, on all accounts, considered the most eligible station that could then be selected. It has not, however, proved to be a healthy location, and from this and other causes, the expectations which were entertained of its rapid prosperity, have been disappointed.

July 29. Left Dibrugur and proceeded down the Brahmaputra as far as the mouth of the Dihing, where I learned that Mrs. Brown had passed down to Sibsagar a few days before, having had a severe attack of fever. Accordingly I changed my course and came to Sibsagar, which I reached on Friday, the 30th. Here I received letters from the brethren at Jaipúr, from which, and the advice of Brother Barker, I have at length decided to remain at Sibsagar. The press, we trust, will ultimately be located here, it being altogether the most central and important station in Assam proper, that is Assam above Gauhati."

The question of removing the missionary station from Jaipúr, whose population had become fluctuating, and was now decreasing, had for some time been under consideration. The tea-coolies could not be induced to settle permanently in the place on account of its unhealthiness, and the missionaries had suffered there from almost constant illness.

Sibsagar, on the contrary, situated in a comparatively healthy locality, on the Dikho river, with a population of five thousand, was the center of a hundred villages which lay within a circuit of six miles, and, were connected with the station by good roads.

Jorhat and Dibrugur also had claims upon the mission, and it was with a view to comparing them with those of Sibsagar, that Mr. Brown had made his recent trips of exploration. The result was a preponderance in favor of Sibsagar. On returning thither he wrote to the missionaries at Jaipúr, July 31 :

"Time is rapidly passing; hitherto I have labored to little purpose; repeated attacks of sickness admonish me that ere long this frail tenement may be dissolved, and I feel unwilling to spend my days at a station where I can have little or no opportunity for preaching, while here there are full streets and crowded villages, where I might labor all the time that I should not be engaged in translating. Kindly take these things into consideration, dear brethren, and give me an early answer, and may the Lord guide us in all our steps."

The Barkers were already at Sibsagar, having removed thither from Jaipúr, in May. They received the Browns into their house on the west bank of the tank, and the two families, for the present, occupied it together. Though considerably dilapidated, and without flooring, this dwelling had the advantage of the tank breeze, being on the embankment, and facing the water.

The family no longer lived on the wing, prepared for attack, with boat and pistol close at hand, as at Sudiya and Jaipúr; they were freed also, to a great extent, from the fever-breath of the jungle which at the latter station reduced mission work to a minimum, and well nigh laid all the workers under the sod. At Sibsagar, wholesome food could be regularly obtained; bread, heretofore an almost unobtainable luxury, was occasionally furnished by a native baker.

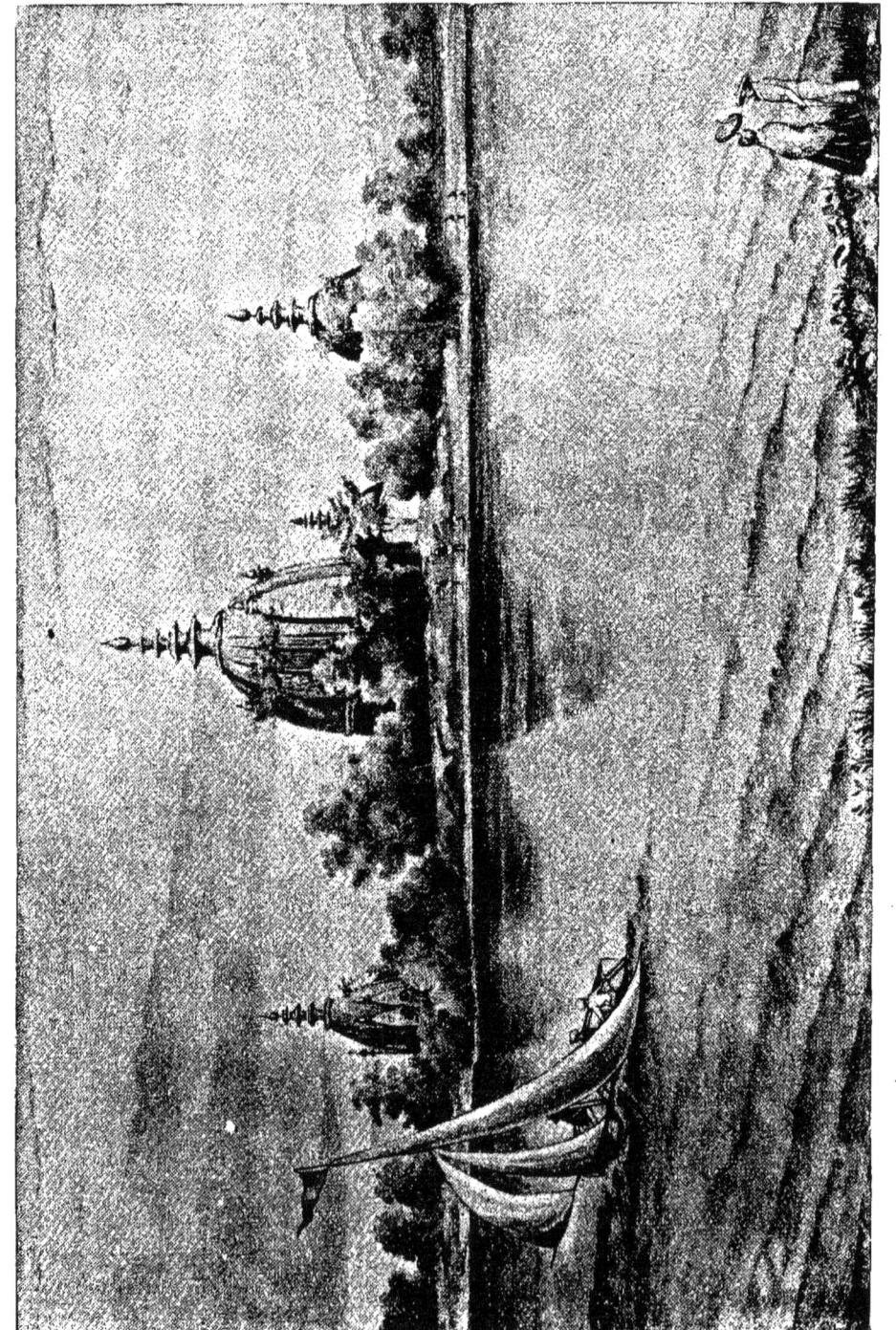

SIBSAGAR TANK AND TEMPLES.

Sibsagar* Tank deserves more than a passing men-tion. Fed from below by living springs, it is a lake large and deep enough to throw up " white caps " in the autumn gales, and its changing aspects are those of na-ture. Mr. Brown used to speak with enthusiasm of the flocks of wild geese, which come with every returning cold season to make it their winter home. These wild fowl were never shot, the Hindus holding that the waters being consecrated to Siva, it would be sacrilege to kill his birds.

" The natives indeed, believe it to be impossible to kill them while upon the tank. Stories are related of nu-merous individuals, English, Bengalis and Burmans, who have died in the most miserable manner, in consequence of violating the sanctity of the tank, or the temples."

This noble reservoir is said to have been constructed about the year 1722, by the Raja Seeb Singh, and comple-ted in a single dry season, in order to avoid the washing of the rains upon the work. He is said to hav eemployed a million men in the excavation, stationing them in ranks, through which the baskets of earth could be rapidly passed from hand to hand. The soil thus removed forms the broad embankment around the reservoir, on which is a road, flanked by temples and residences. The em-bankment is surrounded by a moat called the outer tank. The entire work is a quadrangle, varying but little from a square, the inner tank being nearly two miles in cir-cuit, 114 acres in surface, and from twenty to forty feet deep.

On the southern bank are the grand old temples, three pyramidal structures of solid brick, dedicated respectively

---

*Siva's Ocean. The name Sibsagar, compounded of *Sib* or Siva and *sagar*, ocean, first given to the reservoir, was afterwards applied to the town.

to Siva, Vishnu and Durga.* They are contempora-
neous with the tank. The central, largest temple is that
of Siva, and contains the Salgram or sacred black stone,
an object of peculiar reverence. The temple is 143 feet
high. Mrs. Whiting says:

"Large slabs of stone on which are carved grótesque
images of gods and goddesses, are inlaid from the base to
the height of fifteen or twenty feet. From various crevices, and from the angles around the pretty turrets, grow
large shrubs and graceful vines. The dome is crowned
with a large golden ball, which, at the time I saw it, was
perforated with holes, said to have been made by Burmese
bullets when the Burmese invaded Assam in 1816."

Temples in India not being erected for the accomoda-
tion of worshippers, but for the honor of the gods, are
solid piles. In the interior of this temple is a vault-like
room containing an image of Siva, into which none but
priests can enter. The suppliant brings his offering to
the entrance of the shrine, and prostrating himself, presents it to the attendant priest, who lays it before the
image, ringing a hell to attract the attention of the
divinity.

A mile south of the temples flows the Dikho, a branch
of the Brahmaputra, which it joins by a winding course,
thirty miles below. Along the Dikho lay the native
town, where, later, the mission printing office was located.

Native visitors soon called on the missionaries in considerable numbers, and the priests began to question
what these new teachings might be. One day a school
of Brahman boys came in, with their white-robed pre-

---

* Dúrga (pron. Doorga), also called Káli, and parváti, the wife of Siva
and the goddess of cholera and other epidemics. She is appeased by bloody
sacrifices; the images represent her with many arms—each holding a
weapon—a necklace of skulls, and lips stained with human gore.

ceptor, as American boys would visit a museum or menagerie. The foreign padré showed them his globe, and made the surprising statement that the world is round like a ball, and swings unsupported in space. They thought him a prince of romancers when he described the wonders of the countries underfoot, peopled by white men, and most astounding of all, the marvelous under-ocean, up whose steep slopes he had himself crept in a ship, and which spilled not a drop of its brine ! But when the conversation was led on to the one Creator, and his Son, the only Redeemer of all races of men, the pundit made a courtly salam and withdrew, with his charge.

Occasionally Mr. Brown's visitors were of high rank, and these evinced more bitter opposition than any others, refusing even so much as to touch one of the heretical books, lest they should incur pollution. Some of the intelligent Brahmans, however, were willing to discuss the new theories. The priests told the people that this heresy was long ago predicted.

"October 30. I have recently obtained a copy of a prophecy in the Assamese scriptures, which I have often heard quoted, but never fully understood, not being able to obtain it in writing. It is considered by the Brahmans as a prediction of the introduction of the English rule and religion into this country, and every conversion among the Hindus serves to confirm the prophecy and excite their fears. The passage consists of two verses, the first only of which they are accustomed to repeat in the hearing of Europeans, while the second is what particularly suits the prejudices of the natives. I have often heard them singing it over among themselves with great glee."

The following is Mr. Brown's translation of this portion of the Assamese scriptures :

In Buddha's reign shall cease from earth the sacred Ve-
    da's sway,
And new barbarian shasters lead the sons of men astray;
Thy worship shall they cast away, thy name no longer
    dread,
While foreign rites and heresies the guilty world o'er-
    spread.

But ere the close of Kali-yúg,* great Kàlki† shall arise,
Whose arm shall sweep the impious race from under-
    neath the skies ;
The last barbarian infidel shall sink beneath his sword,
And true religion once again be to the earth restored.

Meantime the "barbarian shasters" were doing their
work. The images on the ancient temples of Siva and
Vishnu looked down upon Christian services and baptisms ; and the sacred name of *Yesu Kristo* was borne
out in song over that still expanse, " long since dedicated
to a heathen deity, now consecrated to the service of
Christ."

---

* Yúg, (yoog) an age or era ; Kali-yúg, the age of Kali ; the present iron
age.

† The tenth incarnation of Vishnu, yet to appear.

XVIII.

"LET us thank God, and take courage," Mrs. Brown wrote in January, 1842. "After having been nearly six years in almost hopeless despondency, a new and blessed era seems to be dawning upon us. There is a rapidly increasing desire among all classes, to learn to read; and we learn from many quarters, that a spirit of inquiry concerning this new religion exists among the people."

While her husband was translating Acts, and going about preaching in the villages, during that cold season, she was able with renewed health to prepare several more school books, among them a reading-book and geography, the latter translated and adapted from Peter Parley.

She spent three or four hours daily teaching thirty or forty boys, till the opening of the new government school drew them away. Meantime the little Assamese girls whose mothers would consent, were glad to come to Mrs. Barker's school ; but prejudice against educating girls was very strong, and not many could be obtained· "In one case, the mother, to prevent her child attending the school, sold it for three rupees ! "

In the early records of the Assam mission, frequent mention is made of assistance received from British officers, both military and civil. The printed reports show

that almost every European resident of the three stations contributed to the support of the mission schools.
Capt. Hannay, on his removal from Sibsagar, in 1845,
presented to the mission his substantial brick bungalow
and premises, to be used for the printing establishment
and residence of missionary printer. The Commissioner,
Major Jenkins, made large annual contributions, and
purchased a press. The professional services of the
station physicians were gratuitously rendered to the
missionaries, and supplemented by many acts of personal
kindness.

Mrs. Brown's large and hitherto complete home circle
was broken by the sudden death of her father, May 25th,
1842, in his 79th year, and on January 18th, 1844, of her
brother Charles. The following letter speaks of death
and birth :

Mr. Brown to Mrs. Elizabeth Ballard :

"Sibsagar, December 25, 1842.

My dearly beloved Mother: A few days ago we received Dorothy's letter giving the melancholy, or, I
should rather say, joyful, intelligence of our dear father's
happy death. . . . The circumstances were so consoling that the sting seems to be quite removed. . . .
How lovely does heaven appear as we approach it, and
how the world fades as we are about to leave it. Our
dear father appears to have felt this most fully, as he
drew near the goal. Happy spirit! He has forever
bidden farewell to sorrow—the trials that beset him here
shall distress him no more.

. . . On the 12th instant we had a little son born,
the first child for more than four years. We call him
William Pearce, after Mr. Pearce, missionary at Calcutta,
the first friend that we found in this hemisphere.

. . . May the blessing of God rest upon you, and the light of his countenance ever be about you to comfort you in all your trials, and, finally, may you be brought safely, with all your numerous household, to sit down with Abraham, Isaac and Jacob in that kingdom where we shall go no more out, is the prayer of your unworthy son.　　　　　　　　　　N. Brown."

Early in 1843 the Singphos came out of their jungles again with spear and battle-axe. The guard at Bisa was captured; many sepoys were killed and wounded in an attack on the night of the 10th of January, upon Ningrú, near Jaipúr. On hearing of the attack, Mr. Brown accompanied Capt. Hannay to Jaipúr in order to assist in securing the mission property, and found that the type had already been buried underground for safe-keeping. The alarm, however, subsided; and the Singphos, with a wholesome dread of British muskets, retired.

It was not far from this time that a number of burial-mounds of the former kings of Assam were opened.

"The tomb of King Godadhor, at Soraideo, as nearly as we could calculate without instruments, was ninety feet high, and so natural in its appearance that a stranger would scarcely have suspected it to be anything more than an ordinary hill. . . . Tumuli in honor of the old Assamese kings and chieftains dot the whole country. These artificial mounds frequently rise to the height of one hundred feet, and the small room in which the corpse is deposited is filled with the king's regalia, his golden dishes and other utensils, and often two or three slaves who were buried alive with their master to attend upon his wants in another world. Thirteen of these royal tombs were dug open during my residence in Assam, and I was told in the flowery language of the country, that when King Godadhor's tomb was opened 'the backs of three elephants were broken with the weight of the treasures it contained;' meaning simply that three elephants were well loaded down."

" The Asiatics, in building a mound, having first made a small heap over the tomb or skeleton, lay on the earth in successive layers from six inches to a foot thick, making every layer even and symmetrical. The first layers are composed of loam gathered from the surface, next the hard pan, clay, sand or whatever lies beneath it ; then, perhaps, surface soil from a new locality, and so on till the desired size is obtained. This naturally produces an appearance of stratification, very different from the virgin earth."

Images and other curious relics were sometimes unearthed, from tombs, temples and palaces, and Mr. Brown came into possession of an interesting collection. A Mussulman once appeared at the study door, holding carefully wrapped in the end of his scarf, a mysterious object. He looked suspiciously about, and finding that the pundit was absent, came in and whispered, " I have got something !"

" Well, what is it ? "

Cautiously unfolding the cloth, he disclosed an oval black stone, three or four inches in diameter, but seemed unwilling to let it pass out of his hands.

" This is the holy Salgram—worth much money—I will sell it to you."

"But you must let me examine it."

With much hesitation, and another frightened glance about the room, the trader in relics allowed the padre to take the stone, which proved to be a genuine Salgram or Sacred Black Stone, believed by the Hindus to be a direct and voluntary incarnation of deity, and hence more sacred than idols, into which the spirit of the divinity is invoked at the will of the priest. It was in fact a flinty concretion around a pretty shell, which having crumbled away, had left its perfect impression within, visible through an opening broken in the end. The three marks by which a devout Brahman recognizes a genuine Salgram were present, the impression of a rosary, minute dents as of a cow's hoof, and golden streaks. The priest who is so favored as to possess or have access to a Salgram, bathes it with religious ceremonies every morning, and worships it as the incarnate Vishnu. For any hands but those of a holy Brahman to touch this sacred object, is death, either instant or prolonged, as the vengeance of the gods may determine.

After some chaffering, the Mussulman parted with his treasure for a few rupees, and Mr. Brown laid it on a table in the center of the room. Some days later there was a flutter of white robes at the study door, and two or three Brahmans came in. Their eyes fell upon the stone ; they started back with hands lifted, and expressions of horror. " Do you know what you have there ?" Then, looking fixedly at the padre, as if expecting to see him fall lifeless before them, " You will die ; you cannot live ; the vengeance of the gods cannot pass over such blasphemy and sacrilege."

Finding the somewhat amused foreigner unmoved by threats, the visitors tried persuasion, but failing to induce him to part with the relic, they took their leave, doubtless convinced that the end of Kali-yúg was close at hand.

The spring of '43 was saddened by tidings of the death of three gifted and devoted workers in quick succession ; Mrs. Theodosia A. Dean, at Hongkong, Mrs. Sarah D. Comstock, at Ramree, Arakan, and Mrs. Caroline (Harrington) Simons, at Tellicherry, on the

Malabar coast.   Mr. Brown paid the following tribute
to the memory of an old friend :

SONNET

ON THE DEATH OF MRS. CAROLINE J. SIMONS,

MISSIONARY TO BURMA.

Beloved sister !   while this region cold
  Thy pilgrim feet on mercy's errand trod,
  So deep was thy devotion to thy God,
So warm the love thy every action told,
We deemed thee formed of a celestial mold,
  And wondered thou shoulds't need thy Father's rod
  To wean thy spirit from this earthly clod ;
Yet o'er thee many a wave of sorrow rolled.
  But now no longer o'er thy griefs we sigh,
Since thou art gathered to the glorious fold
  Where the kind Shepherd wipeth every eye ;
  And radiant there with immortality,
His lovely face thou ever dost behold,
And with the pure and perfect walk the streets of gold.

Four days before Mrs. Comstock's fatal illness, she
wrote from Ramree to Mrs. Brown :

"I have for aught I know, *four* precious children.
Two are with us, and two are far, far away, where I
never expect to see them in this world."

The pen stopped near the top of the second page.
The sheet was finished by her husband on the 5th of
May, telling of her six days' illness, and death, on the
28th of April, and of the two thousand mourners who
thronged the house during the following day.   "How
kind she was to us all," the Arakanese women said,
with many tears ; "she always gave us medicine when

sick. Ah, she came far away from home to die, with no
mother nor sister near her, because she pitied us."

A later letter from Mr. Comstock tells how the two
youngest children followed their mother within a few
weeks. The letter breathes the spirit of heaven, for
which the writer seemed ready. In less than a year, on
the 25th of April, 1844, Rev. Grover Comstock died of
cholera at Akyab, Arakan.

A few entries gathered from Mr. Brown's scanty
diary may indicate the undercurrent of a busy life:

" January 3, '42· "Spent this as a day of fasting, in
accordance with the custom of the churches at home.
Prepared a few remarks on the duty of fasting.

Lord's day, April 17. So rainy that none came to
worship. Read a sermon of J. Scott's on " Satan's
Devices against us." Read one hundred pages in Krummacher's " Elijah the Tishbite "—a beautiful work, and
breathing a spirit of the most sincere and childlike
piety. In it the character of the prophet appears to be
correctly portrayed—how lovely—how faithful—how
strictly obedient was this servant of the Lord! . . .
Elijah " stood before God," waiting for, and executing
his orders—Enoch walked with God, and pleased him ;
Abraham was the friend of God ; and they all gave implicit obedience to his will.

Monday, April 18. Translated remainder of the 28th
chapter of Acts. Had I been diligent and faithful in
my Master's service it would not have been thus long
before this portion of his Holy Word had been completed. But I hope I have commenced a new course,
and by the help of God, I shall be enabled to go on.

April 24. Read in Krummacher's Elijah and Bunyan's Life. Oh, for the grace of repentance.

May 7. Strange that my thoughts should fix with such eagerness on worldly things.

May 17. [After reading the memoir of Harlan Page;] Oh lovely Whitefield and Wesley and Bunyan and Page ! Let my lot be with you, ye people of the Lord.

June 22. My birthday—35 years old. It fills me with confusion to look back upon my life. The coming year shall through grace be devoted faithfully to His service, and O Lord, let an abundant harvest of precious souls be gathered into Thy flock. Translated twenty verses of John 3.

October 24. Finished 20th chapter of John. Went down to see Capt. Hannay. Heard the news of the treaty with China and the retaking of Kabúl. Find that everything has gone wrong to-day, which I believe is owing to my not asking the blessing of God on each undertaking I have begun during the day. Went over to see the Miri who is to be hung to-morrow. Found him crying bitterly. Prayed with him, and he joined in repeating over every sentence. May the Lord have mercy on his soul !

November 21. I find it is good to leave my concerns in the hands of God. He brings light out of obscurity, and clears up the darkest cloud.

December 10. Finished reading over the copy of John—the old teacher wept while reading of the crucifixion. May the Lord grant him true repentance."

The progress of public events in America during these years, could not fail to be watched with interest by her citizens abroad. Mr. Brown read the papers with avidity.

To John Conant, Esq. of Brandon, on the arrival of boxes. "When we get a quantity of reading from home, I almost feel as if transported to my native shores, and breathe an exhilarating atmosphere, altogether different from anything we obtain from any other source. Sometimes when I look back to the loving circles of God's dear children, where I have enjoyed so many happy seasons, my heart is ready to burst with the agonizing desire to revisit those scenes once more."

He was interested in every presidential election, watched the progress of the Mexican War, and already heard the ominous thunders of the irrepressible conflict, noted with satisfaction the growth of the anti-slavery principle, and decided that a gospel of liberty could not consistently be disseminated by means of funds derived even in part from the sale of human beings, or the profits of unrequited labor. Coinage corroded by that "secret rust" he could not believe to be a legal tender in payment of the King's tribute.

Diary, October 1, '43. "Received a letter from the Secretary of the [Provisional] Anti-slavery Committee, asking if I will receive my support from them. . . . I have lived so long in trouble and difficulties, that I dread any further change. However, I will try to go forward if the Lord give me strength."

His answer was in the affirmative. At the same time he desired the funds to be sent through the Board whose mission he served.

October 21. " Sent off to-day my answer to the Anti-slavery Committee, with a copy to Mr. Peck. Have taken an important step, of which I know not what the end will be. Every motive but that of duty seemed to dissuade me from the step, and it has been a painful one to take. I trust I have not followed my own will."

He wrote to Dr. Peck, Secretary of the Missionary Board :

"It appears to me that the Abolitionists, so far as it regards the question between them and slave-holders, are in the right, and that their principles are such as will stand approved when all the prejudices and passions of this world shall have passed away."

The Committee's proposal was withdrawn before action was taken by the Board in the matter, and a few months later, the southern churches withdrew from the society, and organized the Southern Baptist Missionary Convention at Augusta, Ga., in May, 1845.

The arrival of the press and type from Jaipúr in November, '43, removed the hinderance of sending manuscripts and proofs to a distance by uncertain conveyances, and facilitated the issue of the New Testament. Mr. Brown had already marked out the ground for a printing office, going himself to the jungles to select bamboos ; on the 9th, raised the posts, and 10th, put up the ridge-pole of the office.

He then decided to rebuild his own dwelling, the only floor of which was reed matting spread upon the ground and whose posts were now found to be dangerously decayed. He obtained permission to remove his family temporarily to the Assam Tea Company's bungalow, and on December 15th, the workmen began to unroof the house. Much of his time for the next two months was unavoidably occupied in overseeing and directing the coolies and working with them.

"It distracts me, almost, to think how much time I have spent in building my house. I hope two months will never be spent in the same manner again.

March 1, 1844. Moved into our new house this evening. Oh that all my time and powers while I live in it
may be spent in such a way as will be pleasing in the
sight of God. What reason have I for thankfulness for
all the mercies I have experienced while building!
Health has been bestowed, and the means of carrying
on the work, and no accident has occurred to any of the
coolies while at work upon it."

The new bungalow, built of stout bamboos and thatched with grass, was raised several feet above the ground
upon posts. It consisted of three large rooms and a
latticed veranda. Its walls were plastered with mud
and whitewashed; it had windows and venetians. In
front was a semi-circular garden, containing date and
cocoa-palms, the homes of singing birds. Here were
rose-bushes, chrysanthemums, and a sun-dial. Three
weeping-willows thrived beyond all the trees of the garden, sweeping the ground with abundant foliage. These
had sprung from slips planted by the father in memory
of his three eldest children departed. More about the
birds and trees is found in a letter to his little son,
written some years later:

"My darling Willie: What shall I write to you?
About the doves or the robins? We have ten or a
dozen of the former, and about six of the latter. The
former eat out of my hands, the latter are more timid,
and I have to throw the kernels of rice some distance
for them to pick up. The pigeons (or doves) have a
little mat house made for them. The first one that was
made for them, the robins came and drove them out of.
The robins are just like the American robins, only they
have a little white under their wings, which they show
when they are flying.

(15)

Have I ever told you what trees we have growing
around our house? I will try to think of the principal
ones. Weeping-willows, beautiful ones, just before our
door, one called Willie's Willow is right before my study
door. I send two or three leaves of it. It came from
Bonaparte's tomb at St. Helena. Before my study there
are also date trees—one of them bore a few this year ;
almond trees—not large enough to bear yet ; peaches—
had a nice lot this year ; oranges—not ripe yet ; citrons
and limes, pummalo [or|shaddock] a large kind of citron ;
pomegranate trees full of fruit; young cocoanut trees ;
coffee trees ; bear well; betel nut trees ; plantains in
abundance ; young mango and jack trees ; guava, clumps
of bamboo ; tree grape—a very fine fruit ; grape vine of
the country—grapes not yet ripe. All these your papa
has set out since he has been here. I do not think you
will remember how they look, they have grown a great
deal since you left."

The work upon the house was a good investment of
time, outdoor exercise proving to be the best medical
treatment for the weakness of the lungs, and Mr. Brown
was able to write the August following, " My health
has been much better than during any previous hot
season."

Other recreation for the missionary and his family
was found in an occasional hour's gardening and sometimes a two-mile walk around the tank early in the morning, or a sail upon it at evening in the pleasure-boat of
a friendly resident.

Great inconvenience had been experienced in the old
house from the depredations of the white ants, which
had destroyed trunks of clothing, paper, books, and other
valuable articles. The vexatious little invaders would
tunnel any wood except teak, and threatened to eat up
the house itself. Other unwelcome inmates made free

with the house. The numerous harmless lizards were scarcely noticed, unless when they chanced to drop from the thatch into one's dinner-plate; but it was a more serious matter to find a huge centipede or scorpion crawling among the folds of a hanging garment, or lurking in ambush about the joints of the bedstead. One night, Mrs. Brown woke with a sharp pain in her shoulder. A light was quickly struck, but not quickly enough to capture the creature of many legs. A long line of stings found on the flesh showed plainly enough that the invader was an enormous centipede.

One evening at dusk, Mr. Brown, passing from one room to another, heard from a dark corner the peculiar puff! which the cobra emits from its hood just before it strikes. Retreating quickly and shutting the door, he secured a club, a native and a light, and on returning found the creature with inflated hood, and aspect angrily defiant, standing almost upright in the corner, where it was soon despatched.

An exciting incident occurred while the new house was building. Mr. C——, a recently arrived English physician, not yet familiar with the strength and passion of religious conviction in the Hindu mind, rashly flew in the face of it by butchering a cow at cantonments. The sepoys, first horrified and then maddened by this sacrilegious crime—as much worse in their conception than an ordinary murder, as to a devout Roman Catholic the stealing of holy relics from the altar would be worse than common theft—formed an enraged mob, and surrounded his house, from which he was obliged to flee for his life.

" He was afterwards waylaid by a party of fifteen or twenty men armed with clubs, and beaten very severely. The sepoys are now in such a state of excitement and insubordination that Mr. C—— is obliged to retire to the tank with his family, lest he should be again attacked by them. I went down and brought up their bedding to their tent on the tank, whither they have fled for safety."

The Assamese cow is a scrawny, dejected-looking creature. Instead of the fine succulent grasses of the temperate regions, its nourishment consists of a coarse wiry diet of jungle grass, more suited to the native buffalo. Mrs. Brown was obliged to maintain at least twenty cows when her young family was about her. They could only be milked once a day, averaging about a teacupful apiece, and that was considered a rare specimen which could be depended upon for a pint at a time. But what the country fails to furnish the poor beast in the way of nourishment is made up in reverence. The natives call these animals " Mother " and " Father," the most exalted and pure of the spirits of their departed relatives being supposed to inhabit these bovine bodies, and woe to him who lays a sacrilegious hand on them.

During the rains of 1844, Mr. Brown gave weekly lectures at the printing office to the workmen and others on the fallacies of the Hindu shasters. He took the printers out of doors and showed them how to compute the distance and height of an inaccessible object, the Assamese, even Brahmans, being entirely ignorant of this simple problem.

"June 29. Lectured on Truth and Falsehood to the boys and others in Brother Cutter's office at five o'clock. After this showed the boys how to measure distance to a tree without going to it. Calculated the distance two hundred and forty-six cubits, and found it to be on measurement two hundred and forty-seven."

One of his object lessons was computing the height of Siva's temple, which, including the gilt ball on the summit, they found to be ninety-five and a half cubits, or about one hundred and forty-three feet.

After a little practical work of this kind, which the boys were taught to do themselves, they were prepared to take in he idea that the distance of the sun, moon, and stars might be calculated to a certainty. Some further explanations showed how the size of the earth is computed, and gaining confidence in the reasonableness of the sahib's talk, they took away from the lectures the suspicion that a careful examination of the earth's surface might fail to bring to light the four circular oceans of rum, sugar, milk and butter of which the Brahmans had told them, that the shasters had made a slip in saying the sun is only half as far away as the moon, and that there might be a more reasonable theory of eclipses than that a demon takes an occasional bite out of the sun.

Moreover these friendly and entertaining object-lessons made them better acquainted with the missionary, and prepared a channel for religious truth to enter. "Every tour I make," wrote Dr. Bronson in '52, "shows me the value of diffusing a correct science among the people, in order to show them the falsehood of their sacred books. Science, with them, is as much a matter of divine revelation as religion, and both stand or fall together."

On the 9th of March, 1845, the "Sibsagar branch of the Baptist church in Assam" was organized. The year closed with a meeting of the scattered missionaries for mutual consultation and conference. The social intercourse thus afforded was a refreshment to the workers.

The need of help grew more pressing with the gradual enlargement of the work. Mr. Brown wrote to the theological students at Hamilton:

"Brethren, if any of you feel any yearnings of soul towards such a discouraging corner of the earth as this, *Come!* You will find open arms to receive you— brethren who will faithfully cast in their lot with you, and a few intrepid native converts whose hearts will rejoice to travel with you through the length and breadth of the land. Oh, that these simple people could be converted before infidelity and popery make their inroads upon them!"

XIX

THERE was no part of his work into which Mr. Brown threw himself with more zest than outdoor preaching. Wherever he could find a few natives talking together—at the bazar, around a blacksmith's shed, tailor's tent or brazier's shop ; on the river bank, or under a tree—he entered into their conversation, drew out their religious beliefs, and in a frank and friendly way expressed his own. " How I wish I could travel up and down the country, and preach to the people ! " he wrote. " I often feel most painfully distressed that I cannot give myself to preaching, instead of translating and making books. But the latter, I know, is my more particular duty, and therefore I try to be content." When confined at translation during the week, he found his best Sunday rest in preaching-jaunts along one or other of the six or seven radiating roads of which Sibsagar was the focus. Sometimes he followed the banks of the Dikho, the Dimo or Dorika, and other neighboring watercourses, where he found many villages ; while his longer tours took him to the Disang and its tributaries, or south to the Namdang, thence on to the Janzi and the Brahmaputra.

The villagers within a circuit of ten miles must have become quite familiar with the tall, athletic figure and brisk gait of the white padre, going from hamlet to hamlet. They learned to know the serious, kindly face, the dark hair brushed up straight from the forehead, upon which it never could be made to lie down, the deep-set

brown eyes, intense and masterful in argument, but full
of a soft, merry light, whenever the children cautiously
approached, to study his marvelous wearing apparel.

It was a mystery—what he came for.   The officer-
sahibs—*their* business was plain enough, but what could
have brought this one ?   He had nothing to do with tea,
government or sepoys.   It was said he had some strange
undecipherable shasters (full of heresies), in his house.
He was always talking about them, and said Ram,
Krishnú and Dúrga were not to be worshipped, that
there was but one true Avatar, Yesú, the Son of God.
Well, let us hear what he has to say ; there he is now,
disputing with a Mussulman—one as bad as the other.

So the critics would talk to one another, drawing near
meantime, in little groups, till the groups grew to a
circle, and the circle to a congregation ; hearing wonderful things never dreamed of in their philosophy, and
still tarrying to hear more.   The pointed argument, the
clear explanation, the intense earnestness of the speaker,
held their close attention, and generally drew out expressions of assent.   "Come and preach to us every
Sunday," the people of one village urged, when he turned
to go home.

His wayside audiences varied in size from a single
hearer to a hundred, and were of all castes; sometimes
a group of Dooms or fishermen gathered around him on
a river bank ; sometimes a knot of swarthy coolies in
nature's garb, squatted under a tree to rest and stare
curiously at the foreigner ; not seldom, turbaned talka-
tive bazar-men stopped their traffic to join in the discussion, and occasionally a reticent Brahman of impassive
Caucasian features and abundant white drapery, con-
descended by his presence to diffuse a cool, critical and
unreceptive atmosphere among the listeners, for so it
became the accredited teachers of ancient orthodoxy
to do.

The friendly conversation, starting from any topic which chanced at the moment to be uppermost in the minds of the group, often led to a brief exposition or address, illustrated in the most familiar and simple manner, interrupted not infrequently by questions and remarks of approval or dissent—a mode of preaching as unlike as possible to the consecutive, orderly discourse which is suggested to the civilized and Christian mind by the term "sermon," but suited to the circumstance, and adapted to the audience. "*Regular sermonizing* is what we have little occasion for," Mr. Brown wrote in reply to a letter of inquiry ; "talking to people in the street, and exhorting a few disciples in a free conversational manner is what we have to do." This he calls "the peculiar work of a missionary." "Sermonizing in the ordinary method would be nearly unintelligible to those whose ideas of God, sin, holiness heaven and hell were so totally different from ours. We must sit down and explain, and converse and reason with them."

He had a practical, pointed way of talking ; the coolies and fishermen found they could understand him as well as the baboos and Brahmans. "You know how to make clothes for the body," he said one day, entering a tailor's tent, "but can you make a robe to cover your soul at the Judgment?" "Is there any greater heat than this furnace ? " he asked the bystanders who were looking on while a blacksmith was making an axe. "I will tell you of the great *hobah* (assembly) when God shall gather all nations for judgment," he said to a congregation collected at a village festival. Sometimes, when the attention and solemnity of his hearers warranted, he would follow the address with prayer.

"Is there any remedy for sin ? " he once asked a Brahman.

"Yes, by worshipping, making pújas, [sacrifices] and thinking upon God."

The Brahman then proceeded, in the peculiar monotone used by them for religious instruction, to explain the
methods by which the penalties of sin might be escaped.

Then followed friendly inquiries as to the methods and
merits of pújas, in course of which the Brahman discovers that the foreigner is as well-versed as himself in his
own shasters, and knows that some of them forbid the
worship of images.   The Hindu and the Christian were
perfectly agreed that guilt cannot be removed without
atonement, and on this common ground the missionary
then proceeded to preach Christ, the Holy Incarnation
or Avatar, and him crucified, according to the "shasters
that are no fable, but the true words of God."

This conversation had taken place in a blacksmith's
shop, and the old man at the anvil, who had been listening with the closest attention, now spoke:

"Can anything be said against this?   Must not this
be the true religion?"

The Brahman to the missionary's surprise, nodded
assent.

On another occasion Mr. Brown asked a Brahman,
"Are there three Gods or one?"

"One God," was the reply.

"Were Brahma, Vishnu and Sib all the same?"

"Yes, the same God, in three forms."

"Do not your shasters speak of a Supreme God, that
is above Brahma, Vishnu and Siva?"

"Yes."

"Is this Supreme God visible or invisible—corporeal
or incorporeal?"

"He is invisible and incorporeal—without eyes he
sees, without ears he hears, without feet he moves, and
whatever is his will, that comes to pass, was the reply
of this heathen man, who had never seen the Bible,
yet was clearly aware of the existence of the one Supreme
God, and that He is a Spirit."

"This is the God," Mr. Brown continued, "whose religion I have come to preach—the invisible, incorporeal Being, who is the Maker and Lord of all.

"I then told them that all the stories in their shasters about Brahma, Vishnu and Siva, were the work of the pundits, and could never be reconciled with the doctrine of the supreme, invisible God, a doctrine which had been handed down from our first parents and had found a place even in their own scriptures."

At another time, the missionary was walking along the road from Jorhat in company with a traveling Brahman when conversation took the usual turn.

"Oh, I stick to the old shasters," at length remarked the Hindu, good-naturedly. "I shall trust for salvation to Ram and the rest of the Avatars." They had now reached a stopping-place, and quite a number of listeners gathered around them.

"There are one or two things in your shasters," resumed the missionary, "that are false."

"Yes there *may* be one or two," acknowledged the Brahman.

"I am sure there are; I have read some parts of your shasters: they say the earth rests on the heads of elephants, do they not?"

"Yes, there are eight elephants that stand on eight heads of a great serpent, and these support the earth."

"Well, people have been all over the earth in the foreign ships, and examined it on every side, and the heads of these great elephants have nowhere been found."

"You do not mean to say they have gone to the end of the world?"

"Yes, they have been all over it."

"Have they actually crossed the great ocean, and found the other side?"

" Yes, I came from the other side of ·the earth. My country is directly under our feet."

" What! do you mean to say you have come up from the under side? Pray, how did you get here?"

" We sailed directly around on the surface, Just as a fly would creep round an orange."

" Is it possible that people live on the under side?"

" Yes, it is night there when it is day here. Perhaps you will wonder why the people don't fall off from the other side?"

" Yes, to be sure!"

" Did you ever see a magnet which draws a needle so that it adheres to it?"

" Yes, I have seen it."

" There is something like this in the earth which draws all bodies towards the center, so that they do not fall off from it, either up or down, on whatsoever side of it they may be."

" This is very extraordinary. Are these things contained in your shasters?"

" No, our shasters do not contain geography and other sciences found out by human wisdom ; they contain nothing but the words of God, which relate only to religion. This that I have told you of the earth is what men have seen and know, and what you may learn by studying. You will find all the scholars at Gauhati know about these things."

Such discussions were very common, and it is quite probable that many of the Brahmans became secretly convinced that their eight gigantic elephants had a rather small point of support.

" On what does the eight-headed serpent rest?" the padre would sometimes ask.

" He rests on the back of a tortoise."

" And what does the tortoise stand upon?"

"Well you must indeed be unreasonable (with a gesture of annoyance), not to be satisfied yet after all I have told you !'

There were many villages along the Disang and other rivers, too distant to be reached on the Sunday afternoon walks, and to these, during the cold seasons, the missionary made itinerant trips of a week at a time, commonly on foot. He found an encouraging field down and up the Janzi, a beautiful branch of the Brahmaputra, lined with rice-fields and villages. In some places the natives came running a long distance across the fields to meet him and receive tracts. Books previously given by Mr. Barker were found to have made an impression ; some believed they were true." Here and there in town and hamlet were found receptive minds. "Thanks be to my God and Saviour for this day's experience ;" the weary pencil adds, after a day full of travel, talk and preaching, with its alternations of chilling rebuff, eager inquiry and quiet discussion. At Jorhat "the people listened attentively," and there he had abundant opportunity of presenting the Christian doctrines not only to Hindus, but to the Mussulmans who formed a large proportion of the population of that town. Seriously interested companies gathered and followed him on the road and in the bazar ; young men inquired where he would be to-morrow, as they wished to hear "the same words again ;" the people beset him to come and establish schools, promising hundreds of pupils.

Some openly rejected his message ; "a respectable Mussulman, after I had concluded my account of the Saviour, said he should not receive him ; Mohammed was his master and he should follow him. I then read the account of the judgment from the 25th of Matthew. The people gave heed to the things that were spoken."

To some others they were nothing more than the latest entertaining novelty. There were times when it seemed slow, unpromising work—this "creeping around among the villages," toiling through jungles and over streams, and plodding in mire, with the hope of finding a few listeners. When they were found, it was beyond measure discouraging to the preacher to discover that no emotion or thought higher than curiosity was elicited. In a weary hour he confides to a friend (Rev. Dr. J. A. Smith), a missionary's frequent experience:

"After he has unfolded to them the gospel plan of salvation with all the earnestness and ardor he is master of, his audience tell him they have business and must be excused—the Sahib's words are extremely good and proper; his eloquence surpasses anything they have ever heard from their priests; and they have no doubt that for the English it is just as good a way of salvation as theirs is for them. The prophecy of their shasters is fulfilled, that the white people should, through the blessing of Ram, become superior to every other people in wisdom and art, and should become the lords of the East Country; that they have always thought the worship of idols very foolish—it is only the God within them, the spirit that animates us and every creature from the ant to the elephant, that dwells in every leaf of the forest and every particle of dust, this is the God that we ought to worship; but still, as it is so difficult to find Him out, or comprehend this omnipresent Deity, it is the best thing we can do to worship the Brahmans as his representatives!" *

While at Jorhat Mr. Brown had an interview with the ex-raja, Purunder Singh, and his son Kameswor.

---

* For account of "A Brahman's Sermon," see Appendix *B*.

"January 21, 1842. This afternoon I had the privilege of bearing witness for Christ before the old raja and his attendants, and also his son, with each of whom I had an interview of about half an hour. The raja seemed at first to smile at the idea of the foreign padre's coming to change his religion and that of the country. He at length, however, appeared more interested, and made many minute inquiries respecting our doctrines, and the two disciples who embraced Christianity.

His son, whom I called upon first, is a very interesting young man of twenty-five or thirty. He was very inquisitive respecting our theories of geography and astronomy, and urged me very hard to come and set up a school at Jorhat. He is anxious to learn English as well as the sciences. May the Lord give him light, and grace to forsake the religion of his fathers. Promised to send a New Testament to him, and one to his father. The raja and his son are the last remnant of the Ahom race of kings who entered Assam about A. D. 1228. They are supposed to be the lineal descendents of Indra, the king of beavan, and the raja is always addressed by the title of *Sworoga Deo* (Lord of Heaven).

January 22, Saturday. Went out to the Doom * village a little below this. Stopped under a tree and began to speak, when about a hundred people gathered around and listened with great solemnity for about half an hour.

23. Lord's day. . . . Took a crcuit through the villages around Jorhat, about a mile distant from the Tank. Addressed first a company who were inoculating children for the small-pox. The men appeared disposed to listen, but the Brahman who was performing the inoculation succeeded in drawing them nearly all away. Had a long talk with the daroga, a fine old

---

* One of the lowest castes—fishermen and basket-makers.

Brahman, whose son followed us all the rest of the day. At one place we met with several Brahmans who allowed the falsehood of their shasters, especially of the geographical part, to be exposed, without making any effort to defend them ; in fact the principal speaker declared his belief that what we said was true. At sundown again addressed a large congregation in the Doom village. At no place have I ever seen people listen with more attention and solemnity. Subject, the parable of the sower."

On Monday the raja lent the missionary party one of his elephants, which brought them back to the Janzi in a few hours, whence after another day of village preaching they returned to Sibsagar.

During these preaching excursions the missionary was often an involuntary witness of the domestic and social miseries of heathenism. The feathery bamboos of the Disang valley were all alive one lovely April Sunday morning, with birds, busy nest-building, and pouring out floods of musical ecstasy over the poor, filthy huts of human beings. Under low roofs of coarse grass, feebly supported by their often gaping reed walls, absolutely naked children crouched on bare ground, which had been beaten down and hardened for a floor. On what couch they could have slept, not even the birds knew. Pushing back from unwashed, drowsy eyes, their matted and indescribably filthy hair, they woke to turn a greedy gaze—poor little animals—towards the steaming rice-pot, suspended from three khagoris or bamboo sticks driven into the ground around a smoking brand, and fastened together at the top. The young mother standing just without the entrance of her hut, wears one garment, formed of two breadths of white cotton roughly joined at the selvedges, of which the upper portion, unbanded, is drawn to the form, and a corner tightly twisted and tucked in, holds it fast, the short, scant folds hanging a little lower than the knees. Her abundant straight hair, raven black, is twisted into a tight knot behind ; cylinders of colored glass stretch the ear-lobes to unnatural size; strings of bright red and blue beads adorn the brown shapely neck, and numerous armlets and anklets of brass complete the wardrobe. Facing her stands another of her sex ; a duel of words is going on. The shots fly thick and fast; the black eyes flash fury ; every graceless epithet that ingenuity, quickened by passion, can invent, is hurled from one to the other. The little birds overhead sing all the louder as if to down so unnatural a noise. Yet this is no exceptional occurrence—no unusual scandal to be checked by startled neighbors, or quelled by police.

" Strife and railing filled the village with the tones of discord and rage, and not a single countenance beaming with love and benevolence did I see—not a single face which shone as the index of a happy heart—not a single feature lit up with holy devotion and joyous hope."

In another village, the husband of two quarreling wives, enraged by their noise, came upon the scene, and attacking the elder with a bamboo, beat her for some time with the most savage cruelty. The younger of course in the meantime escaped, but returning home later in the day, was seized and beaten in the same unmerciful manner.

Kindly and gentle feelings were not by any means absent however, even among the most ungoverned natures. Motherly love, especially towards sons, was generally strong, often passionately so ; respect, courtesy, gratitude, were often manifest. So far as their scanty means and the rules of caste permitted, the poor natives provided shelter for the traveling missionary.

In general, he was cordially received by the *gohains,* (civil rulers under the rajas, still retaining authority,) but the *gosains* or spiritual rulers looked askance at the encroachment s of the white padres. One venerable priest, however, accorded the missionary a brief inter- view.

" A little after noon I reached the Moramora gosain's place. Found the gosain alone, his chief disciples being absent. It was some time before I succeeded in obtaining an interview, but at length he came and stood in the door of an inner room, so as to allow me a view of his sacred person. He conversed a few minutes, .ac- cepted the books I offered him, and ordered his attend- ant to give me some plantains and a bottle of milk. He is a venerable looking old gentleman, and must be, I should think, about eighty years of age. The young man who was in attendance, was somewhat displeased that I did not address his master by the title of " God," as is their custom. According to the native theory, the deity would seem to be infinitely sub-divided. First Vishnu, Ram, Krishnu, and the ancient heroes partake most largely of the divinity—after them the gosains and and Brahmans, each of whom carries the deity with him —the sun, the moon, the planets, the earth and its rivers, are all gods, and in fine the whole creation, animate and inanimate, is pervaded with a portion of the divine es- sence—in other words, oriental transcendentalism, is the religion with which we have to contend."

At one village two bhokots or disciples of the Auni- ati gosain, a high priest of great sanctity and eminence took tracts.

" This is the first instance in which any of the Auni- ati's men have accepted books, although I have met

numbers of them during this trip. They are now col-
lecting the taxes from the villagers who are under the
Auniati's jurisdiction. Yesterday and to-day, I have
met, I should think, a dozen large boats, which the bhokots are loading with rice for him."

This reverend hierarch had then lately arrived with a
large retinue at Sibsagar, from his residence on the Majúli-
(The Great Island,) between the Lobit and the Brahmaputra. He moved with great state, drum and trum-
pets announcing his approach in a kind of triumphal
procession.

"About two-thirds of the people in this region recognize his authority; the rest are mostly under the Dokimpat. The influence of the gosains over their followers is almost unbounded, and it is considered the height
of impiety to disobey their commands."

On one of these trips, Mr Brown found and preached
to some Ahoms, who still retained the ancient customs
of their ancestors of the Tai race.

"We went out among the villages on the Hologuri
ali [highway]. Was surprised to find many Deonais,
or old Ahoms, who still retain their ancient customs-
live in raised houses like the Shans, and keep up a knowledge of their original language. They were unable to
read Assamese, but had books of their own containing
the records of the ancient religion of the Tais, before it
was subverted by Hinduism in Assam, and by Buddhism
in Siam and Burma."

Mr. Brown was once conversing with an intelligent
Ahom who plumed himself greatly on his ancient caste.

"I have in my possession," said the, latter, "the sacred
records which relate the descent from heaven by a golden
chain, of the first Ahom kings, Kúnlúng and Kúnlai.

"And you suppose that we white foreigners are the descendents of the cannibals of Ceylon, and of the monkeys that went there with the god Ram, to fight the giant Rawon?"

"Yes, it is so written in our scriptures."

"And is it not also written that when Ram had conquered Rawon, he appointed Bibhikon, the brother of the latter, king in his room, gave him his blessing, pronounced him immortal, and assured him that no enemy should ever invade or conquer his country?"

"Yes," replied the defender of mythology.

"And notwithstanding this, it is now well known that the Company have taken Ceylon, and that there was no King Bibhikon alive at the time when the English first arrived in the island."

To this he could make no reply, but acknowledged that if Ceylon was in possession of the English, their shasters must be false. This was a point of so vital importance with the Hindus, that many of them refused to admit that Ceylon was under the Company's government.

During the rains of 1843, a weakness of the lungs so far developed as to deprive Mr. Brown of the use of his voice for a time. In the clear autum weather it was partially restored, and he was out again preaching on the Gorgaung road. Sundays of '44 found him either on one of the main roads, or in the Sibsagar bazar, or among neighboring hamlets, and he continued the practice whenever health and strength permitted, as long as he remained in Assam.

XX

THROUGH THE FORESTS AFOOT.

IN December 1844, Mr. Brown set out on a more extended missionary tour through Central and Lower
Assam. He made the journey of two hundred miles
from Sibsagar to Gauhati, for the most part on foot, in
order to visit the remoter villages, making circuits which
he could not have done by boat.

The little caravan, comprising the missionary, the assistant Nidhi Levi, and eight coolies, started down the
Dikho road on Saturday the 14th, carrying with them
two or three loads of books, and the miscellaneous im-
pedimenta necessary for a march through the jungles.
All were on foot except Nidhi, who, being in feeble
health, rode a pony. Two coolies carried the sahib's
traveling chest between them, suspended from a long
bamboo, but after a few days, re-arranged the load, in
more approved Assamese style, by hanging his clothes
on one end of the pole, and the empty chest on the
other. A single cooly then balanced the pole on his
shoulder and trudged along with the greatest ease.
Dishes, cooking utensils and bedding were transported
in this manner. If at night the party were fortunate
enough to light upon a deserted namghor, which generally consisted of a roof without sides or floor, their
hotel accommodations were considered sumptuous. The
missionary spread his mat and blanket upon the ground,
put up his mosquito netting and carefully fastened it
down ; fires were built and rice aud curry cooked.
Sleep came quickly, after a day's march of twenty or
thirty miles, or the round of a group of villages, distrib-

uting, explaining, discussing, preaching.   The winter air was just cool enough to be bracing, the tropic vegetation was tempered by the season to its perfect beauty, and notwithstanding the annoyances and even dangers of wilder portions of the journey—exaggerated reports of which at one point almost raised a mutiny among Mr. Brown's men—still he found it an enjoyable and healthful trip.

The first stop was over Sunday, at the fisher village near the stone bridge of the Namdang.   Here, under a tree the missionary preached to villagers and passers by, and the next day took the old bund road to Jorha and finding among six or seven hundred coolies who were repairing the highway, some who could read, gave them Scriptures and tracts. Before reaching Jorhat, Tuesday, at sundown, his feet were sore from the long march, and "I was glad," he wrote to Mrs. Brown, " to get my shoes off and walk on the soft grass, as soon as I came upon the Seoni Ali [highway]." At Jorhat bazar there were discussions with some Brahmans of Pope's faith ; they believed that

> " All are but parts of one stupendous whole,
> Whose body, nature is, and God the soul."

"The Divine Spirit," says the Hindu, is inherent in every part of creation ; there is an inspiration of deity in every man, beast, bird and insect ; when they live, it is deity that lives ; when they move, it is deity that moves ; when they die it is the indwelling divinity changing its residence."

One day, Mr. Brown exhibited to some Hindu visitors, a prism which he had made of pieces of window glass, cemented together at the edges, and filled with water.   The light struck through, and lo ! on the wall a fragment of Indra's bow—Indra, god of thunder-storms, who shoots with that dazzling rainbow the demons that would otherwise drink up man's needful rain, and whose arrows strike lightning from the eight rocky mountains that sustain the heavens! An explanation of the spectrum followed, which demolished this highly ornamental buttress of the Hindu creed.

Later in the day Mr. Brown sent Nidhi with the prism to explain the rainbow to the young prince, who on his part, sent to the padre a present of a hanging lamp. This was politely declined, however, lest it should be broken in the tramp through the jungles. Just at dark a moonsif, or native judge called and made many inquiries about these extraordinary foreign stories. He had heard of Captain Cook's going around the world three times, but could not really believe it. Could such a thing be possible ?

"It is true ;" the white man replied. "and the people of the island where Captain Cook was murdered have since been converted, and have embraced the Christian religion."

The moonsif found it hard to comprehend that vessels might cross the eastern ocean from America to China, coming westward all the time, but was so much interested as to repeat his visit the next evening, bringing many new inquirers with him. He and several other Brahmans allowed the Hindu religion to be exposed before all the company without offering to say a word in its defense.

Early the next morning, the foreign preacher was seen to enter the shop of an old goldsmith, an acquaintance of his, and a crowd soon collected. Two Brahmans entered into discussion with him, and finally subsided into silence, but declined to look at his shasters ; and in fact all seemed afraid of the books till after the pundits walked off. Before Mr. Brown left, however, almost every man of the company had a tract snugly tucked into the folds of his súria.

Crossing a small river on his return, he found an audience waiting for him on the bank. To these he talked for an hour.

"Some disputed, but most of them agreed that what I said was true. After exposing the errors of their system, I urged upon them the importance of embracing the Christian religion, and gave away many books and tracts."

A day's march from Jorhat brought the travelers to Amgúri, "a delightful place" on the Dhodor Ali, a highway, here shaded by rows of trees. On the day following, which was Sunday, Mr. Brown made a circuit with Nidhi through the numerous surrounding villages, where they found listeners. Some of the reapers in the rice-fields, however, fled at his approach, supposing him to be an officer coming to seize them for baggage-carriers.

That evening an old *medhi* came in to the namghor with some of his followers. He asked many close questions of Nidhi, who answered all his inquiries and refuted his objections.

"Are all the gods, then, whom I have worshipped, to be given up," the old man finally inquired, "and all the shasters renounced as false? And what say you of the Avatars of Sonkor and Maha Deu?"*

"Sonkor and Maha Deu were only men, and their schemes of salvation are false," replied the young convert.

Instead of evincing anger at Nidhi's plain talk, the visitor turned to his companions and said :

"This takes hold of my mind amazingly!"

---

* Incarnations of Vishnu.' Maha Deu (the great god) pronounced Ma ha' Dow.

"Nidhi then read the last chapter of Matthew and prayed with them, after which the old man began to speculate on what would be the consequence of his embracing our religion, what his bishop (the Auniati gosaim) would do to him if he should refuse to pay his tribute, or to worship the gods, and should live after the abhorred customs of the Christians. He could not read, nor could any of his people, but they seemed with one accord to receive the word spoken as truth. Oh, that some of them might become true disciples! But how can we expect it? They will not, probably, hear the gospel again for years, if ever, and the impression now made will soon fade from their minds."

Monday finds the little company again tramping on through the rice-fields and villages, giving leaflets and books as readers are found. Reaching Golaghat, a finely situated, thriving new military station, on the Dhonsiri river, they put up at the court house, and in the evening Mr. Brown was pleasantly surprised to find among the sepoys of the guard, some Burmans, with one of whom, a former priest of the yellow cloth, he held a discussion till near midnight. The next morning Nidhi found that a tiger had killed and carried off his pony. He left the saddle to be sent back to Sibsagar, and proceeded on foot, having gained strength since leaving home.

The party followed down the southern bank of the Dhonsiri river all day, finding an inhabited and well cultivated district as far as a stream called Doi, and beyond that, jungle to Ponka, where Mr. Brown, footsore, and hardly able to keep up with the coolies, was glad to stop for the night.

Leaving Ponka the next day, they found no villages, and only a footpath throug the wilderness. Wild elephants and buffaloes had been the principal travelers through this region, judging by the foot-prints; but here and there a peacock spread its fan, gorgeous in flickering blue and green and bronze. Wild fowl which abounded here, fluttered from their nests at the crackling of the reeds,and the alarming sound of human voices. Twice the men lost their bearings, and were obliged to retrace their steps. The streams were generally crossed by wading or swimming, except when the travelers were fortunate enough to find a large tree felled and laid from bank to bank. While fording the Kaliani, an excessively cold mountain stream, Mr. Brown was struck with a deadly chill, and narrowly escaped drowning. " Had it not been for the friendly hand of a servant who assited me," says the diary, " I should hardly have succeeded in reaching the opposite bank."

Fortunately they emerged from the jungle soon after, into a beautiful, cultivated region called Búka Khat, and succeded in obtaining a supply of rice, of which they had run short. The next day they reached the principal village; the missionary distributed to those who could read, and saw an immense banyan tree, shading an area 630 feet in circumference. Within one of its hollow trunks, twenty-one feet in diameter, a dozen persons might find shelter in case of a storm.

Their way now lay again through almost impassable jungle, occasionally across a deep stream. On the 28th they came upon a beautiful natural pond, quadrangular in shape, said to be of immense depth, called Deo-dúbi, (Dow-dooby), or Bathing-place of the gods. The Difflu river was found to be full of fish and turtles. Here there was a magnificent view of the snow-capped Himalayas. Open country now, and villages. " A delightful view of the Mikir (Meekeer) cultivation on the hills each side of us. The Mikirs are one of the most interesting tribes in Assam ; they have no respect for the Hindu religion, and are a mild, quiet, industrious race."

The following Sunday's circuit among the neighboring villages, gave opportunity to distribute scriptures and preach : the reapers in the rice-fields, however, were afraid of the strange white man. The next day's march of thirty miles brought Mr. Brown and Nidhi into Now-gong just at dark, the coolies not arriving till the following day. Mr. Brown had come out of the jungle about noon, and the last ten miles of the journey from old Nowgong to the new, was through continuous villages.

" The fine old trees which shade the road on either side, render this one of the most beautiful villages in Assam. The new station is, however, a little detached from the most thickly populated part of the village. I found our dear brother and sister Bronson enjoying their usual health, but worn down with their numerous cares."

To these devoted laborers the past six years had been a time of difficult pioneering among hill and valley tribes.

On the 13th of March, 1840, Mr. Bronson had taken his family from Jaipúr up into the Naga hills, and lived among the wild tribes ; established a school, prepared elementary books in their language. and taught them the way of life, till severe illness and the disturbances among the tribes drove him from the hills. Nowgong was chosen as his permanent field of labor, and to this point he moved his family and goods on rafts, in the fall of 1841, and commenced a most important work. The station was the center of military and civil jurisdic-tion over a thickly peopled district along the banks of the Kulung, an arm of the Brahmaputra, which flowed both from and into the great river. Here Mr. Bronson at once engaged in preaching and distributing from morning till night. By the generous aid of Captain Gordon, the officer in command, and other residents, the

Nowgong Orphan Institution was established ; the object of which was " to gather orphan and destitute children from every part of Assam and train them up under careful Christian influence ; " also to prepare the more capable to be teachers.   A day-school was taught in connection with the boarding department, and an additional school was maintained in the village.   " This institution," Mr. Brown wrote to a friend, " is one of the most important, and as we trust, *permanent* branches of our missionary operations."

Mr. Bronson with elephant and tent accompanied Mr. Brown on the remainder of his tour, the latter, however, still preferring to walk, the elephant's back having the swaying motion of a ship at sea, which was always peculiarly distressing to him.   The twenty days' journey through Durrung and Kamrúp, along the lowlands, north of the great river, proved a most satisfactory one.   Much was learned of the character capacity, language and religion of the various tribes.   The missionaries filled the days full of work, notably among priests, of whom they saw great numbers at their " hostros" and around the temples and shrines.   They found that Lower Assam contained between three and four hundred religious establishments, endowed with lands and hereditary dependents, which formed a powerful barrier to the progress of Christianity and civilization.   These establishments were called *hostros*, the priests *gosains*, and the dependents or disciples, *bhokots*.   The latter were in fact, hereditary slaves of the hostros.   The chief priest was worshiped by them as a divinity.   The gosains, as was to be expected, felt, and sometimes manifested, a hostility to the foreign religionists, which, under the protection of their old friends, the rajas, would have been persecution.   The people, on the contrary, were found generally disposed to listen.   Once when Mr. Brown was showing a company of villagers that

endless repetitions of the name of Krishna could not
insure salvation, a peppery little Brahman spoke up :

"You keep pulling down our system and the worship
of Krishna, but you give us no name instead, by which
we *can* obtain salvation."

It is probable that he knew better, for "having shot
his bolt, he did not wait for a reply, but immediately
ran off, and though we called after him, we could not
induce him to return." This mere *name religion*, as
they themselves call it, has great holdupon the Assamese. The devout have rosaries containing a hundred
beads formed from the nut of a sacred tree, and at each
repetition of the name of Ram, Krishna or Hori, a head
is slipped, and thus the count is kept. Passing a pious
Assamese' prostrate at his prayers, one hears a low monotone of "*Ram—ram—ram*," said as rapidly as the lips
can move, in seemingly endless repetition. Five thousand
repetitions daily are thought to constitute an extremely
righteous man. The most infamous characters, if they
chance to die with the sacred name upon their lips, are
said to go directly to heaven, snatched from the very
clutch of demons, by messengers of the deity thus honored.

Several northern affluents of the Brahmaputra were
crossed between Tezpúr and Gauhati. After wading
through the rapids of one of these, the missionary party
came upon a fine open country, well cultivated, the
inhabitants being principally Kacharis, an aboriginal
race who had but little affinity for the Hindu religion.

"It is greatly to be regretted that there cannot be a
missionary located in Durrung, who should devote his
whole efforts to this interesting people, before Hinduism
spreads any further among them."

No tracts were left with them, as they could not
read. Farther on the missionaries encountered some
Bhutanese traders from the hills, "a Buddhist tribe,"

says Mr. Brown, "somewhat resembling the Burmese."

Here and there Intelligent and inquiring minds were met, and on the whole, it would seem, less prejudice was encountered than might have been expected. A call one evening is noted, from two intelligent *kakotis*, (scribes or writers)who wished to find out the size and form of the earth. After learning how the earth may be measured by a watch and the sun, they themselves calculated its circumference under Mr. Brown's direction, and although the girth of the planet shrank from the shasters' four trillions to 25,000 miles, and great Mount Meru was ciphered out of existence, " they appeared quite satisfied, and rather gratified than otherwise to find that there was some tangible proof that their shasters were false. They made many inquiries concerning our religion, and we sat up till a late hour."

A part of the district of Durrung was found to be "one continuous sheet of cultivation, as far as the eye can reach," the rice-fields being watered by the hill streams directed into numerous artificial channels. At Majikhúsi, a collection of flourishing Kachari villages, hundreds of inhabitants were to be seen coming in groups to inspect the foreigners. They were unable to read, and gave no encouragement that they would send their children to school, if one were established. Mr. Brown tried to interest some of them in his prism, but it looked suspicious, and they shrank back at first afraid to touch it. When they really became convinced it was harmless, the pretty colors delighted them, and afterwards a larger company having collected, they called for "the rainbow" again. At evening worship, several came in, to whom he "read and explained the account of our Saviour's crucifixion, after which Bro. Bronson related to them the story of Dives and Lazarus, and Nidhi prayed." The next day they entered Kamrúp, and stopped over night at Boidorgor, the site of an ancient city built by the kings of Kamrúp. The old town was situated on both sides of the Borolia river, and surrounded by a high wall, which still remained, enclosing an area of about four miles square.

The missionary elephant stopped one day at a school, where sixty or seventy bright boys of all castes were receiving secular instruction in the Bengali language. The whole school followed the padrés several miles to their stopping place, and received from them Christian books. Mr. Brown showed the boys his "rainbow," with which they were highly delighted.

One Saturday night the travelers camped near a large hostro, from which they received many visitors, who were greatly interested in the prism, globe, watch, and accordion. They were anxious for books; but not in Assamese. They were greatly pleased with the Bengali hymns, sung to native and American airs, with accordion accompaniment.

The next day, on his return from a preaching tour of the villages, Mr. Brown was invited by a friendly gosain to come in and see his idols, quite a remarkable group. A full-sized image of Krishna occupied the central place; on his left sat his wife Lokshmi, goddess of love, giving him the betel-nut, and near her, Gorúd, with wings of a bird. On Krishna's right sat Soroswati, the wife of Brama, goddess of intelligence. The priest then requested a favor of the padre, that he would call upon the ladies of his family, who probably had never seen a white face. As Hindu custom forbids high-caste women from leaving their own separate part of the house, the missionary was conducted thither. After showing these ladies his accordion and watch, and talking a little while, he went to see the old chief priest, who was blind. Here he had an opportunity of preaching to an interesting company.

In the evening Mr. Bronson addressed another audience, reading and explaining to them the narrative of Elijah and the priests of Baal, upon which his auditors had many questions to ask. The gosain, in return, concluded the exercises by rehearsing to the weary visitors a story of an hour's length, from the Mahabharata!

On Monday morning the party bade farewell to these frank and kindly villagers. Afternoon brought them to the large village of Hajú, set in a garden of areca and cocoanut trees. From it rises a hill, on which stands one of the most famous shrines in Assam, visited by Hindu pilgrims from all parts of India, and by Buddhists even from China and Thibet, the latter claiming that Saddartha or Gautama once visited the spot, and conferred upon it a mysterious efficacy in removing sin. The worst forms of vice are here carried on in the name of religion. The number of dancing girls attached to the temple is said to be two or three thousand.

The missionaries went up the long flight of stone steps to the principal shrine, and held an argument with the priests. The attendants wished to decorate them with garlands of the flowers that had been offered to the idol, an attention which the visitors declined.

21. "We have spent the day in preaching and arguing with the priests. None of them have pretended to deny the immorality of the place. but they said the sins of the priests and others who visited the temple, were expiated every evening by taking the name and chanting the praises of Krishna. Several times in the course of the day, the priests, feeling uncomfortable from the exposure of their vices, have begged to retire from the discussion, saying they would come to us again and argue the subject thoroughly. We have given away many books to-day, which we hope may do some good.

22. Rose early and came into Gauhati before breakfast. Had the pleasure to find our dear missionary
friends in the enjoyment of their usual health."

It was now about a year since Mr. Barker, in the fall
of 1843, laid the first permanent foundations of missionary work at Gauhati. An effort had been made by
the Serampore Society, but circumstances led to its
early abandonment. Mr. Barker now had several boys'
schools in progress, including one from the Doom or
fisher caste, and another for Brahman boys. Messrs.
Bronson and Brown spent five busy days here. "I
enjoy my visit," writes the latter, "and my work." A
part of the work had to do with the organization of the
first church in Assam. On Saturday, the 25th of January, 1845, the three missionaries drew up the articles
of formation, and on the same day, they, with the native
Christians, constituted themselves into "the Baptist
church of Assam," composed of the three branches of
Gauhati, Nowgong and Sibsagar ; and elected Mr. Barker pastor of the Gauhati branch.

On Sunday morning Mr. Bronson preached in English to the residents. In the afternoon, missionaries
and converts partook of the Lord's Supper, and though
less in number than those who first broke bread in the
"upper chamber," they were strong in faith, and in the
assurance of their Master's presence and sanction. In
the evening Mr. Brown preached at Mr. Barker's house
to the European residents, about twenty in number.

The young Assamese Christians had showed their
colors too openly not to meet with occasional insult
from the bolder and more bigoted of their heathen
countrymen.

N. to E. B. January 27.—"Nidhi says Gour Chand
Day told him and Caleb last night, that he considered
them as hypocrites (*heretics*, I am inclined to think

must have been the word), but the poor disciples were enabled to take it patiently. Nidhi said it *hurt him.* If they have called the Master of the house Beelzebub, how much more shall they call them of his household. To-day. a little upstart Doom belonging to the government school told Nidhi that he *lied,* and repeated it several times during the discussion, and that before the Barkers and me. I was obliged to rebuke the fellow several times, as I would not see Nidhi insulted."

On Tuesday morning the elephant and other pedestrians turned their faces toward Nowgong. That evening a delightful camping-ground was found in the midst of the forest, on a large flat rock, beside a stream of clear running water, and here Mr. Bronson pitched his tent.

29. " Noticed in several places, circular rows of stones set upright, after the manner of the Druidical monuments. In some cases large flat stones were laid horizontally upon the upright ones. These, we are told, are used by the Lalong chiefs as seats, whenever they assemble in council."

The next day, Mr. Brown, being ill, was carried part of the way in a cot. Approaching Nowgong, on the 31st, along the banks of the Kulung, their course lay through its numerous villages, in one of which they staid overnight, and reached the station February 1st.

"Lord's day, February 2nd. Preached at Bro. Bronson's in the morning, and to the scholars in the afternoon, on the New Birth.

3. A severe earthquake this morning at two o'clock, accompanied by a loud rumbling sound."

On Thursday, the 6th, Mr. Bronson and Mr. Brown, accompanied by the assistants, Peter and Nidhi, went twelve miles through the jungle to the sacred lake or pond of Bordoa, whose waters were much resorted to by pilgrims, and devoutly carried off in bottles over the country for the spiritual benefit of the faithful. Only the údahin, or holy monks, however, were allowed to fetch them, and to one of these Mr. Brown handed his prism, and had it filled, whereupon the prismatic colors were regarded as additional evidence of its celestial origin. "Any water would answer as well, if it was only clear," remarked the irreverent foreigner.

"But this water fell straight from Akahi Gonga (Celestial Ganges or Milky Way) during the Sonkor Avatar, three hundred years ago," said its guardians.

The missionary must have longed for a telescope, as he gave the priests and monks some useful facts in astronomy, followed by a brief lecture on geography. Here too the impression in stone of the Sacred Foot of Sonkor is devoutly worshipped. After a long discussion, the missionary party retired to rest in one of the namghors, which proved to be a kind of actors' green room. Overhead, in the dim light, could be discerned effigies of griffins, dragons, giants, tigers and serpents, used in theatrical exhibitions of scenes from the Hindu scriptures. After another day's work among the priests in the neighborhood, the visitors returned to the station.

On February 8th, a branch church was established at Nowgong, and interesting services were held on the 9th. Three days later Mr. Brown left for home, accompanied by "little Mary Bronson," who was much wanted in Sibsagar. Mr. Bronson saw the travelers safely to the Brahmaputra. A letter or two sent ahead by dawk, show how it fared with "Uncle Brown," and his small companion during the ten days' up-trip.

To E. B. ; "Above Tizpúr, February 14th. Having got fairly under way, I lose no time in preparing a line, in case I should find a dawk boat, or any chance of sending to you. I have my boats at last in a very comfortable state. I am in Capt. Gordon's *khel** boat, little Mary in front of me, separated by my great chest, which forms our table. She "thinks our little house will do very well for so small a family." We have lots of bread and biscuits in one corner of Mary's room, and everything is very snug and comfortable.

Evening. We have had a pleasant day's trip, and are now off Koliabor. Hope to reach Bishnath to-morrow, and shall spend the Sabbath somewhere near that place. The men are all anxious to get home, and they work well—six men at work upon each boat—we start at daylight and go till sundown, stopping to eat in the middle of the day. Bro. Bronson left me this morning at six o'clock, to return to Nowgong."

The meager diary makes brief mention of gold washers passed on the way ; of wild buffaloes ; and of long reaches of sand where the voyagers were out of sight of human habitations ; speaks of once going supperless for want of fire and flint ; of the boat met next day on the great lonely river, which supplied their need ; of a Sunday's stop, and teaching of "one and another," and the evening reading and exhortation to the gathered boatmen on the sand-bank ; of a noisy wedding party at Jorhat ferry on the brides' "lucky day," selected with great precision ; of pushing on into the Dikho ; of another Sunday's tarrying, with its talks to village groups ; and finally, "February 24th, the men started before daylight and reached Boliaghat about nine o'clock, from which place little Mary and I came up overland." Home ! glad greetings, and good news on both sides. "Our journey has been one of great interest," he said ; "we begin to feel our ground."

---

*A comfortable boat suited to river-travel.

XXI

A WOMAN'S PLEA.

HAVING discovered much to be done, the missionaries found the question, how to do it, a pressing
one, and not easy to answer. How were all these villages to be Christianized? How were the priestly
establishments to be converted into thrifty, virtuous
hamlets, and polluted shrines into temples of the true
God? What company of preachers would go among the
aboriginal Kacharis and save them from the contagion
of Hinduism? Where were the men to answer the call
of the Miris, now asking for instruction? Who could
go up and save the Nagas from the encroaching influence of the valley priests?

"I often heard the Nagas speak with regret of Mr.
Bronson's leaving them, but this year (1847), we learn
that several tribes have given in their allegiance to the
gosains, and now look upon themselves as a caste of
Hindus.

The gosains are rapidly bringing over the poor Nagas
and Miris to Hinduism, because we cannot cultivate the
field we have begun."

It was a critical time, just the moment to make an
advance all along the line. With what feelings must
the pioneers, who had for ten years been hoping against
hope, have received the information that, owing to a
falling off of funds, the Board were about to reduce their
number of missions. and that Assam, being remote and

(269)

recent, would probably be one of the first abandoned. Mr. Brown received a letter from a Burman missionary, communicating this probability, and urging him in that case, to return to Burma.

For several years there had been a feeling of uncertainty in all the missions of the society. The pathfinders in Burma, Siam and China, having held on through the difficult pioneer period, now saw their hardwon foothold liable to slip from them, perhaps never to be regained. The home mail, instead of words of cheer, brought discouragement. One religious paper told of the probable "suppression of schools, dismissal of native assistants, stopping of the press, translations and tract operations, the missionaries returning, and the work being at an end!" Painful apprehensions had saddened the officers at Boston. "Could you be present," said one pastor to

MOLUNG NAGA-RAJA, OR CHIEF, WITH
SPEAR AND BATTLE-AXE.*

*This tattooed warrior wears bracelets of buffalo-horn, his spear is ornamented with goat's hair dyed red, and his cap with human hair from enemies he has slain.

his church, "at the meetings of our Board, you would feel like weeping, for we do. The heart affecting appeals coming to us for more missionaries, and more money to carry forward their well-arranged operations, while the state of our funds compels us to answer, 'Restrict your operations,' this makes our hearts ache."

And should the little candle in Assam be put out? Should converts be left to the mercy of persecutors, inquirers remanded to paganism, and the lamp of life denied to millions of groping human beings? So grave was the crisis, that Mr. Brown made a special personal appeal to the churches at home, of which the Board ordered 10,000 copies to be printed for circulation. "Few who have read," said the secretary in the following annual report, "can have forgotten the 'Address of Mr. Brown.'" The following are the concluding sentences:

"Should a work of retrenchment be carried on—should Assam be one of the first positions to be relinquished, every missionary, I trust, will solemnly wash his hands of the responsibility. We can part with our families, and send them home to be supported by their friends, and we shall do it, if necessary, but this field we cannot abandon. Should we be reduced to the extremity, be recalled, or left without any regular support in a heathen land, I trust our Lord will not find us wanting in the day of trial. The call to RETURN, is one which we could never obey so long as life and a moderate share of health is granted us: No, the precious converts that are gathered in, and to be gathered, from among this people, are dearer to me than life, and with them by God's grace will I remain to the last."*

And he did remain to the last limit of strength. Mrs. Brown replied to one of the home letters which urged

---

* Missionary Magazine, September, 1845,

them *both* to return to America for a brief rest : "That is impossible. Nathan has espoused the missionary cause as he did his wife, 'for better, for worse, till death us do part.'"

Meantime, to save the lives of her only two remaining children, one of them now rapidly sinking under a protracted illness, Mrs. Brown undertook the voyage to America alone. She was at Dibrugur, where Dr. Long had done all that medical skill could do, when the decision was made. Mr. Brown went across the flooded country from Dibrugur to Sibsagar in twenty-four hours, secured boats and crew for the down trip, hastily gathered the needful articles for Mrs. Brown's voyage to America, and met her at Dikho-múkh. The swollen current carried them down to Gauhati in five days. Here Mr. and Mrs. Barker gave into Mrs. Brown's charge their little Margaret. The parting suggested to Mr. Brown the following lines, which he wrote for Mrs. Barker some months later :

FAREWELL TO A CHILD.

My child ! and is the parting o'er ?
And is thy home the far-off shore ?
And shall I see thy face no more,
  My Margaret ?

Beyond the darkly rolling sea
My heart still wanders after thee ;
I cannot hush its agony,
  My Margaret.

  *   *   *

I hear no more thy footsteps nigh,
I meet no more thy loving eye,
Thy songs no more these tears can dry,
  My Margaret.

And when I put my babes to rest,
I pine for her that once I prest
With fondest love to this warm breast,
    My Margaret.

   *   *   *

No more can mother press thy head,
Nor watch in sickness round thy bed,
Nor know the tears that thou wilt shed,
    My Margaret.

But there is One whose watchful eye
Looks on thee kindly from the sky ;
He bids my heart no longer sigh
    For Margaret.

And I will trust His loving care
For heaven my darling to prepare ;
Oh grant me, Lord, to welcome there
    My Margaret.

The little company proceeded on their way, reached Mr. Marshman's at Serampore, August 14th, and Calcutta on the 17th.

On Monday, August 31st, the father carried his sick child in his arms on board a Liverpool ship, no suitable American vsssel being in port, and the case not admitting of further delay; then, encouraged by his intrepid wife, left her to go on unattended, and returned to his work.

She watched him from the cabin window. A small boat rowed rapidly away from the ship, among the dark figures of the oarsmen, was one in the usual white costume of a European, looking with an anxious face, towards all he loved on earth. The figure grew indistinct: the boat, at last, faded out of her sight, and she turned from the window with a sinking spirit.

When the pilot left, beyond Sandheads, three days later, he carried in his pocket a letter—written from a windy perch of the upper deck—which told of a night of danger from contrary wind and tide on the shoals.

"The strain upon the cable was so great that it cut several inches into the side of the ship, and had it given way we should have been driven upon the shoals. The captain told me afterwards, and has often repeated it since, that the pilot, seeing our danger just before they threw the anchor, 'turned feather white' and said with an oath, 'We are lost, we are lost!' From the confusion, and the noise I heard all night on deck, I knew our situation must be perilous; I could not sleep, and spent the greater part of the night in silent prayer."

When the sands were passed, the staunch new bark, scudding out into the bay under full sail, must have been a pretty sight. But Mrs. Brown longed in vain for tamarind water; wrote no more for some days, and then, only at considerable intervals. Her correspondence required no haste; it would be ninety-five days to the next post-office. The little strength and flesh she had on starting, wasted well-nigh. away during the prolonged head winds, which, owing to the breaking up of the monsoon, beat them about in the Bay of Bengal for an entire month.

This was the captain's first voyage in his tight new ship, and in an overflow of spirits, while still at anchor, he had been all sympathy and attention. "*I am a father,* Mr. Brown," he remarked, with large benevolence, "and you may be assured I will care for your family as if they were my own." When out at sea, this fatherly care proved to be somewhat of the Squeers order. Among the staple provisions for table, were salt pork and beef, well seasoned during preceding voyages, in which they had been accompanied by the sea-biscuit, the latter now nearly ready for independent locomotion. On discovering that a considerable part of the contents of the flour barrel had developed into a species of large woolly worm, Mrs. Brown ventured one day into the pantry, and had a little talk with the autocrat of the rolling-pin.

"Won't you please *sift your flour*, steward? It would be such an improvement."

"But, madam, I have no sieve."

"Well, I can make one. If you will have a sailor bring me a cask hoop, I will find some sheer muslin."

The sieve was made, but no change resulted. To her further inquiries, the steward replied with a significant expression, "We have to use *all sorts of economy* ma'am, these long voyages!"

These luxurious viands were dispensed by the captain with unctuous politeness. "Mr. Humbert, take a little more Pork. Here is a very delicate slice, as thin as a wafer." "Mrs. Brown, try this delicious soup." As the long voyage wore on, provisions which were stale at first. grew almost unendurable, and November 17th the diary notes that they have little to eat but biscuits, salt meat and rice. Of the latter the quantity upon the table was usually sufficient for one child. At times the drinking water was so putrid that it could not be kept in her room, but at last she writes "The water has worked itself clear, and become quite good, lately." The children had an alleviation, in their daily allowance of fresh milk from the cow, and despite hardships, after a time, grew well and strong in the sea air. The patient was on deck in course of a month; all the small travelers found amusement in fine weather, watching the cape pigeons, and on rough days they shouted and danced to meet the seas breaking over the decks, every drenching furnishing a new ecstasy.

The captain showed his best traits in storms ; the still days exasperated him, and flasks from the locker were then in frequent demand. But his courage rose with the wind. " I would rather see a hurricane any time, than a calm,' he told Mrs. Brown. Fearless and really capable, he thoroughly enjoyed the sense of mastery which a storm gave him.

In quiet weather, after the children were asleep for the night, Mrs. Brown sometimes had an hour to herself in her state-room, in which to write to her husband. The following extracts are from this journal-letter, which was mailed to him from St. Helena :

" Friday evening, September 25. To-day being almost a dead calm, and the ship quite steady, I took the opportunity to overlook and repack some of the drawers. On opening the second one, I drew up a handful of articles from the bottom, and out jumped your nice little letter! Before venturing to break the seal, I looked at it for some time with astonishment. To get a dawk at sea was indeed as delightful as unexpected. I have done little else since I received it than to peruse, re-peruse, and cry over it.

Saturday, 26. The kind letter of yesterday led me to suspend the repacking I had commenced, and after breakfast this morning I resumed the business, when lo! to my still greater surprise, I found another letter, marked on the back "A," which solved the enigma of "C" on the first. I know now that "B" is to come some of these days, and when I am melancholy, I shall have a search for it. Perhaps there may be others, and if so, I shall let them come like these, by accident, as I would not like to devour all my sweetmeats at once.

Friday, eve., October 2. After noon, to busy myself, and drive away dull thoughts, I had one of my large chests brought up from the hold to look for some canvas for L— to commence a pair of slippers for Dr. Long. She stood by, helping, and espied another letter marked "D." 'Oh, mamma, mamma,' she cried out, 'here's another letter from papa!'

"Sabbath morning, October 11th. Indian Ocean. I took my large Bible this morning for the first time. The first thing that attracted my attention was a sealed letter under the cover, addressed to 'Mrs. E. W. Brown, Indian Ocean, B.!' No further explanations are necessary. You say it is the holy Sabbath while you are writing, and perhaps I may be reading it on the same precious day. Your words have proved prophetic. How singular that I should have found it on the first *Sabbath* we entered the Indian Ocean. A, B, C, D. Welcome messengers! How many more are there to come?"

Mr. Brown explains the coincidence nearly a year later:

"My prophecy as to note B reaching you on the Indian Ocean was a matter of calculation. I concluded that you would be too sea-sick to take out your great Bible before you entered the Indian Ocean, and that you would probably get it out on Sunday. My guesses as to when I should first receive letters from you proved remarkably correct, but my dreams, as well as yours, seem deserving of little credit. Several times I have dreamed of your being dead—of persons coming and giving the information, and have noted down the times in my journal, but I find that nothing happened to you on the days I noted, and I hope, if it be the Lord's will, that all our dreams of each other's death may prove as groundless as they have hitherto done."

Note B reads as follows:

"Three or four months will be a long time for you to be sailing over the blue ocean, without a word of sympathy or encouragement from your husband, and I am afraid you will sometimes think he is almost cruel to leave you to take such a long and trying voyage alone. I wish I could do something to ease your burdens and comfort your lonely hours ; but I cannot, so I write this hasty note to express my sympathy, in hope that it may afford yon pleasure to find it some day unexpectedly.

It is now the holy Sabbath while I am writing this; perhaps yon may be reading it on the same precious day, and may the God of all consolation be with you and grant you much of his grace during this long voyage.

. . . Let us bow in meek submission to the will of God, and endeavor while we are separated, to please our God, and serve him faithfully. Wherever we are, and in whatever company, let us not be afraid or ashamed to speak in behalf of God and truth. You, my love, will have an influence wherever you go. If you are yielding and compromising, yout influence will be small ; but if you speak out your mind freely and fully whenever there is occasion for it, your words will have an effect; and although you may meet with fewer smiles, you will be more respected, and will have the satisfaction of an approving conscience. If anything on earth has ever afforded me cause of joy, it is that God has given me a true American-hearted wife, uncontaminated with the politeness, frivolity, two-sidedness and no-sidedness of fashionable people ; one who has never held me back from the path of duty because it was unpopular, but has often urged me on when my own natural timidity led me to shrink.

Let us never pull down our flag, my true yoke-fellow, to whatever straits we may be reduced, but let our principles be known and read of all men. Your visit to the dear brethren and sisters in America, will, I trust, do great good. I hope and believe your pleadings will have the effect to bring us help. As you are to go without me, you must do my work and your own too.

How much you will enjoy the delightful meetings at home! They will be life to your soul, and will re-kindle the feelings of former days. How thrilling to listen to the song of praise in the great congregation! To witness the solemn prayer and conference meetings, the heart searching revivals, the monthly concerts—oh, that I could enjoy these scenes with you!

Adieu, Beloved! We have had only a short talk to-day, but it may be it will cheer a lonely hour for you. So on, sweet wife, and darling jewels, over the bounding ocean! You will soon see your native shores—old friends—kind brethren and sympathizing sisters—all will bid you welcome. There will be only one aching spot in your fond heart, and that will be occupied with ten-der anxiety for your long absent and far-distant

NATHAN."

Every resource that could be suggested by a mother's ingenuity was drawn upon for the children's amusement, before the end of the ninety-nine days between Calcutta and St. Helena. Not a few of them were rendered doubly dismal by the necessity of drawing down the "dark-lights" or blinds of her one cabin window, to keep out the sea. The Hindu ayah was sometimes homesick and there was only one other woman on board. The captain was a man of moods; the officers often intoxicated, pro-fane and quarrelsome. The occasional cries of one of the small passengers, scarcely more than a baby, and far from well, were summarily suppressed by threats of a "black bag," and being "thrown overboard."

"Every time the captain hears him cry, he screams out in his coarse, gruff voice: 'Stop that, or I will have the black bag here in a moment;'—or, 'Sam! Joe! bring the bag ; chuck this fellow into it instantly.' I don't know how many times in a day the poor little fellow comes running to me nearly frightened into fits, the blood rushing to his face till it is quite purple. Yesterday I told the Captain the poor boy took all he said about the bag in earnest, and was so much frightened, I believed it impossible for him to stop crying. ' Indeed, mem ? ' was his reply. However, I think the hint has proved sufficient, for I have heard no more about the bag since."

Another occasion exhibits that worthy in a better light.

" On Saturday, P. M., November 14th, a heavy head sea set in, caused by the contending currents of the Atlantic and Indian oceans meeting around the Cape, and a light wind commenced, which continued to increase till Monday morning.

Every loose thing in the ship was rolling from side to side, and many fastenings which had before proved secure, gave way. Sunday night, just after going to bed, my bedstead with myself and Willie in it, capsized, and we were instantly thrown out and landed near the drawers on the other side of the cabin. I was, as you may suppose, nearly petrified with fright ; but instantly recollecting Willie, with the strength of a giant, I pulled him out from under the bed and bedding, and raising him over the back of my. easy-chair, handed him to Mr. Humbert, who sat in the cuddy. I had no light, and as he lay like a log in my arms, and made no noise, I thought he was killed. But he proved to be in a sound sleep, and not a hair of his head injured ! The captain was on deck, but hearing the crash, he came running down to my assistance, and with the help of the carpenter and steward soon put all things to rights again in my room, and cleated down my cot so fast that he says he can warrant it now. My fright, together with the thought of our wonderful preservation, and the continual deep, heavy, rolling and kicking of the ship combined to prevent further sleep. The swell of the sea continued all day yesterday. To-day, 17th, it is gradually suhsiding, and we are again in a state of comparative com-fort. The poor children have not been able to stand upon their feet for three days past without danger of being sent headlong from one side of the cuddy to the other. I have often been obliged to send them to their berths to keep them out of danger. Our captain is in his glory; turns everything into a joke, and in spite of our fears, keeps us in continual laughter. Only a wreck is left of most of the steward's jugs, decanters and glasses, the contents of which have been discharged upon the floor.

"Friday, 20th. Yesterday morning, about 4 o'clock, a gale came on, a heavy sea dashed over the poop, fetch-ed away the hen-coop and nearly washed one of the officers and two or three of the men overboard. A large volume of water burst open the skylight, and nearly del-uged the cuddy. The captain was in his swing cot close by, and got a fine drenching. He turned out in a moment and sung out, 'Bring some buckets, my good fellows and bail away; this is nothing, don't be fright-ened, my lads. Steward, give me a dry shirt.' He then ran up on deck and was the means of saving a boy's life who had been thrown over, and was holding on by an iron rail. The captain says he has commanded ves-sels for twenty years, and only give him a good ship, and he considers himself just as safe at sea in the heaviest gale, as on shore."

On the night of November 24th, the ship entered a hurricane. The skylight was blown off by the first gust.

All hands turned out ; the sails were hurriedly hauled in, not however till the maintopsail had been torn. The captain ordered everything to be made taut, and the vessel was then left to drift. Several men including the captain, were badly bruised. A fearful sea beat the helpless ship about during the rest of the night, and no one, except the children, slept.

On the 8th of December, the cliffs of St. Helena appeared on the horizon. The babas were almost frantic with delight, and the mother made preparations for a visit to the island. " I intend if possible," she writes, "to take the children ashore to see the tomb of Napoleon, and the grave of our sainted sister Judson." At 4 P. M., the anchor was cast, within a stone's throw of land, but the captain objected to putting his passengers ashore. Visitors came on board, and among them, Mrs. Brown had not a friend.

The next day the captain relented, and, on leaving the ship, gave a gruff permission for the sailors to row her to shore when they returned with his boat. The party landed at Jamestown wharf, not knowing a soul on the island, or which way to turn, and walked up through the town, inquiring the way to the burying-ground. At length Mrs. Brown saw a British soldier, and remembering that the soldiers attended Mrs. Judson's funeral, she went up to him, repeated her inquiry, and was directed to the house of Mr. William Carroll, the American Consul. At the word "*American,*" her heart leaped, supposing him to be a fellow countryman. But though he was born on the island, and had never been off from it, he was a warm friend of missionaries, and at once set out with Mrs. Brown to visit Mrs. Judson's grave.

On the way, the kindly, shrewd old eyes of the consul took note of her wan appearance ; he suspected the cause, commented on the salubrity of the island, and advised her to wait over for an American ship. His house was no stranger to missionary guests, going to and from their posts of labor.

The next day Mrs. Brown's baggage was brought on shore, and for two weeks she with her entire family, was made a welcome guest at the house of Mr. Carroll's son. One of the warmest corners of her heart was thereafter devoted to the memory of her visit to the " Yamstocks," for so the natives of St. Helena called themselves.

Among the delights of this fortnight was a drive with Mr. Alesworth, to his farm of a thousand acres, called " Fairy Land," from its beautiful and perfect cultivation, and its variety of forest, fruit and flowering trees. Here, on a December day, the children saw the haymakers at their work, and went strawberrying in Mrs. Alesworth's garden.

The excursion to Napoleon's grave, was on the tapis for December 22nd. On the 21st, a vessel carrying the stars and stripes at its mast-head, touched at St. Helena for a few hours. Chests and boxes were hastily re-packed ; letters written eastward and westward ; arrangements made for the ayah to return to Calcutta ; and good-byes said to many warm friends. At evening, Mrs. Brown and the children were rowed out to the *Rambler*, Capt. Baxter, bound to New York, and the last stage of the seven months' journey was begun.

Fifty days passed on the Rambler, in comparative comfort. Towards the end of them, the mother began to look forward to a narrow New England valley, with conflicting emotions :

"There did a thousand memories roll upon her,
Unspeakable for sadness."

The babas did not help the matter, singing over and over thoughtlessly at their play, the new hymn

learned at their first sunday-school, in St. Helena,—
words almost meaningless to them—

> " Here we suffer grief and pain,
> Here we meet *to part again,*
> In Heaven we part no more ;
>   Oh, that will be joyful ! "

A three days' baffling storm off Sandy Hook, at last
cleared up ; the Rambler put into port, and on the 9th
of February, Mrs. Brown landed at New York. The hour
of memories and meditation had passed; now was the
time for action. She had come on serious errands, and
must nerve herself to accomplish them. From this time
on, till she re-embarked, her energies were bent towards
securing re-inforcement for the Assam mission. The
pastors of New York at once took up her cause ; she
found her husband's "Appeal" had been read and understood.

"All appear most eager to obtain information respecting our mission. Do send me a small box of Assamese
books as soon as possible. I have no copies of scriptures or tracts with me. Everybody wants an Assamese
book, and I have but few to give. . . . I have found a
warm friend in good Deacon Colgate. [From Providence,]
I plead hard for more missionaries, every chance I have.
I tell everybody *I am not going back alone.* Thanks for
your kind letters from Gauhati, and for the pretty loving
verses you composed for your poor E—. I trust we shall
be spared to meet again—keep up good courage, my
lone one."

"Three missionaries for Assam ! " was the burden of
her conversation with pastors, members of the board,
college presidents, professors and students. For the mission, she would go anywhere, face anybody, do anything,
even—hardest of all—" speak in meeting ! " Her first ex-

perience in this—to her—dreadful ordeal, seems to have
been at Providence. "They *will* make me talk in the
meetings whether I will or no." At Boston, she found
kind friends, but not much prospect of success.

",The Board did not give me much encouragement.
Mr. Peck thought *possibly* there might be one family
sent this year, and he *hoped* they might be able to send
two more next—but much would depend upon how
things turned at the Convention, which is to be held at
Cincinnati, the 15th of May." She adds, " I am making
my arrangements to attend that meeting."

In the interval, came the arrival in Charlemont, on
the evening of March 12th. Not one of her relatives
recognized her. "*Can it be possible,*" said her aged
mother, clasping her hands in distress, as soon as Eliza
left the room, after the first greeting; "Can it be possible, that *that is my child?*" She was obliged to become
acquainted anew with her own brothers. "Such joy and
such crying I never did see before;" wrote one of the
children to the father in Assam.

Then followed long talks into the small hours of those
bleak March nights, by the light of crackling hemlock
logs—about a thousand things which letters did not, and
could not, tell. "Dorothy and I have *fourteen years of
talk* to do up, and I don't know when we are ever to get
through with it."

Mrs. Brown had brought in one of her chests, a precious little box, kept these seven years with jealous care.
On the 27th of April, a few members of the family,
with the Rev. Messrs. Remington and Hodges, accompanied her and her children to the burial ground.

"And there, in that beautiful spot on the banks of the
lovely Deerfield, the pleasantest burying ground I ever
saw, there, we for the fourth time, deposited in the earth

all that remains to us of our beloved first born child. A load of care and anxiety is rolled off my mind, now that her precious dust is safely deposited in a Christian burial place, and it is a great satisfaction that they have been brought to her native land and laid by the side of her grandfather. My beloved father! They say his affection for me seemed to increase in his last years, that he never omitted to pray for us in the family, and that he always called me his 'darling,' and seldom spoke of me without tears.

Brother William composed some sweet and touching verses, which were sung at the afternoon services, held at one o'clock in the Congregational meeting-house."

The following hymn by William G. Brown, is the one to which she alludes :

THE FOURTH BURIAL.

A change has passed since last we met
    Beneath the pleasant bowers of home ;
Our eyes have all with tears been wet,
    While parted by the blue sea's foam ;
The hills are here, the silvery wave
    Glides singing still its wonted lay ;
Friends who the hand of parting gave,
    The young, the aged, where are they ?

The flower we nursed is faded now,
    All withered 'neath the sultry skies ;
We smoothed the bright locks on her brow,
    We closed her dark and starry eyes ;
And when the moon lit up the way,
    We bore her to her lonely bed ;
Our hearts seemed breaking, when the clay
    Fell heavy on our first-born dead.

They tore the green turf from her grave,
    Thrice left her to the beasts of prey!
And now we bear her o'er the wave
    With kindred dust her own to lay;
No more shall heathen crimes and woes
    Her gentle spirit cause to weep,
No more disturb her sweet repose
    Whom autumn winds have lulled to sleep.

There comes unto our midnight dream
    Her spirit from the angel land,
We see again her bright eyes gleam,
    We take in ours her cold, white hand;
We hear her gentle voice of prayer
    Round idols where the heathen kneel,
And wafted on the evening air
    Come songs our lips may not reveal!

Our three first-born! Their little graves
    By stream and sea are parted wide;
One sleeps by Salwen's sunny waves,
    And one by Brahma's colder tide;
And one, O native vale, we lay
    Beneath thy green and hallowed sod;
But all shall meet in long array
    With us before the throne of God.

On the first of May, Mrs. Brown started for the Cincinnati anniversaries, making several visits by the way, and seeing old and new friends. After the meetings she wrote to her husband; "Mr. Peck and others are going to set about in earnest to hunt up some missionaries for Assam, to return with me. So hold on and take courage."

During the summer months she went from place to place, everywhere pleading the cause of her beloved mission; so absorbed in her great desire as to forget

weakness, weariness and diffidence. At social recep-
tions and sewing-circles she was the center of listening
groups, moved to alternate tears and laughter by her simple, earnest recitals; Sunday-school children loved to hear
her stories ; and college students were stirred by a missionary motive, as they looked at her motherly face, with
its marks of suffering, and heard her tell of the heathen's "wants and woes." Prayer meetings usually resolved themselves into missionary conferences when she
was present, and a new force and point were discernible
in the prayers which followed her statement. "Hereafter," remarked one of the officers of the Board, "when
the brethren want their missions reinforced, they had
better send home the sisters."

The story had not in those days been worn threadbare ;
and a missionary's wife, *still alive*, was by the mere fact
a remarkable object. Had she not spoken a word, there
would still have been an eloquence of sad reality in the
sight of the lonely woman, who, bidding her husband
go back to his work on the field sown with their little
children's graves, had gathered the small remnant of her
family in her arms, and, unprotected save by heaven,
had borne them "through rude and stormy scenes" to
a place of safety, and was now about to leave them
there, to return. She had no need to talk of sacrifice ;
the warm-hearted western mothers and their children
gathered close around her, looked lovingly into her face
and felt the kindred glow. The churches felt it, and
the response was prompt. Men offered themselves for
Assam ; scholarships were taken for the Nowgong orphans, and many strong protecting arms reached out to
receive her own about to be orphaned children. On the
28th of June, Messrs. Stoddard and Danforth of the
senior class at Hamilton, N. Y., were appointed missionaries to Assam, to be located at Nowgong and Gauhati.

Interest in the mission was not confined to her own denominational connection. Mrs. Brown's childhood and family associations had been with the Congregational churches, hence the bond between her and them was the double one of kindred and of Christian fellowship.

"It is wonderful," (she writes,) "with what interest, sympathy and affection I have, in every place, been received, and in many places, by all denominations. Last Sabbath afternoon, we had a meeting at Circleville, in the Congregational house. I felt very timid, and knew not that I should be able to say anything, but my heart was enlarged, and I talked a good while."

Meantime she visited her three western brothers; made the acquaintance of a second generation of valued relatives, and thus drew many new, bright threads into the web of her life. At Circleville, she was for some time in the company of Dr. Otis Ballard, supposing him to be a stranger, before recognition came through a peculiar smile. The truth suddenly flashed upon her, and crossing the room she took his hand ; the question *Is this my brother Otis*, then needed no answer. On the 29th of June, she was present at the marriage of a daughter of her brother John, at Athens, O., to Rev. William J. Hoge, and accompanied the bridal party as far as Lancaster, O., on their way to their home in Tennessee.

These family re-unions fed and built up a life, which for fourteen years had been almost shut out from social intercourse. Even the scanty notes of the memorandum book sparkle with renewed youth. Rev. Dr. Ballard, son of her beloved brother John, draws from memory the following picture of his aunt, as she appeared to him during this and a former visit:

"LAFAYETTE COLLEGE, Easton, Pa., Oct. 30, 1887.

Dear Cousin :—It was a great event in our family, the visit which Uncle and Aunt made us in Framingham, Mass., while on their way to Boston, whence they were to sail to begin their missionary work in India. I remember the strange solemnity, the pensive sacredness with which they were invested to our minds, as those who had devoted their lives to so holy and arduous an undertaking. I remember the absorbing interest with which we afterwards listened to Aunt's tissue-paper letters, journalizing the six months' voyage, with its many perils and great fatigue ; their arrival at their far-distant field of labor, the hardships and discouragements of the work, their sore bereavements, and the faith and courage which triumphed over all, until permanent success was assured in their Assamese mission.

My childish conception of a foreign missionary as a person of awe-inspiring sanctity, in whom cheerfulness would be almost a crime, remained with me until my acquaintance with Aunt Eliza, many years after, upon her visit to this country. I recall vividly how instantly and delightfully my notions on that point were changed on the Sunday morning (June 6, 1847,) after her arrival, late in the evening before, at the house of my uncle, the Rev. James Ballard, at that time pastor of the Congregational church of Grand Rapids, Mich. Is it possible, thought I, as we were waiting in the breakfast-room, that this can be my demure and severely-serious missionary aunt, who comes down the stairway and through the hall with such elastic step, and whose bright, beaming, beautiful face, as she enters, fills the room with a flood of new sunshine ! I no longer wondered that such loveliness of person and character joined with ardent missionary zeal, should inspire such deep interest in both herself and her work, as that a large audience should listen—as was the case in Grand Rapids—with almost breathless silence for nearly three hours, to the account which the gave of her husband's and her own work in India. To the awakening of a like interest I was witness subsequently at Ann Arbor, at Ypsilanti, at Detroit, and in Ohio. Most forcibly was I struck with the warmth of affection and sympathy with which she was everywhere greeted—an affection so manifestly sincere and earnest, that I could but say to myself as I witnessed it, 'Behold how these (Baptists) love one another.'

Your affectionate cousin,
ADDISON BALLARD."

She returned to Massachusetts in August, after the summer's trip through twelve states, with health much improved. In reply to her husband's expectation that she would start for Assam in December, she wrote:

"I am grieved to disappoint you. . . . My work in this country is not yet done. . . . Danforth and Stoddard with their wives, will, (D. V.) sail about the first of November, and now I am hard at work to get an associate for you—a brother for Sibsagar—and am pretty much resolved not to leave the country till I have the man to bring along with me."

In September, she attended the Franklin County, Windham and Woodstock associational meetings of the churches. When it was discovered that she was present, pastoral deliberations gave way to the motion, that "Sister Brown be requested to speak in behalf of the Assam mission." At the close of one of her talks, a pastor rose and said:

"I have made vows, while listening to the statements of our dear sister, such as I never made before. I shall pray more I shall give more. I never before felt willing that one of *my* children should be a missionary, but now I have given them *all* to the Lord, and hope He will make them *all* missionaries."

Brief visits to Bennington and Brandon took her back in memory many years. "I try hard not to be excited, try not to be glad or sorry for anything," she wrote to her sister Sophia. At Bennington, she received the practical sympathy, not only of her own denomination, the Baptists, to whom the care of the Assam mission specially belonged, but also of the church under whose ministrations the light and inspiration of spiritual life had come to her. A friend of missions urged her to return for a longer visit:

"He would not take no for an answer, but said I must come to Bennington again, and have a missionary meeting among the Congregationalists—my old home— and allow them the privilege of doing something for me or for the Assam mission."

The Vermont Baptist convention of 1847, was held at Chester. Here the Rev. Elijah Hutchinson of Windsor, read her appeal, hastily written in hours stolen from sleep. It told how her errand had been entrusted to her:

"In a letter addressed to me, which I found on board ship, my husband says, "You are going home, you must do your work and mine too, your words will have an influence. I hope and believe your pleadings will have the effect to bring us help." Mr. Barker with his little daughter in his arms, accompanied me to the boat when I left his station at Gauhati. As he took the last look of his beloved Margaret, their first-born child, whom he had just torn from the arms of her fond

mother, and committed her to my charge, to find an
asylum for her in this country, he remarked to me,
with an impressive earnestness I shall never forget; 'I
hope your going home unattended by your husband,
will have an influence which all our appeals have failed
to produce. I hope you will be able to bring back an
associate for me.' Mr. Bronson writes: 'You know how
our hearts are sinking within us for want of help. *Don't
fail to plead for Assam everywhere.*"

I am happy to know that two brethren and their wives
have been appointed, and are soon to sail for Assam.
But the third, for Sibsagar, as an associate for my husband, is still wanting. I would appeal to this convention to know if something cannot be done. I would inquire, where are those dear friends in Vermont, who,
fifteen years ago when they sent Brother Brown forth,
pledged themselves to hold on to the rope? Sorrow
has often filled our hearts, when we have felt that *the
rope had become lax*, and we were sinking. Now is a
sinking time with us.

. . . If one more brother is sent for Sibsagar, it
will be but a temporary supply in carrying on the work
we have already begun. We are anxious to enlarge our
operations. Our orphan school [at Nowgong] which
now numbers thirty, we are anxious to increase. Three
years ago these children were among the most destitute
and degraded of the heathen. They have by degrees
been gathered into this asylum, and now thirteen of
them are hopefully converted to God. We want immediately to obtain one hundred scholarships. We are
also anxious to establish boarding schools, and increase
our day schools. Three missionaries ought to be
sent immediately to the district of Jorhat. Brother
Bronson would tell of other portions equally destitute
around Nowgong, and Brother Barker around Gauhati,
to say nothing of the Nàgas, the Singphos, the Miris,

the Mishmis, and various other tribes inhabiting the
hills around us, upon whom not a ray of gospel light
has ever yet dawned ! Our mission is still in its infancy.
Our work there is but just begun, and shall it be left in
this feeble state, or shall the men and the means be
furnished from year to year, for carrying it on effectually ? And, beloved brethren, *must I go back alone*, and
my husband still labor on without an associate ? "

As Mr. Hutchinson's reading proceeded, an unusual
silence fell upon the house ; many were weeping.
"Sister Brown *must not go back alone;* our brother
must have an associate," was the prompt response on
the spot, and pledges were quickly made.
" I want this address to read to my people at home,"
said the Burlington pastor, and it was unanimously voted
to publish it in the Convention minutes. That evening
she wrote :

"Thus you see, dearest, the sum—all extra—is likely
to be pledged in this convention for the support of an
associate for you. And now I shall give myself no rest
till I find the *man*. I am having correspondence with
Brother S——, and he has promised that he will either
accompany me back to Assam, or take our children to
bring up. If he will engage in either service, I need
look no farther."

The New Hampshire and Massachusetts conventions
followed that of Vermont ; these and the farewell meetings for the new missionaries filled the rest of October.
The Danforths and Stoddards sailed in the *Cato* Nov. 3d.
Mrs. Brown felt that she must make one more effort;
she must present the case of Sibsagar before the executive board at Boston. She was invited to attend one of
their meetings.

"There are other missions," said one of the Board, "and other brethren. Dean, Abbot and Jones have all returned to their fields alone. Would Brother Brown (acknowledged to be a judicious man), if he were here, in view of these other claims, say that Sibsagar ought first to be supplied?"

"*I think he would.*"

"Do you not think he would be willing to wait another year?"

"I do not know; the cause suffers by every year's delay."

"Perhaps you hardly appreciate the claims of the other missions, and of those brethren who have returned alone, and have been waiting so long."

"Has any brother waited on the field *twelve years?*"

"No; but some have *died*, without living to labor so long."

How near her husband, stricken with cholera five weeks before, had come to furnishing this last sad argument for re-inforcing Sibsagar, no one present then knew. Even without this knowledge, it is not strange that during the conversation, Mrs. Brown, overcome by her timidity and disappointment, burst into tears.

She returned to the homestead "to spend Thanksgiving with our dear mother, and as many of the family as could be assembled." Late in December, a journey over Hoosac Mountain in the stage, on her way to Rev. Justin A. Smith's, at Bennington, to leave one of her children, resulted in an attack of lung fever, which brought her very near death. She received for eleven weeks in the family of Dr. William H. Tyler of North Adams, to whom she was a stranger, skillful medical attendance, and such unwearied, affectionate nursing as knit a bond strong as that of kindred. The early spring months were spent in the milder air of Springfield and Hartford, regaining strength, and continuing her gentle, earnest pleadings in private conversation, as opportunity offered. She visited her "much loved and revered teacher," Miss Lyon, at Holyoke Seminary, and enjoyed a few hours of stimulating and affectionate converse with that kindred spirit.   Of interesting visits noted, the following is significant :

" Apr. 9, '48·   Had the pleasure of an interview with Mr. Samuel Miller Whiting, a theological student from Newton, the first one of the Newton students whom I have met.   He is engaged to Miss Elizabeth Flint, of Hartford, and they are pledged to the missionary cause. His heart is set upon China."

Mrs. Brown presented the claims and needs of Sibsagar to the scholarly young student, convinced that he was the man wanted there.   She afterwards had the gratification of welcoming Mr. and Mrs. S. M. Whiting to Sibsagar, as the long-looked-for reinforcement.

At the ladies' sewing circles, Mrs. Brown taxed her ingenuity to interest the young people in the wants of heathen women.   On one of these occasions, during her absence from the parlor for a few moments, a singular figure presented itself.   Wrapped in a long-shawl, gracefully folded about the head and form, the stranger glided into the room, made profound salams, raising her hand to her forehead, and bending low ; then seating herself on the floor, began to stroke the dress of the one nearest her, holding up the fabric and examining it with apparent astonishment ; talking all the while in a softly flowing foreign language.   She examined shoes and stockings with exclamations of wonder and repeated manipulations; then, parting a little wider the edges of the shawl held about her face, looked into the faces of the fair young girls around her, and seemed overpowered with awe and reverence, as if surveying beings from another world ;

and meeting no repulse, went from one to another, salaming and pouring out a flood of musical monologue, with every gesture of admiration. At length the tone changed to one of pathetic entreaty; it was evident she was in great distress, in fact starving, and had a numerous household in the same strait. Finally the Assamese beggar rose, and retired backwards with profound obeisances, and presently Mrs. Brown resumed her place in the circle. The ladies assured her that no written description of eastern customs had ever given them half so vivid an idea as her personation.

By the 15th of May she was able to go to Troy, to the meeting of the Missionary Union, and now began to feel that the time had come to set her face eastward. One of her letters quotes:

"O friend beyond the sea!
How yearns with all its ardent love,
This weary heart for thee.

*　　*　　*

I prize thee, native land—but more
My land beyond the sea."*

But her friends would not consent to her taking another voyage alone so soon after her late illness, and she was detained till autumn. Shaftsbury Association gave her so warm a greeting that she writes to her lonely husband,

"You live as deeply in the memory and affections of your friends—of every soul who ever knew you—as ever, and more so. . . . For want of an opportunity to bestow their favors and sympathy directly upon you, they lavish them upon poor undeserving me. . . .

---

* H. S. Washburn.

Be cheered and comforted with the belief that you are *not forgotten* in your dear native land."

It was proposed that the association should pledge themselves to support a missionary for Sibsagar. A committee of inquiry was appointed to ascertain whether the man would be sent if the funds were pledged, and an especial missionary meeting was to be called, in case of a favorable answer. The answer negatived the specific appropriation.

Mrs. Brown's western friends took her on another missionary tour in that direction. On her way she stopped at Hamilton :

"It was a feast to sit by the bedside of the venerable, devoted Dr. [Nathanael] Kendrick. Oh, how fervently and feelingly he prayed for you and me. The students take turns in watching with him, and they have a prayer meeting every night, at about midnight. I shall never forget his parting blessing. . . . I was so deeply moved, I cannot remember all the words of encouragement and counsel he [afterwards] gave both for you and for me, and the exhortations to continue faithful unto death.

"Renewed my acquaintance with a devoted young brother, *William Ward.* He has two years more, and I think we shall see him in Assam."

From Detroit, Mrs. Brown went on to Milwaukee, having been persuaded to do so by Rev. Lewis Raymond, then a pastor in that city. A missionary impulse was needed in Wisconsin, Mr. Raymond had urged. When her work here was done, she crossed the lake in the *Champion,* and ascended the Grand river in a small boat. Along its banks she found bits of picturesque scenery which reminded her of the Dihing. A last

visit to her youngest brother at Grand Rapids, followed;
then the eastward journey by rail, with ten minute calls
at Ann Arbor and Ypsilanti from friends waiting at the
stations to give a greeting and a parting word. Another
visit at Detroit, and sorrowful good-byes to a large
gathering of friends on the steamer *Canada*.

What a contrast—these easy journeyings, these visits,
with their affluence of refreshing society—to her lonely
travels in Assam! Sometimes, while resting in a floating palace, she would recall a hollowed log on the
Brahmaputra, a piercing sun upon the thatch, and the
utter desolateness of interminable sandbanks.

One night from Rochester to Albany, a distance
equal to the month's pull from Gauhati to Sibsagar!

"Tuesday morning, July 25. I left Albany and
reached Bennington, and had both children in my arms
about three o'clock."

A hard task was now before her. Her hand had
repeatedly refused to write the words which should
resign her children to others, but at last the needed
decision and strength had come. "It is only to keep
our eyes fixed on the cross of Christ," she wrote.

The last arrangements, and the preparations for
departure crowded the early autumn weeks. Then
came the journey to Boston, interviews with friends
and relatives, and a public farewell meeting. Said Dr.
Colver, addressing the departing band of seven—the
Van Meters, Benjamins, Moores and Mrs. Brown—"I
know not how these new missionaries will endure the
fight, but for the old soldiers I have no fears. They
have faced the battle, and are not afraid to try it again.
They know to what they are going, and *they will hold on.*"

At ten o'clock on Saturday morning, October 21st,
Central Wharf, Boston, was alive with waving handker-

chiefs ; and calls of "God speed you !" were sent toward
the outbound *Cato*, then just ready to loose from anchor.
The last passengers were in the pilot-boat, making for
the ship; among them stood Mrs. Brown. Her eyes
were intently fixed upon an object on the receding
wharf. A little boy who had been caught up and seated
on the shoulder of a tall, stalwart friend, and held there,
above the crowd of heads, was eagerly waving both
arms, and calling aloud across the widening water,
"Good-bye, my mamma ! Good-bye, my darling
mamma !" There was something in the scene, at which
strong men turned and wept ; but that cheery good-bye
of her "baby," "the last sweet sound heard from my
native shores," served the mother for comfort through
many a dreary day, and sounded out soft and clear
above the noise of storms.

XXII.

TO return to the occupant of the canoe, which rowed off from an out-bound ship, at Garden Reach, on the morning of September 2, 1846. The cabin window, with its watching faces, grew undistinguishable to him at last : there was a hot glare on the water ; a crowd of Bengal trading-boats ; a general sense of noise, heat and confusion. Presently the jostling of the dingee against the ghaut, the sight of boatmen's hands stretched out for bukshish, and the bedlam of importunate palkee-bearers, recalled the necessity of action. Mr. Brown was, in fact, on the eve of an attack of malarial fever, to which he was obliged to succumb, a few days later. Before he was able to write a letter, he was well on his way towards Assam. By the end of the month, he had so far recovered as to look up his dictionaries and manu-scripts and go on with the translation of Hebrews. At length he could enjoy an evening ramble on a sandbank, after which he would climb to the top of his boat and watch the western clouds, wondering where wife and babas might be. Some of his sunset musings were em-bodied in the following lines :

TO AN ABSENT WIFE.

When on the setting sun I gaze,
 My Love beholds its rising ray ;
On that bright orb could I but trace
 One line for her that's far away,
How tender should the message run,
 As if the loved were by my side,
And I would bid the burning sun
 Transmit it safe o'er ocean's tide.

Or could the moon, with silver robe,
 When sinking in the silent west,
Convey for me o'er half the globe,
 Some emblem on her disc imprest,
How these warm hearts, with joy untold,
 Would soon exchange the greeting word !
But ah ! these letters are so cold,
 Like gems in ocean sepulchered.

Through the October days, the lazy plash of the water made a soft accompaniment to the boatmen's unending, dreamy chant about " Brahm, incarnate Sonatan, and all-awatar causing Narayan," with the oftrecurring refrain,

Ram - bol, Hor i bol, Hey - ey.

The river-air was better than medicine, and during the boat's slow progress up the Brahmaputra he was able nearly to complete the translation of the Epistles. By the time he reached Gauhati, he was again in usual health. There, and at Nowgong, he preached two sermons in English on " The Gospel Message," Mark xvi ;

15, 16; and "Outward Ordinances Symbolical," Romans ii; 28, 29, which were afterwards published together in pamphlet form, at the request of the mission.

He started on from Gauhati, Nov. 9th, in company with Mr. and Mrs. Barker, the missionaries having an appointment to hold their annual meeting at Nowgong, Mr. Brown made the last day's journey on foot, and " reached Nowgong overland at 8 o'clock extremely tired." Here he was met by most encouraging news. The toils and prayers of the Bronsons were being rewarded.

After five years the breath of divine life had begun wondrously to stir the hearts of these orphans born of generations of heathen ancestors. Mr. Bronson thus describes their awakening :

"A great improvement in their daily deportment and a tenderness of conscience began to be visible. I gave them Pilgrim's Progress and the Parables of our Lord. These were blessed to their greater awakening. As they read of the man clothed in rags, burdened with sin, their own falling tears and earnest inquiries showed that they too felt their perishing condition, and need of the Saviour's forgiveness.

The conversation and preaching of our beloved brother Brown were greatly blessed. The time appointed for our yearly missionary meeting had come. We suspended the school, and gave ourselves wholly to prayer and conversation, and declaring the glad tidings of salvation. At sunrise, noon and evening they came together to hear the word of God. It was deeply moving to hear the native Christians plead with their countrymen that they would renounce idolatry and embrace the gospel; and it was still more affecting to see the orphan children, one after another, losing their burdens at the foot of the cross, and rising in the presence of

all, to tell what God had done for them.   Day and
night, whichever way I turned, I could hear the voice of
prayer or the song of praise.   The love of God, the
boundless, mysterious love of God in dying for sinful
men, seemed to be the theme that filled every heart.
The Lord has brought into His church nearly every
member of our highest class, and is now filling their
hearts with desires to preach salvation to their countrymen.   Several of the number have good talents for the
work ; we hope they will follow in the steps of the Karen
apostle, Ko Thah-byu."

"On the 29th of November," wrote one of the missionaries, who was a witness to the scene, to Mrs.
Brown, "ten were baptized by your husband and brother
Bronson.   You can fancy, better than I can tell, what
our feelings were as we stood by the river-side and saw
these dear youth coming out from among their countrymen, making a profession of their faith in Christ by
being buried with him in baptism.   May the good shepherd keep these precious lambs."

Two of them were young women from Sibsagar ;
one the wife of a Shan convert, the other betrothed
to Nidhi Levi.   After the morning service and sermon
by Mr. Brown, the converts assembled on the bank of
the Kulung, with the missionaries, and a company of
heathen spectators.   Among those who had asked for
baptism was Mr. Bronson's eldest daughter, Mary, in
her ninth year.   Only the ripple of the waves broke the
stillness, as, leading her first into the stream, her father
laid his hand upon her head and repeated the solemn
words, "My child, on profession of thy faith in Christ'
I baptize thee in the name of the Father, and of the
Son, and of the Holy Ghost."

"And when, all drooping from the flood,
　　　　She rose like lily's stem,"

the Assamese orphans followed, one by one, in her steps, and took on that name wherein " there is neither Greek nor Jew, Barbarian, Scythian, bond nor free."

Then Mr. Brown baptized the first Christian women of Assam, and a full volume of sacred song rose and floated out over the river toward the villages beyond— a prophecy of the kingdom which ere long is to take in even this dark corner of the earth.

The echoes reached well up towards Sibsagar, for Mr. Brown made hymns nearly all the way home. He translated or composed thirteen while "gliding down the Kulung" and pushing up the Brahmaputra. Among them were " What poor despised company of travelers are these?" "I'll try to be faithful"; "Guide me, O thou great Jehovah;" "Broad is the road;" "Mercy, O thou Son of David"; "When our Lord was crucified." "Nidhi," he says, "has made about as many more, so we shall try to get out a second part of the hymn book early in the year." He went on with the work after reaching home, and on March 5th, 1847, reported the enlarged Assamese hymn book completed.

N. to E. B. "Jorhat Ghaut,. Dec. 31, 1846. . . I can only rejoice in the goodness of God to me during the year that is past. I did not expect at the commencement of it to witness the baptism of twenty hopeful converts in Assam before its close, but so it is. It is the Lord's doing, and is wonderful in our eyes."

He walked home the thirty miles from Dikho-mouth, Saturday, Jan. 2d ; found an empty house, and toys and trinkets scattered around. While sorting over old letters and magazines with which the white ants "had made savage work," he "came across Mrs. Judson's verses to her husband, which made me feel very sad." The heart of his home was gone. The lines must have seemed like a message from one who was now thousands of miles away, nearing their native shore.

" My heart is sad for thee, Love,
　　For lone thy way will be ;
And oft thy tears will fall, Love
　　For thy children and for me.

Yet my spirit clings to thine, Love,
　　Thy soul remains with me,
And oft we'll hold communion sweet
　　O'er the dark and distant sea."

On the 22d of February, 1847, Mr. Brown solemnized the first Christian marriage among the native converts, that of Nidhi Levi and Túkú. It is an interesting co-incidence that while Nidhi was the first male convert, his wife was one of the two women first baptized in Assam. Many Assamese were present at the wedding and "expressed no small surprise at the simplicity of the Christian form contrasted with the multiplicity of their own heathen ceremonies on such an occasion.'

On the 24th the pastor gave a wedding dinner at his house, to which all the native Christians were invited. The guests, neatly dressed in white, sat around the room on mats, their host only being seated at the table, whence he dispensed rice and curry, fish and fowl. The visitors were provided with spoons, knives and forks, and some made polite and self-denying attempts to use them. The majority, however, preferred their accustomed mode of eating with the tips of their fingers. This, as done in an East Indian's deft, neat way,—rolling the rice adroitly into a ball, which is then dipped in curry and tossed into the mouth,—is to him far less objectionable on the score of cleanliness than our repeated use, during one course, of the same spoon or fork. So unappetizing, in fact, is the latter mode to the Asiatic taste that it is said the pupils of a boarding school in Calcutta once nearly starved rather than eat their rice and curry with a spoon.

Quite a contrast to the missionary's little feast at home, were the English residents' evening dinners to which he sometimes accepted invitations. The roomy bungalow, with its doors all wide open upon the verandas to catch the evening breeze ; the airy well-appointed dining-room, and noiseless, obsequious khitmughars, dressed in white, watchful to anticipate every want ; the soft whish of the great punka overhead ; gave all of repose and comfort which could be obtained in that climate. At these dinners of courses and wines, the plain missionary showed his temperance colors, by always drinking healths with water.

Pastoral work and the printing of Revelations, chiefly occupied the rains of 1847.

N. to E. B., July.—"The last communion season here at Sibsagar and the preparatory meeting, were very solemn. Nearly all the converts wept while confessing their sins. M. and H. also spoke very well, and the Búra appears well. K—'s wife too, is quite serious. I hope we may ere long see some of them coming forward."

Around the enlarging nucleus of professed converts, there was a circle of timid believers, who received and accepted the truth in secret, but had not the courage to face opposition, or the moral strength to break caste. One of these, a poor old man, who had been praying to Christ in secret for about two years, was lying very sick. Mr. Brown had him brought into his house, that he might look after him, and give him medicine.

" It was quite affecting to hear him talk and pray after he began to mend. He would lie awake the greater
part of the night, repeating over his sentiments and
feelings, and sometimes attempting to sing—often using
this expression, " I have given up my *whole body* to
Christ," meaning that he had given himself up entirely,
for these poor creatures seem scarcely to realize that
they have a soul separate from their body."

During that summer epidemic, cholera had been again
slowly creeping up the Assam valley, reaching Nowgong
early in the season, and Sibsagar late in August. More
than a hundred died in Sibsagar alone within three weeks;
five of them belonging to the mission printing com•
pound. Húbé, an interesting Naga boy, the first convert from that people, whom Mr. Brown had baptized on
the 12th of September, was one of the October victims.
" I think the Lord will not forsake me, but will come,
and take me to himself to-day," the little lad said, as
Sunday morning ended a night of suffering and prayer.
That morning he fell peacefully asleep in Jesus.

On Saturday, October 2nd, Mr. Brown was taken with
cholera, and for twenty-four hours, scarcely any hope
was entertained of his recovery. The regular Sabbath
services were suspended, but the native Christians assembled and spent most of the day in prayer for the life
of their pastor, while the remedies were being administered. That Sunday seemed to be the most fatal day
among the natives; most of those who were attacked, dying in about twelve hours. Though checked in Mr.
Brown's case, the disease left him much prostrated. On
the 13th, however, he was able to write briefly to Mrs.
Brown, that the epidemic had almost ceased.

" Last Sunday morning, dear little Húbé, our last
baptized convert, was snatched away. He died happy.

I went down in the afternoon and addressed the native converts. They have all appeared extremely well during this time of excitement. Some of the heathen too, have found their trust in their gods fail them in the hour of trial, and have expressed their belief in Christ.

How much I have missed you in this time of sickness and distress. All have been very kind to me. . . . Sabbath night, the 3rd inst., sister Cutter came up and spent the night here with brother Cutter, thinking it was probably for the last time. I did not however think myself so sick as they considered me. But God has in great mercy spared me, and what reason I have to bless and praise His holy name !

October 22nd. Here I am, just going to pack up for Nowgong and Gauhati, and am only waiting for letters from you, which I expect by the overland to-morrow or next day. . . . I find the cholera has left me much weaker than I had any idea of being. I trust the trip on the river will do me good, as well as the others, who have all been very poorly. . . . G——, has come out and declared himself to be on the Lord's side, and we hope he may soon be baptized. His wife and mother also are favorable. Túkú's mother has given up her opposition, and says she believes the Christian religion is true. Her husband says the same. Horuram, who married Túkú's sister, Sokú, is a hopeful convert. May the Lord carry on His work, until Assam shall become a garden of beauty to Him. We expect some baptisms at Nowgong, when we go down.

October 26th. . . . Last Lord's day was a solemn and interesting day to us. G—— and Horuram, were baptized, after which we had the communion. G——, you know—he was the greatest opposer we had. . . . After their baptism, the candidates said they had never had such happiness in their life. At the communion there was a good deal of weeping among the disciples.

We now number sixteen—twelve natives, three missionaries here, and one in America ; besides the little Húbé
now in heaven."

Horuram had been a secret, timid christian for a year.
When at last he gained strength to face the contempt
and opposition of his relatives by a public profession,
they bewailed him as they would the dead. His mother-
in-law took her daughter Sokú away from him. The
day after his baptism he met in the road his own mother
and a large company of friends coming to remonstrate
with him.

"Have you lost your reason, or have you no longer
any regard for your mother and friends, that you are
willing to bring such disgrace upon us ? "

The convert was able to give "a reason for the faith
that was in him," and to plead with them to follow him
in renouncing heathenism. His relatives replied by de-
nouncing him as an outcast who could no longer be
permitted to enter their houses or even to eat again with
his aged mother.

The missionaries were accompanied to Gauhati by
Horuram and Nidhi, the latter having been licensed by
the church to preach. A pleasant visit with the Bronsons at Nowgong followed, then the annual meeting of
the mission at Gauhati. Converts were added at both
stations.

N. to E. B., Gauhati.—"We met around the Lord's
table forty in number, and I thought if you could have
suddenly come in upon us, you would not have known
where you were. The Bronsons remained and labored
here the following two weeks. I went down to Goalpara, and there baptized our old friends, Mr. and Mrs.
Bruce, November 28th. It was a precious season. We
sang Mrs. Sigourney's hymn at the water side."

Mrs. Brown was missed here at the brief reunion of so many of "our old Sudiya company." On Monday morning, the 29th, Mr. Brown, in company with a party of friends, had the novel experience of a steamer trip. It brought them up to Gauhati in two days. Thence he took the familiar little boat again, which, after all, he liked better than the noisy, pretentious steamboat; passed the long, monotonous sand-reaches, breathed cool air from the northern hills, spent days of quietness, and, at length, on the last evening of the year, reached home.

"Jan. 1, 1848. The old year's setting sun found me just entering Sibsagar from my trip to the south. Was taking tea at the Thorntons' when your long, loving letter of 27th Sept. was handed to me. Your previous one reached me only a fortnight ago at Tezpur, just after I had sent one off to you."

The new year came in with but doubtful promise to Mr. Brown. It was true two missionaries were on their way, but they would be stationed hundreds of miles distant from him on other fields, and upper Assam, with its village-lined rivers and peopled hills, remained, and was likely still to remain, after twelve years of occupancy, destitute of a preaching missionary! Physically wearied with the struggle to fulfill the duties of translator, pastor and itinerant preacher with one brain, one voice and one pair of hands and feet, and sick with hope deferred of an adequate force to Christianize the neighboring hill tribes, his strong heart almost sank, when the message came that no helper, even at this late day, was to be sent to Sibsagar. The "mountains of ice" seemed to close around him and shut him out from the human sympathy which a missionary so particularly needs. He felt like Elijah in the cave.

Jan. 4. " When you come out I hope you will bring a good stock of faith, hope and patience. Mine are nearly worn out. I have scarcely any heart or courage left. . . . The Lord bless you, and comfort you in every trial. Feb. 3. . . . All these things, my darling, in addition to this protracted and painful separation from you, often make me weary of my life—but what is to be done I do not know. If you can get a missionary to come out with you, then come; and if not, I can only say you must act on your own judgment, after seeking wisdom and direction from our Heavenly Father, who tempers the wind to the shorn lamb, and will, I trust, bring us out of all our troubles. 4. I had made out a list of books which I wanted you to get me, but on the whole I think it is not best to send for them, as I can very well do without them. . . . We must have a missionary, or the mission must be given up. The appointment of Danforth and Stoddard to places between two and three hundred miles off, will afford no assistance to us here. 7. Should a stay of a few months longer than you wish, afford a reasonable prospect of obtaining help, you had better stay and wait for it."

And now came the bitterest trial of this bitter time— the news of Mrs. Brown's dangerous illness at North Adams, followed by a month of suspense.

May 1. " The tears fall fast as I begin to write, but what to say I know not. Mr. Peck's letter, giving extracts from yours of the 13th and 15th of January, reached me yesterday. To-day is May-day, the anniversary of that day two years ago when we got leaves and flowers and filled my study with them to please our sick L——. . . How much it is to be regretted that you could not have come out with the new missionaries, then you would have escaped the dreadful winter's cold. If your life is spared, I trust you will be on your way to Assam before this reaches you, but if it should find you in America, hasten out immediately. Let no temptation induce you to remain another winter; your only chance of recovery from your complaint is in getting on the ocean immediately. Mr. Peck writes about my coming home, and that he expects I am on my way, having heard that I was sick. I tremble lest you should get the idea that I am coming, and so be waiting for me, and thus prolong the time of our separation. No, I shall stay here and do what I can, as long as I can see any chance of doing good, and when there is none, then I shall go home for good. Do not, my darling, wait for missionaries, or undertake to do anything more among the churches. Your efforts have no doubt been one great means of bringing on the disease of your lungs. My prayers ascend for you constantly—the only relief I can find is in committing you to our Heavenly Father's care."

Among the wonderful inventions which had appeared in the civilized world since Mr. Brown's exile was the daguerreotype. While waiting for the mail which was to bring the news either of his wife's death or recovery, he received a package, brought from America to Gauhati by Mrs. Danforth. He opened it, and met the life-like image of the face which he now scarcely dared hope ever again to see on earth. It was as if she had come to him from beyond the grave. The shock of conflicting emotions was so great that, like Joseph, he turned away and sought where to weep aloud, and for a long time cried with a "great and exceeding bitter cry." But he was able the next day to write, "I am calm now; the picture is a treasure. I keep looking at it almost all the time."

" Sabbath evening, June 10. Have been walking out this evening up and down before the house alone. The flower trees in front appear to bloom more beautifully than ever—it makes me feel dreadfully to look at them. . . The other day I received a *New York Recorder*, mentioning your sickness, and saying that thousands would offer up prayers for your recovery. This gave me some comfort and makes me hope that the Lord will hear these prayers, and restore you once more to health. . . His goodness in sustaining your mind in peace and comfort when in the prospect of death, forbids us to fear that He will ever leave or forsake you."

Gauhati and Nowgong had already welcomed their new missionaries. " Our hearts were made glad," wrote one of the orphan lads to Mr. Stoddard while he was coming up the river, "when we first heard of your leaving your beautiful country, dear parents and friends, to teach us and to preach the Saviour's precious gospel. Hasten—come soon, that our dark country may receive light and salvation."

" Had not Brother Stoddard arrived when he did," wrote Mr. Brown, " the Orphan Institution must have been abandoned." Mr. Stoddard wrote home after his arrival at Nowgong on the 18th of May, "I felt that I was not worthy to communicate such joy to the lambs of Jesus ; and that I now could say, as I looked at the flowing tears of gratitude and heard the unrestrained exclamations of joy—' Lord, it is enough ; I am fully compensated for all I have, or all I may be called to endure for Thee.' "

Mr. and Mrs. Bronson's departure had been far too long delayed. After initiating the new missionaries into their work, they regretfully sought renewed health in a voyage and visit to America. Mrs. Cutter, greatly enfeebled by repeated illness, accompanied them.

Mr. Brown writes, June 10th, 1848, to the Woodstock Association, "We have had the pleasure to hear of the arrival of these dear brethren at their field of labor in safety, and at a time when they are greatly needed; as Brother and Sister Bronson will be constrained to return to America this cold season, on account of her health. I sincerely hope our dear Brother Bronson, who has long been a most laborious and faithful missionary, may visit Vermont before his return. He expects to take with him to America two of the orphans, [Lucien Hayden and James Tripp,] to be educated for the purpose of laboring among their countrymen."

During the summer of '48 Mr. Brown was revising the Testament, and writing an Assamese Grammar, and in consequence of the illness and absence of Mr. Cutter, had in addition to all his previous duties, the printing-office on his hands. At the close of the year, he alone remained in Assam, of all the old missionaries.

To Rev. E. B. Smith, "All my old brethren are gone, and the two new brethren alone remain with me. I say *with me*, though they are as much separated from me as a minister in New Hampshire is from one in Ohio, and so far, that it is impossible for either to render the others any assistance; in fact it is as if we were in a different field altogether."

With reference to the paucity of workers he wrote some months later to Rev. Pharcellus Church:

"Some of our missionary operations at the present day appear to resemble the conduct of an emigrant who on reaching the headwaters of the Missouri, instead of clearing an acre and planting his corn, should attempt to distribute his seed equally through the surrounding forest, a few kernels to each acre."

To Dr. Peck, Dec 13, "I am engaged as usual in the common routine of business, having in addition to other things, the printing-office to look after, which I should not be able to do, but for the invaluable services of our principal assistant, Batiram, who oversees the concern. We are now printing the second edition of the New Testament, which is about half completed, and I am partially revising it as we go on."

Mr. Danforth wrote : " The management of the press and the work of translation, in addition to the general mission work of the Sibsagar district, now hung upon the uncertain life of a single missionary."

The complete desolateness of spirit that settled upon the lonely missionary after sixteen years of toil without a vacation, can be best understood by those who have been in like circumstances. A veteran of China under the head of " Missionary Vacations," outlines with a startlingly truthful pen the conditions under which such a missionary keeps on working :

" His farewell has in it an unfathomed abyss of meaning. No associations or institutes for him, no Monday conferences. Down he goes into the social mire, the intellectual torpor, the spiritual death, of heathenism. He dwells among the tombs. Henceforth it is to be with him a perpetual giving-out, never a taking-in. The heathen around him don't live in his atmosphere ; they don't think his thoughts ; they dont breathe his spirit. He is alone. The word never had a meaning before ; it has now. True, he has papers and books, and they are passably well for a time, but they never talk ; they never respond to what he is saying; they are never conscious of his presence; they never take him by the hand ; they never smile or shed a tear ; they are voiceless and pulseless and bloodless. . . . All this while the climate is racking and debilitating. His nerves become unsteady. The unvarying sameness of things around him is endurable for a few years ; but at last, like iron-rust, it eats into his soul.

. . . Is it strange that after eight or ten years of such service as this, a missionary should ask to be let off the wheel for a time ? There is an overwhelming sense of exhaustion. Is it strange that he should be so human as to wish to breathe for a while once more the upper air of a Christian land ? Or that, like David, he should long for one good drink from the old well at Bethlehem, where he had been brought up ?*

The following is one of the letters written while thus holding on by the slackened rope :

"SIBSAGAR, Jan. 13, 1849.

My Dear Brother Bronson:

Feeling sad and lonely this evening, I sit down to scribble a few lines in hopes it will help to drive away melancholy thoughts. Not a word have I heard of the Cutters, nor have I received anything from you since you reached Calcutta, but I heard through Brother Stoddard of your safe arrival, and long ere this, I have no doubt, you are tossing on the billows of old ocean. Alas! many a long day, ere we shall meet again, if ever, in this work. My dear wife has now been absent from me two years and a half, and I often fear I shall never see her face again. I have heard nothing from her for near two months. Assam seems desolate indeed now you are all gone. I am only clinging to the wreck, while

---

* Dr. Ashmore in Missionary Magazine, September, 1876.

the surges are dashing around me, not even attempting to do anything more than to hold on, if possible, till some of you return. I am going on with the printing, and the regular seasons of worship among the native converts ; this is all I can do. Brother Bronson, if you and I are spared to meet again, we must go through the length and breadth of this country, and lift up the gospel trumpet as we have never yet done. We must take a more aggressive course ; go out amongst the people ; bring the truth home ; and show up the contradictions and absurdities of their shasters. When you come, let us spend every cold season in traveling, and the rains in making books. In fact, I have determined that unless Providence blocks the way, I will not spend another cold season at home. I cannot go out *this* year ; that is impossible, for I cannot leave the station alone. Brother Nidhi and one or two with him go out every now and then a few days ; but it is hard work. I have not much faith in sending out our young brethren without some one to back them up when they get into difficulty, and are abused and brow-beaten, as they are sure to be, by overbearing Brahmans.

May the Lord direct your way, my dear brother and sister, and soon restore you to us again. You will find it a dreadful trial to break away from your dear children, and that happy land, to enter again upon your cheerless and disheartening labors, but this work must be done by somebody, and as nobody else will assist us, why, we must do it alone.

With kind Christian love and sympathy,

Ever your affectionate brother,
NATHAN BROWN."

To another friend : " Oh, when will the day come, that the gospel shall be preached to the poor Assamese ? "

XXIII

THEIR WINDING WAY.

TIDINGS came at length, that Mrs. Brown had embarked from Boston, and her husband set out on
the 12th of February to meet her. The *Cato*, with its
cargo of ice and missionary passengers, reached Calcutta
on the 23d, after a happily uneventful voyage. The
most severe storm was the hurricane of November 11th,
when six sails were stripped to ribbons. To Mrs. Brown
the journey had been one of mental suffering. She felt
like the wife of a Siberian exile, who, leaving her children behind, traverses dreary tracts to join the husband
whom she may or may not, find alive. Reassuring letters met her on her arrival in Calcutta. She writes to
her sister Dorothy :

" I was obliged to wait three weeks in Calcutta before
my dear Nathan's arrival. But I found letters in waiting
from him, to say he was on his way, which was a great
comfort. Our meeting, when he did come, I shall not
attempt to describe. The dear missionary brethren
and sisters who sailed with me, all left Calcutta for their
respective stations before Nathan arrived. It was hard
parting with them, especially the Van Meters, to whom
I had become very warmly attached."

The Browns left Calcutta in the heat of the season,
at the change of the monsoons, on their winding way to
Sibsagar. It was an unsafe time of the year for the
journey ; the same time at which Thomas and Bronson
started on their disastrous trip twelve years before. The
rains were flooding the upper streams, and their friends

in Calcutta anxiously urged a delay. But time was
precious, the laborers very few, and they decided to take
the risk.

Their one-masted, eight-oared craft, nine feet wide,
accompanied by a cook-boat, started up with the evening tide, Friday, April 13th ; and, standing in the midst
of a disordered medley of chests, boxes and bedding,
the latter covered with grime, mold and red ants,
Mrs. Brown, fatigued by her day's work, and dispir-
ited by painful good-byes, it must be confessed, cast
a lingering look back on receding civilization. She
could not help remembering regretfully those pleasant
trips the summer before, on the lake steamers, with
their neat staterooms, airy galleries and cool, breezy
decks, but her attention was soon diverted by a clamor
outside, and she watched through the deepening twilight, "the boatmen attempting by dint of threats and the
points of their bamboo poles, to force their way through
the narrow canal, which was completely blocked up
with native boats of all shapes and sizes ; some close to
the water, with flat, others with sloping tops; some
towering to an immense height, and of a most ridicu-
lously uncouth appearance. It took till nearly midnight
to force a way through this motley crowd."

The noise, heat, and intolerable odor overcame her
courage for a moment.

"I never can live to reach Assam," she said, "pen-
ned up three months in this uncomfortable hole, under
the heat of a tropical sun."

"My dear," replied the husband, (unspoiled by lake
steamers) "I am afraid your visit home to America has
unfitted you for coming down again to missionary life."

"Really I began to tremble," she afterwards wrote to
the Colvers, "lest even the *'old soldier'* would not be
able to *' hold on.'"*

Both became ill during the week they were in the Sunderbunds, slowly crawling through hot slime and sand and tangled water-weeds, in and out, back and forth, along multitudinous unclean streams, that scarcely seemed to know which way they ought to flow, but all alike emitting a blinding glare and stifling miasma. "I cannot ascertain what the heat is," Mr. Brown wrote, April 28th, "as my thermometer only extends to 104 degrees, and therefore I am obliged to put it in a drawer of clothes in the heat of the day, to prevent its breaking. For several days after leaving Calcutta, it reached 102, but latterly it has been much hotter."

Reaching the open river, they began to revive: Mrs. Brown shook off lassitude by a "desperate effort," "determined to make the best" of such conveniences and accommodations as the boat afforded. She had by long experience, gained a fine knack at converting almost any "hole" into a home. She opened an old teak chest, containing her small stock of household belongings, found her red Shan work-box, with its trays full of a woman's tools; and the rude cabin was transformed as if by magic. The pater-familias found himself in a cool white suit seated writing by a window, which somehow, now seemed to catch a breeze. He could hear outside, a refreshing splash and gurgle of water against the boat, and within, felt a consciousness of curtains, cleanliness and comfort.

And such days for talking, as those were, on the boundless topic—America! He grew young again, hearing about Vermont hills, and the old folks at home. Letters are written by that window, full of merriment, and with the abandon of a boy.

N. B. to S. B. B., May 8, 1849. "Eliza—poor thing!— I am afraid is but poorly prepared, after all your *gooding her up*, to go back to a jungly life in Assam. Already she begins to wonder that I can use an old rusty tin can for a sugar-bowl; and laughs at me when I tell her the apple-barrel has lasted for apple-sauce during her absence, and is not exhausted yet—she having rejected it before she went home, because the apples were a little wet and wormy. She will have it that the butter of this country does not taste like American butter, nor the milk like American milk—(I should hope not, if it is all like a canister we opened the other day—one that was brought from Boston last year by Mrs. Danforth.) And whenever she sees the floating carcase of a cow, or any signs that a human body has been thrown into the river, she says, "*We cannot drink the water any longer!*" I expect nothing but that when she gets home, she will think she cannot drink our beautiful tank water, just because the washermen and other natives wash their clothes in it, which gives it rather a soapy taste!

I suppose you will think this a miserable letter for a missionary to write—a real sentimental, melancholy one would probably be considered much more appropriate. Perhaps I ought to say a few melancholy words about the children, but I am so pleased with the arrangements for them, that I cannot even sham a single whine."

Mrs. Brown to Rev. Justin A. Smith, from Siraj-gunji, May 1. "Our temporary residence in this little boat seems more like *home* than any place I have found for the past three years. It was hard to bring my mind to submit to all its discomforts and inconveniences, but they are already so nearly forgotten, or I have so adapted myself to them as to make the little boat seem a dear and pleasant place." To Mrs. Smith. "Yet I cannot help thinking of the nice wells of fresh cool water with which you are all blest. We have none to use but the river water, and in these small streams, it is very impure, the rivers being burying-places for the dead, and reservoirs of all the filth from the villages which skirt their banks."

E. B., Home-journal. "It is not unusual to see a dead cow or a dead human body floating upon the surface of the stream ; and being obliged to use the water for all drinking and cooking purposes, the idea is horribly repugnant. This afternoon we passed a place where the bank, for some distance, was strewed with old garments, pillows, mats, waterpots, etc. ; the possessions, no doubt, of the dead, whose bodies had been brought from the neighboring villages. Articles used about the deceased in their last illness are considered defiled, and are carried with them to their place of burning or burial, and there left to decay. Even the meanest beggar will pass by, leaving them untouched."

The following was written to be mailed at Goalpara :

N. B., to daughter : "A few days ago, I met your dear mamma at Calcutta, and since then we have had a good long talk about the babas, and all the relatives in America, and I have become very much interested in the descriptions of all that she has seen. America is a noble country—I am afraid Assam will never be like it, at least not in our day. And now for a

RIDDLE ; ABOUT A NEWSPAPER.

I have lately received a newspaper from home, full of intelligence. I have been reading it for above a month and have not finished it yet. It contains some of the most interesting stories I have ever heard ; it tells all about America, its wealth, its houses, its people, its politicians, its ministers, its churches, its monuments, its rivers, its lakes, its steamboats, its cataracts, its prairies, its railroads, its cows and oxen, flour, pigs and

poultry; it tells me all about my relatives, all my old
friends that I knew twenty years ago, and what has become of them; all about my own children—a history of
them ever since they left me; all their travels and
tricks, their cries and kisses, their plays and prattles,
their hops and hurts, their tears and troubles, their
kicks and capers, their mischiefs and their music, and
other things more than I can think of. This newspaper
attracts my attention in the morning before breakfast,
it keeps up its stories all day and often during the night,
even without a candle to read by ; it is confined to no
particular subject, but furnishes me information on any
topic I am anxious to inquire about ; it often describes
things over a second time, especially things which I do not
well understand, enlarging and commenting upon them ;
it gives not only the words but the accent and emphasis, and teaches me the pronunciation of names of
places and new terms that I do not find in any dictionary ; it tells me what are the various opinions of
distinguished individuals upon the most important subjects, and a great many private speeches of various
persons that never find their way into the public papers
generally. Now, pray, what is the name of this wonderful newspaper? Guess, if you can, and then I shall
call you papa's own girl."

While going by sail up the Jamuna, the travelers were
suddenly overtaken by a genuine Bengal hurricane, apparently blowing from all points of the compass in
whirling succession, and driving the rain and hail fu-
riously through doors and windows, whose frail fastenings were of little use against the tempest. The
manji put the boat ashore and stationed a man at each
mooring stake to hold on. Meantime the cook boat
containing all the provisions disappeared, having twice
broken loose from her fastenings and drifted down

stream. She was recovered, and with the exception of bruises to the crew and some damage to craft and baggage no injury was sustained.

They spent their wedding-day, Sunday, " in a waste desert place," and talked of the Deerfield river, the cool shadows of the maples, and nineteen years ago.

E. B., May 6th.— " We not unfrequently see the tracks of buffaloes, tigers and elephants, and sometimes get glimpses of them and hear their fierce roar in the distance. 9. Entered the noble Brahmaputra, and came in sight of the Assam hills! Another severe storm last night. The thermometer has fallen several degrees since we entered the cool waters of the Brahmaputra. The current has been fearfully strong in some places to-day, the high banks often caving into the stream, so that our boats were in danger of swamping."

On—past picturesque Goalpara, where they mail and receive letters, and feast their eyes on hills. Passing projecting rocks, they see the cave-home of an old hermit, who lives upon boatmen's charity and in return prays the gods to give them a safe passage.

Met by Mr. Barker early on the morning of May 22nd, they reached the mission house at Gauhati, in time for breakfast. A pleasant week was spent here with their old friends and the new recruits ; the former, Mrs. Brown reports, "bear the marks of 'old soldiers'." " The roses are faded from our dear sister's cheeks—the health of our dear brother has been declining for several years. They must soon leave for a season of rest and the invigorating breezes of their native clime, or we fear they will sink irrecoverably. The few days we remained at Gauhati, were indeed a refreshing season. The girls' boarding-school which has been established by Mrs. Barker, is in a flourishing condition. A com-

modious brick building, has just been erected and nearly
paid for by the contributions of the English residents
at the station.

On the first and second days after our arrival, the commissioner and other English residents visited us. Wednesday, Thursday and Friday were mostly spent in returning these calls. The religious exercises on Sabbath
were well attended although the day was rainy. The [na-
tive] girls' and boys' Sabbath-schools were very interesting. Mr. Danforth preached in the chapel in the morning to an English congregation of thirty or forty, and
Mr. Brown in the evening.

Monday morning, May 28th, the Browns left Gauhati,
accompanied as far as Nowgong by Mr. and Mrs. Danforth. The projecting rocks, washed by a whirling current, now offering no footing for the men who towed the
boat, they resumed their long bamboo poles, and worked
with might and main, pushing her up stream.

E. B. "On Thursday, the manji, wearied with this
laborious process, bought a canoe, in which two men were
sent ahead a few rods, to carry on the rope, and having
fastened one end to some snag or bush, to return with
the other end ; all the boatmen then laying hold of the
rope, would slowly pull us up, to the point where it was .
fastened."

Entering the Kullung, they were 'completely shut
in by the dismal jungle of tall reeds, growing close
down to the water's edge." The neighborhood of
trees again, later on, was a refreshment to the
eyes, and the sight and sound of innumerable
monkeys frollicking, chattering, and swinging themselves from bough to bough, gave a sociable aspect
to the wilderness. Much better was the company of
human beings, when at evening they reached the first

village above Gauhati. The head man was friendly, but unable to furnish them milk, as milking-time would not arrive till ten the next morning. Milk, as well as fowls, ducks and vegetables, were forthcoming at Jagi, a considerable settlement two days' pull farther up, where the head-man showed the travelers much civility. The missionaries spent Sunday among the villagers ; conversing and preaching. Some disputed, some ridiculed, and some said "*Hoi*," "all true." At evening the missionary party took a long walk beyond the village, and found a swarming population living in circular groups of huts ; so arranged, apparently, for mutual protection, the spaces within, being used as enclosures for cattle. The sudden apparition of white faces spread terror among the women and children, who ran like wild deer to their hiding-places. But as soon as they discovered that one of their visitors was a woman, they began to be inspired with more confidence. Mrs. Brown succeeded in drawing them forth from their lurking-places, and after a little encouragement, they became quite familiar.

Nearing Nowgong a few days later, they met two Christian lads from the orphan school, one of whom delivered, in behalf of the pupils, a graceful address of greeting to Mrs. Brown, welcoming her back to Assam. "Prayers have daily been offered," he said, "by all the Christians in the school, for your safe return." Stopping over Sunday, June 10th, at this station, they witnessed the baptism of Kandura, by Mr. Stoddard, the high bank of the Kullung being crowded with heathen spectators. "The three days we spent at Nowgong, were among the most interesting of my life," Mrs. Brown wrote. Monday morning, they went on their way, accompanied for three days by Mr. and Mrs. Stoddard, the Danforths, remaining meantime in charge of the Nowgong station.

The scenery along the Kullung was varied and interesting. Villages and rice-fields, and groves of the cocoanut palm, jack-fruit and plantain alternated with forests of peepul, banyan, teak and rubber-trees. Sometimes the boat-rope, gliding like a snake along the reedy bank, disturbed the stately sharp-beaked herons watching for fish, and scared the wild ducks feeding along the edge of the stream. Entering the Brahmaputra again nearly opposite Bishnath, the travelers for some days threaded a dense jungle of reeds fifteen or twenty feet high, by means of setting poles or the hand over hand hauling in of the gooning-rope. On the 17th of June, they stopped at a settlement of Miris.

"They were truly children of the woods, says Mrs. Brown, living in the rudest manner, children half-grown going unclad ; men and women with but one garment each. Many of the women had their necks and wrists covered with beads and bangles of glass and silver ; and the opening in their ears stretched to so enormous a size as to admit a silver ornament of the circumference of a dollar! They were not at all shy, but flocked around our boat, curious to see and examine everything within their reach. We took a few picture-books and tracts and went out in front of their houses, (which are built upon stilts) and talked for some time, endeavoring to give them some idea of God and religion."

Finding among these villagers a few who had been taught to read—one at a Sibsagar mission-school, and others by a Hindu pundit—Mr. and Mrs. Brown gave them books, and "left them in their simplicity and ignorance."

The progress of the boat now became seriously impeded. Recent rains had caused a sudden swell of the immense river, and the rush of the current on the 20th, was fearful beyond description. Quantities of drift-wood swept by, while the men tried with main force to get the boat on by hauling in the rope fastened some distance above, to a clump of reeds. The chorus of "Allah! Allah! Allah!" rose above the roar of the rapids and swirl of rushing flood-wood. All felt that their fate hung literally upon a thread. A floating tree of unusual size was seen ahead, bearing down upon them. It struck the frail boat, which shook under the collision.

E. B. "The manji instantly left the helm, ran below, and tore up the floor to ascertain whether the boat was filling. To our great joy we learned that no serious ac-cident had happened to her, and the men resumed their pulling, but the force of the water had been so much increased by the passing and striking of the tree, that there was not sufficient power to carry us on. The rope broke ; and we were hurled back with great velocity, till we were at length rescued by means of the rope which was attached to the cook-boat."

While the canoe went ahead again with two men and the gooning-rope, a favorable breeze sprang up.

"Our manji with all the quickness and inde-pendence of thought of an experienced sea-captain, or-dered the sails to be hoisted, and cutting loose from the rope, headed the boat round. With a fearful rush, we were forced through clumps of brush and floating trees, and soon safely reached the opposite shore, the cook-boat following in our wake."

Later, the two men in the canoe were recovered, and for the remainder of the day, tracking-ground was found. At dusk, the boats were moored by dense jungle ;

(21)

the night passed with continued rain, thunder and
lightning. The next day, the gooning-rope again became the only resort; falling banks and drift-wood
clogged the stream, which was hourly rising. At length,
on the 25th, a strong, favorable wind took them on rapidly; what would have been nearly a week's journey by
poling and gooning, was made in a day by sail. They
soon after entered the Dikho, and reached Sibsagar the
28th.

A large company of natives were collected at the landing, each eager to give the first welcome to their returning pastor, and with their own hands to unload the boat.
Their words of affection and delight at sight of the long
absent *Memsahib*, expressed in exuberant Assamese,
recalled by contrast her first reception fourteen years
before. "Then," she says, "all the people looked upon
us with suspicion, and some ran away with fear, at the
sight of us."

The boats having been unloaded, "a precious little
company" of Christians gathered for an impromptu
praise-meeting.

XXIV

ONE by one, these men and women had crept timidly towards the light, out of the tangled jungle in which they had been benighted. Their path had been difficult ; none had gone that way before ; they had discerned the light faintly through a fog, and sometimes stumbled in the thicket, or sunk in the mire. It was the duty of the guide to hold up the lantern with one hand, and with the other to open a path, meantime keeping close watch lest any should stray back into the darkness. He must sometimes stand between his charge and the beast of prey or wily serpent, and all the while look to it that none fainted for lack of nourishment. They were indeed "a precious little company," a sacred trust, the burden of his hourly thoughts. " Our little flock are left like sheep without a shepherd," he wrote, during the recent brief absence of all the missionaries ; " I feel a great desire to meet them again, and to find that they are still steadfast in the truth."

The relation of the pastor to the infant church was that of a parent to children. He was familiar with their temporal as well as spiritual necessities. The church prayer-meeting, held on Saturday evening, was a weekly family gathering for worship, singing, confession and counsel. When kneeling in prayer, these children of the east prostrated themselves upon the ground. Any other attitude would have seemed, to them, irreverent. Their prayers and confessions were not seldom broken by sobs and tears ; " God be merciful to me a sinner," was the frequent burden of their petitions. Their ad-

(331)

dresses and exhortations to each other were the spontaneous expressions of their simple faith. Years after, Mr. Brown thus recalled, in a missionary address, some of these scenes of his ministry :

"Nidhi Levi, the first native preacher, was converted from the schools. I frequently receive letters from him of the most affectionate kind, all breathing the warmest attachment to the blessed religion of Jesus. How many times I have seen him weeping, in our prayer and conference meetings. Batiram was another converted pupil and preacher, now gone home to glory. He was always timid in regard to his own conversion, though all around felt that he was a true child of God. I have seen him, at our conference meeting preparatory to the communion, throw himself prostrate on the floor, according to the custom of the country, confess his sins, and in an agony of grief, trembling all over, beg the prayers of his brethren and sisters, that he might not prove a hypocrite, and go to eternity unprepared."

"Kolibor is a true child of nature," writes Mrs. Brown, "but appears sincerely pious. His conversion took place in mature life, so that he has not enjoyed the advantages of early training which Nidhi and Batiram have. At the prayer-meeting last evening, when he came to mention his recent bereavement, (the death of an infant) he cried aloud like a child. And this he often does when confessing his sins in prayer. In him it is so natural and unaffected, that it is the brightest evidence of a broken and childlike spirit."

Of a Friday evening covenant meeting she makes note that there was "much weeping among the members ; " that one native brother, who had been excluded, "confessed his faults and was received back to the church;" and another "confessed having fallen again into opium-eating." Another entry says :

"Last evening we had a real old-fashioned revival conference, such as we used to have in America; one after another rising in quick succession to relate the exercises of their minds, as if they were afraid of losing the opportunity. The meeting continued later than usual, and after it was dismissed there was a great lingering, as if unwilling to leave. At length a number gathered around the table and commenced singing hymns. Some stayed till nearly midnight."

These hymns, composed for them by their pastor and set to English tunes, were a delight to the converts. The smoothly-flowing Assamese language, with its large proportion of broad vowels, melted into the noble old melodies as if itself a part of the music. The new hymnal completed in 1850 contained one hundred and eighty-two hymns, about half of which were either translated or composed by Mr. Brown, and most of the remainder by Nidhi Levi and Batiram. "The converts are constantly singing them," writes their pastor; "singing appears to be their life." Especially did he enjoy their rendering of his favorite air, "*My Native Hills*."

On Sunday evenings he preached to a mixed native audience in the chapel near the printing-office. Sometimes companies of villagers from a distance, visiting the station, came in to hear. In 1850, Sunday Assamese services at ten and two o'clock were commenced at the old house on the corner, where four ways met, midway between the tank and the river. He held a Sunday Bible class at the bungalow for the instruction of converts, and Mrs. Brown had her own Sunday-school for women and girls. After the new zayat was put up on the river-road there were daily religious services there.

Mrs. Brown to Mrs. Stoddard.—" We have an English and two native services on Sunday, besides the Bible class in the evening, and when Nidhi is not able to preach once on Sunday, Nathan has to conduct them all, and then sometimes goes out at four o'clock, after the afternoon services, into the streets or bazar or zayat with the native Christians to oversee their preaching and put in a word to help them along as occasion requires. . . . This is prayer-meeting day, and I must read over my chapter and make preparations for that, so you will excuse this hurried note."

Mr. Brown's sermons to a regular Assamese audience, whether heathen or Christian, were in a practical and pointed style. The existence of sin, its horrible and loathsome nature, and the helpless bondage to its rule, of the unaided human spirit, were plainly set forth ; then the one redemption, the blessed avatar, Jesus Christ, was presented. The pastor was very apt to preach on every-day right-doing. A religion of emotion, without strict, practical morality, met with but little encouragement from him, and his plain, searching statements of scriptural godliness were not without the fruits of repentance and subsequent reform.

Mrs. Brown writes after a women's meeting, May 3, '54: " To-day one after another confessed with weeping and distress some old sins long hidden. Mr. Brown has lately been preaching a course of sermons on the Commandments. They seem to have set consciences at work, searching out old sins of lying, stealing, deception, etc., and the working has brought forth voluntary confessions of sins which had hindered them and blinded their minds."

These "spots of moral verdure already reflecting the richness and beauty of the garden of the Lord," refreshed the hearts of the workers.

On Sabbath mornings a little assembly of Europeans, similar, except in numbers, to those at home, met in the large middle room of Mr. Brown's bungalow. It comprised the few English residents of Sibsagar, most of whom felt it a duty and pleasure amid the surrounding paganism, to join in Christian worship with the missionary families. Mr. Brown usually read a sermon from Scott or Simeon, the voice of prayer was heard, and the old familiar hymns were sung, which almost took the exiles home.

"Although there are but few of us," wrote Mrs. Brown, "seldom over fifteen or twenty, these seasons of Sabbath worship seem more like home than anything else that we enjoy here."

The pastor's study was always open to inquirers; quill and manuscript were at any time gladly pushed aside for a friendly, earnest talk with native visitors. whether Brahmans or coolies, baboos or school-boys, courtly retainers of the old rajas, or the occasional tattooed Naga chief from the hills, carrying his spear and battle-axe, and resplendent in necklace of buffalo horn, and door-knob earrings. How he stared about him, and started back, aghast, from the mirror, then gazed in admiration! How he listened and stood aloof, with eyes fixed on that machination of demons, the clock! One of these chiefs, who often came with a party of his people to the missionary's house, was persuaded one day to stand for the accompanying portrait. By degrees confidence was established, questions were answered, and conversation was led to the great simple truths of religion, for this was the object of all these talks, and it was

the missionary's principle to let no native visitor leave
without hearing of the way of life.

The translation of the New Testament being finished,
Mr. Brown took a brief rest from pen and head-work,
and refreshed a weary mind by making water-color

KEYONG, NAGA CHIEF OF KONGON VILLAGE.*

pictures of a number of Assamese birds. "Painting
these birds," he writes, "was my medicine after the terrible fevers I had in Assam. They were painted in the

*From Assamese engraving in the Orundoi of Feb. '55. Original water-
color by Rev. N. Brown.

Sibsagor August 13. 1849

My dear little Son
Look at your hour
old Father and see how
he is crying because
he had got no little
letter from Willie.
The hair brush you
sent me by Mamma
I have got. It is a
very nice one. I
have a scythe too, and mow with it in
the morning. The toads are as thick as
ever. Do you have many in America?
I hope you do not handle them. A few
days ago an Asamese woman set down
a dish of rice upon the ground, where
a snake lay coiled up. She did not see
the snake and set the dish right upon
it back. It bit her and in about two
hours the poor woman died. A man
was drowned to day while swimming
in the river, trying to catch some
floating wood.
Have you had any blackberries
this summer? We have had plenty
here and strawberries too. Mamma

brought them out with her. Did you nor
think it was a pretty rocky place when
you went up to Grandpa's at Woodford!

The Donkey, poor Beauty, alas was
carried off by a tiger. He came
up behind her, it is supposed,
where she did not see him, and
carried her away into the jungle.
She was never seen afterwards.
Savage looking creature, is it he
Poor Donkey ought to have kept watch

better, and had her eyes open, and
not gone where the tigers were.
    Your affectionate Papa
        N Brown

"NO LETTERS FROM THE BABAS."

fall of 1849. I came across an old camera obscura which helped me in drawing the outlines."

His letters to his children were enlivened by hiero-glyphics, puzzles and conundrums, and frequently illus-

GIGANTIC CRANE.   (Telia Hareng.)*

trated by pen-and-ink drawings. The specimen here given, was written when the dawk once came in with its grown-up correspondence, but with no small letters from the babas.

---

* From Japanese engraving, after original water-color by Rev. N. Brown. Length, tip to toe, 6 ft. 4 in.; wings spread, 7 ft.; height, 50 in. Head and throat blue, legs red, wings and body black and white.

Advancing civilization had for some years puffed and whistled up the great river, but it was not till Sept. 3, 1850, that the muddy waters of the Dikho splashed under the paddles of a steamboat. The boat was the *Damouda*, bringing Bishop Wilson and Mr. and Mrs. Pratt.

The aged bishop's sermon was one of his characteristic ones—plain, pointed and solemn, carrying appropriate warning or encouragement to each member of the small European congregation, gathered at Capt. Brodie's house that afternoon. It was his "dying message," he said, knowing that he should see their faces no more. It contained words of affectionate appreciation of the sacrifices and labors of the missionaries before him, so far exiled from friends and country for "a good and glorious cause." Mrs. Brown speaks of a pleasant interchange with Mrs. Pratt after the service, of plans and hopes for the Christianization of the women of India. At evening, taken in by Bishop Wilson to dinner, she finds him "very affable," making "kind inquiries about our missionary operations, number of converts, schools, books, etc."

She adds, "We all went on board the steamer to bid them good-bye. An immense crowd of natives had assembled on the bank of the river to see the wonderful *Jue'jahaj* [fire-ship]. Some pressed on board, and fell down and worshipped the engine as a god."

That same summer had brought to Assam intelligence of the death of Rev. Cyrus Barker, of Gauhati. Forced at last, by rapidly declining health to leave his work, he had sailed with his family for America, died at sea, and was buried in Mozambique Channel on the 31st of January, 1850.

"His last thoughts [Mr. Brown's Mission Report] were upon the dear people of his charge ; his last message an exhortation to them to be faithful to the end. Death had to him no terror; for the same blessed Saviour he so fervently commended to others, became in that trying hour his support and ground of triumphant hope."

To Mrs. Barker: "His reward is on high; he has gone to join the assembly of the faithful; to join in the hosannas of the saints and angels above. . . . Remember me affectionately to the sweet little Margaret, little Eddie, Ruthie and all. May their father's prayers be speedily answered in their behalf, and may they all be early converted to God."

A memorial sketch of Mr. Barker's life and labors was written by Mrs. Brown in Assamese for the benefit of the native Christians.

Strong young recruits pressed in to fill the broken ranks. In May, '51, news came that the new missionaries, Ward and Whiting, were on the Brahmaputra. "Brighter days are, I trust, in store for us," wrote Mrs. Brown, recalling her acquaintance with all four of the new-comers, in America, three years before; "I consider them all, jewels of the first water. I fancy I was the first one who put it into their *heads* to come to Assam, and I trust the Lord has put it into their *hearts*." Mr. Brown wrote to Mr. Whiting:

"Welcome, dear brother and sister, to these heathen shores—may your lives and health be precious in the sight of the Lord, and may your labors in the Master's vineyard be crowned with a success and influence that shall extend far down into the ages of eternity. You come out knowing well that missionaries have to contend with trials and discouragements, and therefore I trust you are not destined to be disappointed when you

find that many of your hopes and wishes fail of being realized. We have to labor for the future rather than the
present—still I believe that by the exercise of a more
truly self-denying and missionary spirit, we might see
great things accomplished in our day. . . . In these
days of bustle and excitement we are too apt to lose sight
of that simplicity of effort and that patient continuance
in well-doing which are so essential to the success of
every minister, and especially every missionary. Had
we the meek, lowly, self-sacrificing spirit of à Schwartz
or Brainerd, what a happy example of Christianity
would be held up before the heathen and before our
native converts. But alas, the church is becoming too
much like the world—shorn of her lovely radiance, and
stripped of her primitive power. We can preach, and
we can pray; but the question is, do we act out Christianity? Do we exhibit a fair specimen of it before the
heathen? In proportion as we do this, we may expect
that our efforts will be accompanied with a life-giving
energy similar to what was witnessed in the apostle's
days. . . . I am impatiently waiting to see you. I
have finished the New Testament, and have partially revised it, but it will still have to undergo another revision after a few years' fresh experience. My arrangements for the future I do not intend to settle definitely
till after your arrival."

During these years of alternate drought and refreshing, the isolated missionary pastor had drawn strength
from the thought that he was at one with the great
church militant, and, like a man on picket duty, sometimes
ran over, mentally, the batallions, brigades and divisions of the army behind him, and looked ahead to the
details of the coming campaign.

He wrote to the Woodstock Association, May 10,
1850. "It is a great thing to live in the world now; it

is a great thing to be spectators of the scenes that are now enacting on the surface of the globe; to witness the transition from a state of darkness to the brightness of a millennial day : it is a great privilege to be allowed to labor and exert an influence in such a crisis of the world ; to join the armies that follow the Prince of Victory and help strike the blow that vanquishes the power of Antichrist forever. It is not one sphere or department of labor that demands the energies of the church now ; it is not the home field, it is not the heathen field, it is not the European field, that has an exclusive claim upon us ; we must look at the *whole world*, and extend the warfare in every direction if we would meet the emergencies of the age, and accomplish our part in the work which Providence has marked out for the present generation."

To Rev. Elijah Hutchinson : "Yes, God's house is now beginning to take in the whole globe : as it rolls around, the prayers of all people are ascending to fill the high vault of heaven."

Mr. and Mrs. Ward were located in Gauhati with the Danforths, who had been there alone since the Barkers left. The Stoddards at Nowgong were gladdened by the return of the Bronsons, who found there a valuable accession to the mission force in the person of Rev. G. C. Daüble, a Lutheran missionary lately stationed at Tezpúr, who, on changing his views and uniting with the Baptists, joined the Nowgong mission and labored with devoted earnestness and success in the school and in outdoor preaching. He afterwards married Miss Mary S. Shaw, of the Nowgong mission.

As the Whitings were making their way up the river towards their future field, they were met and welcomed by Nidhi Levi, and on Saturday afternoon, June 7th, a boat

came alongside containing Batiram, who had been sent
by Mr. Brown to look up the travelers, now somewhat
delayed beyond the expected time.   He and the Thorntons, resident friends, followed later by the road, accompanied by a crowd of Assamese, so eager to see the new
Sahib and Memsahib that they climbed the trees to
catch the first glimpse of their boats coming up the
Dikho.   Seven miles below Sibsagar the new-comers
caught sight of Mr. Brown under his broad-brimmed
solar hat, standing in the jungle-grass on the bank, and
hailed him with exclamations of delight.   Touching
shore, they left their boats for an evening ride by elephant and pony into the station, their escort of delighted
natives running to keep up with the elephant's ponder-
ous, slouching gait.   Thus, at 10 o'clock in the moonlight of that Saturday evening, the Whitings entered
Sibsagar, the goal of their hopes, the central point of
their future seed-sowing.   Presently outlines of ancient
temples loomed indistinctly before them ; a dim gleam
and low plash of water marked the edge of the great
tank ; a little further, and a light appeared from the
mission bungalow, and a hearty welcome from Mrs.
Brown closed the eventful day.   On Monday they entered their own house, and prepared to commence work.

All the missionary brethren, new and old, from the
three stations, (they were now *seven* in number !) together with native delegates from the churches and
other Christian Assamese, met in convention at Sibsagar, in October 1851.   It was the most important meeting of the kind yet held; during its three weeks' continuance, the various forms of work were systematized
and uniform methods adopted ; foundations of church
order were laid, and provision made for more extended and
permanent evangelistic labors in the outlying districts.
Seven native brethren were, after careful examination,
formally appointed to missionary service as assistant

preachers and colporteurs, and assigned to their respective fields. Mr. Daüble was set apart to his work, Mr. Brown preaching the sermon from the text, "Son go work to-day in my vineyard." Many important questions involving efficiency and unity of labor were settled, on such subjects as books, buildings, teachers, schools ; course of study, trades, lectures, examinations, and lyceum of the Orphan Institution ; duties of native assistants ; industrial education of girls ; regulation of general expenses ; erection and enlargement of mission chapels and namghors ; enclosure of burial-grounds and method of interment. In connection with the latter, the following recommendation as to the burial of native Christians was adopted ; and may serve as a sample of questions constantly coming before an isolated missionary, on which he needs the advice and sanction of his brethren :

"That the body be wrapped in a simple white winding sheet and new mat, and that it be conveyed on a common bier to the grave for interment. Should, however, any native Christian wish to bury his friends in a more expensive manner, with coffin, etc., your committee would not deem it advisable to make any objections."

In accordance with a recommendation of the mission made in July, the three branch churches of Gauhati, Nowgong and Sibsagar, were now recognized as separate and independent bodies, and afterwards organized into the "Baptist Association of Assam." In that capacity the ministers and delegates convened in the chapel October 30th ; elected Rev. N. Brown moderator, and adopted a constitution. "The letter from the Sibsagar church was read by Bro. Batiram D. Peck ; and those from Nowgong and Gauhati, written in English, were read in Assamese by the moderator." The association listened the next day to a sermon in Assamese by

Nidhi Levi Farwell, from Matthew xiii, 31 ; " The kingdom of heaven is like to a grain of mustard seed ;" took
up a collection for the Missionary Union ; resolved, on
motion of Brother Nidhi Levi, to recommend the sending of preachers to the north bank of the Brahmaputra ;
and on motion of another Assamese brother, to thank
American Christians for " sending beloved missionaries,
who have come among us to make known the path of
light." " The church and Christians of Assam salute
you ; " was their message, "thanking God that he has
ever put it into your hearts to send this blessed hope
which we have found in believing the Lord Jesus Christ
our dear Saviour."

On Saturday, October 18, the overland had brought
news of the death of the fathers of both Mrs. Bronson
and Mrs. Whiting.　The Convention adjourned for the
day, and on Sunday all assembled " to listen to a most
excellent, touching funeral sermon from our dear Brother
Bronson." The funeral of Mrs. Brown's sister Dorothy
took place that same day in Heath Mass., and though it
was three months before she heard of this bereavement
she dressed in black and sat with Mrs. Bronson and
Mrs. Whiting as a mourner, "drawn towards them with
deep sympathy in their affliction, and also feeling that
very possibly, at that time, there was fresh cause for
grief either in the case of our dear sister or mother.
I felt a strong impression that there was a fitness in
joining myself with the mourners, little thinking, however, that my dear sister was being buried that day,
and that all my family were dressed in black, at her
funeral."

" January 19, 1852.　To-day received the sad news of
my precious sister Dorothy's death.

' Our hearts so perfectly incorporate in one,
　That not the shadow of a thought e'er marred their
　　unison.' "

Mrs. Tucker was one of the many missionary spirits who never cross the sea. The same devotion which nerved the younger sister to endure hardness in a heathen land, held the elder one to the self-sacrificing service and loving neighborly ministries of a quiet country life at home. Her death was followed, on the 15th of the following February, by that of "Mother Brown" at Whitingham. In all these years, her spirit never had been parted from her far-away son. "You are scarcely out of my mind any of the time," she wrote, "yet God has strengthened me so that I have not been distressed as I expected to be. To his almighty protection I commend you, with all the dear missionaries of the cross." When "Eliza" came to visit her in '47, *without Nathan*, the disappointment was almost more than her heart could bear; and there were long, tearful talks in the old farm-house, between the mother and the wife, before the idea that he ought to have taken a furlough after fourteen years service, was given up. "Nathan," on his part, never ceased to be an affectionate mother-boy. "That is a beautiful spoon, mother," he wrote her, on receiving a keepsake, "it has only one fault, it chokes me."

In 1851, a suggestion was made by the Commissioner, that the Sibsagar missionaries should found a native Christian village in the neighborhood, by taking up government land, laying it out in plots, with a common for pasturage, and lots for a church and school-house; and providing the families with cane-cuttings and young fruit-trees, thus encouraging them to make a livelihood by agricultural pursuits. While this plan was not adopted, still, for the benefit of such native Christians as might choose to avail themselves of the opportunity, Mr. Brown and Mr. Whiting took up grants of land for them to cultivate. With regard to the proposed village Mr. Brown enquires :

"Whether when our converts are more numerous, it would not be better for them to settle upon farms at their own discretion, and live entirely upon their own resources, rather than to depend upon the missionaries for assistance and direction in their minor affairs?"

To Dr. Long, March 3, '51: "I shall be very happy to join in any effort to induce the native Christians to cultivate. They did so to some extent last year, and if a suitable piece of ground can be found, to which all their cultivation can be transferred, I shall most willingly afford them all the encouragement I can."

Mr. Cutter's connection with the mission closed in 1852. The charge of the printing establishment fell upon Mr. Brown. This involved the overseeing of the affairs of the office, and keeping both presses running, besides preparing most of the matter for them.

An important branch of the pastor's work consisted in teaching and training young men to be preachers. He believed "the plan of sending in native laborers, as fast as converts shall be raised up and qualified, to be the true mode of conducting missions in eastern countries."

"The native preacher has a thousand advantages which the foreigner has not. He stands on a level with his countrymen; he is neither above them nor below; he is familiar with all their feelings and prejudices; he appreciates their difficulties, doubts, arguments, fears; he conforms without inconvenience to their customs, dress, and manner of living; his constitution is adapted to the climate; and the expense of his support is but half, or perhaps a fourth, of what would be required to sustain a foreign missionary and his family."

These young men came to his study for instruction, and accompanied him into the villages for itinerant preaching and colportage, thus gaining aptitude and confidence for their subsequent work alone.

"Our native brother Nidhi Levi is an energetic and excellent preacher, and well qualified to meet the arguments by which the Brahmans endeavor to defend their system."

To the Secretary, Dr. Bright, Jan. 16th, '51· "I have been obliged to give up making excursions into the country this cold season, as I hoped to have done, but I have given permission to Batiram and Biposú to lay aside all other work whenever they feel disposed to go into the villages, and I have been happy to find them disposed to embrace the offer with a frequency and zeal that is very encouraging, and shows what they would do if they had a missionary to go out with them and lead them on. I had anticipated having Brother Nidhi constantly employed in this business, but he has been in the doctor's hands the greater part of the time for the last two months—disease of the lungs, which will probably carry him to an early grave. In the meantime he has embraced the opportunity to finish and correct for the press a tract against Hinduism which he had nearly completed on his way up from Nowgong with me last year. It is now printed : 'Conversation between Pundit and Preacher,' and is, I consider the best tract we have. . . . For the mission, besides Nidhi's tract above mentioned, we have had printed, 'Error Refuted,' a tract by Batiram, besides a Primer or Spelling-book, and a series of Juvenile Tracts, translated by Mrs. Brown from Bengali and English, nine numbers of which are already completed and the remaining three are nearly ready. We are now at work re-printing the 'Second Catechism,' a useful tract now out of print. I shall send you copies of all these by ship."

Later, the assistants received additional instruction
from Mr. Whiting.   Batiram was one of the first members of the Sibsagar church.   He belonged to the writer
caste, was formerly Mrs. Cutter's pupil at Sudiya and
Jaipúr, and in Sibsagar was for several years foreman
of the printing office.   Mr. Brown wrote in 1845 of his
conversion :

" He has been a secret worshipper for about a year,
but has never found strength to come out till a few
weeks ago.   He appears remarkably clear in his experience, and we hope he may be a zealous and useful
preacher of the gospel among his countrymen."

A serious illness, from which he was then recovering,
had led Batiram to his decision, and he maintained it with
courage and consistency.   He summoned his fellow-
workmen and friends to his house, and thus addressed
them :

" For two years I have been convinced that the Hindu
religion is false, and the Christian religion *true;* but
shame and fear have kept me from acknowledging it;
and till I was recently laid aside by sickness, I did not
fully see my sins, and feel my need of pardon.   I think
the Lord Jesus Christ has now had mercy upon me—
has given me light, and a heart to love him.   For the
last two years, I have daily prayed to Him in secret;
and now publicly before you all, declare my disbelief in
Hinduism, and my cordial belief in the blessed truths
of Christianity, and call upon each of you, my brothers
and friends, to think of these things, and pray for yourselves."

On the 9th of March, 1845, he was baptized by the
pastor in the Dikho river.   A large number of his hea-

then acquaintances witnessed the rite. Every effort had been made to prevent his defection from the religion of his fathers, but he had remained firm amidst both reproaches and entreaties.

He addressed his companions at the water-side in the most affecting manner, urging them to forsake their idols, and embrace the religion of the true and living God. After his baptism, he was shunned by all his former acquaintances. His cousin Ramsing, who lived with him, and was also employed as a printer, manifested great hostility, and renounced further connection with him, but was subsequently himself converted.

XXV

SUNLIGHT IN HAUNTED LIVES.

THE pastor's wife received frequent visits from heathen women, usually of the lower castes; to whom
she was an object of mingled curiosity, wonder and reverence. Entering with profuse salams and prostrations,
they would pour forth some piteous complaint, partly
fact and greatly romance, often a tale of domestic misery of a painful description. She waited patiently and
pleasantly, while three senses bore each its separate
annoyance, thus buying her opportunity to give a little
instruction. Their visit over, they would creep up to
stroke her dress, and beg for pice* or paddy.† On
receiving the latter in a fold of the sador or head-cloth, ˙
they rewarded her with the most extravagant compliments, accompanied by prostrations, and kissing of her
dress and feet. The maimed and diseased were no
strangers to her door. Her hands were not too dainty
to dress their sores when necessary, and she was skilled
in preparing and administering remedies.

But the sick and suffering spirit—how should she
reach it? To her efforts to teach them, the poor creatures would often reply :

" It is of no use to talk to us ; our husbands can
understand these things, but we can't learn to read;
we have no souls !"

This cruel doctrine has been impressed upon the low-
caste Assamese woman, until it is really accepted, with
a pitiful acquiescence. She looks forward to a future
life, it is true, but that boon is to be granted her only

---

* A small copper coin.   †Unhulled rice.

through her husband. Her mental and moral faculties are asleep. She is the prey of a cringing fear of evil spirits, having the most implicit belief in their actual appearance. She lives a haunted life. Her ideal of womanhood is the hundred-armed Dúrga or Kali, a coarse, brutal impersonation of destructive material force. The Assamese woman, in her prayers and offerings to this goddess and to the demons, has no better hope than to mollify their malevolence, and avert some threatening evil. Dark thoughts and fierce passions possess her own spirit ; hard work and insufficient food, seasoned sometimes with blows from the husband assigned to her while yet a child, without her acquaintance or consent, are her environment.

Mrs. Brown had pleasant smiles and kindly words for them which raised their self-respect and made life easier to live. By degrees they began to take in the meaning of her teachings ; old women loved to sit at her feet and look at her, and listen while she told them about the Friend of Martha and Mary, of the widow of Nain, and of the woman who was a sinner.

E. B. Oct. 21, '50· "Two of the women, (one a member of the church, the last baptized) finished 'the First Reading Book' to-day ; a great day for Assam ! I do not think the Herculean task of two married women having learned to read, has ever before been accomplished in this province. The women after having grown up in ignorance, are fully impressed with the belief that they cannot learn. Besides, the ridicule to which they are subjected, makes it very difficult to induce them to continue. Our old Brahman pundit often comes along by my little school-room, and laughs at the idea of my spending my time teaching *women* to read."

"The Sahib's house has been asleep for three years," said one of the women visiting the bungalow on its mistress' return from America; "but now the Memsahib has come back it will wake up again." And so it did; the north room being the headquarters of a kind of unchartered Woman's Employment Bureau. Here, almost any day, and at all hours, might be seen seated on the matting, young Christian women, neatly dressed in white, making garments for themselves and their children, which Mrs. Brown had cut out for them, and taught them neatly to stitch together, instructing them in the intervals, as to the bringing up of their little ones, and advising them in improved modes of housekeeping; for all this, in her view, was important missionary work. These young women, till they came to the mission, had never seen a needle, except the coarse bodkin made by a blacksmith, with which their scant garments had hitherto been put together. The affectionate creatures in return looked upon her as their mother, and to their children she was a grandmother; her house was home, resting-place and hospital for any of them as occasion might require; they told her their troubles and received her advice and sympathy. When ill, they sent at once for her; no medicine or food could be quite equal to that which the Memsahib prepared and brought to them with her own hands. She bathed and dressed their infants, watched with and nursed the sick, and laid out the dead. In short, they were her family. On Wednesday afternoons they gathered in her room for a quiet hour or two of prayer. She writes to her sister about these friends of hers, soon after her return:

"I have had much to do, in getting the old house and its musty contents in order for housekeeping, besides much time has been spent in receiving calls and visits from my old friends, the women of the surrounding villages. They come to welcome me back, as their custom is, with some trifling present of rice or fruit, and to express their joy and surprise at my return. . . . But oh, the children! They make doleful lamentations at my having left them behind, and say they don't know how I am to live without them.

Since writing the above, I have had the native Christian women in for a prayer-meeting. . . . Seven praying Assamese women in Sibsagar! All seated around me on mats spread on the floor, dressed in cleanly and becoming attire, consisting of three garments, skirt, jacket and scarf of white muslin thrown over their heads, and caught gracefully under their arms; all able to read the Testament in their own language, and to sing. They prostrate themselves on their hands and faces when they pray—this would be a novel sight to you, but we who live among this people, prefer to see them continue their national customs, unless there is something objectionable in them, to adopting ours."

Mrs. Brown describes the Assamese woman's *mekala* or skirt, as made of two breadths of cotton, or native raw silk, sewed together and hemmed top and bottom. "It is not gathered into a band, but bound straight around the waist, with a deep fold in front." When at work in the house or in the rice fields, this is her only garment. In full dress she wears also the *ria*, a strip of cloth two or three yards long, bound closely about the chest and shoulders, and the *sador*, a broad scarf about the same length as the ria, worn over the head, one end hanging down in front nearly to the feet, the other thrown gracefully over the left shoulder. She is fond of ornaments, and wears a profusion of beads, rings, bracelets, anklets and ear ornaments. The high-caste women wear jewelry of gold, silver, amber and precious stones, while the poor dúmúnis are satisfied

with imitations, in brass, gilt, and glass. "They usually
have a luxuriant growth of hair, which they dress with
cocoanut oil, comb straight back from the forehead and
twist into a large knot behind, often adorning it with
fragrant flowers." The national costume admits of no
change of style; it is the same from generation to
generation.

The full dress of the men consists also of three garments, the *súria*, a strip of cotton cloth "three or four
yards long, one end girdled closely around the body, the
other laid in folds in front, reaching nearly to the feet;"
the *sador* or scarf, which by the men, is "thrown loosely
over the shoulders, crossed in front, and the ends thrown
back over each shoulder," and the *pagori* or turban, a
strip two or three yards long, twisted and bound around
the head. Both men and women go barefoot, except
that wooden sandals are sometimes used out of doors.
"The men pluck their beards, and shave their heads,
except a long tuft some six inches in diameter left
about the crown, and this they twist into a small
knot."

Assamese etiquette requires the guest on entering
the house of a superior, to call out, "Lord, O lord, we
have come," then to make a salam by touching the fingers
of the right hand to the forehead and bowing the head
half way to the ground. After visitors are seated on
the floor, betel-nut is served to them as a mark of hospitality. On leaving, the salam is repeated, and when
outside, the retiring visitor calls out, "*Iswor, O Iswor,
ahirbad dia.*" God, O God, give Thy blessing!

The morning greeting to a friend is "*Bhat kala na ?*"
Have you eaten your rice? Women kiss by joining the
ends of the fingers of the right hand, kissing them, and
waving or throwing the kiss.

No family names are known. Even the given name
is seldom used. The wife is addressed by her husband

as *peio* or *honai,* dearest or golden ; he speaks of her as
the mother of his oldest child, for instance, *Sokú-mak,*
the Sokú-mother. A wife considers it so irreverent to
speak the name of her husband, that it is almost impossible to persuade her to tell what it is. She speaks of

ASSAMESE FISHERWOMAN WITH SCOOP-NET.

him as *Teu,* the honorific pronoun for "he." Whatever his affection for her, she fills a servile place. In
the lower castes, she performs field and other outdoor
labors, waits upon her husband when he eats, and afterwards partakes of what he has left.

Of the mothers' meeting in her own room, Mrs. Brown says :

" I do enjoy these weekly prayer-meetings more than almost anything else, and we have lately established a mothers' meeting. The first Monday evening of every month the concert for prayer is held, so I thought Monday P. M. would be a favorable time for the mothers' meeting, as the sisters would be on hand for the concert. . . . They have entered into it with a great degree of interest. Kúnti's mother also joins us, for her two unconverted children."

This Wednesday prayer-meeting was held weekly almost without interruption as long as she remained in Assam, and afterwards continued by Mrs. Whiting. The seven praying women soon became a score; a number of heathen mothers and grandmothers soon " took to coming ;" and sometimes it would happen that thirty or forty women and girls crowded the bedroom floor on Wednesday afternoons. Doubtless, those were not the least helpful and impressive occasions, when, toward the last of her labors, the pale, wasted Memsahib at times presided over the meeting, lying on her couch.

Meantime Mrs. Brown had gathered to herself little vicious-looking children covered with unclean rags and vermin, washed and clothed them, and day after day with persistent patience and for a long time without apparent success, drilled them in correct principles and habits, facing the revilings of their parents and friends. It was the real " grindstone of missionary work."

On the 9th of December, '49, a large number of natives gathered on the banks of the lower tank, near the printing house. A tent was pitched and outdoor services of singing, prayer and sermon held, after which the pastor baptized Sokú and Púni, the former the wife of Horuram, who was taken away from him by her mother on his conversion. Púni was a young girl, the betrothed of Biposu. Their marriage took place at the bungalow the following March. Seventy or eighty native guests were invited; the large middle room was decorated for the occasion with rose and orange branches, in honor of the young bride and groom, thirteen and nineteen years of age, who were both dressed in white. Mrs. Brown, the day before, had invited all the Christian women up to help make the little bride's wedding-cake, which, after the ceremony, Nidhi and his wife Túkú, served to the native Christians and any others who would partake, all comfortably seated, of course, upon the floor. The surname of Judson was afterwards given to this pair, married about the time that the great missionary died at sea.

A year later is recorded the death of Túkú, at the age of seventeen, leaving a little daughter, Hannah, two years of age.

E. B. "April 2, 1851. Poor Túkú died about ten o'clock this evening, after a suffering illness of nearly a month. I went down and assisted in preparing her remains for the grave. Cut down in the bloom of youth— her husband and his home left desolate! 3. Attended the funeral of Túkú about 11 o'clock this morning. It was distressing to hear the hideous wails set up by the heathen mother and other relatives on the days of her death and burial. It formed a striking contrast with the deep, silent grief manifested by the Christian friends. . . . We have buried her in the little mission burying-ground, by the side of Húbé, the young Naga convert."

Batiram's widowed mother, a strong-minded, intelligent woman, devoted to her son, and indignant at his abandonment of the religion of his fathers, had manifested the most bitter opposition to his profession of Christianity She never afterwards ate with him, but he supported her in a house adjoining his own. They lived in the mission compound of the Whitings, who became much attached to this intelligent young convert, taking him with them as assistant preacher on their missionary tours to Jorhat and the country villages.

In May, 1853, being attacked with what proved to be his last illness, he was carried down to Dikho-múkh by Mr. Whiting for the benefit of the Brahmaputra air, but died while they were on their return. "I am going," said the dying man, "to my father Abraham, to Isaac and Jacob, and the whole family of saints; I am going to dwell with Jesus my Saviour forever and ever." He then turned to his widowed mother, who stood weeping by his side, and most pathetically exhorted her to become a Christian, and meet him in glory.

Mr. Brown was absent in Burma at the time. "Give the Sahib my salam," Batiram had said to Mrs. Brown before going down the river; and while he spoke his face lighted up with a heavenly radiance; "tell him I long to see him again. I had hoped to hear his voice again in our little chapel, but if I never more meet him in this world, I hope to meet and sing praises to my *prio Probhü* [beloved Lord] with him hereafter."

Mrs. Brown to Mrs. Danforth, May 28. "I am just dispatching a line to my dear husband, to give him the sad news of poor Batiram's death. He died on board the boat, at Boliaghat this morning at four o'clock, and his cold remains now lie on a table in our veranda. All are assembled for the funeral, and now there is a little delay about the coffin, which is being made, and lest the others have no time, I grasp a moment to drop you a line. The little church has met with a great loss. . . . Moina, poor child, is a picture of distress, and the wailing of the old mother is enough to break a heart of stone."

Years after, she thus described the scene:

"In the veranda of the mission bungalow, lay the remains of Batiram. The missionaries had constructed for him a rude coffin, and were about to give him a Christian burial in an enclosure near by, which had been set apart as the mission burying-ground.' The news of his death had spread widely around, and a large number of his native acquaintances and friends were gathering about the house with saddened countenances, to witness his burial. Already the little flock of his brethren and sisters, comprising the native church at that station, had assembled, and stood with moistened eyes around his coffin. In the midst of the gathering assembly could be seen an emaciated old woman, whose face gave evidence of a marked and determined character. Attired in soiled and scanty raiment, her whitened locks disheveled, walking to and fro about the grounds, alternately shrieking, howling and beating her breast with her hands, often prostrating herself and beating the earth, calling upon her heathen gods to give back to her her son—she bore all the appearance of a maniac. At length rushing through the crowd into the veranda, and laying her tawny shriveled hand upon his brow, she burst forth with a shrill, unearthly voice, in the most pathetic ejaculatory strains, intermingled with howling and wailing, addressing herself alternately to the departed spirit of her son and to the gods. 'Oh, my son—my beloved, my only one ; my stay and my support! Oh, why have you left me? Whither, oh, whither art thou gone? . . . O ye gods ! where have ye borne him? Why take a poor widow's only son, and leave her without any support? Oh, bring him back to me, or let me go to him!'"

The hour for the service having arrived, Mrs. Brown, in the hope of quieting the old woman without doing violence to her over-excited feelings, stepped out into the veranda, and laying her hand upon her shoulder addressed her in Assamese with the title of respect and affection, "Búri Ai," or Grandmother :

"O Grandmother, your son has gone to be with Jesus, where he is far happier than he ever was in this life. Do you not remember his dying exhortation to you, to forsake your idol worship, and cease to trust in heathen gods, who cannot hear or answer your prayers, and to listen to the words of the missionary teachers, and learn about the true God, Who alone has power to wash away your sins and make you happy after death ? O Grandmother, cease your wailing and moaning, and give your mind to the true religion. Batiram has gone to be with Jesus his Saviour, and with the saints and angels who surround the throne of God. Come to my house to-morrow, and I will teach you what the true shasters say about heaven, the abode of all the good, and where your dear son has gone."

The words, the touch, or the tone must have been soothing to the broken and distracted spirit, for she listened attentively, seemed somewhat subdued, and promised to come and hear more to-morrow. Then wearied with excitement, and faint from long fasting, "she seated herself among the weeping converts, remained quiet during the funeral services, and followed with the assembly the remains of her dear son, to witness the interment."

Still the mother-heart was sore from its terrible anguish and questionings. Where was the spirit of that son ? He had died an apostate from the faith of his ancestors. "*I hate your God,*" she said to Mrs. Whiting, later, when visiting her.

Mrs. Brown describes in a letter to a friend, another scene, to which she was witness, some months after :

"Batiram's mother knelt down and prayed in our little woman's meeting this afternoon. It was the first time she ever prayed before any *human* being. It was a hard struggle for her, and I cannot but hope it was the turning-point in her conversion. A few weeks ago, she appeared in a most bitter, unreconciled state of mind. One day when she came to see me, I asked her if she prayed. "Prayed!" said she, "what is there for me to pray for? I get nothing but *dŭkh* (trouble) here; the Lord has taken away my son, my beloved son who had promised to take care of me in my old age, and if I pray for anything, it is that He will take me too." Her prayer to-day was simple and childlike, like that of a new beginner, using the singular instead of the plural pronoun. "The Lord has taken my own dear son—the will of the Lord be done. Have mercy upon me, a poor sinner, and fit me to join him in heaven. Have mercy upon my step-son and two daughters, who are in total darkness, and bring them to the light and knowledge of the gospel." Here she stopped to weep, and I believe nearly all in the room were affected to tears."

She was soon after baptized; Batiram's last prayer was answered.

XXVI

WHENEVER it was practicable to leave the Sibsa-gar work, Mr. Brown was off on preaching tours to the villages. In January, 1850, he accompanied Mr. Hesselmeyer, a young Lutheran missionary then recently stationed at Dibrugur, on a tour into the Jorhat district. A tent, elephants, and a large number of coolies relieved the difficulties of travel on this trip. The next cold season he and Mr. Stoddard went out together.

In February Mr. and Mrs. Brown and Nidhi Levi went by boat to Tezpúr, and thence on Mr. Bruce's elephant to Nowgong, accompanied by Mr. Daüblé on horseback. Their course lay through grass jungle, in some places higher than their heads when sitting on the back of the elephant, and showing many paths trampled by wild beasts. Natives who had attempted to settle here, it was said, were compelled to leave on account of the depredations of tigers, who carried off their cattle, and in some cases, children. Coming to a deep, narrow river, they found a broken canoe, half filled with water, and one man in attendance. They ventured over, one at a time. The elephant was unharnessed and his trappings put into the canoe, then with his keeper on his neck, he started to swim across, but repeatedly turned about, paying no respect to the punches of the iron spike. At length some one discovered that the cause of his fear was the pony on the opposite bank. The cautious pachyderm looked with suspicious eyes on this unfamiliar creature, and a tremor thrilled through the huge frame. Perhaps in the wild jungle life of his youth, his hide had shivered under the claws of a tiger, and he may have suspected the pony to be a beast of the same species; at all events, he declined closer acquaintance, but when the horse was removed to a distance, swam over without reluctance. A company of sepoys required the services of the ferryman, before the coolies had crossed with the baggage, and as it was growing late, the travelers left them on the further side and proceeded along the high broad bund, to Nowgong; Mr. Brown and Nidhi walking the rest of the way, while pony and rider galloped on out of sight, greatly to the relief of the elephant, who, towards evening, made no objections to fording the Kullung, with Mrs. Brown and two native women on his back.

A fortnight was spent in Nowgong and vicinity, and afterwards Mr. and Mrs. Brown visited the high priests of Assam at their homes on the Majúli. This large island contained three priestly establishments or hostros, each having a population of some four or five hundred monks and a large number of bhokots or hereditary dependents, who with their families lived near the monasteries. The high priests or gosains of these establishments were distinguished respectively by the titles of Auniati, Komola Bari, and Dokimpat.

Stopping the boat nearly opposite the Auniati Gosain's village, the travelers crossed a mile or two of sand bank on foot, and were carried in the boatmen's arms across two small streams, reaching then a road, densely shaded with large old mango, jack and plantain trees. A mile more brought them to a spacious, rather dilapidated namghor or worship-house, surrounded by a covered brick platform. On ascending the steps and walking around the platform, they were joined by several Brahmans from within, who obligingly allowed them to look in at the doors and windows, but could not permit them to defile the sacred apartments by stepping over the

threshold. One of the rooms was a theater. On the
stage were the usual adjuncts of an Assamese play-
house, consisting of grotesque gigantic masks, some
of which represented deities, and hollow images of
an elephant, horse, lion and other beasts, to be entered and manipulated by the actors. Among the
musical instruments were huge drums and cymbals.
Other apartments contained images ; one idol peculiarly
sacred, was in a darkened room, into which it was a
matter of considerable doubt whether the foreigners
could be permitted to look at all. At length, however, a narrow crack was made in the door, through
which the form of the sacred object, veiled with a
red cloth, was dimly visible by the light of a taper
which was kept burning night and day. It stood upon
a throne of carved wood, daubed with gaudy paints,
and which rested upon a mound of earth ; and beside it was a brass vessel with a ladle, containing a
milky fluid. Within the shrine a taper was kept burning night and day. Mrs. Brown describes two large
semi-human figures in another room seated on pedestals, as having outspread wings, and beaks, as of
birds.

The news of the arrival of foreign visitors having
spread through the village, a crowd of men, women
and children surrounded the veranda, particularly anxious to see the " Beebee Sahib" or white lady, the
first specimen of that curiosity ever brought to the
island. One courteous old Brahman with a silver-
headed cane, ordered chairs, but the establishment
afforded only one, whose dust and cobwebs showed
its infrequent use. Mr. Brown and Nidhi now commenced conversation on the Christian religion, but met
with no encouragement. Even a copy of the gospels
was refused. The interview was soon interrupted by
an invitation to visit the Auniati's representative—he

himself being absent on a visit to Gauhati. On his veranda, a few rods distant, the sacred personage was seated upon one of the royal mats, dressed in pure white, and surrounded by numerous *kawolias* or monks. He received his visitors with a slight salam, and ordered sweetmeats and flowers for them. While the missionary entered into religious conversation with the high priest, Nidhi became engaged in an animated discussion with the attendant monks. On their way back to the boats, they saw many devotees lying on the damp ground, where they had sunk exhausted under heavy loads of rice and other offerings brought from their homes to the shrines. Under a shed was the Auniati's sacred boat, ninety feet long, kept guarded from profane touch. Rows of tired pilgrims lay sleeping along either side of this sacred object.

The next day the missionary boat stopped at the ghaut leading to the monastery of the Dokimpat Gosain, who was believed to be a divine being, and approached by his worshippers only with prostrations. Finding this august person busy with baggage and accounts, having just landed from a trip to Sibsagar, Mr. and Mrs. Brown, after a brief visit during which they were treated with great civility, proceeded to the monastic establishment. Here the old priests, prostrate on the ground chanting prayers, were too devout to take any notice of the white foreigners, but a swarm of young Brahmans gathered about them, and took them to a shrine containing some remarkable images, which Mrs. Brown, being allowed to examine from a respectful distance, thus describes:

"The images here were of the full size of men, and superior in quality to any we had ever seen in India. They were made of finely wrought brazen metal, some overlaid with gold, some with silver, and arranged in rows, standing enshrined in separate recesses of wood frame-work.   Placed before them were various offerings of flowers and food.   On inquiry I was told that the food offered to the gods to-day, is removed and eaten by the Brahmans and priests to-morrow, and the flowers used to adorn their hair ; the perfume of the offerings serving for the food of the gods.   In one corner of the room I saw a platform surrounded with curtains, which I was told was the place where they put their gods to sleep at night.   After the door was closed, our dear brother Nidhi, who is ready upon every opportunity to defend the faith, commenced preaching.   He was often interrupted by contradictions and remarks, but his patience is unbounded.   While carrying on the discussion I noticed his countenance seemed to kindle with a brightness as of Moses on the mount."

Leaving the monastic enclosure, they were encircled by a crowd of bhokots,—men, women and children—to whom Nidhi preached from under the shade of a wide-branching tree.

" Many listened very attentively, and some took our books.   On our return to the boat, Mr. Brown and Nidhi again called upon the Dokinpat and his people, and preached to them for half an hour.   They made no attempt to dispute, and behaved very civilly, except that the disciples, who were themselves kneeling, ordered Nidhi to kneel also, telling him it was not respectful for him to stand in the presence of so great a personage.

The gosain very politely sent on presents of rice, *dhail* (a kind of split peas), milk and sugar for ourselves and the boat people, according to the etiquette of the country."

As the travelers were making good headway up the Dikho two days later, all the men except the manji being on shore towing, Mr. Brown's writing was interrupted by a singular phenomenon. One end of the chest which served him for a table, began slowly to lift itself up, without apparent cause or provocation. What could it mean? Surely the table-tipping spirits just now reported so active in America, had not invaded old slow-going Assam! A splash of water about his feet, and a dangerous gurgling sound under the mat, left no time for speculation, and a very material cause was not far to seek. The boat, moving rather rapidly against the current, with a sleepy captain at the helm, had struck a sunken tree, which stove a hole through the bottom, an accident not uncommon on Assamese rivers.

E. B. "The water came rushing in at a fearful rate. Mr. Brown tore up the bamboo floor and commenced bailing with all his might, till the boatmen swam to his relief. 'We were in deep water, and had great cause for fear that the boat would fill and go down before we could get her to the shore.'"

N. B. "The boat remained fixed on the snag, which prevented its sinking. The water was very deep, and although we were near the shore, we had no means of reaching it, till at length we succeeded in swinging the boat round until the front end nearly touched the bank. Mrs. Brown was thus enabled to jump ashore, after which I succeeded in getting out our boxes, clothes and books, most of which were thoroughly saturated. Just at this time a small boat came up, into which we loaded the goods and conveyed them ashore."

It was now nearly night, a storm was approaching and the boat was a wreck. Mr. Brown hastened on afoot towards a neighboring village. For fear of breaking caste the villagers could not admit the boat-wrecked travelers to their dwellings, but he found anu took possession of a small open shed which had been used either as a stall for cattle, or a market place. Here the wet blankets were hung up to keep off the wind and rain, the drenched books and clothing were opened and spread out, and a bed made upon the ground. The boatmen kindleJ a fire outside, and after a cup of tea and a dish of boiled rice, Mrs. Brown lay down to sleep, " thankful for even so comfortable a shelter as this from the approaching storm." Rain began to come down at midnight ; the next day she writes :

" Nathan sent me on in this canoe with a part of the baggage, as soon as the rain held up, and was to follow himself with the rest when he could procure another canoe. . . . At sunset met Capt. Brodie's *bolio*, come down for our accommodation. I was very glad to exchange the little canoe in which I had been so cramped all the afternoon, for this nice, commodious boat. . . . About 9 o'clock one of the men cried out to my surprise, " *Sahib ahil !* " [The Sahib has come], and in a few minutes I had the pleasure of welcoming my dear husband on board, much fatigued, and up to the knees in mire, having walked some ten or twelve miles after sundown—no road but a footpath which was full of mud from the heavy rain we had the night before.

Saturday, 16. Met with a warm reception from all the dear native disciples. We reached our own home in season to get a little settled before the Sabbath."

XXVII

A FAMILY SCHOOL.

A MUSSULMAN beggar with two children clinging to his neck, appeared at Mrs. Brown's door one day in January, 1850. The man was feeble ; the children's mother, he said, had been devoured by a tiger; and, prostrating himself on the ground, he begged that the younger one might be taken and adopted by the missionaries, as the only alternative from starvation. The hungry, bright-eyed little creature, three years old, was taken in, and became the nucleus of a small family school.

On her return to India, six months before, Mrs. Brown had resolved to adopt a few little Assamese girls as her own, that she might give them the nurture which children have in Christian families at home. "These girls," she said, "I shall hope to train up, by the blessing of God, to know and love the Saviour, and hope that they will become the wives of native Christians, and the most promising, of native preachers, and that they may live to do good to their fellow-countrymen long after I am gone."

In order to carry out this plan, it was necessary to receive from parents or guardians a written agreement, giving the children absolutely to her, and containing the important provision that she should select their husbands and give them in marriage. They were to be under her constant oversight, and to regard her as their mother, receiving from her not instruction only, but their clothing and food, some to be boarded in native Christian families within the compound, and some in her own house. This necessitated their becoming outcasts; to secure children on such terms was not easy, and her efforts to obtain them had been for six months entirely unsuccessful.

Hence a place and welcome were already waiting for the little waif, brought in this unexpected manner to her arms.

Jan. 11. "In the afternoon the father of Akesúri came, and the pundit drew up the.agreement for his giving her to· me. It was signed by seven witnesses, and I paid him three rupees for bukshish; then the father and all the witnesses went through the ceremony of eating tamúl * together, to seal the agreement."

At daylight one morning, a few months later, a slave-girl escaping from her master, a native chief, came to the bungalow and cast herself on Mrs. Brown's protection. The Fugitive Slave Law anent such cases, not reaching thus far, she was taken care of, and soon after married to the gardener. She became a day-pupil, and was baptized the next year.

In August, another Mussulman girl, six years old, whose father was in prison at Dibrugur for theft, was brought and given to Mrs. Brown with a written agreement by the mother, who was on the way home to her father, a sepoy at Gauhati. She left her daughter without showing any regret or affection. "I look upon the dear little child," writes Mrs. Brown, "as another gift from the Lord. Oh, may she be early converted to him, and spared for usefulness." The father, on his release came and demanded the child. "We all betook ourselves to prayer that the Lord would incline the heart of the father to leave her. He com-

---

* The *tamúl* or betel-nut, is chewed with a spicy and astringent leaf, lime and tobacco, which stain the teeth and lips red.

menced a lawsuit. ... The thought of parting with her produced a great excitement in the school, as her amiable disposition had won the hearts of all." The next day the father came, consented to leave her for ten rupees and signed the writing. "Oh, the Lord has been gracious in sparing the sweet, curly-haired, bright-eyed little Koromsani to us."

Mrs. Brown tells the story of another of her adopted family, the child of a Bengali sepoy:

"The mother was the daughter of a learned Brahman at Jorhat, one of the most distinguished pundits in the country. Having been left a young widow, with this her only child, she took another husband, contrary to the laws of Hinduism, which allow no second marriages. By this act she incensed her father and other relations, and was driven from their doors an outcast. She came with her husband to Sibsagar, still having high aspirations for her daughter, and seeing the elevated position of the native Christian women here, she was induced to give up her child to be educated in the school.

Mrs. Brown had only thought, at first, of taking six children, but the number gradually swelled to fifteen, including two or three day-scholars. In reference to the expense of maintaining this increasing family, though there was but small visible means of doing so, she says, January 20, 1851, when she had seven; "My faith fails not; my Father in Heaven, Who by His good providence gave them to me, is rich, and I do not think He will withhold the necessary support."

They were of several castes and nationalities; Mohammedan, Hindu. Doom, Brahman and Eurasian. The school was carried on by Mrs. Brown herself, with occasional assistance from the pundit, who gave the children

lessons in writing and arithmetic when he was not otherwise employed, though looking upon the whole project
with incredulity. Teaching boys was all very well, but
girls! These insignificant *sualis*—what could the Mem
expect to make of *them?*

Mrs. Brown, however, saw gleams of a soul in the
bright black eyes of little Akesúri, Koromsani and
the others, and she meant to reach it. She found, especially with the older ones, many accumulated obstruc-
tions to be cleared away from the stifled faculties. She
often felt the delight of a miner, whose eye, trained to
darkness, catches an occasional sparkle in a pile of ore.
She found not only mind and affection, but conscience
in these girls. Her work grew upon her. Married
women, coming to visit, staid to learn, taking their
places among the children; some of them attending
school regularly.

And a strange sound came to her ear through the
school-room door one morning while she was writing a
line to Mrs. Danforth in the adjoining room; and, after
listening a moment, she writes: "Hark! what do I
hear? As sure as you are alive it is the voice of our old
Brahman pundit singing *hymns* with the school-girls!
It is not the first time I have heard him. Poor old man!
He appears to love these hymns." No wonder the
weary heart of the old Brahman, starving on husks of
pompous fable, found refreshment in singing those simple
Christian songs. Like the heart of a little child, it
opened to receive the truth thus presented. He caught
a gleam of soft celestial light clearer than any he had
found in Vedic hymn or Dharmashastra, and, like the
ancient Magi, bowed down and worshipped. It was
noticed that he sometimes stole away from the study
into the school-room, and knelt or bowed his head when
the children were at prayer. He had serious talks with
Mr. Brown about the wondrous Eastern story which he

was helping him put into Assamese; the divinely simple words sank deep into the refined, sensitive, unsatisfied spirit.

N. B. "Since becoming acquainted with our Scriptures, he declares his belief in them, and often weeps while reading particular portions of the New Testament, but says he cannot give up the religion of his fathers, forsake his relatives and acquaintances, and be without a friend to visit him in sickness or bury him when he dies."

A curious little relic of him remains in the shape of a letter to one of the children in America, quaint with the courtly grandiloquence of the days of the rajas, in which he had been brought up.

"Your family pundit, the old Brahman Takúr, sends his innumerable loving compliments. I have been in your family service since you and your most excellent little brother learned your A B C's. I was here when the most noble Memsahib took her journey to America with you, her children. Only myself and the Sahib remained. Since the return of the most excellent lady, she has formed a school of young girls, and now that there are ten, the house has again become a little cheerful. The Sahib has taken up a hundred púras [acres] of land, and is getting people to cultivate it. In the month of May he had a portion of it sowed with paddy, and another portion has been planted with fruit trees.

But the greatest and best thing we have here is the little church of Christian men and women, who meet together to worship God. The women meet at our bungalow every Wednesday, two o'clock, with the Memsahib, and remain with her till five, praying and singing praises to God.

When I hear good news from you and the Willie Baba, my mind is always filled with joy, and I send you, with my best compliments, this little chit, that you may continue to remember me.   Finis.   English date 13 June. [1852].

Sri Sridor Hormar Pundit,

TAKÚR."

A year later the pundit died of cholera, during Mr. Brown's absence in Moulmein.

E. B. "The poor old man gave us much reason to believe that he had embraced the Christian religion, but secretly, for fear of his associate priests.   Hearing of his illness, I sent one of the native Christians to learn how he was, and to offer my services, if I could be of any use.   On the first visit, he found him surrounded by priests who were making offerings to the gods for his restoration, and had no opportunity to speak to him.   The next day he went again and found him dying.   He had been stripped by the priests of his warm blanket, and everything valuable ; carried to an out-house, and left alone to die.   On hearing my message, and inquiring whether there was anything he wished me to do for him, he aroused himself and said with great energy : 'Tell the Memsahib to furnish the wood for the burning of my body when I am dead.   Unless she does so, I shall not have a decent funeral ; the priests are so penurious that they will not furnish the wood.'   [This request was complied with.   The pundit soon after expired, and on the following day his body was burned.]   Poor old man, I feel as if one of the family had gone !   We sent men and medicines, and did all we could for him in a native's house, but to no purpose.   Mr. Bronson went to see him twice."

The sound of hymns and prayer continued to be heard in the missionary bungalow and compound. "As soon as these little girls began to read the Scriptures," is the pastor's testimony, "they began to pray. For the last five years of my stay in Assam, I was awaked nearly every morning by the sound of their voices singing and praying in various parts of the house. Oh, it was sweet to witness these buds of promise, starting forth in the wide wilderness of heathenism."

The three oldest girls, Búdhi, Jogóri and Kúnti, (pronounced Boody, Jogóri, Koonty,) were baptized by Mr. Brown on the morning of July 6, 1851, and "after the baptism," he writes, "we met around the communion table, and had the pleasure of receiving into our little church, our dear friends, Mr. and Mrs. Whiting."

E. B. "The circumstances of the conversion of these girls, so recently gathered in from heathenism, were deeply interesting. About the commencement of the year Búdhi and Jogóri appeared to be seriously affected with a sense of their sins. Their distress of mind increased for some days, till eventually they expressed a hope that their prayers had been heard, and their sins forgiven. Their hearts were then filled with joy, and their greatest delight was in singing hymns of praise to . their newly-found Saviour. From this time a number of the others were aroused from their former indifference, and commenced pleading earnestly for the Saviour's mercy. Whenever the exercises of the school were suspended for a short time, they would seek some retired corner to pray, and would often ask leave to hold a little prayer-meeting by themselves. At all hours of the day, might be heard the low voice of prayer, or songs of praise. Thus for some weeks our house was literally made 'a house of prayer' by these newly-converted heathen girls. Even the little ones from four to six years old, appeared to catch the spirit, and we cannot suppress the hope that amongst them will be some genuine fruit that shall ripen for the great harvest."

Kúnti, now thirteen years of age, was the daughter of a prominent Brahman, and the first of that caste baptized in Assam. Her mother, being now a widow, and reduced to extreme poverty, though strongly prejudiced against Christianity, had been induced for the sake of a support to betroth her daughter to Ramsing, the cousin of Batiram, who was now a professed Christian, and to allow her to be placed in the school for instruction.

No sooner did this little girl comprehend the story of the Redeemer's life and death, as it fell from Mrs. Brown's lips, than her heart was touched with a sense of her own sinfulness and need of such a Saviour. During a severe illness, she confessed an intelligent faith in Jesus Christ, and allegiance to Him, expressing a confidence that if she should die, she would go to be with Christ and the holy angels ; urging her school-mates to seek the same salvation, and dictating a pathetic letter to her mother, at that time too feeble to visit her child, in which she exhorted her to renounce idolatry and embrace the true religion.

Kúnti recovered, to confirm her vows by a public profession, meeting, strange to say, no objection from her mother, who even "rose from her sick bed, and with the assistance of her little son, walked with tremulous steps some distance to the water." A year later the little girl's heart's desire for her mother was fulfilled. This proud-spirited Brahman widow took her place as a pupil among the children in the school, learned to read the Bible, and ultimately renounced heathenism. "It is wonderful," Mrs. Brown writes, "how fast she has gained spiritual knowledge since she gave up all hold on caste, sat down and ate with the Christians, knelt with us and prayed, and disclosed all the struggles she had in her mind."

In the meantime, another pupil, a little girl of the lowest or fisher caste, was reaching up for crumbs of the same life-giving truth. On the first Sunday in June, 1852, the gathering villagers witnessed a marvelous spectacle. The Brahman widow and the little Doom girl were led together into the baptismal waters, which washed away the ancestral barriers, and made them kindred in Christ, ready to partake of the same loaf and drink from the same sacramental cup. No one but a Hindu can realize what all this meant.

"I wish you could have been here," Mrs. Brown wrote to her daughter, "to see the proud Bamúni with the lowly Dúmúni—the highest and the lowest—both clothed with the same spirit of humility, go into the water together, and become of one caste!"

This little girl was greatly beloved by her teacher, and was afterwards married to one of the Nowgong Christian lads.

"Will the Memsahib read, and send this to my mother?" she asked, one day, handing a folded paper to Mrs. Brown. It proved to be a letter, which she had written of her own accord. Translated into English, it read as follows:

"Mother, if you have any wish to hear the word of God, please come to me sometimes, and I will make it known to you. I entreat you to pray always to the Lord Jesus, for the forgiveness of your sins. My beloved mother, if you will believe the Lord sincerely, and take refuge only in Him, then you will find happiness to your soul, and in the world to come, life everlasting. I pray you, do not delay any longer! Think not, mother, that in coming here, I have forgotten *you.* I love you as tenderly as ever, and pray for you always. And do not think this separation makes me unhappy. Our dear teacher loves us very much, and I feel always happy with her. Whatever I find, I find all good for me. And to my dear brother say that I have not forgotten him. Say to him for me, 'My dear brother, renounce your idolatry at once, and embrace our Lord. Pray only to Him for the salvation of your soul.'

Will my very dear mother please accept this bag which I have made for you, and keep it always in remembrance of

Your loving daughter."

This mother and brother were both converted. The latter was baptized by Dr. Peck in January, 1854.

On the occasion of Kúnti's marriage, the pastor's house was gay with greenery and flowers.

E. B. "On Christmas-day, our dear Kúnti Caroline Simons was married to Ramsing and moved to her new home. Biposú's house has been built over for them and makes them a very neat, comfortable place. Kúnti leaves a large vacancy in my school. I miss her more than I can tell. . . . Our house was filled—about a hundred guests in all. We had bushes and flowers hung up all around the hall, and after the ceremony, cake and oranges passed around to all who would partake. Kúnti behaved with perfect propriety, and very prettily she looked. She is a most lovely girl; I hope and pray she may be happy and useful at her new home."

The little bride still found her way daily to her beloved school, and continued to develop in intelligence and piety. The following is a part of one of her letters to Mrs. Brown's daughter, translated from the Assamese. It was written in October, 1852:

"This is the month for the Dúrga Púja [Doorga Pooja]. I will describe it to you. In this country the people make many idols which they worship on different occasions. On this occasion, they worship the goddess Gobani. This goddess has ten arms and hands; the images are made of straw plastered over with mud, anointed with oil, and painted to represent the human form, and then people buy them of the image-makers for worship. This goddess has a great many names—a thousand, I believe—Dúrga and Gobani, are the principal, and the worship is called *puja*. The púja is made by killing animals, such as buffaloes, goats, ducks and pigeons; the blood and some of the cooked meat is set before the images, which are fed by the odor. Then the assembled multitude prostrate themselves before the images and pray for the blessing and protection of the gods; and so deluded are the people as to think that their dumb idols have power to kill or keep them alive. Parents take their little children with them and teach them to worship in this way. This púja is the one they are now celebrating here, and we hear day and night, from every direction, the sound of drums, fifes, tomtoms and other heathen music, and all the people are rushing to the pújas as if they were mad. And oh, my dear L——, I was once so foolish as to go to these pújas and worship with them, with all my heart. I took great delight in the heathen worship, and verily thought them the true gods, and that they had power to save me from every evil, till since I came to your dear mamma for instruction. I have now learned that the heathen

religion is all false, that there is but one living and true
God, and but one way of salvation, through Jesus Christ
His Son.   I have now no desire to go to these heathen
celebrations, the sound of them even at a distance is
very painful to me.   Pray for me dear L——, and for
my little brother who is still a heathen.   My dear mother
was baptized in June last.   She sends her loving salam
to you, and all the school-girls join in sending their best
salams.

    · Your Christian sister,

              KUNTI CAROLINE SIMONS."

In place of the heathen pújas Mrs. Brown provided
entertainment for the native Christians in ·little home
treats, and joined them in an occasional picnic.

To daughter, January 1851 :—"I wish you could have
been here at our New Year's picnic, I think you would
have enjoyed it.   Dr. Long, Mrs. Thornton and her sister, ourselves and the native Christians formed a party
and went over the other side of the river, to visit Rungpúr, the former capital of Assam, where still remain the
old palace, theatre, treasury, two temples and other
smaller buildings of the king.   Although it is only three
or four miles distant from where we live, yet it has been
so long deserted that it is overgrown with high grass,
and bush jungle—over our heads on the elephants—which
is the haunt of wild beasts.   Some of our party saw a
tiger sunning himself on the roof of the piazza of the
king's treasury, and in one of the dark rooms of the old
palace we found the bones of a buffalo.   The palace is
an immense building, two or three-stories high, with
many rooms or dungeons underground, where the king
kept and *imprisoned* his numerous wives !   One of the
temples at Rungpúr, is said to be the largest and most
expensive one in the province.   It is built of stone

carved with images, which represent the Hindu gods and goddesses. There is a tank near it almost as large as the Sibsagar tank, but no wild geese resort to it. On our return, we stopped at the Rung-ghor or Raja's theatre, a fine large airy building, where we spread our picnic table of sandwiches, oranges, biscuits, cakes, etc., distributing a part to our native friends, which they appeared to enjoy right well. When this was over, they sang a few Assamese hymns. The echo of the sacred songs from the walls of this old building once devoted to idolatry, and by voices which but a few years ago were devoted to idol-worship, was very cheering and delightful. Oh, may the time be hastened on, when all the heathen shall turn to the Lord, and all heathen temples be devoted to His praise."

On their return, the native Christians and their friends were invited to Batiram's house to a dinner, provided by Mrs. Thornton and Mrs. Brown, the day's festivities thus closing with what we might call a "church sociable." Thus Christian families and a Christian social life had been established. Mrs. Brown endeavored to correct the custom of child-marriage, retaining her own pupils not previously betrothed, to the age of fourteen or fifteen—as great an innovation as could at first be brought about. The girls were trained in household labor, and taught how to make home pleasant. Those who could not be accommodated in the bungalow, were boarded in Christian families in the compound, an arrangement which was found very beneficial to the young married women who took them, and thus felt a share of the responsibility of training the children, and brought into constant action "the principles of forbearance, kindness and self-denial, the result of which, it is hoped, will be the establishing and ripening of their Christian characters."

Mrs. Brown considered the details of neatness, order
and economy an important part of a Christian education.   The girls dressed becomingly in native style, nor
did they find themselves led into any violent or painful
change from their national customs or manners.   They
were still allowed to sit on the floor at their books, or
work or meals ; they still ate deftly with their fingers ;
made their accustomed salams, and otherwise comported
themselves in the same manner as other well-bred Assamese were taught to do.

Those who lived in the bungalow took care of the
school-room, prepared work for the others, and for
amusement, had their own little flower-beds in the garden.   Mending and making their own clothing, learning
cross-stitch and embroidering samplers on canvas with
the pretty wools and floss given them by the second
Mrs. Hannay, were other employments.

Missionaries' letters are usually written at odd minutes, often when the tired brain ought to be at rest.   In
such a letter written late one evening, Mrs. Brown
gives a friend an account of the day's experience, "for
want," she says, "of something more interesting." This
had happened to be one of the long rainy days of an
Assam June.   A hot moisture, provocative of mold,
insects and slimy creatures, pervaded the bungalow, and
permeated every porous substance.   Far from well, the
worker "rose late ;" her day began with the usual eight
o'clock Assamese worship in the large middle room, at
which the school and servants assembled.   Then comes
a hasty message ; one of the Christian women is sick;
wants the Memsahib.   Breakfast ; directions and materials hastily given for dinner ; dirjee's day's work
quickly prepared ; school promptly assembled and put
in charge of oldest monitress, with injunctions to be
good children ; then off, on her sure-footed little Brahma pony, under pouring rain across fields and ditches,

to visit her patient. After she is made comfortable, pony carries his mistress on to the Whitings'—to take "tiffin with these dear good people." On reaching home, she finds the dawk has arrived, with a daguereo-type of her "baby" in America, and "lots of letters to read, which I had hardly time to hurry through, and dinner too, which was waiting, before time for our Wednesday female prayer-meeting. Notwithstand-ing the mud, we had a full attendance of natives, and a very good meeting, which held till almost dark."

After Mrs. Brown moved with her school from the tank down to the river, a messenger arrived one day to an-nounce the coming of a visitor of rank. Some days later the curiosity of the children was gratified by see-ing a boat, fitted up with unusual elegance, touch at the landing, and an Assamese lady dressed in silk and real jewels come up the veranda steps, assisted by obsequi-ous attendants. She was the daughter of an ex-raja and wife of a chief gohain, maintaining—as far as practica-ble in those degenerate days when rajas were no more, and the foreigner infested the land—the rank and state of a native princess. She had heard of the wonders of the white woman's house, and came on a tour of investi-gation; possibly a faint hope that she might find some-thing to brighten a dreary existence entered her mind. Secluded as she had been, all her life, within monoto-nous surroundings, and weary, perhaps, of the barriers of rank which kept her from knowledge of the great world outside, she had made up her mind to take one step, at least, into wonderland.

Mrs. Brown found her intelligent, gentle and receptive. Everything surprised and interested her—dress, furni-ture, mirrors, watch—above all, the beautiful books! The visit was an exceedingly pleasant one, and when the princess returned to her boat, it was to carry home thoughts that would throw at least some light into a shadowy life.

Mrs. Brown passed the summer of '52 in much suffering and apprehension of a speedy breakdown.

She says, July 4th : "My health appears to me to be a wreck. . . . I pray that I may be resigned to the Lord's will. If He has anything more for me to do in this heathen land, He can restore my health and prolong my life and give me cheerfulness in His service. I see nothing in the world worth living for except the up-building of Christ's kingdom. My soul is in raptures at thoughts of that.

' To work for God and man, thyself forgetting,
    Be this thy life—thy life is heaven on earth.' "

About this time she read the memoir of Mary Lyon. "The contemplation of her character has made me feel such stirring of soul that I want to begin anew like a child, and live my life over again." She hopes she may "at least have the privilege of shaking hands with her and others of her spirit in heaven," and notes the characteristic and appropriate inscription of Miss Lyons' own words on her monument : " *There is nothing in the universe that I fear but that I shall not know all my duty, or shall fail to do it.*"

In 1850–51, Mrs. Brown had found time to prepare for the Assamese children a series of twelve brief illustrated narratives, chiefly translations from English and Bengali, with some additional original matter of her own. Among them were, " Old Saul, the Praying African," " The Warrior Chief Converted," " Happy Death of Bajon," " The Orphan Girl," " The Eagle's Nest, or A Mother's Love," and a " Memoir of Húbe," the little Naga boy. She was fully repaid for the labor bestowed on these little story-books when they came from the press and a copy was presented to each of her delighted pupils. They were so dainty and small, type so clear, after a child's own heart; they were the first story-books ever made *on purpose* for young Assam—and moreover they were *true* stories ! When the news spread, the house was thronged with eager faces of heathen children from the neighborhood, crowding in to beg of the Memsahib that they, too, might have one of the beautiful little books.

E. B. "The two little girls so small that they could not read them, carried theirs about, kissing and caressing them as children in America do their dolls, while the older ones searched theirs through and through, looking at the pictures, and the different colored paper in which they were bound, each contending that she had the prettiest, till having satisfied themselves on those points, they commenced reading them aloud, one to another, commenting largely, and disputing upon the meaning of what they read, often referring the question to me. The reading continued after candle-light, till it was time to assemble for our Saturday evening prayer meeting. ᵣOh, that these little memoirs of pious children and others, may prove a lasting blessing to the dear children of Assam !"

The prejudices of heathen parents and relatives against giving up their girls, began to melt away, and it was not long before both Mrs. Brown and Mrs. Whiting had as many under training as they could take care of. Before she left Mrs. Brown had numerous applications from the higher castes, which she was obliged to refuse.

May 3, '54. "The widow of a Brahman came a few days ago with a beautiful girl eight or nine years old,

and cried to have me take her. . . . I told her that
if life was spared till the cold season I would try to make
a place for her, if she would bring her then."

It was perhaps among the girls of the more neglected
castes, that the strengthening and beautifying power of
Christianity was most plainly shown. Búdhi Lizzie was
one of these. She was a Hindu girl, born in Sudiya
about the time of the massacre, and given to Mrs. Brown
at Sibsagar by her relatives when she was in her twelfth
year. The little untrained creature had a passionate and
wilful temper which cost her teacher and herself much
anxiety and trouble. On this soil the blossoms of heavenly planting showed the fairer. After her conversion
she too became a worker, and her brief life bore sound
fruits of patience and courage. She wrote in Assamese
to the American baba, of whom Mrs. Brown had told her,
"I have my old grandmother and aunt, who are not
Christians, therefore I beseech you do pray for them,
that they may also become Christ's disciples. Pray,
dear Baba, that I may walk in His path, and obey His
command in all the days of my life, and that I may do
something to help your mother in her small school."

Búdhi was betrothed when about fifteen, to Peter
Boardman, one of the Assamese workmen in the printing office, formerly a pupil of Mr. Barker in Gauhati.
A year later she and her school companion Húbhodro,
were married at the bungalow on the same day, the
latter to one of the Nowgong lads, on which occasion
Mrs. Brown opened the bungalow for another wedding
feast.

To daughter. "It was very hard for me to give away
Búdhi. She had been with me nearly four years, and
we are much attached to her, and her assistance in the
school I miss greatly. She lives in the compound,

within call from my bed-room window and will board two or three of the school girls. Although they had corresponded for more than a year, she had never spoken to her lover previous to their marriage. This, however, I did not know till a few days before they were married, or I should have managed to have that heathenish custom broken. The other couple were old friends, and had had frequent interviews."

Peter was converted and baptized after his marriage, and later, when he went into government employ at Dibrúgur, Búdhi with many regrets, left her little Sibsagar house, fitted up with comforts and kept in order and neatness, as her dear "Brown Memsahib" had taught her, for a cheerless home among strangers. Mrs. Whiting, under whose care all the women and girls came after Mrs. Brown left, kindly furnishes the facts of Búdhi's subsequent history.

At first she was treated with suspicion and then with abuse, by her heathen neighbors at Dibrú, who called her "*that Christian dog,*" and persecuted her by every expression of coarse contempt, but she lived out her faith with such consistency and meekness, as to be a real missionary in the neighborhood. She had no heart to unpack her box and take out the pretty trinkets so associated with happier days, but she could and did read over her precious books, and her voice was heard at evening from the dreary uncomfortable hut, singing the sweet old Sibsagar hymns. When Mr. and Mrs. Whiting came to Dibrú on a brief trip, and were the guests of Colonel ——, Peter's employer, Búdhi found her way to her beloved teachers, and regardless of the presence of guests, threw herself at Mrs. Whiting's feet in an agony of weeping. "Oh," she sobbed, "the Lord *is* good; I thought you were never coming, but the Lord has heard my prayer; I look once more upon the faces of my dear teachers!" After Búdhi had left the room, Col. ——— remarked, "I want no greater evidence of the power of Christianity over the heathen than this woman's life during the two years she has heen here. Not an angry word has been heard from her lips ; in the neatness of her house, and consistency of her deportment, she has been a perfect example to her heathen neighbors, and her singing of Christian hymns has done me more good than sermons."

The conversations and instructions of the beloved missionaries during their fortnight's stay, brought comfort and strength to this tempted Christian, who had stood loyal to her profession under a furnace heat of trial. Some months after, while she was making preparations for a visit to Sibsagar, Búdhi was taken suddenly ill. Calling her husband to her side she said: "I shall not go to Sibsagar to meet my brothers and sisters there, and the missionaries. My precious Saviour is calling me, and I shall soon be with Him. Give my love to the dear Whiting Sahib and Memsahib. God sent them to comfort us, did He not? Tell them I go trusting in Jesus, for *I have the white stone* on which the new name is written."

The terrible trial was all over now ; the loving, sensitive spirit was taken home, away from the dreary surroundings, and cruel scoffing, to better mansions. Her short life of twenty years set its seal to the reality of the Christian's faith.

Of the fifteen taken frcm heathen homes to her sheltering love and instruction, Mrs. Brown herself had the privilege of seeing ten baptized while she was still with them, and it has since been learned that the entire number renounced heathenism and embraced the religion of Jesus. Nearly all their heathen mothers, also, seeing the change in their daughters, were drawn to the true light, and became Christians.

"Sow in the morn thy seed;
   At eve hold not thy hand;
To doubt and fear give thou no heed;
   Broadcast it o'er the land.

Thou cans't not toil in vain;
   Cold, heat, and moist, and dry,
Shall foster and mature the grain
   For garners in the sky."

XXVIII

THE second Burman war resulted in the incorporation into the British possessions, of the province of Pegu, including the towns of Rangoon and Bassein. Southern Burma was thus opened to Christianity, and a conference of Burman missionaries was called, to meet at Moulmein in the spring of 1853, for consultation on the best means of prosecuting their extended work. The Rev. Messrs. Peck and Granger were sent by the Executive Committee from America, as a deputation to represent them in this convention, and to visit other missions. Early in February, Mr. Brown, having received a request from the deputation to join in the deliberations, left Sibsagar for Calcutta.

Reaction from an unusual press of cares resulted in much suffering on the lonely boat, and the coolies at their oars heard, without understanding, the padre's plaintive hymn :

> "Thou our throbbing flesh hast worn,
> Thou our mortal griefs hast borne ;
> Thou hast shed affection's tear,
> Jesus, Son of David, hear !"

Presently he writes to Mrs. Brown :

" This is beautiful ! Here at the Múkh—the fishes are leaping up in every direction, and the ramporas and gonga siloris [Assam birds] are trying to catch them, while now and then a fat porpoise is shooting up his

(392)

snout. I always feel at home when I get into a boat upon the Brahmaputra—it is next to being at home on the side of the Tank.

Below Bagwa, February 20th. This is the holy Sabbath day, and I have enjoyed it more than almost any other day since I started, although the weather has been tempestuous and the wind has rocked the boat very much. I told the men they might loose the boat and let it float down the stream, but there has been so much wind, they have been obliged to make it fast again. . . . How many have been my thoughts of home, and you, sweet love, to-day! . . . I have been thinking of the goodness of God to poor unworthy me, until it seems as if my heart would break. It is not often that I can speak or write of my feelings, it agitates me so—but on the whole I have a sweet peace of mind, that leads me to trust and believe, and personally apply God's promises."

Almost daily fever had made the journey down, one of some physical discomfort, to which was added the lack of suitably prepared food. Still he had been able at Gauhati, on the 13th, to preach in Assamese, and in the evening, in the new chapel. On the way from Gauhati to Calcutta, he was taken with acute erysipelas of the face.

He darkened his boat as best he could, to shut out from the chinks the hot reflections thrown up by the water—a thousand flickering suns below and around him—bandaged his eyes and lay down. A note-book and pencil within reach, enabled him to write, a little at a time, without opening his eyes, or removing the bandage.

Mar. 3. " After coming into a small stream below Kulna, heard a continual rapping under the boat, as if ten thousand woodpeckers were tapping on the bottom of the boat—only the sound was not loud.   On inquiry, I found it was caused by myriads of little fish, called the tepa-mas, who were tapping their snouts against the boat, in order to eat whatever substance they might find collected on the outside.   One or two hundred boats have been along with us to-day.   Duraj says there have been lots of monkeys in two places, very near the boats, that have appeared perfectly tame, eating under the trees, fifty or a hundred in a place.   Friday, 4. Reached Dailobari, where is a bazar, and 100 boats stopping.   Wanted to look out and see, but dare not. Near noon we entered a broad stream running south-ward, called the Gumoti.

Sunday, Mar. 6.   Did not get in last night as I hoped. Found the stenchy marshes and channels excessively disagreeable as we came near Calcutta.   Came on this morning to Boliaghat, hoping to go in with the evening tide, but the canal was so perfectly blocked up, there was no getting along.   Concluded, therefore, to start before daylight and come into town."

Mr. Brown passed a fortnight in Calcutta with his kind and hospitable friends, Mr. and Mrs. Thomas, during which the inflammation subsided, and on the 21st of March he embarked for Moulmein on the crowded war steamer " Berenice."

Sat. March 19.   "Was agreeably surprised by the arrival of Dr. Dean from China, on his way to Moulmein.   Went to see about getting a passage on the steamer."

A cordial friendship grew up during the voyage between the two veteran missionaries, who discovered that they were within one day of the same age.

"March 26. Akyab. I arrived here in the *Berenice*, with Dr. Dean this morning, and am now at Brother Moore's, where we have just taken breakfast, and are going on board again in an hour or two.

Wed. 30. Reached Rangoon at half-past ten, A. M. Went to see the Kincaids, and Brother Vinton at Kemmendine in the evening.

31. Left Rangoon at 8, A. M. Anchored at Amherst in the evening. Apr. 1. Went up to see the Dawsons. Went to see Mrs. Judson's grave. Learning that the *Berenice* would not get up to-day, engaged a small boat to take us up, for three rupees. Reached the ghaut near Brother Ranney's at 8 P. M., and soon found myself housed with my old friend Simons.

Sat. Apr. 2. Saw Dr. Peck, Mr. Granger and most of the missionaries. Kincaid, Simons and Bennett are the only ones here that I had ever seen before. Attended a prayer-meeting at Obo, Newton, in the evening. Apr. 3 Had the pleasure of once more hearing a Burman discourse, which I understood and enjoyed. The preacher was Brother Kincaid."

To Mrs. Brown. Apr. 4. "The marble slab for Willy's grave is all right. I am going to have it put at the grave. I long to get home, but fear I shall not be able to go so soon as I hoped to do. It is doubtful whether the business is through before the end of April, and then I must stop a while to get some music type and some stereotyping, &c. . . . *Evening.* Have just got home from the Burmese monthly concert. Mr. Wade asked me to address them, so I did."

Mr. Brown had the pleasure of finding still alive a number of Burman Christians whom he had known eighteen years before, and of talking with them. "I can understand Burmese when I hear it," he says, "about as well as ever, but of course cannot speak it readily."

"May 1, Sunday. To-day I tried to preach in the Burmese chapel; got a good deal confused in the first prayer, but was more at liberty after I had fairly begun my discourse. Kincaid says the natives understood all I said. I did not, however, feel at home in the language, as I do in Assamese."

Several of the Christian women of Sibsagar sent letters by the pastor to their Burman sisters. Mah Doke, a venerable sister of the Moulmein church replied :

"To the brethren and sisters, disciples, who reside in Wethali (Assam), sending affectionate salutations :

Beloved friends, although in this world we are far separated in body, yet in spirit we are near, for in a short time we shall meet in one city. Now, we have never seen you, and you also have never seen us, and indeed, if we should meet, we should not understand your language, nor you ours. But when the sons of earth shall arise, and from all nations and countries the saints shall enter into the kingdom of our beloved Lord Jesus Christ, there will be but one language, and all will unite together in adoring and praising God. Then shall we all, if we are true disciples, speak the same language with you, and sing with one accord the praise of the Most High.

. . . I, Mah Doke, was brought to the faith by the Teacher Judson, who came to Rangoon from America, and was baptized by him more than thirty years ago.

Dear friends, our female church members meet for prayer and the worship of God, every Wednesday morning at ten o'clock, at the house of Mrs. Wade, the pastor's wife. On Sabbath mornings the boys and girls meet to receive instruction in the law of God.

I am now very old, and when God will take my spirit hence, I know not. Until my life closes, I shall continue

to have the same desire to meet and see you, as you
have to see me.

MAH DOKE.

In the Burmese year 1215, [1853.] 4th day of Nayong,
increasing moon."

The introductory sermon was preached before the
convention on Monday, April 4th, by Dr. Peck, from
Joshua 5 ; 15. The first session was held on the next
day, Dr. Wade being chosen president. About twenty
missionaries were present ; among them Rev. Messrs.
Kincaid, Ingalls, Stevens, Haswell, Simons, Ranney,
Brayton, Bennett, Harris and Moore. They were men
of opinions ; " almost all good and strong men," Mr.
Brown wrote ; independent, outspoken, most of them
experienced in the service ; men who had laid foundations and knew whereof they spoke. The deputation
were also men of intellectual power and of conscientious
convictions : views on methods of work were found to
differ, and before the close, discussion at times grew
very sharp. Among the topics were the re-occupancy of
Rangoon and Burma ; the claims of Tenasserim and
Arakan ; church organizations and discipline ; modes of
evangelization ; schools ; publications.

As chairman of the committee to which was referred
the general system of schools, and particularly the expediency of teaching English, Mr. Brown presented a
report which recommended the careful training of a
native ministry to carry on the work begun by the missionary. "We are convinced that native agency is to be
the principal instrument in converting the masses in
heathen countries." "If we would introduce among
our native churches a healthy, vigorous, stable Christianity, we must have a *portion* of our native ministry thoroughly educated and enlightened—men whose
talents and acquirements shall be, as far as the circum-

stances will admit, equal to those of the missionaries themselves." To this end the report recommended the teaching of English to such theological students and translators as could obtain a thorough mastery of the language; " a partial knowledge of English is of no value whatever, in a missionary point of view."

" We should ever bear in mind that the time will eventually come, when we must leave these churches to their own resources, the supply of missionaries will cease, and native pastors and teachers will fill their places. We must bend our energies to prepare our native converts for this period. We must raise them from their state of pupilage as fast as our means will allow. To leave them before they have leaders of their own, to whom the treasures of English are fully open, able to draw from our standard authors the weapons to serve them in any emergency, would, in our opinion, be unwise. All the reasons which would induce us to plead for an educated ministry in our own country, apply with ten-fold force to the education of our native preachers. . . . Besides those engaged in the ministry, the advantages of having a few thorough English scholars for the purpose of transferring our most important books into the native tongues, will be at once manifest. . . . The disadvantages under which the missionary labors, in translating into a foreign tongue, are great; and without a native to examine every sentence, he cannot be sure that his translation is idiomatic. Add to this the utter impossibility that our missionary societies should ever be able to furnish the men and means, that would be required for the preparation of a vernacular Christian literature, such as the wants of a newly converted people demand."

The report advised the limitation of village day-schools to one at a station, unless perfect supervision could be given to a larger number; that there be none but Christian teachers and Christian books, and that they be opened daily with religious services. But boarding-schools, that is, schools in which pupils are removed from heathen surroundings and kept under Christian family influence, the committee regarded as "an important branch of missionary labor," the object of such schools being first, the conversion of the pupils, second the raising up of Christian school-teachers, and the preparation of students for the theological school. Messrs. Kincaid and Dean, with the Deputation, were opposed to boarding-schools as a means of evangelization. Messrs. Brayton, Bennett, Haswell and Stevens favored them. A warm discussion arose. With reference to the relative success of preaching and schools in Assam, Mr. Brown stated that three-fourths of the whole number of converts, which had been about sixty, were from the orphan and other boarding-schools, the remaining fourth were servants and other persons, mostly in employ, who had been living for some time with missionaries, scarcely any converts having been from village schools.

On adaptation of methods to the character of the people and peculiarities of their religion :

"Where a people have no long-settled national religion, we can operate directly upon individual minds, but where society is bound together by an ancient and strongly established religion, the action upon the mass takes place much more slowly. To go out among the Karens is like going into a wood and cutting down the trees one after another; not so in regard to the old religions like Hinduism and Buddhism; these are like a solid pagoda; with great effort you must pull it away brick by brick, and can scarcely see any impression made for a long time, but when the period for its fall comes, it will go with a rush. In India a great work has been going on, and now Hinduism as a power upon the better and educated classes has lost its hold. By them it is despised and contemned. The struggle in India now is not with Hinduism, but with infidelity. It will be the same in Burma ere long."

Mr. Granger proposed to amend the section under consideration by adopting a substitute of an opposite character, and the discussion was continued by Messrs. Kincaid, Ingalls, Brayton and Thomas. Mr. Brown opposed the amendment as sweeping away schools from several missions without the consent of those missions, and said:

"It was not in the power of this convention or of the Executive Committee to carry out these restrictions. The bow might be bent until it should snap. The brother from Rangoon [Kincaid] would be one of the first to walk right through the rules, the moment he conceived them to interfere with the conscientious discharge of his duty."

The result of the discussion was a tie. Dr. Dean, the vice-president, being in the chair, gave the casting vote in favor of the amendment. Mr. Brown asked leave to record his protest against the amendment, so far as its operation might affect the Assam Mission. The subject was reconsidered at the next session by Dr. Peck's request, and a second amendment limiting the resolution to schools in Burma, was carried.

The Convention adjourned May 17th, after about sixty sessions, lasting through six weeks. There was a pleasant social gathering of native Christians, and missionaries at Dr. Wade's that evening at which Burma, Assam, China and America shook hands.

"Tuesday, May 17. Went down in the evening to Dr. Wade's. Dr. Dean addressed the church and read a letter in Chinese, which he had received since his arrival here. Mr. Granger also addressed the native converts. Both were interpreted by Bro. Stevens. Afterwards Ko Dway addressed the assembly in a Burmese discourse. As there were three persons in one God, so there were three favors bestowed on man, and these were also one, viz., Creation, Redemption and Sanctification. Interpreted in English by Bro. Stevens."

Business, and visits with the missionaries and the brethren from America occupied another week.

"Friday, May 27. Got off on the *Fire Queen* with Dr. Dean. Left the Simons' with a feeling of regret, also the other friends. Sat. 28. Reached Rangoon in the evening. Sister Kincaid and Bro. Van Meter leave us here. Spent the night at Bro. Kincaid's, he gave me two wooden images and a palm-leaf book. Sunday morning. Went up very early with Dr. Dean to Kemmendine, and took breakfast with the Vintons. Could not stay but an hour, as we had to be on board again at 9 o'clock.

Wed. June 1. Have been beating about off Kyouk Phyu ever since midnight, not daring to come in. Came to anchor about 10 o'clock. It is a beautiful place amongst the islands. We wanted to go on shore to see if there were any remains of the mission, but the captain allowed no time.

Calcutta, Tuesday, June 7. Missionary Conference this morning. Topics were Street Preaching and the new Marriage Act ; the latter was universally condemned as being most oppressive, and not applicable to native Christians. Street preaching is made an obstruction, according to the new law. . . . Dr. Dean gave a description of the new movement in China, and was heard with great interest. About twenty-five or thirty missionaries of all sects were present.

June 9. Went up to Serampore with Dr. Dean. 10. Went out in the morning to see the inscriptions on the missionary tombstones, also to see the pagoda which was Henry Martyn's chapel, and the great banyan. Returned in a native's palkee carriage to Calcutta. Sat. 11. Went with Mr. Wenger and Dr. Dean to see the Presbyterian and Free Church schools, and to see the Mint, a great curiosity. There were, I think, a dozen engines at work, stamping a coin every moment. The overseer told us they could strike three lacs in a day. 12. Preached, or rather, read, for Mr. Leslie in the morning, Dr. Dean preached in the evening, " Which of you intending to build a tower," etc. Sunday, 19. Preached (read I mean) for Mr. Thomas the same sermon I preached for Mr. Leslie last Sabbath : " My sheep hear my voice," at the Lall Bazar Chapel. Sat. 25. Much trouble in securing boats. 28. Have finally got my boats ready and went on board with my things to-day. Wed., 29. Started about 5 P. M., and reached Serampore about 9 in the evening. Went to see Mr. Murray, to get the paper put on board early in the morning.

Monday, July 4. Celebrated Independence Day by reading the " White Slave," and marking Burmese letters. The White Slave is a terrible picture, and no doubt a true one; the dark parts are given in all the horrors, but it is not so effective as " Uncle Tom's Cabin ; " it has not the tenderness, the pathos, the *religion*, that give a charm to that book. 8. Entered the Ganges a little after noon. Mond. 11. Came down the Pubna, small river. Tues. and Wed. Head winds ; obliged to lie by. 14. Began to go up stream. Sat. 16. Reached Sirajgunge. Remain here over Sabbath.

. .. Sun., 24. Read the Burman Hymn book nearly half through and was delighted with it. A wind spring-ing up in the afternoon, we went on by sail, a few hours. 25. Finished the Lord's Prayer * in Burman verse, which I begun yesterday. Also partly did another, the " Happy Land." Tues. 26. Finished the " Happy Land." Prob-ably there are a good many faults in the idiom, which I could correct, if I had a Burman by my side, but I will send them on to Bro. Stevens, and see what he can make out of them. 28. Strong, high water, and head winds. Spent about half a day in going half a mile, pulling by the cable. Came on till a late hour before we found a stopping-place. In the evening commenced the hymn, " Who are these in bright array ? " 29. Came by frightful rocks, arrived within about half a day of Goalpara, they say. Finished the hymn on the Glorified Saints.

July 30, Sat. Spent most of the day warping round the rocks ; in one spot the current rushed down by a rock, making a fall of about a foot at once. Reached Goalpara near night. Aug. 1. Rained hard till three o'clock. Then the men said they must have a small boat or they could not get on. Bought one and came on just above the village, where we stopped for the night under the hill. Have finished to-day the hymn which I commenced Saturday, " Death of the Righteous." Aug. 2. . . Made a translation of the hymn " Guide me, O thou great Jehovah."

Under date August 4, the diary contains the hymn " Zion's Travelers," like the others, in his own Burman handwriting. Mr. Danforth met him on the 6th, and Mr. Robinson's elephant brought them up to Gauhati the next day.

Here he met Mrs. Brown. She had written him much, and had more to tell, of all that had happened

*See page 420.

during his five months' absence; of the removal from
the bungalow on the tank to the one on the Dikho; of
the arrival of the Bronsons at Sibsagar; of the death of
Batiram; of the breaking out of cholera and the busy
weeks of attendance on sick and dying natives. A number of persons in the mission compound, including some
of her own servants, were attacked, and the excited natives were "mad, making pújas." She had written her
letters by snatches, amid calls to the sick and dying.

E. B. to S. B. B., September 3. "The cholera broke
out almost simultaneously all over Assam. At Sibsagar
and Nowgong it raged fearfully—some fifteen or twenty
thousand of the natives were swept off, besides a number of the foreign residents.

At Sibsagar many of the workmen in the printing
office and their families were attacked, also a number
of my scholars. Teachers and assistants were constantly running to me, night and day, for medicines."

Later, Mrs. Brown records four deaths in the mission
compound. Upon this scene of distress and excitement
the Bronsons arrived March 18th, and were the greatest possible comfort. Mrs. Brown had been so absorbed
in her labors for and with the Assamese that in the
absence of her husband, she had partially lost the use of
her own language, and it was some days before she
could talk English with her old friends without a large
intermixture of Assamese. Dr. Bronson, went "heart
and hand into the work," doing the thousand things
which in the emergency needed to be done; visiting
cholera patients, repairing buildings, and attending to
the printing department; "working himself almost to
death," Mrs. Brown says, May 11th.

E. to N. B. March 28. "Last night's dawk brought
us mournful news. Poor Brother Daüblé is no more.

He was taken with spasmodic cholera Monday 21st—in three hours after was insensible, and died the 23rd. Pingault attended, and Stoddard was over him to the last. What a breach is made in our mission!

The cholera does not appear to be in the least abated, although we now have frequent showers. Ghinai's Mary is gone. Yesterday Nidhi went up with Peter and Than to bury her. In the night poor Hannah, [Nidhi's motherless daughter, a pupil in the school,] was attacked violently, and Nidhi was sent for. Dr. Long kindly came to see her this morning. Pray for us, darling. May the Lord bless and sustain you in all your sickness and sorrows. Hannah says, ' *Sworogoloi jüing—Probhü nebo.*' [I am going to Heaven—the Lord will take me.] "

The children's lessons were suspended, while little Hannah vacillated between life and death for more than a week, kept from sinking through Mrs. Brown's care, and careful nursing.

March 31. "I have her in the school-room ; Nidhi and two or three of the school-girls are with her all the time. Nidhi's servant-boy died at his house yesterday, after an illness of only a few hours. This week the cholera has broken out in the jail on the tank. It is raging at Nazira, Jorhat, and all around us."

'The cholera raged in every part of the country," says the Missionary Magazine, July 1854, "to such a degree as literally to decimate the population of Sibsagar district. The mortality of Nowgong district was over 9000, and of Gauhati much greater. It was, in every sense, a land of death."

Mrs. Whiting says, of this season of pestilence :

" Our home adjoined the temple grounds. Daily we saw the worshippers going with their offerings to wor-

ship, seeking to propitiate the favor of their gods. . . .
Large companies of women formed themselves into a
procession, and with their heads covered, went twice
daily to the temple, with their offerings. It was a sad
sight as they passed and repassed our house daily.
Three little girls, one bearing a dish of flowers, followed
by another with fruit, and the third with a dish of rice,
headed the procession of a hundred or more women.
One woman in a most piteous, mournful strain chanted,
"O Siva, O ye gods, have pity! Hear us, save us. Our
husbands are dying—our children are perishing—our
cattle are being destroyed. Siva, have mercy, O Siva,
save us!" Then the whole company would join in the
thrilling sad refrain, "O Siva, have mercy, Siva, O Siva
save us." Four times daily, for many days, this mournful procession passed our bungalow." *

It was on the 4th of April, that the pundit Tákur
died. Mrs. Brown had paid but little attention to her
own overwrought condition ; had kept on night and day,
nursing the sick, when she should have been herself in
a patient's place. At length she was completely worn
out. On Sunday, April 3rd, she felt a dizziness immediately after the communion, which was followed in the
night by alarming symptoms ; but they were arrested
in a few hours, before the disease fastened itself upon
her.

She afterwards wrote, " I felt that I was quietly sinking away into the arms of my loving Saviour." "Death
seemed near, Christ my Saviour also seemed near;
He was very merciful in removing my fears. I felt
that I could rest my weary, helpless soul on Him."

To Mr. and Mrs. Stoddard, April 11th. " Dear Sister Elizabeth [Mrs. Whiting] came down for three days

---

* *The Helping Hand*, October, 1887

and nursed me carefully, and on Friday took me home with her, and kept me till last night ; and to-day I am home again."

To N̈. B., 7th. "Have had the girls in to see me, and the little invalid Hannah, to lie awhile by my side on my bed. The poor child is like one raised from the grave. The cholera is all around us still, but it has left the bazar, and we trust. nearly left the station. . . . But the relatives of the office-people have been sick and dying, and a number of the workmen have taken leave for a few days, on that account."

She soon resumed her usual duties, often conducting morning worship and the women's prayer-meeting, hearing the girls' lessons, and preparing their sewing for them, while lying on her couch, keeping her sick pupils, Húpahi and little Akesúri, meantime, with her in her own oom.

The steamer *Jumna* came almost to her door in June ; and being invited to occupy one of its state-rooms on the down-trip, she left Sibsagar on the 14th, taking Búdhi and Húpahi with her. Hannah, now recovered, went on ahead with her father Nidhi, in his canoe.

Mrs. Brown enjoyed some social weeks in Nowgong and Gauhati with her friends the Stoddards, Danforths and Wards, and made the acquaintance of several new missionary-babas, among them a "grandson" namesake of her husband at Gauhati. After Mr. Brown's arrival there, he had a fall that injured his right arm and shoulder, disabling them so that he was obliged in the autumn to learn to write with his left hand. They left Gauhati on the 17th of August, after some difficulty in inducing the natives to go on up the swollen Brahmaputra.

N. B. 19. "The boatmen refused to go over to the Kullung—for the purpose of going by Nowgong. Was

obliged to let them take their own course, and a wind
springing up a little after noon, we came on to Ronga
Mati. 24. Fine wind, came on nearly all day. Very
strong water. Towards evening got into a whirlpool at
the junction of two channels. 27. Copied off my Burman hymns, nine in number, for Brother Stevens, and
wrote a letter to go with them."

And now commenced a month of delays, perils and
escapes, unexampled even in their frequent experiences
of the great river's angry moods. The daily progress
varied from "a few rods " to "two or three miles," a
head-wind sometimes adding its obstructing force to that
of the rapids. Dangerous as "gooning" was under
such circumstances, they were obliged, in places, to resort to it. The roaring current was so terrific that the
boatmen repeatedly refused to go on, glad even to find
a fastening-place where they could secure the boat from
being washed away. On the 7th of September, one of
the men spied from the mast, the white bungalows of
Tezpúr, but a northeast gale held them under a jungly
bank all that day. Torrents of rain continued to fall
during the night, and the water had to be bailed out of
the boat:

E. B. Sept. 9. "Yesterday P. M. the wind somewhat abated ; the men on the cook-boat being out of rice,
and there being on our boat but one maund [abou 25
lbs., almost the sole remaining sustenance for seventeen
persons,] to divide with them, seeing death by starvation
staring us in the face if we were to remain here in the
jungles many days longer, we left our moorings and attempted to go around the point of land before us."

N. B. . . . "The cook-boat went on first; after it had
got round, they sent back the canoe for us. We went

only one pull of the goon, the men on the cook-boat
motioning us to advance no farther. So we moored
directly under the point. Soon the cook-boat broke her
cable and came drifting by, her manji being left on shore.
I tried to get our manji to move back, feeling that the
place was insecure, but he determined on remaining for
the night, and put out cables in front and stern, and then
the anchor. The boat seemed very uneasy, and about 8
o'clock she rolled and labored in a manner to alarm us.
I went out and was frightened to see the velocity of the
waves; they rolled by like a stream of lightning. The wind
appeared to have shifted a little so as to throw the main
strength of the river directly upon that point. Soon the
earth began to cave in ; large masses, several yards in
depth, would disappear in an instant, rocking and almost
swamping the boat by the surge. It seemed as if land
was as unstable as the water ; all appeared like waves in
motion. Immense masses of bank followed each other in
rapid succession, till all the cables were brought into the
stream, and nothing was left to hold the boat but the
anchor. Two or three of the men were carried down
under the boat with one of these masses, but they came
up at length, and caught by the sides of the boat, but
were found to be much bruised. The boatmen now
stood helpless on the deck, crying, 'What shall we do ?
What shall we do?' and calling upon God to rescue
them ; the Mussulmans saying, 'La Illah il Allah,' and
the Hindus, 'Ram, Ram.' I felt sure that the anchor
would soon give way, and tried to persuade the manji to
let loose as soon as possible, and trust the boat to the
stream, but they all said the boat would be instantly
swamped if let loose. For a moment I thought perhaps
it might be best to go on shore with my dear wife and
the girls, and leave the boat to its fate, but I saw this
would be almost certain death ; to be left in the jungle
in a storm, and without any prospect of being found, for

days perhaps, by any passers-by.   Although we were in
sight of Tezpúr, it would be quite impossible to communicate our situation.   While I was urging the men to
stand at their oars, ready for action if the anchor should
give way, we saw the boat beginning to move down the
stream; the frightful rocking and struggling of the boat
ceased, and I felt relieved when I found the anchor was
disengaged.   The men succeeded in dragging it up into
the boat, and on we went, with great velocity, for about
a mile, passing the cook-boat on our way, and at length
entered a small stream, where we again moored for the
night.   It was a merciful deliverance, and we felt that
Providence had surely interposed for us.   We had not
been long moored, when we heard cries from the cook-
boat.   They, too, had been set adrift by the falling
bank, and were brought down into another small stream
near where we were.   It was a cheering sight, with the
earliest morning light, to see their mast appearing above
the intervening jungle.   About 10 o'clock Duraj came
on in a small boat with our breakfast, such as it was, for
we are almost entirely out of provisions, as well as the
boatmen.   After breakfast we sent off Duraj for supplies,
and the chuprassee, [native officer], to Mr. Hudson, to get
another small boat to help us on.   The wind continued
unabated, but there is less rain than there was yesterday.

Sabbath morning, 11th.   Came on and reached the
station at 2 P. M.   12.   The boatmen refusing to go on,
I have concluded to wait for the steamer.

Saturday, Sept. 17.   Last evening Brother Stoddard's
boys, Kandúra and Debiram, came in about 5 o'clock.
They have brought Brother Stoddard's elephant for me
to Laukwa ghaut, and Brother Stoddard thinks I can
start Saturday morning and go over to Nowgong the
same day.   This I find will be impracticable, as they say
it will take from daylight till noon to get crossed over.
The boys got off a little past 9 o'clock.

Lord's day, 18th. Preached for Mr. Hesselmeyer in Assamese. 19. Last night about midnight we had a smart shock of earthquake."

The kind Hesselmeyers had invited the storm-bound missionaries to their home, but the Bruces being absent and their house vacant, it was decided to occupy it till the arrival of the steamer, and thankful indeed were the tired travelers for so commodious a shelter.

E. B. Sept. 12. " Perishing as we all were, with excitement and want of provisions, yesterday (Sunday), being a favorable day, we thought it a work of mercy to come on. It was joyful to hear that there is a steamer expected to go to Upper Assam this month. It seems truly a godsend, as that is now our only hope of getting home. 30th. You can hardly conceive our delight on hearing that the smoke of the steamer was seen from the station last night at dark, after having for more than a week been on the tiptoe of expectation, and for two days almost in despair of its coming at all. It reached the ghaut between 9 and 10 this morning. . . . We shall sleep on board to-night, and be off, I trust, early to-morrow morning. We have had clear weather the last two days, and all bids fair for a fine passage up. The Lord be praised for his goodness in hearing our poor prayers, and sending us this means of deliverance from our confinement here."

The steamer *Brahmaputra* left Tezpúr Oct. 1st, and landed the Browns at their own steps in less than three days, the captain kindly running up the Dikho for their accommodation.

XXIX.

M R. BROWN began the translation of the New Testament into Assamese, January 1st, 1838; but the years immediately following, were so filled with commotions, distress, and removals as to afford but scant opportunities for settled work. To secure even an intelligent pundit in the remoter stations, was difficult. The plan of work made out at Sudiya, met with much overturning ; it was three and a half years before the first gospel was finished. With much effort, and at the cost of an illness, he finished Matthew before leaving Jaipúr.

Jaipúr, June 9th, 1841. "Still confined to my room, though somewhat better, I hope. Completed the translation of Matthew in Assamese, to-day. We have printed only a small edition, as we wished to have an opportunity for an early revision. In this translation, I have adhered to the resolution of the Board, and have not found it necessary to transfer any terms, except the word Christ, which may partly be regarded as a proper name."

He had already received Judson's Bible.

May 13th. " Received to-day the new edition of Mr. Judson's Burman Bible. I think this will be found to be the most faithful, correct and finished version that has appeared in any of the eastern dialects. It is the result of many years' severe labor, and it appears to have been revised in a most thorough manner—the alterations from the former edition are very numerous. In translating, I always keep the Burman Bible before me, and often find it of great assistance."

He translated most of the New Testament during the years 1841–7, at Sibsagar. Native visitors used to find him standing at a high, broad shelf extending along his study wall, quill in hand, and before him a much-corrected manuscript in Assamese characters. Dictionaries and Greek texts lay open upon the shelf at either hand, Bibles in several languages within reach, and a heap of printers' proof pushed one side. This shelf was Mr. Brown's study-table; here in the rainy season, when uninterrupted he often worked eight or ten hours a day turning the Greek of Luke and John and Paul into idiomatic Assamese. On the floor sat his pundit looking over work done, and ready to answer questions.

His diary notes show that Acts was the second book taken up, being finished in April, and John in October, 1842; Mark. Romans, Corinthians and Galatians in '43 and '44' and the remaining epistles in '45 and '46' Sometimes the study-table was the top of a chest in a canoe on the river; Hebrews and the epistles of James and Peter were thus translated in the three last months of '46 while returning from Calcutta. Luke and Revelation. completing the Testament, were finished in 1847. He afterwards made three revisions of the whole in '48' '49 and '50' and one of the last of his labors in Assam was the fourth revision, completed during the summer of 1854.

July 10, '54. " Have been looking over my alterations in the New Testament, collected for the next edition, and find I have noted between six and seven hundred, mostly of minor importance. Have gone through and examined them all with the pundit."

Dr. Ward characterizes his style as "clear, terse, and Grecian." He loved the work; he found, the deeper he studied, the diviner the glory that

> " gilds the sacred page,
> Majestic, like the sun,"

and considered the oriental languages peculiarly adapted to the expression of scriptural thought.

To Rev. Pharcellus Church, January, 1856. " I have often been struck, while reading the Scriptures in the languages of the east, with the peculiar force and per-spicuousness of many passages in the New Testament, especially in the Epistles, which in our version are ob-scure, ambiguous, or perhaps absolutely erroneous. I recollect a remark of the second Mrs. Judson, that she should consider herself amply repaid for studying the Burmese language, had she derived no other benefit than that of perusing the Burman Bible ; so clearly and forcibly was the meaning of the sacred text exhibited in that version."

In December, 1854, Mr. Brown completed the " Har-mony " or " The Life and Gospel of Christ " in Assam-ese, a continuous narrative from the text of the four evangelists. Before leaving Assam he had translated a considerable part of Bunyan's Pilgrim's Progress, and left it in the hands of Nidhi Levi, to assist Mr. Danforth in completing it. It was illustrated by a native engraver, and published in 1856. He also translated a few por-tions of the Psalms, and prepared considerable other matter for the press, revising necessary books for the schools, making catechisms, tracts and hymn-books and a pamphlet of tunes.

Making a book, like making a house, in the early Assam days, meant going away back to the beginnings.

The printing department included a small foundry for casting type, lead mold, and lead-cutting machine. Of one of the first issues at Sudiya—a Khamti cate. chism—he says :

"The delay in printing it has arisen from the diffi. culty of preparing the Burman type and cutting new characters for the additional sounds in Shan, beyond those which are common to the Burmese. In points that admit of question, we have generally favored the forms which are most common around Mógaung and Ava, rather than those which are peculiar to the Khamtis, who being at one of the extreme points of the Shan region, may be supposed to have diverged farther from the general orthography than those tribes which inhabit the center." A few days later he says :

"Have distributed quite a number of catechisms among the Khamtis the past week. Find that they can read them much better than we had feared. Although many of the letters were manufactured by altering and remodelling the Burman type, and a large portion of them cut and cast anew, under every disadvantage, yet there is scarcely a letter which the natives find any difficulty in recognizing."

He made a catechism for the Assamese at about the same time, which fifty years later, Rev. E. W. Clark translated for the Nágas. Notwithstanding hinderances, nearly 200 pages of his translation and other work were issued from the Sudiya press in small editions before July, 1838, as the first two years' work. amounting to 4600 copies of books and tracts, averaging twenty-five pages each. At Sibsagar there were fewer difficulties to contend with, and from the beginning at Sudiya up to 1851, eight and a quarter millions of pages had been issued. This included some works of the other missionaries, Mrs. Brown's school and juvenile books, and several useful translations by Nidhi and Batiram.

In January, 1846, Mr. Brown prepared the first number of the *Orunodoi* (Dawn of Day), "A Monthly Magazine, devoted to Religion, Science, and General Intelligence," which he edited in the Assamese language during most of the remaining years at Sibsagar. It was copiously illustrated by native engravers, whose work was pronounced in Calcutta superior to anything that had then been produced there by Bengali workmen. The reading natives liked this wide awake magazine; the Brahmans found it interesting, and obtained some new ideas in an attractive form, besides information on topics of general interest. Such headings appear as Turko-Russian Hostilities; The War in China; Revolution in Spain; Battle of the Alma; Remains of Sir John Franklin Found; Telegraph from Calcutta to Bombay; Louis Philippe; Gen. Winfield Scott. Illustrated articles on Astronomy, Geography and Natural History conveyed useful and needed instruction, while temperance, veracity, self-reliance, family government and other appropriate themes received attention. Through its columns Christian hymns, translations of psalms, chapters of "Pilgrim's Progress" in serial course, Scripture narratives, sketches of martyrs, "A brief history of the Apostles," "Parable of the Sower," and "Account of Our Saviour" found their way into heathen homes, where the Christian scriptures in their usual form, would not have been admitted.

Mr. Brown admired the Assamese language; its open, agreeable vocalization, its picturesque Sanscritic characters, its quaint inflections and idioms, became almost native to him. Above all, he delighted in its marked family likeness to the European tongues. He vindicated its independence of Bengali, and maintained

its legitimate descent from the ancient Sanscrit. To
systematize the facts he had gathered by oral use of
Assamese with the natives and reading their books, he
prepared in 1848, a few sheets of grammatical forms,
and the work extending beyond what was anticipated,
an Assamese grammar of eighty pages was published,
under the title of " Grammatical Notices." They " do
not claim," he says in the preface, " to be regarded as a
grammar of the Assamese language ; nor were they prepared with a view to publication in their present state."
The Grammatical Notices were a welcome help to newly
arrived missionaries and other foreigners ; the book was
called for before it was bound, and the thanks of government were conveyed to the author. One of the his-
torics of the country by native authors, was prepared
for the press by Mr. Brown, in 1844, and issued for the
benefit of the schools at the expense of the resident
magistrate.

Looking forward to the probable future predominance
of the Bengali language in the lower provinces, he had,
in 1842, strongly urged that the press be retained in
Upper Assam, foreseeing that its removal would lead in
time to the relinquishment of the mission to the Assamese ; a measure, to which, he could never, for a moment, bring his mind. Paralyzed as the mind of the
valley-people had become, through centuries of the
worst form of heathenism, and requiring perhaps generations of patient and unrewarded effort before results
should appear, he believed in *continuing the effort.*

"I cannot think it is our duty to relinquish the Assamese as a distinct mission, while there is at our doors,
so large a population speaking one uniform, copious,
and beautiful language, and as yet unsupplied with
laborers at all adequate to the occupation of this wide
field."

The connection between the Sanscritic and the European languages early attracted his attention :

" To a botanist or a naturalist in a foreign country, it affords peculiar pleasure to discover a plant or animal with which he has been already familiar in his native land; and still greater is the delight of a mis- sionary, when, after several years residence in India, he first begins to discover the sounds of his native tongue mingled with the rude accents of the heathen tribes around him, thus obtaining practical evidence that he still labors among the same human race—his brethren of that "one blood" of which "God hath made all na- tions of men."*

He traced a considerable number of test words from the Assamese, Bengali and Hindustani back to Sanscrit, taking in side relations of the Burmese and Shan, and comparing with Persian, Russian, Greek, and the Latin and Gothic languages of Europe, noting affinities of Assamese, Sanscrit, Greek, Latin, Erse, Gothic, Ger- man, Saxon, English. Some of this seems to have been done on a river trip.

February 19, '53. "Compared and wrote down words in first book of the Æneid corresponding with the Assamese—also Burman words in Revelation."

A somewhat more extended work in the same line, was his comparative vocabulary of three hundred com- mon words, commenced on the way to Assam, and ex- tended in the course of years with the co-operation of missionary friends in Burma and Siam, to about thirty different eastern dialects.†

---

*For Principles of Lingual Affinity, see Appendix C.

†For Max Müller's letter on labors of Mr. Brown and other mission- aries, see appendix D.

The Lords Prayer in Burmese

HYMNS AND TRANSLATION.

For the above in Roman letters see opposite page

The Burmese hymn is a reduced facsimile from

I. Pitri, Probhu sworgodham,
   Houk pujonio tómar nam ;
   Barhók tómar raijy oheh,
   Isa púr houk dehe deh ;
   Sworgot ji rúp kora hól,
   Hei rúp houk ei bhumondól.

II. Dinor ahar kori dan,
   Rokhya kora amar pran ;
   Ji rúp khemón lókor dhar,
   Khema kora pap amar ;
   Porikható kori tran
   Dóhor mukut kora dan.

DOXOLOGY.

Raijy, probhaó mohima jen
Hodai tómar houk.   Amen.

MATT. VI; 9-13, WITH INTERLINEAR TRANSLATION.

He amar sworogot thoka Pitri,   tómar nam pujonio
O our heaven-dwelling Father,   Thy name hallowed
houk ; tómar raij   houk ;   jenekoi   sworogot
be ; Thy kingdom be [*established*]*;   as   in heaven*
tenekoi prithibito tómar isa púr houk.   Ajir
so   on earth   Thy   will fulfilled be.   This
dinor ahar amak dia.   Aru amar dhoruahontok ami
day   food to us give.   And our   debtors   we
jenekoi khema korón, tenekoi amaró dhar khema kora.
as   forgive,   so   our debts forgive.
Amak porikhaloi ni niba,   kintú dóhor   pora
Us into temptation do not lead, but evil   from
rokhya kora. Kionó raij,   aru mohima, probhao, ci
save.   For kingdom, and glory, power, these
hokoló horbodai tómar.   Amen.
all   ages Thine. Amen.

XXX

THE year 1854 opened under circumstances of encouragement. "Several have asked for baptism;" Mr. Brown wrote to Mr. Whiting, after his return from the Moulmein convention. "I hope some of them may be able to go forward while Dr. Peck is here. He baptized one in Arakan, and I should like to have him perform a similar duty in Sibsagar."

E. B. Jan. 13, '54. "This morning I had the pleasure of meeting and greeting Dr. Peck, from America, at my own home in Assam! How fresh it brought to memory my last parting with him, and other dear friends on board the 'Cato,' in October, 1848! The Whitings arrived in about an hour after Dr. Peck, and we had the pleasure of having them all at our table to breakfast.

Sunday, 15th. A very interesting and memorable day. In the morning Brother Whiting preached in the native chapel, to an audience of about 75, including all the church members and school girls. At eleven o'clock we all repaired to the tank in the mission compound when the ordinance of baptism was administered to Than, (Húpahi's brother), Húbhodro, Parboti and Lucy, by Dr. Peck, in a most solemn and impressive manner. His address in English, Nathan interpreted to the Assamese. One or two hundred of the heathen were present. When he led the little girls down into the water, he repeated those affecting words of the Saviour, 'Suffer the little children to come unto me.' It was a tenderly impressive scene.

In the afternoon Brother Danforth preached in the native chapel ; in the evening the sacrament was administered to twenty-four communicants, eighteen of whom were native.   Before the communion, Dr. Peck addressed the church on the love of Christ in making such a sacrifice for sin, and dwelt much on his sufferings, especially his mental agony."

Dr. Peck having called a conference of the mission at Nowgong, Mr. Brown and the Whitings went down to attend it, and Mrs. Brown was alone in charge of the station for several weeks.   Inquirers came to be instructed, church members to tell their troubles and receive advice ; she had the printing establishment to superintend, hands to manage, proofs to correct, and her school to teach.   On Sundays, the morning and evening services were carried on by the native preachers, and their Sunday afternoon street-preaching went on as usual, while the women and children came to Mrs. Brown at the bungalow for a Bible-class and prayer.

E. B.   "Jan. 19.   Jogori came to have one of her good family talks.   Her heart is brimful of joy and hope, through the recent conversion of her husband, for whom she has so long been laboring and praying.   She now boards four of the school-girls, and seems to delight in the charge, and in being able to do anything for Christ's sake.   Gave her the new hymn-book, and sent one to her husband ; told her she must encourage and assist him now in learning to read the precious truths of God's word, which from the mouth of others he had learned to love.

Búdhi came in with Peter this evening, the first time they have visited me together since their marriage. Búdhi and Húbhodro have both exerted a most salutary influence over their husbands."

Jogori and Búdhi witnessed the baptism of their husbands by Mr. Whiting on the first Sunday in April.

Mrs. Brown records the conversion of a gray-haired day-pupil, Sokú-mak, (Sokú's mother) the grandmother of Nidhi's little Hannah, the same who had manifested such bitter opposition to the baptism of her son-in-law, Horuram. Six years had passed since that time; and four since she had seen her daughter embrace the despised religion. When Dr. Peck baptized Than, Húbhodro, and the little girls, she was one of the crowd of heathen on the bank. Something in the scene touched deeply the weary, suffering woman. She left the spot, with three other old women, retired to pray, and from that day was punctual in attending all the meetings, especially the Wednesday female prayer-meeting. At one of these, in February, " in the midst of sobs and tears, she avowed her determination to forsake the Hindu religion and embrace the religion of Christ. Since that she has often spoken with deep feeling, and acknowledged her great sinfulness." "Batiram's mother, Than's mother, and now Sokú's mother have all, one after another, come into our female prayer-meeting, confessed their belief in the Christian religion, and asked for prayers." A month later Sokú-mak and Than-mak presented themselves before the church and asked for baptism.

"About this time Sokú-mak commenced attending my little school as a day-pupil, and sometimes I have hardly been able to credit my senses on going into the school-room and seeing the haughty Hindu woman sitting down on the mat with the little children, sometimes employing one of the smallest of them to teach her to read the word of God. She took great delight in being present at the religious exercises with which the school is opened, and she had a number of times led in prayer herself."

At the last prayer-meeting which she ever attended, Mrs. Brown called on her to pray, "which she did without hesitation and in a very feeling manner." She was soon to leave earth's sorrows. As long as she was able she came to school—up to a week before her death. A few days of acute suffering, cheered by the Memsahib's visits and prayers, and then the aged Sokú-mak went to her Saviour.

The meeting at Nowgong was an important one, involving questions vital to the orphan institution. The Assam missionaries were a unit in the conviction that this school was a wise and scriptural agency for propagating Christianity among the heathen people, as well as an indispensable means of training converts to be missionaries to their own countrymen. In view of the fact that three-fourths of the converts in Assam had come from this and other schools, notwithstanding the precedence always given to out-door preaching over other modes of evangelization, they strongly deprecated any measures tending to limit or cripple its operations.

Dr. Peck, on the other hand, representing the Executive, and some other devout and earnest thinkers at home, who believed oral preaching to be the only scripturally authorized method of evangelization, found himself in the difficult position of variance from the views of the mission.

Mr. Brown was chosen moderator of the conference ; the discussions continued from January 21st to February 7th, both deputation and missionaries plainly defining and defending their views. The opinion of the executive, backed by the stringent pressure of economic considerations, prevailed ; the Orphan Institution, as an asylum for heathen children, was, in effect, abolished.

"Contrary to the unanimous judgment of the missionaries on the field, the Nowgong Orphan Institution

was so far modified that its practical abolition was a
question of only a few years' time.   Since its abolition,
no organized, systematic training of Assamese converts
for mission work, has been carried on."*

After reaching Tezpúr, on his way home, Mr. Brown,
who had long been suffering from the sprain of the
right shoulder, decided to follow friendly advice ; turned
about and went to Gauhati for treatment.   His letters
are now, for some months, written with his left hand.

To Mrs. Brown, Tezpúr, February 13, 1854.   ' How
little we know what a day may bring forth !   An hour
ago I wrote to you that I was going to Sibsagar, and
now I am about starting for Gauhati.   It was my opinion that I ought to go and see Dr. Simmons, but my
anxiety to get home, and the anxiety you felt to have
me come home, made me decide otherwise, but now this
letter from Dr. Peck turns me about again.   My heart
is sick and sorry at the idea of going, but it appears to
be duty.   The Whitings will take up Monroe and Ra-
tibori.   I have given brother Whiting two hundred rupees, which he will make over to you.   Brother W. will
get out one number of the Orunodoi—please make over
to him the articles that have come for it.

Gauhati, February 16th.   I have had Dr. S—— look
at my arm to-day.   He thinks it will get well, but may
be some five or six months in doing so, as the sprain
was a very bad one.
I think probably I shall start for home on Monday."

The inflammation appears to have increased on the
way up ; the heat, confinement and motion of the boat

---

*Report of Assam Jubilee Conference, held in Nowgong. Dec., 1886.

caused so much distress that he walked the sands a good part of the way, arriving at Sibsagar, March 9th; he found Mrs. Brown quite ill, having been suddenly taken the previous night with inflammation of the right lung. She says :

" I was in the house all alone except two or three ot the little girls, so soundly asleep in the school-room, I could not wake them. At length I heard the chokidar [watchman] in the veranda, and after much trouble got him to call Numóli. . . In the morning early I sent for the *Bej Borūa*—[native doctor] there being no other doctor at the station, for some leeches. My dear Nathan came home Thursday night, March 9th, greatly to my surprise and joy—and his kind watchful care over me since his return, has, I believe, with God's blessing, been the means of saving my life."

The summer of 1854, was one of unusual heat, and mortality from fevers and dysentery; five of Mrs. Brown's school-girls were down with fever at once. The air was so full of pestilence that domestic animals were swept off by scores, and even wild beasts fell a prey to disease. Mr. and Mrs. Brown sometimes resorted to their old bungalow at night, for the sake of the tank air. They passed through the rains in great weakness and depression, though not obliged to suspend any of the usual labors. It became daily more and more evident that the two were doing their last work in Assam. Mrs. Brown seemed to hear inward whispers, saying, " Work while the day lasts," " It will be *but a little while,*' "This may be your last year."

These twenty-two years without a vacation had shaken Mr. Brown's robust constitution. The sailor may nerve himself to stand at his post through many nights of buffeting winds, but, little by little, the winds and the breakers will beat the strength out of the strained sinews and the breath out of the body. It was not hard work and exposure alone, nor wholly a malarial climate, that had sapped the iron strength; mental anguish had done its part; repeated discouragement, and hope often deferred, had not been without their physical effects, and now the time had come when they could do no more, and a return to America, for at least temporary rest, became necessary.

To daughter, June 1st, '54: "Your dear papa is very infirm, his nervous system quite shattered, crippled in his right arm, diseased in his eyes, his sufferings at times intense, and he becomes so nervous, he cannot sleep nights; walks the rooms and verandas to and fro. The glare of the sun for the week past has so affected his eyes that he is threatened with another attack of erysipelas in the eyes and face; obliged to keep the room darkened, and wears continually a green silk shade. Notwithstanding all this, he still has the use of his voice, and can have the men in the office come to him for orders, etc., and so manages somehow to keep the wheels moving."

The trembling chirography of this letter told its own story; still more, the statement, " I fear we shall not be able to write you very regularly. The heat and glare of the sun so distracts my head that I scarcely know what I am about, and the little strength we have, we must husband with the utmost economy, to get along and not let the interests of the mission suffer."

E. B. September 22, '54. "Spent the day at Sister Whiting's—have slept there for the last two nights for change of air. The night air on the tank seems much purer than here on the river bank. My health is evidently running down. Oh, that as the earthly house of this tabernacle decays, the building which is eternal may be strengthened day by day !

We begin to think seriously of leaving Assam and returning to America for the restoration of our health. My heart shrinks from the trial of leaving my dear school and prayer-meeting—all our little interests here, even for a season, and the uncertainty of life and return makes me tremble at the thought of taking the first step towards breaking up our home here. My constant prayer should be : 'O, Lord, prepare me for all Thy will and pleasure.' I find I have a very strong will to remain and labor a few years more for these dear destitute people.

October 15. Sunday. P——, K——, and J——, [three more of her pupils] were baptized by Mr. Brown in the tank after the services at the chapel this P. M. Lovely girls—may they prove true lambs of the Saviour's flock ! These girls and women married from the school, are very dear to my heart. Having had the whole charge and care of them so long, they look up to me as to a mother, and they are as dear to me as any adopted children can be—and those who have been converted are bound by a double tie. The thought of being obliged to leave them at no distant day, is more trying than any one can conceive who has not had a similar charge under similar circumstances. . . . It sometimes seems as if my heart would break."

The little school was now so systematized, and the gentle Assamese girls so obedient and affectionate, that it was not necessary to dismiss them even for a day. The older pupils helped the Memsahib in the care of the little ones. Mrs. Brown writes :

" The monitors bear nearly all the burdens; H—— is a dear good girl, almost like an own daughter to me;

she is so careful not to give me trouble, and to look after my health and comfort. She appears to draw strength from above daily. When I am ill she manages the younger ones to a charm."

It was the opinion of both Dr. Long and Dr. Barry, that Mr. Brown could not expect his eyes to recover while he remained in Assam, but it was long before he himself yielded to that conclusion.

To daughter in September. "The cold weather is now coming on, so I trust we shall not be obliged to go home just yet, though it is doubtful whether we are able to spend another hot season here."

About this time the mail began to bring him letters oddly superscribed, and he noticed that his plain democratic name flourished an honorific appendage. "I see that somebody has been attempting to adorn your poor old father with a couple of ecclesiastical epaulets in the shape of two D's. I have good reason to believe it was a mistake ; at all events they don't belong to me."

To his intimate friends he returned the compliment by affixing the ornamental letters to their names also, and thus succeeded for a time in recovering the plainness he preferred. On learning later, by an official communication from his Alma Mater, that the title was a bona fide one, he wrote to her as follows :

"To Hon. Daniel N. Dewey,
            Secretary of Williams College.
                    Goalpara, Assam, Mar. 10, 1855.
    Dear Sir :—I have the pleasure to acknowledge the receipt of your favor of August 16th, furnishing me

with a certificate of the degree conferred on me by the Trustees of Williams College.

Among all the recollections of my native land, there are none more pleasant than those connected with my residence in the classic vale of Williams, and there is no institution from which a literary title would be so gratifying as from my own Alma Mater.

I shall ever think of Williams College as a nursery of missionaries ; her walks and her groves have been hallowed by the prayers of Gordon Hall and Samuel J. Mills, and many of her alumni have followed in their steps. It is with peculiar gratitude that I am able to refer to the preaching of that venerable man, Dr. Griffin, the former president, as the means, under Providence, of directing my own mind to the missionary field.

I have long felt, in common no doubt with many others, that the customary use of D. D. as a mark of distinction among ministers of the gospel, or as an appendage to the common address of an individual, is liable to serious objections. Regarded simply as a college honor like the title of A. B. or A. M., its application would be attended with fewer inconveniences. Entertaining these views, I trust I shall not be regarded as wanting in true respect for my Alma Mater if I request my friends, in writing or speaking of me, still to use the plain title of *Mr.*

May I beg that you will present my kind regards and best wishes to the Trustees of the College, and to its excellent President,* of whom I retain the most pleasing and grateful recollections,

With sentiments of high esteem,

believe me yours very truly,

N. Brown."

---

* President Mark Hopkins.

The question of returning home had already been settled by increasing infirmities. The decision had cost Mrs. Brown a hard struggle, and her husband severed no ordinary pastoral tie in leaving the flock whom he had led with many tears and prayers, and with a father's trembling anxiety for ten years.

E. B. Feb. 11, '55. "I can do no more. May the Lord watch over them and us, and if it is not ours to return, bring us all safe home together in heaven. . . . Kúnti's poor old mother has died and been buried to-day. I hope she has found rest to her soul in heaven. She has suffered much and long on earth. This is also the anniversary of our darling Nathan's death. His dear remains sleep in the old garden at Jaipúr, now overgrown with jungle, and probably the haunt of wild beasts."

As soon as it was light on Tuesday morning, February 13th, the native Christians began to collect around the pastor's house. The whole church was soon on the veranda; gray-haired, decently-attired aged matrons, quiet-mannered young mothers with wondering children clinging to their skirts, and wide-eyed infants in their arms; converts, preachers, and office-hands; Kolibor and his wife Númoli, Jogori and her husband, Ramsing and Kúnti, Peter and Búdhi, Horuram and Sokú, Húpahi and Dehiram, the little Akesúri, creeping up to be caressed; Jessie, Parboti and Lucy; and Nidhi Levi, looking the last upon his friend and pastor of many years, and holding his little weeping Hannah by the hand.

E. B. Feb. 13, 1855. "It was one of the hardest partings (and I have had many), I ever experienced. The native women and girls wept as if their hearts would break. . . . We sorrowed most of all that we should see each other's faces no more. We prayed and sang, and lingered from early dawn to near 11 o'clock before we spoke the final good-bye. A lovelier band of native women I doubt whether can be found in all India. . . . If God in mercy restores my health so that I can again be useful, I will return and labor for them till life ends, with all my heart."

The Whitings, at first with the Danforths and afterwards alone, carried on the Sibsagar work till 1861, taking occasional missionary tours into the surrounding country. In 1858, they were the only laborers left in Assam till the arrival of Rev. Cyrus F. and Mrs. Mary Bronson Tolman. For a whole year Mrs. Whiting did not see a white woman's face.

During a brief stop at Tezpúr, Mrs. Brown went by elephant to Nowgong to say good-bye to the missionaries and "dear native disciples" there. She and her husband reached Gauhati on the 28th. On the down trip the two were out one evening, walking by moonlight on a sand bank, absorbed in conversation, and taking no note of the points of the compass, when suddenly they discovered that clouds were fast gathering, a thick mist rising, the moon obscured, and their boats nowhere to be seen! The jungle with its wild tenantry was not far; it was an awkward place in which to be benighted. They called along the sandy reach; no answer! As they hastened toward the river, the snags protruding from the sand, assumed to Mrs. Brown's eyes, in the fast gathering darkness, the forms of wild elephants, buf- faloes and tigers. Some seemed fixed, with their im- mense trunks and horns pointed-upward ready for battle; others seemed running directly towards them. At length, turning a sharp point of the bank, they came suddenly upon the boat, and found its small interior,

lighted by a cotton cord in a cup of oil, just then more
attractive and picturesque than the grand moonlight
stillness of a Brahmaputra sand bank.

E. B.   At Gauhati.   "Another painful parting, with
the dear Wards and native disciples.   Here, too, we
parted with the servants, cook and bearer, who had come
down with us from Sibsagar, the last of our Assam
friends.   Went on board sick and sorrowful."

Many loving words from associates and converts followed them, with prayers for their return.   Nidhi's
farewell verses in Assamese closed with this hope :

" Beloved Mother, when you return,
    May you be accompanied by many servants of Jesus,
    Who shall wield the sword of the gospel,
    And destroy the reign of Satan.

Now, Mother, with a full heart
    I bid you farewell.
    May the Lord be with you sailing ;
    In all your journeyings preserve you from danger.

That in all your trials and sorrows
    Jesus may be your comforter,
    Restore your health and hasten your return,
    Is the prayer of your son."

From Gauhati, the steamer *Thames* shortened the
distance to Calcutta.   Passing Goalpara, on the 9th of
March, they soon after left Assam behind them.   "Poor,
benighted Assam ! "   Twenty years before they had
passed this spot, to enter a country where there was
not a ray of gospel light.   Two decades had not brought
daylight to Assam ;   it was still benighted ;   but mid-

night had slowly given place to the beginning of the fourth watch, and there was a star in the east. Even streaks of a slow dawn were apparent, bearing testimony to these "sick and sorrowing" hearts that their labors were not in vain.

"We have the sure word of prophecy," [were Mrs. Brown's last words written in Assam,] "that the time will come when the remaining darkness shall be dispelled; when these heathen temples shall crumble to the dust, and the self-righteous Brahmans shall become the humble followers of Christ."

At Dacca, Mr. Bion, a German missionary, called on the travelers and took them home with him to remain during the steamer's stop.

E. B. "In the evening Mrs. Robinson took us for a drive, to show us the city and ruins. We visited the tomb of the old queen, the palace and mosque, fortifications, and a beautiful tank, all greatly dilapidated, and said to be hundreds of years old."

Three weeks passed in much weakness at Calcutta; here Mr. and Mrs. Brown had the pleasure of seeing Mr. Beecher of Bassein and Mrs. Vinton, who was sending her children to America. April 16th, the Browns embarked on the *Ringleader*, an American clipper, bound for Boston via London, both so feeble that it seemed a matter of considerable doubt whether they would endure the voyage.

While they were still in the Hoogly, Mrs. Brown crept from her berth to the deck, to see the *Rambler*, which had carried her from St. Helena to New York in 1847. The good old ship was now a melancholy sight. She had been caught and wrecked on the sands, and lay on her beam-ends, forsaken by officers and crew, three of whom were drowned, and the vessel was expected hourly to fill and sink. "Only the pilot remained by the ship," says the diary. Did the worn-out missionaries trace some analogy between the storm-beaten vessel and themselves? If so, it still held true, that "*the Pilot remained by the ship*," in spite of shoals and tempests.

Their hope of return was never realized; but written on their hearts was the name *Assam*. A second and a third generation of miners have gone into the darkness, and now the mountains are bringing peace to her people, and the hills, in righteousness. "Wild, devil-worshipping savages, are transformed into staid, substantial Christian men." "*A new Assam* by faith we see." * Eastward, northward and southward her shut gates are creaking on their hinges; she cannot long be isolated; the day of her redemption draweth nigh.

---

* Report of the Jubilee Conference, 1886.

XXXI

THE *Ringleader* pushed out in the teeth of the southwest monsoon ; two months of gales in the bay and around the cape—well named of old, the "Cape of Storms"—rendered existence to her passengers at the best a blank, except for one melancholy event, the illness and death of the steward. At ten o'clock on the morning of June 1st, officers and men gathered at the ship's side, while Mr. Brown conducted the solemn burial services, at the close of which the dead man's body was gently lifted over, and

> "His heavy-shotted hammock-shroud
> Dropped in his vast and wandering grave."

After passing the Azores, kind-hearted Captain Matthews had the satisfaction of seeing his invalid passengers begin to show the benefits of the voyage. As they neared the mother country, their strength and spirits sensibly revived. Entering the Thames, Mr. Brown felt like Rip Van Winkle waking into a changed world. It was difficult to take in as fact, the moving picture of triumphant commerce, civilization and Christianity which now opened before him. He had never seen a railway train or locomotive, and having gained the impression from newspapers that a majority of the passengers were killed by accidents, had affirmed a determination never to ride behind "one of those engines

(437)

of death." They disembarked; out of the midst of confused movement and noise, he found himself somehow spirited into one of the deadly projectiles. A jerk—a rush, a few minutes of whirling irresponsible helplessness, then out again, *alive!* But silence was nowhere to be found, by day or by night; she had met her fate at the hands of civilization and the century. Fortunately good Mrs. Moore's house was not very far from the British Museum; in its peaceful, unprogressive galleries the ghost of silence wandered; the old East Indian followed it, and studied Nineveh marbles.

The *Ringleader* took its passengers on board again on the 27th of August, and a month later they were in Boston Harbor. There was the State House dome unchanged, but spires and masts had thickened within the quarter-century, and an obelisk had shot skyward—the granite memory of a past, the last fringe of whose robe was just vanishing behind a cloud of steam. Then followed more days of hurrying to and fro; greetings, meetings, cordial handgrasps, loving welcomes. At length the still center of the whirlpool is discovered in the Deerfield valley, and then comes a moment in which to take breath; to try to trace in altered faces the looks of long ago, and to hear and tell what had happened in twenty-three years. Mr. Brown wrote some of these reminiscences in the album of a friend a few months later:

There's a book I've been reading for many years,
    Turning the leaves with the hours;
Some of its pages are blotted with tears,
    Some painted with golden flowers.

Oh bright were the pages that life's young morn
    Begemmed with its early dews!
But the pictures now are soiled and worn,
    And gone are the golden hues.

And the leaves have been turned in a tropic clime ;
   Sad, sad has been many a scene,
With the cloud, and the shadow, and mourning time,
   And the sunrays thrown between.

Reading on, I revisit the northern shore,
   Where no vassal bends the knee ;
And the rainbow page is painted o'er
   With the progress of the Free !

But alas   I stand by my native hearth,
   And the forms that I loved are gone ;
Changed, changed unto me is this beautiful earth;
   Let me pass with the passers on !

A few more lines on the fading scroll,
   And the tale of life is o'er ;
But its impress, typed on the inner soul,
   Will abide forevermore.

Falls of Schuylkill, March 25, 1856.

Few of those "friends who the hand of parting gave" in Vermont and Massachusetts during the autumn of '32, remained. "I hardly know whether the joy or the sorrow has predominated," Mr. Brown said in an address before the Missionary Union. "Parent, brother, sister, friend, acquaintance, have passed away since we bade farewell to the home of our youth.

     ' The mossy marbles rest
      On the lips that ours have pressed
        In their bloom,
      And the names we loved to hear
      Have been carved for many a year
        On the tomb.' "

Letters received in London had brought intelligence
of the death of Deacon Albert G. Smith, of Rochester,
N. Y., from whom and Mrs. Smith their daughter had received parental care.   Missions, University and Theological Seminary lost a friend in Deacon Smith ; and
his memory lingers like a fragrance in the church which
he long served with faithful affection.   His widow, Mrs.
Julia A. (Burrows) Smith, was called home on the 6th
of January, 1890, after filling out nearly fourscore years
of quiet, unselfish service in mission and other departments at home.

One of the painful circumstances which Mr. Brown
met on his return home, was the strained relation between the Board and some of the Burman missionaries.
When motor and wheels are far separated, if any of the
bands become stretched, part, or slip from the gearing,
much confusion results.   Such a disaster had happened
in the society's Burman operations.   The cordial connection and perfect understanding which in the early
days existed between executive and missionaries, and,
like a clear oil, caused the wheels to move easily, had
become somewhat chilled and clogged with dust.   In
the whirl of much work, the connecting bands of the
machinery became strained, loosened, and in some cases
slipped, and when zealous hands seized the gearing,
spliced and tightened the bands, they no longer fitted.
A deal of friction, creaking and hinderance of work was
the result.   Some of the Burman missionaries were
censured by the executive for assuming too much responsibility as to their own labors and movements ; the
executive, on the other hand, were censured for unprac-
tical theories, and too great pressure upon the missions
in the attempt to carry them out.   Mr. Brown's convictions were on the side of the censured missionaries.   A
committee-meeting in Boston late in December recalled
him thither for a week.

To W. G. B. Charlemont, Jan. 10. "I got into Boston in season for the Christmas meeting; found about ten committee-men there from various States. The sessions held a week, three times a day; it was very fatiguing; no definite results. The accused missionaries came off clear from any real ground of censure, as far as I could judge."

In January, the fierce winds drawing through the Deerfield valley as through a flue, with mercury below zero, made havoc upon the small remnant of strength which the missionaries had brought home with them. In a mild interval, they were able to travel to Philadelphia, where kind friends nursed them both till time for the May anniversary of the Missionary Union with the Oliver St. church, New York. A letter from Brooklyn, written in great bodily weakness, says:

"If I should live two or three years, I have no doubt of seeing the truth prevail, but am so feeble, I may not live to get through the struggle,"

Still he preached, at Strong Place and 16th Street churches, and addressed the Union in defense of their missions and missionaries, and the denominational principle of "soul-liberty." Perhaps he spoke with the more freedom because he had not happened to be himself personally concerned in the questions of "responsibility" and "insubordination."

Unable to subscribe to the policy then controlling the Executive Committee, Mr. Brown withdrew from co-operation with it, pursuing his own independent course. He preached for the churches when he had strength to answer such calls, and delivered occasional missionary addresses, illustrated by Hindu and Burman idols.

His open letter on the restriction of the mission press in Burma, had appeared in the Chicago *Christian Times*

the year before his return, and in the spring and summer of 1856, was followed by a series of "Letters on
the Management of Missions," in the same journal,
urging a return to primitive methods.

In August, Mr. Brown, though in extremely feeble
health, became engaged in editorial work on the *Journal and Messenger* of Cincinnati. Here he writes, "A
mountain load seemed pressing on me." "Never mind;
if it is necessary to begin life. anew, I think we can do
it." His scattered family, and suspended life-work, bore
heavily upon him. "I do not feel at home," he wrote
to his daughter, "any more than poor Telemachus did,"
I am a wanderer—

> "Exilé, et malade de cœur,
>   J'erre toujours sur les flots !"

And now there was thunder in the air. The stormy
election of 1856 was at hand. Under the heading
"The Coming Crisis," he wrote in the *Journal and
Messenger*, August 29th :

"Portentous clouds are rushing together, in opposite
states of electricity, and their premonitory rumblings
give us distinct warning of the immense power of the
destructive elements with which they are charged.
Where shall we look for another Franklin to raise his
·magic wire and penetrate that black reservoir of destruction, conducting its energies into safe channels ? . . .
Under whatever names present parties may be ranged,
Slavery and Freedom are the only real antagonists on
the field."

While Mr. Brown was in Cincinnati, he visited the
head-quarters of the "Underground Railroad," and received from its president, Friend Levi Coffin, and his
excellent wife, the hospitable attentions so needful in

his condition of physical suffering and feebleness. It was this same Friend Coffin, who had offered a refuge to the fugitive slave, "Eliza," after she had fled across the Ohio river, on moving blocks of ice, with her infant in her arms.

A letter from him, dated "2nd, 21st, 1857," informs Friend Brown, then in New York, that the "car"—a capacious covered wagon—had recently made a valuable trip.

"The locomotive [Friend Coffin's good grey mare] performed well, notwithstanding the inclemency of the weather. The freight consisted of a mother and five daughters, (six in number). One daughter made her escape last year and is safe in Canada. If she arrives safely with her five children, she will have all her children with her except her only son, who was taken from her some years ago, and is yet a slave in another part of Kentucky. She was separated from her husband some two or three years ago, and brought to Covington, Ky."

Upon his return to America, Mr. Brown had become more fully acquainted with the principles and objects of the Free Mission Society, organized in 1843, and found they agreed with his own. Of these principles, the most prominent were, a separation "from all connection with the known avails of slavery, in the support of its benevolent purposes"; the sovereignty of the churches over their own missionary organizations, and the representative character of the latter; and an "uncompromising opposition to all oath-bound secret brotherhoods as being utterly opposed to the genius of Christianity and a republican government."

An additional principle, brought into prominence by recent events and claims, was "that Christian missionaries are the servants of Christ and not of men." **The** society claimed only to be a channel through which the churches might conveniently do their appropriate work of evangelization.

Its organ was *The American Baptist,* an anti-slavery missionary newspaper, edited by Rev. Wareham Walker, who was now putting a period to eleven years of conscientious editorial work. Mr. Brown, with health somewhat improved, was, in February 1857, associated with Mr. Walker, whose resignation, a few months later, (followed by his death from consumption in 1860,) left the returned missionary sole editor.

The circumstances which led to Mr. Brown's connection with the paper, are found related in a letter written to him twenty-seven years after, by Rev. A. L. Post, president of the Free Mission Society :

"I have been dreaming over our long and happy acquaintance, and the manner of its origin. Not long since, you mentioned the fact of the change a short note from me effected as to the last half of your life. I have always believed that there was a sort of inspiration in the writing of that note. How, on my way home from New York, where I had been for a while, helping Bro. Walker in the editorial department of the paper, downcast and sad, in view of the fact that Bro. W. could not be depended upon there much longer; my ejaculations were going up all the way in the cars : 'Lord, who shall take Brother Walker's place?' After a while it seemed to come to me like an inspiration; Nathan Brown, a returned missionary, is somewhere in the country, who, if he could be gotten, would be the right man for his successor. How I got the impression that you were in Cincinnati, Ohio, I do not now know, but such was the fact ; and I concluded, that as soon as I reached home, I would write you. That was the origin of that note. When I reached home, I immediately wrote and sent off that note to you. After a week or two, I have still in my mind, the picture of a man getting out of the stage in front of our house, and coming up on our front walk. Who is that? was the query in our minds. It was not long before all was explained. He said, 'My name is Brown; I received a short letter from A. L. Post, in relation to the editorship of the *American Baptist*; made up my mind that it was a call from higher than human authority, and obeyed at once, and here I am to learn more as to the meaning of the call.'"

It is a noticeable concurrence, that Mr. Walker, who was Mr. Brown's successor in the *Vermont Telegraph* twenty-five years before, should now be succeeded in the editorship of the *American Baptist*, by his former predecessor, then about to go on a mission to the East.

He longed to go back there now; he had not forgotten the people of his early enthusiasm, the Shans:

"I intend when I return, and as I hope, on a more unfettered platform, to push on into the country between Assam and Ava, and hope to form a junction with Brother Rose or some other brother at Bhamo, a large Shan town on the borders of China. Bro. Kincaid and myself have baptized several Shans in various places, and I feel that this great race, superior in character as well as numbers, both to Burmese and Karen, ought not longer to be neglected."

From the society's meeting at Cleveland, Mr. Brown wrote, May 28, 1858:

"At our Board meeting this forenoon, I brought forward the request I have long purposed to make, respecting my return to labor among the Shans of Burma. The brethren all sympathized in my feelings, and are in favor of my going, but think I ought to stay at least another year. I leave the question to be decided by the open ings of Providence."

The questions that had disturbed the foreign work were still far from settled; earnest men held clashing opinions; "the subject of foreign missions and the right way of conducting them," said the *Christian Times*, "has reached in our denomination the interesting status of a perfect imbroglio." A leading denominational paper of New York said of the new policy of restriction, that it "cost our treasury from ten to twenty thousand dollars, and the life of one of our most valuable pastors; and what is more than all, it has produced an untold amount of division among us, and a great falling off of contributions to the missions."

To Mr. Brown's duties as editor were added those of Corresponding Secretary of the Free Mission Society. He now found himself thrown into the heat and heart of a struggle for the principle of freedom in the churches and their missions. To stand against the tendency to centralization, and to do what in him lay, towards a restoration of the original methods, appeared to be his immediate duty.

Of the withdrawing Burman missionaries, some became connected with the Free Mission Society, which now acted as their channel of supplies and intercourse with the churches. Their communications were cordially and promptly published in *The American Baptist*, and in 1858 there was issued a pamphlet in their defense, compiled by Mr. Brown, which was entitled, "Baptist Episcopacy, as developed in the Proceedings of the Deputation and Executive Officers of the American

Baptist Missionary Union: embracing Letters from Messrs. Vinton, Brayton, Beecher, Brown, Ranney, Rose and Cross ; Kincaid's Vindication of Missionaries and corroborative testimony; with other important documents."

The editor-secretary's hands were filled with work, and his heart, at times, with a heavy load of care. The responsibilities he had assumed, must have cost him many a sleepless night and anxious day. "No one knows but God," writes one of the missionaries, "how much we all owed then, and others have owed since, to his eloquence and firmness."

Rev. J. S. Beecher had returned to Bassein, Burma, in the spring of 1857, Mr. Brown addressing the farewell meeting held at Roxbury, Mass., on his departure. After his death in 1866, he wrote of him:

"He returned to his beloved Karens in 1857, and was received by them with an enthusiasm and delight that seemed too great for expression. His chief work for the last nine years has been to elevate and prepare for usefulness a band of faithful and able ministers of the New Testament. In the department of education his success has been wonderful ; although he himself was never satisfied with the advances made, but was continually pressing to raise the standard higher. . . . All will mourn for him as a good man gone, a strong man fallen on the battle-field."

News came in June, '58, of the death of Justus H. Vinton. He had returned one day, " very tired," from a difficult mountain journey to an unhealthy region, hitherto unvisited; his last mission being to locate native preachers in the villages. There came that evening, to the weary servant, a glimpse of unearthly glory;

then a brief illness and "he was not, for God took him." Mr. Brown wrote, in *The American Baptist* of June 8th :

"There is sorrow in the Karen jungles. Tears fall in the school of the prophets assembled for morning prayers on the Kemmendine hill. Shway Dagong looks down on weeping companies of rude men and women from the forests of Pegu, as they wind their way towards the grave of their beloved teacher. VINTON and INGALLS sleep side by side, until the great drama of earth shall have ended."

Rev. Norman Harris, having laid his wife Miranda Vinton Harris, to her long rest at Shway-gyen, and stricken down himself by fever, was compelled, in 1857, to resort for a season to his native land. Becoming identified with the Free Mission Society, he returned under their auspices the following year. Services were held in New York, on Sunday evening, June 27th, at which Dr. Thomas Armitage made a powerful plea for the apostolic plan of missions. It fell to the lot of Mr. Brown, as corresponding secretary of the society, to address the departing missionary :

"Brother, you well know whither your steps are tending. You know that the moment you place your foot on Burma's strand, death will have his archers pointing at you from every jungle, and from the rank grass and reedy swamp, fever will look out with its serpent eye, and hiss upon you with its poison tongue. But lo, I am with you, says the mighty Conqueror, and under His banner you may well venture where the shots fall thick and fast. I do not wonder that your nerves are firm, and your heart strong, when I think of the object for which you are selling life.

. . . Going out on such a mission, the bearer of such a message, with such responsibilities resting upon you, with such motives urging you on, with such witnesses above and all around you, with death and the judgment standing before your face, is it for me, my brother, to give you orders and instructions in your work? For a thousand worlds I would not stand between you and your conscientious convictions of duty to the Master. For a thousand worlds I would not take the responsibility of answering in your behalf at the judgment bar, for a single deviation from what your own conscience dictates. No, brother, you must answer for yourself at that day. This society cannot answer for you, nor you for them. Go forth, free and unfettered, as the messenger and herald of the Most High. Go, and labor where Providence opens the door. Go to the home of Vinton and look at the flocks he has left. If they require your care more than any other portion of the field, obey the call of Providence. If the young prophets most need your attention, sit down under the shadow of the towering Shway Dagong, and perform the humble office of a teacher. But we know you will not forget Shway-gyen, or the dying request of those whose remains you have there entombed."

Mr. Brown was a strong believer in woman's work in missions. The American Baptist of June 7, 1859, thus answers the question, "Is Woman an Appendage?" . . . "Priscilla was as much a missionary as Aquila; her name is generally mentioned first. The beloved Persis labored much in the Lord ; also Tryphena and Tryphosa ; not to speak of the Marys and Phebes, and Dorcases who were all assistants in the work of evangelization. . . . Ann H. Judson and Sarah Boardman and Deborah B. L. Wade, Mrs. Helen M. Mason, Mrs. Comstock, Mrs. Simons, Mrs. Bennett, Mrs. Vinton,

Mrs. Brayton, and many others we might name, did not go out as family appendages ; they were missionaries in name as well as in reality ; and their communications for the Magazine in days when the missionary enterprise had a heart and a soul, were read with as much interest as the communications of their husbands.

 . . . We do not believe in exacting service from missionaries' wives; all we ask is that they may have the privilege of engaging in such voluntary work as they may think proper, and of having their labors recognized; and that when their husbands are taken away, they shall have a standing of their own, with the option of laboring on as missionaries or of returning to their native land, as they may choose."

In January, 1862, there came in one shock a double domestic grief; the sudden death of Deacons Nathan Brown and Jonathan Ballard, "loyal hearts and true" in every cause of human progress. The following is found in the files of the paper, under head of editorial correspondence : .

" Charlemont, Mass., Jan. 23, 1862.

Dear Brother Duer:—When I left you yesterday, being called suddenly to attend upon my dear father in what was supposed to be his last illness, I had little thought of the scene that would meet me on my arrival here. My sister's house is indeed a desolation. Her father and her husband both lie in the same room, cut down within eighteen hours of each other ; yet both but little more than a week ago were in the enjoyment of good health and with as fair prospect of passing through the year unvisited by the pale summoner as any of us. But they are gone; snatched away in a moment, yet not unprepared. 'Lovely and pleasant were they in their lives, and in death they were not divided.'

My father, Dea. Nathan Brown, formerly of Whitingham, and more recently of Bennington, Vt., was in his
eightieth year. He died about noon, on Tuesday, the
21st. His disease appeared to be an oppression of the
lungs, accompanied by a slight fever, which, however,
would probably not have been fatal, but for his extreme
age.

My brother-in-law, Dea. Jonathan Ballard, was somewhat worn down from watching and anxiety, but went
to bed on Tuesday night with the expectation of a sound
night's rest, and so far as known, his sleep was quiet till
near six in the morning, when his wife heard him breathing very hard, and rising to assist him, she found him
in the agonies of death. He was not able to utter a
word, and soon expired. His age was sixty-three.
Thus have passed away two strong pillars of our earthly
Zion, to fulfill,. no doubt, a higher and more important
service in the heavenly temple.

The funeral is to be held on Sabbath afternoon. Elder
Chapman, pastor of the Baptist church here, preaches
the funeral sermon.

Yours in haste,

NATHAN BROWN."

Mr. Brown's foreign work reached along through all
the years at home. Whatever else he might have to do,
he never ceased to be heart and soul a missionary. To
encourage, cheer and sustain workers abroad, formed a
great part of his service ; the current of his own desire
never ceased to set strong toward the foreign field, while
his wide correspondence and life-long friendships kept
him always one in spirit with the veterans of Assam,
Burma, India and China. There was not a field or
station in whose welfare he was not interested; but
next to the Assamese, the Burman mission seems to
have been most cherished. The very name, Burma, struck

a responsive chord. Its people, its language, its missionaries, its converts were peculiarly dear to him. He seemed to have, as he once expressed it, "a passion for everything Burman."

March 30, '69. "We do not believe there has ever been a company of missionaries better fitted as a whole, for their work, more thoroughly practical, faithful, self-denying and judicious than the missionaries in Burma, from the time of its founding until the present day. They have not only been laborious workers, but in ripe scholarship and preaching talents, they have generally been very superior men. As authors, where is there another mission that enrols on its list more thorough scholars than Judson, Wade, Mason, Stevens, Cross and Haswell? As preachers, where have there ever been men of greater power than Kincaid, Boardman, Vinton, Beecher and Thomas? Of those now living where shall we find examples of more successful perseverance in labor, beyond the ordinary term of service, than in the devoted Brayton, Harris, Simons, and Bennett, who having spent their twenty, thirty, and forty years, still remain to finish their work, and lay their bones beneath the soil they have trod so long?"

[Address to departing missionaries, Rev. and Mrs. William M. Scott, in 1865.] "Burma has been consecrated by holy men and women who have labored, toiled and died. There Judson has left the bloody tracks of his painful march to the prison of Oung-pen-lá. There sleeps the wife of his youth beneath the Hopia tree There reposes the dust of the sainted Boardman. His widow, the second Mrs. Judson, who went upward from St. Helena, has left a line of light in her passage to the starry world. There rest the ashes of that lovely missionary Mrs. Helen M. Mason.

There sleep Justus H. Vinton and Mrs. Vinton, and others equally devoted. There sleep the first Karen convert, Ko Thah Byu; the first Karen martyr, Ko Thah Gay; the Burman martyr, Ko San Lone; the old Burman pastor, Ko Thah Ay. Already a long array of bright spirits have toiled, died and won the crown. Oh what hallowed associations cling around the land of your adoption—what sublime examples for your encouragement as you press on in your arduous warfare!'"

The following hymn, written by Mr. Brown, was sung at the designation services of Mr. Scott, May 26, 1865.

GOD SPEED THEE.

God speed thee on thy mission,
    Bearer of holy spell; *
Thou, on whose midnight vision
    Come dreams of heaven and hell!
Beyond the bounding billow
    Thy God hath bid thee tread,
Where waits no downy pillow
    To rest thy weary head.

Go where the Yóma ranges
    Are sparkling in the light;
Go where the desert changes
    To fields with verdure bright;
On banks of rivers olden,
    The ripening harvest spy;
And bind the bundles golden,
    To garner in the sky.

---

* Good-spell, God-spell, or gospel; i. e. good tidings.

Go where, mid temples hoary,
    Unchanged, the rude Karen,
With faith in ancient story,
    Looks for the Book again;
There spread its glowing pages,
    There pour the gospel ray;
The misty dawn of ages
    Now brightens into day.

Lo! seraph wings are floating
    Adown the azure sky;
All tokens now denoting
    Messiah's kingdom nigh;
The angel bands descending
    Earth's happy hymnings meet,
And human songs are blending
    With theirs in chorus sweet.

Haste—for the coming glory,
    Prepare the chosen ones;
Mount Calvary's banner gory,
    Shall gather Burma's sons.
Hoard up the jewels sparkling,
    And thou shalt find each gem,
Brilliant when worlds are darkening,
    In Christ's own diadem.

The files of the paper also contain the following lines which he wrote on the departure of Mrs. M. B. Ingalls, for the third time, for Burma, Aug. 31, 1867. Mr. Brown says of the circumstance to which they refer:

"I reached the wharf too late to go on board, but was able to speak with her as the vessel moved off. I asked her 'how long before we might expect to see her again?' She replied by pointing her finger upward."

Adieus are waving from ship and shore ;
"Say, sister, when shall we meet once more !"
No voice ; words fail the thought to tell,
But the lifted finger answereth well,
    Pointing aloft.!

She has buried her dead on a foreign strand,
Buried, to her, is her native land ;
Cheerful she welcometh billow and storm ;
Through the blackening tempest I see that form
    Pointing aloft!

Away with the reapers on Burma's plain,
Like Ruth, she gleaneth the golden grain ;
She gathereth pearls ; each orient gem
A star for the King's own diadem,
    Pointing aloft !

In the city's whirl, in the pagod's shade,
In the hamlets that skirt the everglade,
In the maddening rush to the idol's shrine,
Wherever immortals can catch the sign,
    Pointing aloft !

The scene is changed, and Death reaps now;
Groups are gathered and strong men bow ;
On her brow the death-damp gathers chill,
But the skyward finger is steady still,
    Pointing aloft !

Gone—to the glorious cherubim,
Gone where the sun and stars are dim,
Crowned, she walketh the golden street,
While in Burma her teachings they still repeat,
    Pointing aloft !

XXXII

A T sound of the shot on Sumter, men sprang to their feet, and discovered they had but one business on hand. The resistless torrent of patriotism drew all interests, all questions into itself. The missionary-editor found his field at home, wheeled his batteries into line, and enlisted for the war. With him it was a war of ideas. Above the scream of shells and smoke of mortars, he saw another arena, a moral battle-field, where the opposing forces were freedom and slavery; where God's hand was the moving power, and the victory was not that of section over section, but of eternal justice, the friend alike of North and South, over a system which was the enemy of both.

Commenting on the term "intensely abolitionist," applied to the Free Mission Society, he had early claimed for "The American Baptist" the same honor:

Feb. '57. "It is intensely opposed to slavery in every form, and to all other kinds of moral evil. This is our mission, to bear our testimony, intense and undiluted, against prevailing errors. Let those who are with us in sentiment join in the work, and never cease their efforts till the very principle of slavery is abolished and abandoned, whether physical or mental, in the nation, in the churches, in the ministry, or in the management of missions. *Delenda est Carthago* is our motto; "Carthage must be obliterated."

The readers of the paper discovered on January 5th, 1858, under its name, the text, "*Say ye not, A Confed-* .....

*eracy, to all them to whom this people shall say, A Con.
federacy.*" (Isaiah viii ; 12.) Subsequent events threw a
very literal emphasis upon this prophetic motto, which
remained at the head of the "Baptist's "columns through
the war. On the subsequent enlargement of the paper
into the "American Baptist and Freeman;" it appeared
with the motto, " He is the Freeman whom the Truth
makes Free."

In the annual report of the Society, May 1860, he
pointed to slavery at the present crisis as a more
formidable enemy of the Christian church than paganism.

"We look out upon foreign lands, and our hearts are
moved by the degradation, superstition and sufferings of
our race. We look at the Karens emerging from dark
waters, struggling for life, calling on us for help; they
must not plead in vain. The call from Japan echoes
across the western ocean ; to that Macedonian cry we
must not prove unfaithful. Haiti and Africa are stretch-
ing out their imploring arms ; heavy is the debt we owe
them ; with no stinted offerings let it be repaid.

But another cry comes up ; a heavy swell rocks sea
and land ; the sound of a mightier conflict vibrates on
the air. We have a mission at our own doors; here
stands our enemy, fiercer and more bloody than any
form of paganism. Every age has its great questions;
some paramount issue that controls all others ; strike
that, and we touch a million destinies ; give a wrong
impulse there and we ruin all.

. . . Shall our country be saved or lost ? This
republic is destined to exert a commanding influence
among the nations ; shall that influence be life or death?
With slavery in our embrace, the transference of American Christianity to other lands will be no gain to the
cause of morality and religion. Even pagans despise

the hypocrisy that utters no word of sympathy for three millions in chains at our threshold, and yet compasses sea and land to proselyte an idolater. The American missionaries in Syria had just succeeded in gaining the confidence of the natives, when news reached the inquirers that several of the American states had enacted laws compelling the free people of color to choose between exile and enslavement for life. Instantly the chapels were deserted, the missionaries shunned, the books they had circulated were examined no more. The Catholic friars declared that all the preachers sent forth by the Propaganda could not have struck so heavy a blow at Protestantism in Syria.

There is no missionary field on the globe which compares in importance at the present moment, with these United States. Could the churches of America but perceive their opportunity, did they comprehend the magnitude of the crisis, would they but rise up in their strength, draw the separating line between justice and oppression, and bear an honest testimony against the wrong, the great question of the nineteenth century would be settled, and this nation and the world would move on in a career of religious, intellectual and moral development worthy of a brotherhood of rational and immortal beings. . . . While truth has yet a foothold among us, while the nation is yet plastic, now, while the great heart throbs with youthful fire, is our time for missionary work. To prevent apostasy is easier than to cure it. . . . Here then is our field of labor ; here our appropriate mission work. While our brethren abroad are pressing the battle to the gates in the war against pagan idols, let us be equally faithful in the warfare against Mammon and Moloch in their Christian dress. . . . We may be few and feeble, but we are not doing an insignificant work. Moral power is not measured by money or numbers, but by the strength of principles.

Christ's church is the divinely appointed agency for carrying on the contest with the powers of darkness; that church will never be superseded while time rolls ; her foundation is the eternal Rock ; and the last chapter in the world's history shall be her triumph over the gates of hell."

Mr. Brown's editorials would perhaps be the best record possible of his life during the battle-years. They answer the purpose of a journal—for which in those days there was scant time—and, taken together, form a series of instantaneous photographs of current events, being generally written in haste, often while the press-boy waited at his elbow to take them in fragments, with ink yet undried, to the compositor. The following extracts may serve to show their drift :

"A world united could not legalize the possession of a slave. . . . The New Testament is the charter of true liberty. The spirit of freedom breathes in every page." April 16, 1857.

"In His first recorded sermon, Christ proclaimed liberty for the captives, and any gospel which ignores this grand principle, though preached by an angel from heaven, is another gospel than that of Christ. Freedom and Christianity move on together, through all the world's history." March 9, 1858.

"The truths enunciated by Luther were no more important ; nay, the first persecutions of early Christianity by the Roman emperors involved no principles more vitally essential to religion than the condemnation of American slavery; for he that denies the brotherhood of man, denies also the fatherhood of God." January 24, 1860.

" It is the religious element alone that gives strength to the anti-slavery movement ; the deep conviction that slavery is a sin against God, is the only principle that makes any real advance in the warfare with oppression." March 5, 1861.

Garibaldi seized upon the great principle, which is yet to control the world's diplomacy, that "*every oppressed human being is entitled to relief and protection.*" January 1, 1861.

"The Problem of Government." April 1. 1862. "A million of men in arms, most of them men of high moral and intellectual as well as physical power ; and standing in the front rank of modern civilization, cannot do battle for a twelvemonth without sending pulsations of life or death to the remotest portions of our planet.
. . . . If we can show, contrary to the expectation of European politicians, that the despotic element in our republic can be not only restricted and defeated in its ambitious designs, but absolutely subdued and extinguished, it will exert a mighty influence upon the downtrodden masses of Christendom. . . . They and we shall alike understand that we are not isolated nationalities struggling merely for separate independence, but that we are members of the same great family, combating against the common enemies of human rights.
. . . We cannot recognize the right of fraud, violence and robbery to exist anywhere, without endangering the peace of the world. The entire circle of humanity must be linked together on the basis of equal rights. In the world's great commonwealth, no nation that tolerates the degradation and oppression of any class of its population can be allowed a place. Its representatives can have no seat in the great parliament of universal freedom."'

May 27, '62· "The passage to Richmond is not more beset with obstacles than the way to Freedom. What then is necessary to our success? We want the spirit of Heintzelman : ' Stand in your places if your guns *are* empty.' . . . There is danger of yielding to the length of the struggle. But we may never lay our weapons down till victory perches on our banner. If we must live over the days of mobs and gibbets, let them come ; but to allow slavery to survive this war we must never submit to, cost what it may. What we do, must be done lawfully, but it must be done."

Nov. 11, '62. "The pressure now being brought to bear on the President is tremendous. The probation of slavery gives to the opposition hope and courage, and there can be no doubt that every possible appliance will be used to render the emancipation proclamation a nullity. . . . Resistance to the Federal government is boldly predicted and advocated, in case the pro-slavery policy now marked out for it is rejected ; ' disgrace, dishonor and defeat' are declared to be the ' certain, inevitable destiny' of the President. With such elements to contend with, will it be possible for him to carry forward the war? . . . Can a government be victorious over the enemy in front, while thus attacked by treason in the rear? Manifestly the time has come when the President must assume a policy of extraordinary energy, or the nation falls.

. . . Those who have the best means of judging, believe that the President is the Man for the Hour. His tenacity of purpose is such as to warrant the confidence that he will not be frightened by Fernando Wood and John Van Buren. His remanding of Gen. Hunter to the South, for the purpose of carrying out the policy he formerly inaugurated there, is regarded as an index that on the First of January the work of liberation will begin in earnest. There is, moreover, no indication that the President will tolerate any slackening of the war. The generals are pressed forward, and new expeditions on a large scale, are being sent southward. So long as the government maintains a firm front, so long will the country stand by it. Now that the proclaimed emancipation policy places the war, from the commencement of the new year, on the basis of eternal justice, it is fit that we should enter on the struggle with renewed energy and confidence :

> ' Since Right is Right, as God is God,
>   And Right the day must win,
>   To doubt would be disloyalty,
>   To falter would be sin ! ' "

Nov. 18, '62. " We look upon the union as one and indivisible ; a nation raised up by Providence, and bound together in its material interests by the natural configuration of the country. We are also linked together in responsibility for the guilty system of slavery, and together we must work out the problem of its extinction. We cannot stand aloof, and say to the four millions whom we have kept in bondage, ' We wash our hands of your blood ; we make you over to the sole control of your owners ; on them be the guilt of your oppression ; henceforth we are free.' No ; a nation cannot play Pilate in this way ; this government cannot relieve itself of its responsibilities ; it must accept them, heavy though they be ; it owes a debt to the colored race that can never be cancelled but by their freedom. In God's book of justice it stands charged with the rectification of this wrong, as the unalterable condition of national prosperity."

Dec. 9, '62· "The hours of our political probation are gliding away unnoticed ; the sands are nearly run out, and yet we trifle. A hand has passed over the wall ;

MENE, TEKEL—*Thou art numbered, weighed and found wanting*—glows in letters of fire; U—and—is faintly visible; other letters are coming out; tell us, ye wise men, do they spell PHARSIN?"

Dec. 30, 1862. "Such a year of sorrow, lamentation and woe never before passed over our beloved country. We now see what slavery is, by what it has done. Mother, daughter, sister, wife, why are you dressed in robes of mourning? Who has quenched the light of hope in your dwelling? Who is it that has dug the trenches and piled the sod over a hundred thousand brave men? It is slavery that has done this. The whole country transformed into a workshop of war; its grim and murderous associations crowding out the gentler emotions of the soul; kind and loving natures becoming callous under the roughness, recklessness, profanity and suffering witnessed in camp; the prostration of honest industry, the disappearance of the precious metals, the greatly enhanced cost of living, enormous taxation: these are the price we pay.

Such is cost of slavery to the North; what does it cost the South? We should be selfish, indeed, if we looked merely at the miseries endured by ourselves alone. If our cup has been bitter, that of the revolted States has been one of tenfold vengeance. The flower of their chivalry are sleeping in premature graves; almost every aristocratic family mourns its dead. Through all their borders there is no security of property; much of it has been sacrificed, the rest may at any moment be seized or destroyed. Penury and starvation hang over the whole population; plague and slaughter stand on either hand.

But are we, as the result of all this anguish and sorrow, to welcome the birth of the expected man-child, pure, unsullied, national freedom?"

At an anti-slavery meeting, held Dec. 22, 1862, in the Church of the Puritans, New York, Dr. Cheever, Mr. Goodell and Mr. Brown were appointed a committee to memorialize President Lincoln in reference to the terms of the forthcoming proclamation of emancipation. His diary contains the following account of the interview:

"Dec. 30. 1862, Dr. Cheever and Mr. Goodell sent in urging me to go on to Washington with them, as a telegram had been received from Senator Harlan, that an interview could doubtless be obtained, and that it was important for the Committee to come on and present the memorial—that adopted at the meeting of ministers and others at the Church of the Puritans.

I declined going, Bro. Duer being absent. Besides, I thought the time had passed, the Proclamation was doubtless settled and finished by this time. Dr. Cheever came in himself, a little after noon, and was very pressing, so I agreed to go.

We started from the Jersey ferry, at six o'clock. Rode all night and reached Washington in the morning. Found Senator Harlan at the National Hotel. Went up to the White House in the afternoon, Senator Harlan conducting us, but could not get an interview. The Cabinet were in session.

About six in the evening went up again. Senator H. seated us in an ante-chamber, and went to ascertain from the Private Secretary if we could be admitted. After being gone fifteen or twenty minutes, he came giving the intelligence that the President could give us but five minutes, as he had agreed to meet the West Virginia deputation, at 7, and it was now very near that hour. So we followed the Senator to the President's room. We were ushered in where the tall man stood up near the fire, apparently waiting to receive us. Were introduced and shook hands. Mr. Harlan excused himself and passed out of the room.

'Well, gentlemen, be seated.'

The President sat down in a large chair near the fireplace, Dr. Cheever in a chair on his right hand, near the table and under the gas, Mr. Goodell in another chair next him, while I took the big chair opposite the President, at the other end of the fire. Dr. Cheever got out the memorial and began to introduce his subject, explaining our object—was afraid the memorial was too long to read. (It wanted then just five minutes of seven by the clock that stood on the mantel.)

'How many pages are there?'

Dr. Cheever began to turn them over and count—the length was formidable. He did not venture to tell him how many pages there were.

'Well, read on ; if it is too long I'll tell you when to stop.

The doctor began : the President stretched out his legs across the fireplace, leaning, or rather lying back in his chair, in such a posture as a tired man or an invalid would assume in order to rest. He fixed his eyes upon me mechanically, and did not, as far as I could judge, take them off, except in a single instance, during the whole reading. In order that I might not appear to be watching the effect of the reading upon him, I directed my eyes to the reader, looking up but seldom towards the President. He listened with imperturbable attention ; the memorial was read by Dr. Cheever in a somewhat rapid manner, not with that terrible emphasis with which he had read it in his own church—that of course, would have been to insult the President. The soft unimpassioned tone did not, however, take away the edge of its severity—but the President showed no emotion. Only once did he interrupt that part of the memorial which said that if emancipation was a military necessity in any States, it was in all.

'That's a non sequitur,'* said he, hurriedly, raising himself up in his chair and turning his look upon Dr. Cheever—'that's a non sequitur.'

Dr. Cheever thought the statement was correct, and the President dropping the subject, allowed the reading to go on till the memorial was done, and Dr. Cheever began to follow it up with further remarks. At length a pause gave the President opportunity to begin. The sleepy eyes opened, the dark complexioned face assumed an expression of interest; a consciousness of mental power, perhaps of superiority, gleamed from the eye, the wide mouth disclosed a seemingly half-sarcastic smile, and if I could read the countenance, it said, 'Now, gentlemen, I have borne a pretty severe lecture from you, and you don't get off without something of the same sort yourselves.' His first words were:

'Well, gentlemen, if you could *prove* to me *one half* of what you have read in that memorial, I should be a happy man!'

He then went on to show that the wonderful effects which the memorial predicted would follow the proclamation, in ending the war, were imaginary and without any foundation.

'I *know* it is not so,' he said with much emphasis. 'You have addressed me a letter through Mr. Greeley, in behalf of twenty millions, assuring me that as soon as I issued the proclamation, the whole country would rally round me, and thousands of volunteers would rush into the ranks. The proclamation was issued, and see what the result was in the elections; the opposition gaining strength and carrying the majority against us. Instead of the proclamation having brought support to the administration, it has done the reverse.'

Mr. Goodell and Dr. Cheever remarked that there was another cause, 'that the proclamation was not a pro-

---

* The President pronounced it as if written " sekkitur."

clamation of immediate emancipation, but a postpone-
ment of it.'

'Yes, I know that is the reason you give for its failure.'

According to previous agreement Mr. Goodell and
myself left it chiefly to Dr. Cheever to carry on the
argument, knowing that the time was so limited. The
President said :

'You state in the memorial that the whole country
would be united on emancipation, that they would be
unanimous.   How could we believe that such men as
were leading the opposition in New York city, would be
unanimous in approving emancipation ?'

Dr. Cheever contended that it would have been so if
the blow had been struck at once, instead of deferring it
three months. 'Your enemies in New York city, even
the *Herald* and Fernando Wood would have quailed
under it.'

The President said one or two victories would do a
great deal more towards disarming the *Herald* of its
opposition than any proclamation.

While the discussion was going on, one of the President's children, (Tad) a smart little boy, six or eight
years old, came bouncing into the room ; 'You must go
away, my son, you can come and see pa by and by.'

The President said the Committee were unwilling to
allow him to be the judge of what would be best ; their
memorial assumed that they knew better than he did,
what measures would save the country.

'You come to me as God's ministers, and you are
positive that you know exactly what God's will is. You
tell me that slavery is a sin ; but others of God's ministers say the opposite—which am I to believe ? You
assume that you only have the knowledge of God's will.'

'No, Mr. President,' said Dr. Cheever, 'we only refer
to God's word, which speaks plainly on this point. The
Golden Rule is sufficient.'

The President said to Dr. Cheever, that he presumed he was the writer of the memorial. Mr. Goodell said that the other members of the Committee had a part in it.

'Well, Dr. Cheever, I must say that you are a very illogical reasoner, at least, that is my opinion—ha! ha! ha!' The President seemed to have a habit, whenever he said anything sharp or sarcastic, of finishing it up with a sort of forced, mechanical laugh—a pretty good imitation, too, of a right hearty, spontaneous laugh—to show that he was in good humor. This made his sarcasm appear not at all offensive, but rather as good natured pleasantry, and Dr. Cheever could not but thank him for his frankness. Several times his laugh was so earnest, that, mingled with his wit, it succeeded in bringing the whole Committee into a tolerably sympathetic he-haw.

The President said all his convictions and feelings were against slavery. 'But,' said he, 'I am not so certain that God's views and feelings in respect to it are the same as mine. If His feelings were like mine, how could He have permitted it to remain so long? I am obliged to believe that God may not, after all, look upon it in the same light as I do.'

The Committee answered that this would prove too much—it would excuse any crime which God permits, adultery, murder, treason. Does God's failure to interpose, relieve the government of its obligation to punish these crimes?

As the time wore away, the West Virginia Deputation became impatient, and the Private Secretary came in to say they had come. 'Tell them to wait a little,' said the President, and went on with his conversation.

'Your memorial represents that a decree of emancipation would produce a *transfiguration*—but I have no evidence that it would produce a 'transfiguration.' 'I do

not know that the British decree of emancipation produced any such transfiguration in England.'

Dr. Cheever: 'Was there not a transfiguration in
the British West Indies? Nor in the Sandwich Islands?'

The President said the idea seemed to be that there
would be something miraculous in the effect of emancipation, but he had no evidence of miraculous events in
our times. The memorial attributed our military defeats to our generals who did not favor emancipation,
and predicted that if other generals were in command,
of the same sentiments on abolition as the Committee,
we should be sure of victory. He supposed, as a general thing, an officer who was hearty in the work he was
doing, would do rather better than one who was not,
but when we looked at facts, he did not see that the
generals who were in favor with that part of the community which we represented had done much better
than others. Some of the generals of this class had
done pretty well, and some had not done so well. He
did not see that there was on the whole much difference.
Such generals as Reno, Stevens and Kearney had been
denounced as pro-slavery, and abused as if they were
traitors, but there was this proof of their patriotism,
that they had given their lives for their country.

The President did not appear to be at all sanguine
as to the results of emancipation. He said, however,
that the experiment would be commenced to-morrow on
a scale of some two or three millions, and if it succeeded with them as the memorialists anticipated, they
could then with propriety call on him to emancipate the
rest. He thought the proclamation would do something; that it was, on the whole, the best course that
could now be pursued, and therefore he had adopted the
measure.

The Committee urged upon the President the duty of
carrying out emancipation as a measure of justice; and

not as a mere military necessity. He considered that he had no power to do it except as a military measure ; he would be glad to have slavery done away with, but he knew no authority by which he could interfere, except as a measure of war.

Dr. Cheever appealed to him whether if one of those children of his should be kidnapped and carried into bondage, he would not feel that there was authority in the National Government to rescue and restore them to their parents? This seemed to affect the President, it was a solemn question. He hesitated for a moment, then said hurriedly, as near as I could make out the expression, that it was a case not provided for.

The clock had now reached about twenty minutes to eight, and the topics seemed to have been nearly exhausted, Dr. Cheever having, as chief spokesman, well sustained the argument. Thinking that we had held the President quite as long as we could, with propriety, I remarked that perhaps we ought not to trespass upon his time further, so we rose to go. He rose and continued his talking—we thanked him for his frankness and candor. He seemed in perfect good-nature, and not at all anxious to hurry us off—made several pleasant remarks, and wound up with an anecdote to show that proclaiming slaves free did not make them free.

. . . I told him we were very thankful for the proclamation, and I hoped it would not prove a mere proclamation, but that it would be fully carried into effect. Mr. Goodell said a few words on the importance of having generals that were heartily in favor of carrying it into execution, and we took our leave, the President shaking hands with us as we left.

The next morning everybody was on tiptoe to get a sight of the morning papers, as it was understood they were to contain it, but the document did not appear till three o'clock in the afternoon, and when it did appear it contained the extraordinary declaration that emancipation was an act of '*justice!*' Was that word added subsequently to the reading of the memorial, and the discussion of this subject with the Committee?

P. S.   It appears that the word was added by Mr. Chase with the President's acquiescence."

[EDITORIAL CORRESPONDENCE.]

"Washington, Dec. 31, 1862.

Dear Bro. Duer:—The memorial adopted at the meeting in the Church of the Puritans, we presented to the President to-day. . . . He is evidently an earnest man; frank and candid, but his sentiments on the great question of the day are by no means of the radical stamp. Perhaps he is, in this respect, a fair type of the sentiment of the nation. The public conscience has become so demoralized by slavery that we have come to look upon human laws as superior to justice, instead of recognizing justice as the source and fountain of all law, and the only ground upon which any human enactment can be rightly enforced. I have been surprised at the manner in which some abolitionists, even, admit and proclaim that the President, in adopting emancipation as a war-measure is not at liberty, under the Constitution, to take into consideration the claims of the blacks to justice, but that if freedom comes, it must come as an accidental, unsought result of war. Now, the fact that emancipation is a military measure, instead of depressing it to a lower moral plane, elevates it, and disencumbers it of the restrictions of statute law. When an appeal is made to the sword, the routine of legal forms is confessedly abandoned; instead of waiting for redress by prescribed and circuitous processes, the strong arm and ready weapon strike directly at one end, *justice;* overleaping everything else, we aim our blows directly for this one object.

War can never be defended on any other basis than that of strict and absolute right ; if it stands not on this, it is but wholesale murder. So far from ignoring or conflicting with justice, the war-power knows nothing but justice; for this it even makes revolutions; it overthrows constitutions, and history enrolls as heroes the actors in these struggles for the right. Our fathers planted themselves on the fundamental, eternal principles of equity, and mankind do them homage. For any other cause than the establishment of right, the war they waged would have merited and received the execration of all nations. We cannot conjoin military law with the disregard of human rights without making a despotism. General Hunter was perfectly logical when he said that under a republican government, military law and slavery are incompatible.

. . . This evening I had the pleasure of meeting Brother Welles in his school, where a most interesting scene was presented, the sparkling eyes and quick voices of the pupils showing with what eagerness they embrace the opportunity to obtain that knowledge of which a cruel system has so long deprived them. Some of the pupils were from Fredericksburg and other parts of Virginia, some from South Carolina, and they exhibited a vivacity and intellect which we should not find exceeded in any northern schools.

Yours for the oppressed,

Nathan Brown."

Jan. 5, 1863. " Having concluded to remain in Washington over the Sabbath, I will give you a running sketch of my observations during the past five days. New Year's was spent very pleasantly, the only drawback being a generally expressed disappointment at the non-appearance of the President's proclamation. All expected it in the morning papers ; instead of it we had a report that it was to appear at noon ; it did not come out, however, till after three o'clock. The President probably held it under advisement till the last moment, and though it must have been substantially completed on Wednesday, it is not unlikely that there may have been a final revision on Thursday morning. At any rate, the New York memorial was in season to exert whatever influence it was capable of exerting, in shaping or modifying the terms of the proclamation. I confess that I was greatly surprised, after hearing the President's views the previous evening, to see in the proclamation the unequivocal declaration that emancipation was "an act of justice," as well as a military necessity. So far as I have learned, the proclamation gives general satisfaction here. Still there is much bitter though latent pro-slavery feeling in the city. On New Year's day, when many were beginning to doubt whether the proclamation would be issued at all, I heard a lady who professes to be a Unionist, express her exceeding delight that the President had abandoned his foolish design of freeing the slaves. But the proclamation came, and every murmur was hushed.

During the day, I visited several of the army hospitals, in company with Bro. Welles, and Bro. and Sister Read, formerly missionaries in New Mexico. The management of the Washington hospitals is beyond all praise. They are admirably lighted, clean, and well-ventilated, and the wounded soldiers told us that for comfort and prospect of recovery, they could not be better off at home. Most of these hospitals are the large, splendid churches, where but a short time ago a pro-slavery divinity echoed through the spacious arches, and beneath whose domes no prayer for the destruction of slavery was ever breathed. Now, the gorgeous pulpits and stained windows look down upon the preaching of a better gospel by those kind ladies who act as ministering angels in visiting and supplying the wants of the sick and dying. . . . Among the noble women who have devoted themselves to this cause, should be mentioned Mrs. Senator Harlan, Miss Helen S. Gilson and Miss Clara T. Barton. The latter may be regarded as the Florence Nightingale of America. She remained under fire for hours during the battles of Antietam, Chantilly and Fredericksburg, taking care of the wounded soldiers who were picked up as they fell on the field of slaughter, and brought to her extemporized hospital."

Before leaving Washington, Mr. Brown preached on "Emancipation and the Millenium," to a crowded congregation, and visited the colored schools in Alexandria, where he found a proficiency in the pupils which augured well for the future of the freedmen.

Editorial, Jan. 13, 1863, under heading "An Act of Justice:"

"'JUSTICE'—we thank the President for that word. It elevates the nation to kinship with the heavens. It writes the name of ABRAHAM LINCOLN among the stars. That single word changes the whole tenor of the proclamation. The emancipation of God's crushed, torn and bleeding children, is decreed not merely as a 'military necessity,' not merely as an 'act warranted by the Constitution,' though it is unquestionably both, but as 'an act of justice.' Our civil war is now in form what it has always been in reality, the struggle of freedom against oppression."

May 26, 1863. "This nation is now ripening for victories. The singular career of our armies, our defeats and barren victories, cannot be explained on the supposition that we have been inferior to our enemies in number, skill or bravery.

. . . How marked is the course of Providence. Why has our great army, the greatest and best in soldierly drill, the Army of the Potomac, not been able to advance one step towards Richmond? Why was it driven back from the very streets of that heart of the rebellion? Why has Rosecrans and his courageous host advanced so slowly? Why have these great armies been able to do nothing but keep the rebels from invading us? It is because, first, the submission of Richmond endangered the cause by forcing a peace; and second that our army from New Orleans might march up through the heart of the great slave-holding cotton and sugar plantations of Louisiana and Mississippi, and thus secure the slaves and insure their freedom by actual conquest of the soil, and bring them into our lines just at the very time we were ready to enlist them. A little, earlier and we should have been hiring them out on plantations; now they enter the Corps d'Afrique. . . . In Louisiana and Mississippi, under the converted Banks and the experienced Grant, are the places most proper for our victories to be achieved. May no foolish sin drive us back to the wilderness."

Dec. 29, 1863. "'The Discipline of Three Years.' For three years the Almighty has been educating this nation on a grander moral scale than He has educated any other nation since the time of the Jews. Kingdoms, it is true, have risen, kingdoms have fallen, hecatombs have been slaughtered, but the issues at stake were not so directly as ours between liberty and slavery, right and wrong, the universal brotherhood of mankind on the one hand, and the tyranny of a favored class upon the other. Hence, none of the previous wars since the Christian era have held suspended such momentous influences upon the destinies of humanity for all coming time.

. . . During these three years, has all been accomplished that might reasonably have been expected? In the direct act of war, perhaps not. The country has been impatient ; the administration has been impatient ; our troops have been impatient, at what seemed to be useless procrastination. But God has a purpose. . . . There was a moral change to be wrought, a revolution in old ideas, of far mightier consequence than triumphs on the battle-field. And who shall say that everything has not been exactly timed and ordered to produce the greatest possible result?

. . . Colored men are not the only slaves that have been liberated by this war. . . . The school in which God has been educating us for three years, is making men of us. We shall never again be the bond-slaves of King Cotton."

March 7, 1865. " 'The President's Inaugural.' Out from the miry grounds of expediency, out from the fogs of state-craft, out from under the black and thunder-charged cloud, President Lincoln emerges into the clear sunshine. Climbing to the top of some hoary rock, he stands like one of the sublime old prophets, the submissive instrument of the Divine will."

April 25, 1865. " Obstinate, indeed, must be the infidel that cannot recognize the influence of the celestial weavers in the web we are weaving this day. No human wisdom could have planned, no human skill could have executed the grand drama which is working out the redemption of our country.

President Lincoln had almost reached the goal of his hopes. Four years of brave struggling had given him the victory over his foes. Weary days and sleepless nights had worn his nerves, weakened his step and wrinkled his brow with furrows, and now the prospect of a free, glorious, happy country, began to dawn on his vision as the clear shining sun after a night of storm. In obedience to the nation's will, he is seated in the chair of empire for another four years. Deep and solemn are the words he utters. They are borrowed not from books of law, but from the Divine oracles. He spoke as Moses would have spoken; he talked of justice and eternal principles; in all the mighty panorama passing before our eyes he could only recognize the hand of a Divine Being, guiding the destinies of mortals and measuring out righteous retributions. But he did not seem to share the confidence of those around him, that the dark and bloody day was over. Prompted, as by some heavenly monitor, he intimated his apprehension that the reckoning would not be closed, '*until every drop of blood drawn with the lash should be paid by another drawn with the sword!*' Ruler and high priest of a nation, thy words are prophetic. The clouds which roll up before thy vision are divine premonitions. An angel's pen will underscore that prediction with thine own heart's blood. The age of sacrifice has not yet passed away. Liberty has her altar, and upon it thou must lie. The hundreds of thousands already slain will not suffice. There must be a royal victim; the blood of the nation's ruler and representative must mingle with the crimson flood that washes the curse from our land."

May, 1865. Secretary's Annual Report of the Free Mission Society. — "Every great moral earthquake heaves the human race to a higher plane. This is God's law for the elevation of mankind. Sorrow and suffering work out redemption. The blood of martyrdom enriches a nation's soil. Every coming generation will possess higher and nobler views in consequence of Abraham Lincoln's grand career and glorious death."

In 1866, Mr. Brown wrote a brochure for young readers, entitled " The History of Magnus Maharba* and the
Black Dragon," purporting to be based on some quaintly
spelled old manuscripts which had fallen into the hands
of one Kristofer Kadmus.   The young people were not
slow to discover by reversing letters, and detecting resemblances in sound or sense, that some well-known
characters figured under the odd looking names on these
pages, and found that the story had a meaning, as they
followed the adventures of the fugitive, lovely Fredeema,
pursued by the dragon, Slavery, and delivered at last
by the intervention of good King Magnus ; heard the
tramp of the Dragonian armies in Virginland, laughed
over Bulskampur flight from the specter Pan ; cheered
for commander Rightfoot and the Granite Duke, on the
Fatherwater ; held their breath while Boldrobin dashed
through the mountains by the Shiningdoor, crossed the
Boundarimark river and plundered the Penwood valleys,
till overcome on Deathsburg field.

The death of Maharba and the mourning of Fredeema
are thus narrated at the close of the story :

" And the king's servants removed him to a private
chamber and laid him down to die.   And his lords and
they that loved him, and Fredeema, stood around his
bed, and watched him until the morning.   And because
his vitality was strong, the king lingered in his dying,
and the body and spirit struggled in their unclasping.
And when the sunlight looked in at the window, the
weary throbbing ceased ; and the king gave up his ghost,
and it became disentangled from its attachments, and
floated upward to dwell with the immortals.   And Fredeema put her lips to the king's clay and kissed his cold
face, and she said, Alas, alas, that thou shouldst die for
me ! For if thou hadst not pitied this sorrowful child and

---

* The word *Maharba* is a reversed anagram.   The book was published
both in the common and in the phonetic spelling.

taken her part when there was none else that could deliver her, thou mightest still have lived, powerful and
honored among the kings of the earth, and my poor
name would have perished from the memory of men.
And she covered her face and poured forth her anguish
in a torrent of tears.

And a voice of wailing went up from the royal city,
and it spread and increased in volume as it rolled over
the land. And all the gay cities were suddenly draped in
the weeds of mourning; and the sun grew dark and
gloomy; and the warders of the sky stretched their
clouds of crape over the pillars of the east and west;
and a pall was spread over the mountain tops and over
the lowly vales, and all the trees of the forest were
fringed with funereal tassels; and men spoke not for
horror, and every pulse paused in its beating, as if the
crack of doom had sounded from a clear sky.

And when the terror had abated, a cry of vengeance
arose on the air, and the Black Dragon heard it in his
hiding place. And he at once comprehended that there
was no den so dark, no gulf so deep, no mountain so
high, as to give him a quiet resting place on the planet
where he had done this deed. And he raised up his
lofty form, and spread his pinions for the home of his
father; and the mold of oblivion settled on his wings as
he disappeared beneath the thunderclouds that skirted
his downward way.

. . . Now there was in that country a massive and
lofty column, on which it was the wont of Historia to
record the names of departed heroes and statesmen,
and all the great and good that were deserving of remembrance. It was pyramidal in form, and vast in
dimensions, and the clouds rested on its summit. And
after the multitudes had returned from viewing the king's
corpse, they gathered around the monument, to witness
the inscribing of his name. And Historia took her

longest ladder, and set it up against the side of the column, and they watched her as she ascended ; and Fredeema climbed up after her to see where she would put
the name of her favorite.   And while she was passing
over the spot where the names were most thickly written, the people gazed intently, expecting every moment
that she would stop and begin.   But she went on and
on, until she had left the vast crowd of statesmen and
warriors beneath her feet.   And she passed the long
line of kings, King Adam and King Jeffer and King
Andrew, and King Adam ben Adam, who befriended
Fredeema in her childhood, and Osami the martyr, and
all the philanthropists and martyrs that had given their
lives to the welfare of their race.   And when the people
saw that she still kept ascending, they gave a loud shout,
for they then understood that it was a great and noble
king that had passed away from among them.   Now
there was written far up and distinct from the rest, just
under the clouds, a single name, in large characters, yet
scarcely visible for the distance ; the name was

PATER PATRIÆ.

And they watched Historia as she fixed her eye upon
the spot; and Fredeema closely followed her.   And
when she had reached the place, she took from her gir-
dle an iron style and placed her hand on the rock to
write just beneath the solitary name.   And while the
multitude were shouting, and before the rock was pierced,
Fredeema spoke and said: 'My sister, do you remember
the four millions of liberated Kushans?'   And Historia
dropped her eyes and remained for a moment in thought,
then stepped upon the next round and placing her
fingers just over the ancient letters, began to carve the
rock with a clear, bold stroke.   And all the people were
amazed and confounded, for it was a fixed belief of all

the men of the Occident that no name ever could be written above that of the father of his country. But when Historia withdrew her hand, and they saw the name of

MAGNUS MAHARBA,

and knew that it was written for all time, in characters enduring as the eternal hills, their minds were illuminated, and they saw with new eyes, and their shoutings were changed to tears of glad and wondering emotion, and they clasped their hands in prayer and gave thanks to the God of heaven that He had allowed them to look upon the face of so noble a king and martyr, the deliverer and savior of his country."

XXXIII

ONE RACE, ONE FAITH, ONE SPEECH.

THROUGH all this varied experience, the missionary's sense of universal kinship increased year by
year. "This is what the world was made for," he said
when the Atlantic Cable was laid.

"It was not made to be forever the abode of scattered
groups of isolated nationalities, with no common bond
of sympathy, worrying, wasting, enslaving and destroying one another. It was to become a united whole, a
grand fraternity, a body instinct with one life, of which
a single member cannot suffer without affecting the
happiness of all. We may liken the hitherto isolated
condition of the human family to the imperfect organization of an embryonic existence; but that condition
is now changed; the heart begins to throb; its pulsations are conveyed to the world's extremities, and they
carry with them the fresh, warm blood of a common
life. The effects which this change is to produce can
as yet be hardly appreciated; nor will the greatest of
these effects be immediate.

. . . Analogous to the effect of the telegraph on
small, isolated governments, will be its effect on the
multiplied languages of mankind. Civilization is already
reducing their number. The process will go on hereafter with greater rapidity. The leading language of
the world will ultimately become the language of the
telegraph. Translation from one dialect to another is
not suited to the business demands of a telegraphic age.
It is too slow a process for a people that send their
thoughts by lightning. They must have a general com-

(482)

mercial medium, and that medium will gradually absorb and supersede other existing tongues. The languages of Babel have had a long reign, but their successor is nominated. ENGLISH is the candidate in whose favor all the probabilities center."

On the Franco-Prussian War and International Arbitration, Dec. 27, 1870. "The control of different people by a government of arbitration is not a mere matter of speculation; this republic is actually built upon such a basis. . . . We have a court which has thus far decided many controversies between States larger in area than most of the European States. Its decisions have effectually settled every question that has arisen. New York has appealed to this tribunal against Connecticut; Alabama and Florida against Georgia; Maryland against Virginia; New Jersey against Delaware.
. . . Let the philanthropists of the world memorialize the great powers that are soon to form treaties of peace. Let congress, cabinets, ambassadors, be instructed to press upon contending powers the expedience and necessity of inserting in all new treaties the principle of arbitration. Such treaties once made, the cause of peace might safely be left to win its own way, and a great commonwealth of humanity would follow in due time as the necessary result. Kings, emperors, presidents, there might be, of various names and degrees of authority, but all would be under the dominion of law. Thus the savagery, the ambition, the lawlessness and selfishness of tyrants would be effectually restrained, and we should have the dawning of a millenium in which there should be but one government and one system of laws for this one world.
Jan. 10, '71. So far as human vision can discern, the leading tendency now is toward a republic of nationalities, and a cessation of war. This seems to be the one

great need of the age; an umpire clothed with power that shall settle all differences between nations, in the same manner as the judicial bench now settles quarrels between individuals. For the union of all nations in a common brotherhood, with a supreme court to insure perpetual peace, let us labor, pleading with our own and other governments, to bind themselves by treaty to the principle of submitting all disputes to an impartial court. We cannot doubt that universal peace is one of the blessings included in God's plan of the future, and happy they who act in the same direction with His providences.

. . . Everything tends towards the establishment of a grand commonwealth of nations, a republic for the globe. All we want further is Christian principle, the acknowledgment of Jesus as our King and Lawgiver, and then would be realized the establishment of that kingdom of righteousness which has been foretold in prophecy. Shall we not pray for its speedy approach?

As humanity reaches forward in its career of progress, the tendencies will be more and more toward one government, one language, and one religion."

He believed that the vital pulse of regenerated humanity will heat from the heart of God.

On "The Christian's Life." "It is the reunion of God and the soul. . . . His Spirit takes possession, infuses vitality, occupies as a residence, the soul of man. . . . We are expressly told that Christ is our life. Not merely the sustainer of our life, but an integral, essential element of that life. He, by his Spirit, pervades the soul. Believers are united to Him, not as the parasite grows upon the oak, but as the branch is united to the vine. They and Christ are one. Paul declares in his epistle to the Galatians that the life he was then

living was not his own life ; it was Christ living in him.
It is impossible to reconcile such passages with any
other supposition than that God and the soul are absolutely united in such a sense that as the human mind
possesses and controls the members of the body, so God
by a direct influence takes possession of the mind.

It is an essential condition of life that one of the two
elements uniting and co-operating should be under the
perfect control of the other. So far as the human or-
ganism ceases to be under the control of the mind, so
far it ceases to live. In the higher life, the soul must
be equally passive under the controlling power of God.
It must offer no resistance to the superior influences.
In other words there cannot be an unwilling participant of
the divine life. It is not a union of force. God does not
by an irresistible act of power, take possession of the
human soul and use it as a machine. . . . The soul
must, to the extent of its capacity, be a co-worker. It
must give itself up to be an instrument of God's will.
This act of submission is in Scripture called faith, or
trust ; not merely a belief of truth, but a cordial sur-
render of the heart and a confident reliance on divine
promises. Such reliance is always represented in the
sacred writings as an indispensable requisite to the
Christian life. . .. Regeneration cannot take place
without it. Eternal life is suspended on reliant and submissive faith. The Holy Spirit can be resisted. The
gracious influences may be repelled, and salvation rendered impossible by the sinner's opposition.

Hence we may perceive that the union with God does
not interfere, in any degree, with the proper freedom of
the soul in its earthly relations. The higher life does
not supersede the lower, but sanctifies, elevates and
refines it by holy influences.

. . . Verily, brethren, there is a lack in our Christianity. We are striving more for numbers than for holy

power. Faith droops her wing. Ordinances are observed, but too often Christ is undiscerned; many are weak and sickly, and many sleep."

On the practical test of Christianity; after claiming its harmony with the comprehensive and settled science that is to be: "It is not on learned treatises and philosophical argument that Christianity depends for its preservation and spread among mankind. . . . The physician may discourse eloquently on the virtues of his medicine, and persuade the patient that it is adapted to his case; but it is the cure which gives the proof. Such is the Christian's evidence for the faith within him. Thousands and tens of thousands have tried the medicine and they know it has given them peace and happiness. They know there is no other joy to be compared with that of religion. It meets their nature; it meets their wants; it satisfies their longing aspirations. . . . Let the pained, anxious, doubting soul try the remedy which others have found efficacious; and he will find himself possessed of emotions which he never felt before; of joys beyond any previous conception.

This is God's mode of evidence; this is the means by which He perpetuates faith; this is the anchor by which He binds the soul amid the storms and tossings of life's perilous sea. . . . What we need, is not better or more learned defenders of Christianity, but more meekness and modesty in our opinions, more Bible and less creed, more of the practical and less of the controversial.

. . . Only the living Christian is properly prepared to resist the assaults of infidelity. He has the witness within himself; the supernatural inflowing of the divine life. This is the best of all evidence. While the merely intellectual believer is perpetually weighing human testimony, harrassed with doubt and anxiety, lest some new discovery of geology, or astronomy, or history, should be found to conflict with the sacred record; he that has the Spirit feels no such perturbation; no speculations or reasonings of philosophers can shake the basis of his faith, for it rests on personal experience; he can as soon be persuaded that his physical life is a dream or a delusion, as that the higher life infused into his soul by the Spirit of holiness, is not a blessed and divine reality."

Holding to a world-wide brotherhood, Mr. Brown took a stand in *The American Baptist,* as he had formerly done in *The Vermont Telegraph,* against all narrower clanships. In 1867–8, he made a careful study of the subject of oath-bound secret societies, and plainly expressed his views in a series of editorials.

Apr. 7, '68· " The clan system is a relic of barbarism. It does not belong to the present age, much less to the advancing civilization of the future. It is in direct hostility to the universal brotherhood of man."

June 11, 1870. Address before the Anti-secret Convention at Cincinnati. "The Gospel is at war with every system of clique or clan, caste or combination, that seeks to create distinctions in the human family. . . . The spirit that binds men in secret, oath-bound clans is an anachronism; it belongs to the dark ages; it belongs to heathenism; it is no child of Christ, His gospel or His church, and should forever be banished from among His saints.

. . . But it is said that we are fanatics who expect to uproot this venerable institution; that it is spreading in the country, the church and the government with a strength that nothing can resist; that it is becoming the commanding influence in all our movements for

reform , giving its grand titles and its methods of pro-
cedure to all our temperance societies, which in turn are
becoming feeders for the mother organization.   Fifteen
years ago, Mr. President, I came to this city, a sick and
worn-out missionary, to find a warm shelter from the cold
New England winter, and hearing that there was a good
man here who kept an underground railroad, I made my
way to his house, where he and his excellent wife housed
and nursed me, and he told me stories of the fugitives
he had helped forward from a land of bondage to a land of
freedom.   The general opinion was that Friend Coffin
was doing a very small business ; that if he was not a
wicked lawbreaker, he was at least engaged in a foolish
and fanatical attempt to do what there was not the
slightest chance of accomplishing.   But I am here again
to-day, in obedience to his call and the call of other
Christian friends, and what do I see ?   I look across
the Ohio river, and there is sunshine on that shore.
. . .   I look elsewhere, through this great republic, and
what do I behold ?   Those little trickling rills of pity that
flowed down the cheeks of pious Friends, and Christians of
other names, have swelled to a mighty river, whose broad
wave rolls freedom from Niagara to the gulf.   Mr. President, there is nothing impossible, if it is only right."

On "The Religion of Masonry," as developed in the
higher degrees, "The distinctive features of Christianity
are shut out.   There remains what Theodore Parker
called the 'permanent' in Christianity, that is, the religion of nature, and nothing more.   The 'transient,'
that is, the special or distinctive features of the gospel
system, are stigmatized as 'sectarianism,' 'false piety,'
an 'imaginary worship.' . . . The skepticism that prevails
among the upper classes in our own country and in
England, is in perfect harmony with the teachings of
masonry."

The past was found to reveal evidences of race kinship. It was the editor's evening recreation after a busy
day in New York, with a well-shaded lamp on the table,
and his family about him, to draw from his treasures a
copy of some old undeciphered inscription, and by
piecing out defaced letters, and comparing one with
another, little by little to come at the meaning. Those
were social and enjoyable evenings. Family and guests
were drawn into consultation, while his enthusiasm lent
to sculptured legend and pictured urn a most lively
human interest. Nothing genuinely old came amiss to
him, whether Mexican hieroglyphics, Mohavé picture-
writing and rock-etchings, Karthaginian votive tablets,
or Marseilles offering-table, with tariff of sacrifices
made to Baal ; epitaph from Echmunazar's coffin, or
Moabite stone, "fresh with the finger marks of King
Mesha's chiselers." To him, each was a glass which
brought a distant but living age into view. He almost
heard the mallet strokes on Dighton Rock, and almost
saw the engraver's intent face that once bent over the
Mexican Calendar stone ; he was brother alike to the
sculptor of Runic obelisk and Cypriote mortuary column.

Sometimes the table was covered with East Indian
and other ancient coins, of which he possessed some
rare specimens, and here, the results of inquiry were
always definite and valuable. "Geography and chro-
nology," he said, "are with much truth called the eyes of
history, but without coins for spectacles, their dim and
defaced lines could never be traced." It was not a
"dead past," which he delighted to study.

"The past is of surpassing value only as it serves for
a scaffolding upon which humanity may rise to a higher
plane." .

He took great interest in American antiquities, especially burial mounds. On seeing one of these mounds

for the first time, at Marietta, Ohio, he was so struck by its resemblance to the burial-places of the Assamese rajas, that he involuntarily asked, "Whose tomb is that?" He was told that it was an old Indian watch-tower, but no argument could persuade him that it was not a burial mound of the same kind as those from which images, utensils and ornaments were unearthed in India. He afterwards learned that his suspicions were correct, similar mounds having been opened and found to contain bones, images and various utensils. On Dr. Wilson's description of the opening of mounds in the "Old Fort" near Newark, Ohio, he says:

"The bearing of this discussion on the early connection between the eastern and western continents will be seen at a glance. With the help of our missionary friends in Asia, we expect yet to prove what all our savans so stoutly deny, that the Asiatics and Americans are twin brothers."

The study of relics and inscriptions was closely connected with that of languages. The comparison of these and the tracing of their individual growth, their laws of life and their relationships, were subjects of never-failing interest.

The "American Philological Society" was an outgrowth of these and similar studies and recreations. Its objects were "to cultivate the science of language; to establish, perfect, and propagate an orthographic kosmoglot; to trace the origin, growth, and relationship of languages; to collect grammars, vocabularies, and specimens of ancient and modern tongues; to encourage the study of hieroglyphics, mythological emblems, temples, images, old inscriptions, coins, and in general, all the records and relics of the past; to investigate problems of ethnology; to publish a literary journal, and such other works as the Society may deem proper."

REV. NATHAN BROWN, ÆT. 64.

This social circle held monthly meetings at the residences of members, and Mr. Brown was their president as long as he remained in the country. The society dated its organization January 1st, 1863, and was incorporated in 1868. Papers were read on antiquarian and philological subjects, attention was directed to the improvement of English spelling, and two new books were printed in a rectified orthography, adapted to universal use.

"The researches of philologists have happily prepared the way for the introduction of a uniform phonic system into all the languages of the globe. Much of the work, indeed, is already done. The missionary alphabet, as it is usually called, prevails with little variation throughout the islands of the Pacific, is used extensively in the languages of Asia, and in the recently established missions of Africa. The system is everywhere substantially the same. The prominent and essential feature of this orthography is the correct classical use of the vowels a, e, i, o, u, which are invariably sounded *ah, ey, ee, oh, oo.*"

At the Poughkeepsie meeting in 1869, of the American Philological Association, of which he was also a member, he took part in a spirited discussion on the pronunciation of Greek and Latin vowels, advocating the classical sounds, and believing it possible to arrive at the original pronunciation.

The universal alphabet had been a subject of life-long interest to him. On his way to Assam in 1835 he had done some of the foundation work which led to the adoption of a phonic system in the east, as appears from correspondence of the East India Romanizers. Referring to an international alphabetical conference held at Chevalier Bunsen's, Sir Charles Trevelyan writes in February, 1854, to Mr. Brown, that the latter was there "mentioned as an authority in respect to the application of the Roman letters to the languages of Asia.'

In 1865-6, Mr. Brown arranged and published his " Kozmik Alfabet." It corresponds, in the main, with the original " Missionary Alphabet " of Max Müller. It has but few diacritical marks, and no characters other than those in common use, the reversed capital, ᗡ, serving for the sound of *th* in *th*is, and ᗺ, for *th* in *th*in. C with the cedilla—ç—indicates the sound of *sh* in *sh*all. In the use of this alphabet, only one rule of spelling is required, namely, "*Let every letter have its own sound: and let every sound have its own letter.*" The classical or continental sound of the vowels is retained.

KOZMIK ALFABET OV FORTI LETURZ

SOUNDED AZ IN ᗡE FOLOIN̦ WURDZ:

A	a	Adam	M	m	madam
Á	á	párt	N	n	nonsens*e*
B	b	b*u*ild	N̦	n	sinkin*g*
C	c	*ch*ildren	O	o	*h*ono*u*r
Ç	ç	ç*h*agrin	Ò	ò	br*ò*ad
D	d	dou*b*t	Ó	ó	g*h*óst
ᗡ	ᗡ	ᗡ)*th*is	P	p	plou*gh*
ᗺ	ᗺ	ᗺ)*th*ink	Q	q	Qurán
E	e	men	R	r	ri*ch*
È	è	bè*ar*	S	s	só*u*l
É	é	vé*i*l	T	t	troubl*e*
F	f	fò*ugh*t	U	ᴜ	m*u*rm*u*r
G	g	g*u*es*s*	Ʉ	u	put
H	h	head	Ʉ́	ú	rúl*e*
I	i	pitiful	Û	û	sû*e*
Í	í	fi*e*ld	V	v	vers*e*
J	j	joint	W	w	wicked
J	j	bij*o*ú	X	x	Xristos
K	k	kindred	Y	y	yeóman
L	l	ais*le*	Z	z	*z*ealo*u*s

N. B.   Italik or sailent leturz tu bí diskárded.

MIÇONARI HIM.

From Grínland'z aisi mountinz,
  From India'z koral strand,
Hwèr Afrik's sʋni fountinz
  Ról doun ɑèr góldn sand,
From meni an énçent river,
  From meni a pámi plén,
ɑé kòl ʋs tu diliver
  ɑèr land from error'z cén.

Hwot ɑó ɑe spaisi brízez
  Bló soft ór Sílon'z ail,
ɑó everi prospekt plízez,
  And ónli man iz vail ?
In vén wiᴅ laviç kaindnes
  ɑe gifts ov God ar strón,
ɑe hiɑen in hiz blaindnes
  Bouz doun tu wud and stón.

Çal wí húz sólz ar laited
  Wiɑ wizdom from on hai,
Çal wí tu men binaited
  ɑe lamp ov laif dinai ?
Salvéçon ! Ó salvéçon !
  ɑe joiful sound proklém,
Til erɑ's rimótest néçon
  Haz lerᴎt Mesaia'z ném.

Waft, waft, yí windz, hiz stóri,
  And yú, yí woterz, ról,
Til, laik a sí ov glóri,
  It spredz from pól tu pól ;
Til ór our ransomd nécur
  ɑe Lam for sinerz slén,
Ridímer, Kiᶇ, Kriétor,
  Riturᴎz in blis tu rén.

(31)

Of these language-studies and efforts for phonetic reform, Prof. Max Müller says in a letter to Mr. Brown of July 7, '66, here published by permission:

"It was a great pleasure to me to receive a letter from you, and to hear that you have recovered from your illness and are able again to take an active part in those studies which owe so much to your former labors among the tribes of Assam and the valleys of the Irawadi. I was quite disappointed at not meeting you when you touched England on your way home, for there were several questions which I should have liked very much to discuss with you, which it is difficult to discuss in a letter. But I hope you will sooner or later throw the results of your linguistic studies into a more accessible and permanent form. Your experience with regard to the rapid changes of dialects left to themselves without literary or traditional restraints of any kind, is invaluable. Soon there will be no more chance of studying the growth of such dialects, for even the work of a solitary missionary will interfere with the natural development of savage speech. And yet is not that the true life of language, and ought it not to be studied with the greatest care, when there is still a chance of so doing? Please do not allow your experience on this subject to be lost.

. . . I shall be curious to watch the success of your alphabet. It contains some very practical features, and does not differ essentially from my own missionary alphabet. I am glad to find that the simple principle on which my missionary alphabet is founded, begins to be recognized even by those who at first opposed it. I do not care *how* modification is expressed; all I contend for is that there should be *one* uniform way of expressing the rough fact of modification without any attempt at coining diacritical marks for every variety of sound that may be discovered. Letters should never photograph sound, but only suggest sound. Give people a clear idea of the typical vowels and consonants of human speech, express the typical vowels and consonants by the ordinary letters, and then, if in any language a missionary hears, besides the ordinary t, for instance, another t, whether of Sanscrit or Arabic, let it be represented by a modified t. What that modification is, does not matter; whether italics, or capitals, or inverted letters, makes no difference, only ·let it be uniform.

. . . The interest in the science of language is certainly on the increase; there is hardly an English review which does not discuss the subject in its different bearings on history, ethnography, philosophy and religion.

. . . Believe me with sentiments of sincere admiration,

Yours very truly,

MAX MÜLLER.

The Rev. N. Brown."

The possible future unification of languages was a favorite idea with the returned missionary, and he believed in English as the basis of the kozmoglot or world-tongue that is to be. In an address on "The Saxon Language—its Eclipse and Relumination," he traced our mother-tongue back to its various widely removed sources, and closed by forecasting for it a grand destiny.

"The era we are approaching is one of light, simplicity, truth, beauty harmony. The tribes of earth are to become as one household. And that household must speak a common tongue. 'Then will I restore to the people,' says sacred writ, 'a pure language;' not many languages, but one. The curse shall be removed; the babble, Babel, Babylon—in other words, the spirit of confusion—shall pass away, and the reign of peace and right, unanimity, order, beauty, truth, be everywhere consummated.

... Unquestionably, the first step towards a universal language, is a universal alphabet. Let us give our noble tongue a comely dress, and it is all we need to do; other nations will use it as fast and as far as they perceive it to be worthy. When its alphabet is rectified, it will readily coalesce with its kindred tongues, the various branches of Sanscrit, Greek, Latin and Norse. Not improbably it may, mingling still farther with these, receive other important additions and modifications, before it becomes the permanent language of the future.

The idea of a happy, harmonious universal brotherhood has been for ages the theme of poets, the vision of philosophers, and the subject of divine revelation. The obstacles to this great consummation are rapidly disappearing, and as we watch the downfall, one after another, of the mighty bulwarks of strife and wrong, we would devoutly exclaim,

> ' Oh for the hour when, like a millstone cast,
>   Babel shall fall, and Discord's reign be past.' "

XXXIV

BEYOND THE SOWING AND THE REAPING.

MRS. BROWN never entirely recovered from the effect of the hardships and exposures of her Assam life. Yet she longed to go back; those dear girls and women who, when she left, had pleaded with tears to be allowed to follow her wherever she went, always kept their place as children of her heart; she wanted to see them, and was homesick for Assam. "I can fully sympathize with you and Sister Stoddard," she wrote to Mrs. Danforth in March, '63, "in the *heart-longings* to spend the remainder of our days among that people."

It gradually became evident that her unusual vitality and endurance were permanently undermined, and she met one of the severest trials of her life in giving up at last, the hope of return to the foreign work. Yet she took up in much physical feebleness, the task nearest to hand; the energetic, cheerful spirit, getting more work out of the frail body than some in perfect health would have attempted, and perhaps holding it in life the longer, by the tonic of an unselfish purpose. During the years spent in America, she entered heart and soul, into all her husband's missionary and anti-slavery labors. The National Freedmen's Relief Association, with its auxiliary Women's Committee, organized in New York in the winter of 1862, was one of the objects which enlisted her sympathies.

To a friend, March 20, '62. "Can you not get together a sewing-circle in your society and do a littl something? The reports which reach us here, of the destitution, sickness and suffering of the thousands at Port Royal and elsewhere, are heart-rending. We sent off about sixty men and women as teachers, doctors and nurses, with a large quantity of clothing and supplies, on the *Atlantic*, about three weeks ago ; but that is only a 'drop in the bucket,' among so many."

"Remember me in your prayers, mother ; good bye ;" writes a young soldier in the Army of the Potomac from "Camps near Stafford Court House, Va." He was a Eurasian boy from Siam, who had shared her care and counsels, and found it natural to call her "mother."

The brave men had marched, fasting, through wintry rain and knee-deep mud, fording the freezing streams. "It was hard work in this march," he wrote, "and a good many are sick and the ambulances are full of men that are not able to walk." A later letter of May 17, '63' tells of the move to Kelly's Ford, of more hard marching, and of wading the Rapidan, "the water so deep and swift we can hardly stand on our feet," and capturing forty bridge builders on the other side; of the night's picket duty in wet clothes, no fires being allowed to tempt a reprisal; of the next day's advance on Chancellorsville, and the disasters of Saturday and Sunday ; of some of his comrades killed, and his own "slight wound in the head."

The "mother's" replies carried hope and courage to the friendless stranger lad through his army experience, which included Gettysburg and a hospital bed in Alexandria. After the war, on returning to Siam, he wrote her, "I will not forget my Redeemer, Who died for me, and I will do all in my power to spread His gospel truths."

"I have a new charge ; [she writes to her daughter, May 6, 1866,] two Karen boys, arrived last Tuesday from Bassein. . . We had not heard that these boys were on their way, till Dr. Brock brought them to Papa's office, and made the charge of them over to him. . . . After I had got them some supper, and been with them a little while, they seemed so lovely, so like my Assam children, I had no wish to part with them. They are now quite at home with me, and I with them. The eldest, M——, is nineteen ; Y——, sixteen ; both sons of Karen pastors, sent here to finish their education, and go back to preach to their countrymen ; are both church members, baptized some years since. . . . We shall keep them till we get directions from Brother Beecher as to the school to which they are to be sent." .

It was a little reminiscence of old times to Mrs. Brown to care for and teach her new charge, helpless for a time, in a foreign country, among customs very strange to them. After they were sent to school, she was " Mama" still to them, writing and receiving frequent letters.

Women's missionary meetings formed just the atmosphere Mrs. Brown delighted in ; and though she did not often make a public address, she loved to sit and listen, and at the close, to grasp the hands and look into the faces of fellow-workers. As one of the managers of the " Five Points Baptist Mission," she at one time found strength to do some work for the little waifs of lower New York.

Missionaries, young and old, home and foreign, outgoing and returning, knew that they could give her no greater pleasure than their presence ; it was a real delight to her to plan outfits, and render what aid she could. She listened to many chapters of unwritten sorrows ; her motherly heart carried many burdens, fears and hopes unheard by other ears. She felt a peculiar tenderness for returned missionaries, veterans from the front, hiding their wounds and necessities, and often laboring beyond strength to enlist new volunteers.

To her own family and kindred, her life was one of affectionate devotion. The home, which for most of those years was in Jersey City, was lighted and warmed by the glow of a real mother-heart; and like a beacon, it burned the brighter in the tower, the farther it sent its beams out over the sea.

The yearly visits to the homes in Charlemont were bright spots in her life. Not only her own beloved kindred, but the kind townfolk and neighbors were very near her heart, and she loved every inch of ground along the banks of the Deerfield. During one of these visits, her mother, in her eighty-ninth year, passed on to the homestead above. " What word would you like to send to your absent children and grandchildren, mother?" Mrs. Brown had asked, when it became evident she must soon go. Mrs. Ballard replied with emphasis: " Tell them to put their trust in the living God, and in His Son, Jesus Christ;" and breathed her sweet life out into the bosom of her God, in assured faith. " Lord Jesus, I commit my trembling soul to thee," were among her last words, uttered with a countenance reflecting the heavenly brightness.

Mrs. Brown often recurred with gratitude to the unexpected privilege after her long wanderings, of being at home, to minister to her mother during her last illness. Mrs. Ballard had been a " shut-in " sufferer for many years, from lameness occasioned by a fall from a carriage, giving a long example of uncomplaining patience. Her death occurred Dec. 7th, 1857. " Her children rise up and call her blessed."

On the 4th of February, 1867, Mrs. Brown met with a similar accident, falling in the icy street; the straining of a tendon confined and crippled her for many months, and rendered the remaining two years of her life a gradual decline. It was not without some pangs of disappointment that one so active accepted the shrinkage of life ; " the power of endurance I once possessed for laboring ' long and strong ' has left me," she writes under date of her sixty-third birthday. But the cheery spirit triumphed over pain ; few even of near friends suspected what she endured ; there were not many days even in the last two suffering years, in which she did not perform deeds of precious service. She had an elasticity of temperament which kept her youthful to the last ; always in quick touch with whatever young life might be about her, her childlike gayety was still the charm of friends, and she seemed to be even growing younger, in a heavenly sympathy and cordialness that had no boundary-line. This peculiar combination of the social and spiritual in her character gave it a unique flavor, a kind of wild-rose delicacy, which became more and more noticeable with advancing years. Perhaps this may be best illustrated by inserting here her own account of a dream which impressed her with much vividness.

" Jan. 22, 1870. Last night I dreamed a dream so unlike any previous one, that I desire to record it before it escapes my memory.

I dreamed I was in the midst of a large settlement or colony, where were numerous people—men, women, and children—peacefully and quietly pursuing their varied avocations, without distinction of rank or color. All were dressed in comely attire, cleanly and comfortable, but none in the gewgaws of modern fashion. Walking about through streets and avenues, I saw in the distance, beautifully variegated scenery, hill and dale, farms and gardens, cattle grazing on the slopes, and farmers cultivating their fields. People in the streets were pass-

ing and repassing; all seeming bent on their own pursuits. I entered a number of large buildings, where,
in the different departments, were teachers and pupils,
and workmen engaged in the various branches of science,
arts and trades. Peace and order prevailed; no hurry or
bustle, or harsh words, to offend the eye or ear. In
other rooms were children with their teachers engaged
in learning elementary branches. All sorts of people
were passing and repassing in the streets—I recognized
among them Mrs. T—, and several other old acquaintances, with whom I had formerly been associated in
works of benevolence and charity. But there was one,
a stranger, of medium stature, comely, but not remarkable in looks and appearance, whom I had never met before. He had been present in the school-rooms and
work-shops, and seemed everywhere cordially recognized
as general overseer and superintendent. At length,
having been for some time standing in a large room
where groups of happy children were seated, and parents
and others were standing round, joyful listeners to the
mild and loving instruction of their superintendent, I
went again into the street, where, among others, I met
my old friend Mrs. Seddinger. She, with a characteristic
expression of benevolence and love beaming in her face,
turned towards me and inquired if I knew the person
we had just left talking so earnestly with the children
in the school-room? I replied, No, that he was a stranger. It is the *Lord Jesus,* she replied; and looking to
see my surprise, added, 'You are not very well,
would you like to have him go home with you and spend
the night?' 'Most certainly,' I said, 'but could not
think of asking such a favor.' 'He will be happy to
go,' said she; 'he is always ready to go where invited,
I will speak to him about it.' Here we separated; I
went to my home, where I found quite a gathering of
people; children in the front room and Jesus in their

midst. standing on a small platform at the corner of a desk, interesting them with his pleasant and encouraging remarks. None seemed to be afraid or awed in his presence. In passing I stopped a moment to view more closely the person I had now become so deeply interested in. At this moment he raised his eyes and looked on me with such a look of love that I felt my heart drawn out to him, filled with the purest affection. Immediately he resumed his instructions, and I passed on into the adjoining room, where were gathered several of the sisters I used to know in Dayton, Ohio. Mrs. E— held in her hand a copy of the New Testament, which, she said, she wished to present to Jesus, if she could be sure he would accept it. Mrs. B—, taking the book from her hand, said she would go and ask him. She soon returned with it, saying he gladly accepted the gift, with the request that Mrs. E— would write her name in it, which she did, adding also some texts of scripture, and laid the book upon the mantel-shelf. Soon Jesus came into the room, and said he must go. I then spoke to him and asked if he would not spend the night with us. He said he would but for a previous engagement to return to his own house. Feeling surprised to hear he had a *house of his own*, I inquired where his home was. He said he owned half a house about three blocks from ours. Then taking from the mantel the Testament presented by Mrs. E—, he departed. Just at that moment the morning bell awoke me from this, the pleasantest of dreams. I could but wonder if it might not be a foreshadowing of the coming millenium."

"The dream is remarkable," wrote Mr. Brown, "for one thing—the nearness with which she thought of Christ; no person who was not in the habit of constant familiarity with a present Savior, could have had such a dream—so it seems to me."

In June, 1870, she accompanied her husband to Ohio,
enjoying with relatives, brief visits which she knew
must be her last. Her affection embraced them all in
one strong bond. Though unable to sit up all the time,
the warm hand-clasp and welcome cheered her spirit,
and she lighted up every home she entered. Of this
visit she wrote :

"We started for Ohio, June 3rd, accompanied by Mr.
and Mrs. Duer. Attended the Free Mission anniversary at Cincinnati, and visited in returning, our friends
at Columbus, Circleville, and Tarlton ; and while Nathan went to Newark in search of Indian curiosities
from an old fort there, I went to Springfield to visit
Charlie and Eunice. In my feeble and crippled state,
I felt but little courage to start on such a long journey,
but the Lord has been better than my fears. We
reached home Friday, 24th, after an absence of a little
more than three weeks. . . . I have looked forward with
hopeful anticipations to making this visit to the dear
Ohio relatives for several years past, but since I received
the injury to my hip, had nearly relinquished the idea
of ever being able to take so long a journey again. *I
have been*, and enjoyed the visit more than I can tell.
Friends everywhere seemed to vie with each other to
give us a warm welcome, and do everything possible to
make our visit enjoyable. This visit to Ohio will
ever be attended with grateful remembrances to them,
and more so to the Divine Giver of all our blessings."

Her husband, finding that the little outings of July
for change and sea-breeze, failed to bring up her ebbing
strength—after her partial recovery from a severe illness in August, took her to the old homestead once
more, in the hope that she might derive benefit from a

Eliza W. Brown

few weeks in her native air. That failed too ; but her .
letters to him written there, are full of word-pictures of
the bright indoor life. From the window of "the same
room where she was born, and also her darling Sophie,"
she watched a pair of young lovers walking on the river
bank under the maples, "as you and I were wont to
do." That was forty-one years ago! "It was spring-
time then ; the time of blossoms and the singing of
birds, and our young hearts were filled with song and
hope." In spite of pains and weakness, she felt she
must have the privilege of taking some part in the marriage preparations. She enjoyed the calls of the dear
old neighbors, and the quiet evening talks with her
brother.

E. to N. B. Oct. 16, "There is to be a gathering
of *old folks* in the upper village this week Wednesday
—all over seventy—and I have heen invited. Brother
J——says I shall pass well for that age !"

"I went, and enjoyed the day very much. Met almost
all who remain of my old class of schoolmates."

This was the last social gathering she attended while
with her friends. The November winds and rains
brought on an attack of pneumonia, through which she
was most tenderly nursed at "Sister Sophia's." On the
18th of December she sat by the death-bed of her own
oldest brother William, and commended the departing
spirit in prayer into the hands of a loving Savior. She
shortly after went home in company with her daughter,
to Jersey City, to await the return of the silent messenger for herself. The oldest and youngest of that
group of eleven brothers and sisters crossed the dark
river within six months of each other.

After her return home, Mrs. Brown passed several
months of alternate acute suffering and intervals of com-

.fort ; she desired little waiting upon, beyond what her
husband could do for her, while one by one the strands
of the silver cord gave way under the tension of pain.
In February, 1871, a visit, "not half long enough," from
her youngest brother, Rev. Dr. James Ballard, brought
up many Bennington reminiscences.   She wrote him, in
March, "It is good to have a living man come among
us, and stir us up to love and good works. . . .   Don't
forget the one letter a week—let me, in my prison-house
of pain, enjoy the visit with you, it would be better than
medicine."   Of this genial brother, and the old Bennington days, William Lloyd Garrison wrote, in 1873, after
reading a letter of Dr. Ballard's to a mutual friend :

" It was next to looking in his pleasant face, reviving
as it did, the memories of " Auld lang syne,"—delightful
memories, too, and saddened in the retrospect by nothing but the seemingly premature death of his sister.
Happily the gain was hers ;

'Tis the survivor dies ! ' "

March 8th, Mrs. Brown wrote to a friend :

" Plans and prospects—I want to hear all.   I cannot
bear to have such a long interval between our letters.
Time is winging us away, and we shall not have a chance
to exchange a great many more.   With me, I have recently been brought so near death's door, that I feel the
time may be very short.   Pray for me, dear sister, that
I may have patience to endure these sufferings to the
end."

She was still able, occasionally on mild days, to go
out.   March 26th was her last attendance on public
service, but it was not till May that her family began to
feel immediate alarm.   Even then she was so bright in
the intervals of pain, sitting up a part of every day to

the last, that when the call came on Sunday, May 14th, it was unexpected.

[N. B. Diary, 1871]. "As the Sabbath morning dawned, she inquired what day it was, and seemed gratified when I told her it was the Sabbath. I took the Bible, read a chapter and prayed, at the end of which she said in a slow, distinct voice, 'Amen, and Amen.' She no doubt meant by this, that her prayers were ended."

"Jesus has been our Friend thus far, and I believe He will be our Friend all the way through;" she said to her husband, during one of the last nights of extreme suffering.

The Sabbath sunrise was cloudless. Waking from a brief slumber, she listened while a dear friend repeated some verses of the hymn, "When streaming from the eastern skies," and at the close, in reply to the remark, "Our hymns are such a comfort," said, "Yes, they all speak of Jesus—precious, precious Jesus;" then, after a pause, repeated:

> "Jesus lover of my soul,
> Let me to thy bosom fly,"

and dropped asleep again.

Returning to her bedside after a short rest, her husband saw that she was fast going; and the earnest tone and look with which she tried to comfort him in her farewell "Sweet Love!" the only words she then had strength to speak, showed that she was aware that the time of departure drew near.

Learning an hour later, in reply to her own inquiry, that the physician thought she would not pass another night, she received the intelligence without surprise, and seemed satisfied. At length utterance failed.

"At this stage she made great efforts to say something, striving to move her lips so as to produce the
sound, but could only get as far as the word "Death."
Three times she began the sentence, evidently desiring
to say something to comfort the weepers by her side,
but she has left us to fill up the blank. We know from
the sweet peace of her countenance, that she was speaking of something that was pleasant to her—something
that she had no dread of—something that she welcomed
as her deliverer. ' Death—has no terrors,' or something
equivalent, was doubtless the idea which she wished to
express. I had repeated to her a little before, a verse
from L——'s lines on the death of Vinton :

> ' To the dim pass her feet have come,
> .   The steps are stony cold ;
> But yonder are the temple dome,
>   And courts of shining gold.'

Willie came in and took her hand, but it is uncertain
whether she recognized him. The breathing grew more
difficult, the intervals longer, until at last, without a
groan or struggle, we found that she had passed away—
the throbbing heart was still—the anguished bosom forever at rest !

> ' She mounteth to the eternal gate ;
>   Earth can no more confine ;
> She worships where the angels wait
>   Before the inner shrine ! ' "

It was now the hour of the Sabbath morning service,
and the sound of singing came over from the church
opposite.

On the evening of Monday, after a short service at the
house, conducted by Rev. Dr. William H. Parmly, Rev.
John Duer, and Rev. Frederick Evans, the sad journey

back to the old home in East Charlemont was commenced.
On May 17th, relatives and neighbors came to look once
more on her face. The apple trees had burst into early
bloom at her bridal forty-one years before; now they
had tarried late, that they might deck her bier. The
delicate blossoms nestled lovingly on the last pillow,
against the pale cheek and crowned the trees with sym-
bols of resurrection. '' Yes, lay the flowers about her,''
said an early friend, '' she was herself one of the sweetest
flowers God ever made.''

Rev. Dr. E. H. Gray, assisted by the Congregational,
Methodist, and Baptist pastors of the village, conducted the funeral services at the neighboring church,
and preached a sermon from the text, '' Where is God,
my Maker, who giveth songs in the night?'' (Job xxxv;
10), closing the discourse with a brief sketch of the
life so closely interwoven with that of the many surviving companions of her early youth, who had assembled to lay with kindred dust all that was mortal of
their friend. Dr. Gray said, in conclusion:

'' Thus has passed away this dear, dear friend; one
of the loveliest and most devoted of women. She was
just such a person as would be sure to attract you at
once, and make you feel, instinctively, that you had
met a true friend.

Mrs. Brown was rigidly conscientious; she was
ever true to the principles of right. Right with her
could not be compromised; she took her conscience,
especially, into all her religious duties. With her the
inquiry was, not what men say, but what does God require? As the needle points unswervingly to the pole,
so she never lost sight of Jesus, as her ' Prophet, Priest
and King.'

Having entered upon the missionary work, she never
faltered. She might have wavered when, with her husband

and their two associates, they started on their perilous
journey of four months in a small boat up the winding
Brahmaputra, through perils by robbers, by venomous
reptiles, and by deadly malaria.   She might have faltered when, one by one, her children were snatched away
by death, and their graves violated by wild beasts and
barbarous natives.   And when health failed, and with
two remaining feeble children, she undertook a lonely
voyage home, hoping to save them, and then turned,
desolate and sad, to go back to her companion and to
her work in dark India, she might have cried out : 'O
Lord. I pray Thee, have me excused.' But Mrs. Brown
said, ' Lord, if I am worthy, let me work on ;' and the
Master said, ' WORK ON.'   And she did work, faithfully,
until health and strength and constitution all gave way,
and then God directed her home to finish her work and
here to die.   'Blessed are the dead who die thus in
the Lord.' "

In a leader headed, " Martyr Lives,' *The Watchman
and Reflector*, of September 21st, 1871, wrote of Mrs.
Brown's death :

" If the blood of martyrs is the seed of the church,
the spirit of martyrs is its life. . . .   We have life-
long martyrs who, like Paul, die daily.   Our female
missionaries, in general, are such.   They are holocausts
on God's altar.   We need only to know woman in her
delicacy of make, her keenness of sensibility, her
strength of attachment to home and country, her clinging love for husband and children, to be able to forecast
the sufferings involved in her going forth to a life of
toil amid the darkness and degradation of heathendom.
We thank God for such martyr lives ; they help lift
the whole church to a higher plane of thought and
action.   Here and there, from time to time, one catches

the holy inspiration and comes forth from the secret altar, with the vow of consecration on her heart, saying calmly, 'Here am I, send me.' They are a living proof that Christianity is, to-day, all it ever was. And suffering with, they also reign with Him, not hereafter only, in supreme glorification, but here also, in true royalty of soul. We are not of those who say, 'Why was this waste?' The ointment of their broken vases fills all our homes with the fragrance of their spirit. The whole world is a gainer. But to the church they are of as priceless worth—not the dead alone, but they also who lie unconsumed on the altar—as to the nation are the heroes of its history and the living heroes who have but to hear the call of their country to go forth, to do and dare, and die in its service.

We have been led to these thoughts by reading the sermon preached at the funeral of Mrs. Brown, wife of Dr. Nathan Brown, and with him formerly the founder of the mission to Assam. We condense from it a brief sketch.

. . . We greatly sympathize with the sufferings of such, but their martyr lives, over and above all the immediate results of their labors, are among the richest blessings of the Christian church."

"The missionary career is ever a martyr possibility," says George Dana Boardman. "When we remember the exposures to which most missionaries are subject— exposures of fatigue and heat, and damp and fever, and anxiety and heart-sickness—exposures oftentimes actually entailing premature death — we may literally speak of the missionary career as a libation of martyr-blood."*

---

*Address to Missionary Union, May, 1881.

XXXV.

WHEN the Sabbath breeze carried toward the steep wooded shores of Uraga harbor, on the 10th of July, 1853, the strains of "Old Hundred" from the deck of the war-ship *Mississippi*, a key was set in Japan's prison-door, whose turning meant more than open ports and treaties of commerce. Workmen on the fort, and gathering soldiers must have caught faint, high notes floating landward across the sparkling water of the bay from instruments and voices of men, that were lifting on a full harmony the words:

> "Earth, with her ten thousand tongues
> Shall fill Thy courts with sounding praise."

Was it less—that hymn sung just then and there—than a note of response to the angels' song over Bethlehem? True, there intervened a period of ferment, confusion and bloodshed—but the force of ideas at length prevailed. Mr. Brown wrote in an editorial of May, 1872:

"We welcome this beautiful Gem of the Sea to the family of civilized nations. She has joined the great empires of the west, and now stands on the common platform of a free and equal humanity. An empire of thirty-five millions, nearly equal to France or the United States, compact, homogeneous, and speaking a single language, her future career is almost certain to be one of honor."

(516)

Sermon, Aug., '72. "All the religious elements, as well as political, are now in a state of solution, ready to crystalize around any nucleus that may be thrown in. . . . Can we be so blind as not to see that now is the critical moment, now the turning-point, now the golden opportunity, when we must seize the gospel banner and bear it aloft before the millions of Japan, or lose the priceless treasure, betray our mission to a ruined world, disregard the plain pointing of the providential finger, and leave those inquiring millions to grope in darkness, and become a prey to deism, atheism, and every snare by which Satan lures mankind to death? No, we must not, we cannot be so false to our Master as to let the golden moment pass unimproved."

Missionaries of the Protestant Episcopal, Presbyterian, and Reformed Churches had gone to Japan soon after the opening of the ports, and were followed by those of the Congregational and Methodist Boards. The Free Mission Society had also for some years had an interest in Japan, and now that the main causes of separation within the Baptist lines had ceased to exist, it was deemed best to unite their two missionary societies, and that measure was practically effected in the spring of 1872. In a full and enthusiastic meeting of the Missionary Union, Japan was taken up, and Mr. Brown was designated to begin its work in that field. He had for years been specially interested in the progress of events in that country; not a few of his editorials had discussed its history and religions ; and for some months past he had felt an irresistible desire and call of providence to go forward and finish his chosen life-work there.

" The call came providentially," he said, "at a time when no insuperable obstacle prevented me from once

more leaving my native land.   I have therefore decided
to go.   My early vows bind me to the mission work.
Restored health favors."

To attempt to become acclimated again in India, at
his age, would have been hazardous ; but it was thought
the cool climate of Japan might prolong his life and
usefulness. He was sixty-five years old ; still the fire
kindled in his college days burned as clear as ever ;
and he set his face to cross the ocean, with all the old
enthusiasm. "If I can live ten years," he said on leaving home, "and can give the Japanese the New Testament, and see a Baptist church of fifty members in
Yokohama, I shall feel that it has paid to send me
out."

Mr. Brown closed his fifteen years' editorship of *The
American Baptist*, May 28th, 1872, severing with mutual regret, a connection of almost equal length with
his genial associate, Rev. John Duer, a true-hearted
friend of the colored race.   Mr. Duer died in Brooklyn,
Sept. 6, 1875.   Another long and tried friendship was
that with Rev. Albert L. Post, for seventeen years
President of the Free Mission Society.   With solid,
yet brilliant talents, and a promising future, Mr. Post
had, in 1849, abandoned the bar for the pulpit ; had
devoted ample means and an undivided heart to the
anti-slavery cause, and in his own words, "had known
something about the underground railroad, brickbats,
and stale eggs."   On his retirement from official duties
in 1870, Mr. Brown said of him :

'In presiding at our annual meetings, in the prudence and moderation of his rulings, in his inimitable
tact and skill in checking all tendencies to acrimonious
or personal discussions, in the clearness and breadth of
his definitions and statements of great principles, how

often has it been said, " We shall not look upon his like
again.'

On the 24th of July, 1872, relatives and friends
gathered in Jersey City, on the occasion of Mr. Brown's
marriage to Mrs. Charlotte A. [Worth] Mariit, Rev.
Dr. Parmly officiating. The weeks which followed were
partly occupied with preparations for the new missionary enterprise, partly with watching by the dying bed
of a sister at Charlemont. Her death occurred in September. Thus while the eldest brother of the Whitingham family circle of fifty years before, heard voices
calling him from over the Pacific,

> "She, the youngest of the band,
> Had crossed a darker sea."

While she lay waiting for the signal to embark, old
friends came, one Sunday, late in August, to the Congregational church, in East Charlemont, to hear her
brother's farewell sermon. He gave a sketch of the field
that had opened before him, and said in closing:

" Farewell, beloved country ; farewell, dearly beloved
friends. We may not meet again in time, but we shall
meet in the glorious world, where Greek and Jew,
European and Asiatic, Briton and Chinese, Japanese
and Hindu, and the whole assembly and Church of the
first-born shall be gathered to chant through eternity,
the song of redeeming grace ! "

The missionaries left New York in November. Many
friends bade them " God-speed," on their westward way.
During a detention in San Francisco, Mr. Brown
preached missionary sermons, the last, at Union Square
church, Oakland, Jan. 5, the day before sailing, on the

text, "God reigneth over the heathen ; God sitteth upon the throne of His holiness." Forty years before, he had preached from the same words, at Dr. Sharp's church, Boston, on the eve of sailing for Burma. How changed, since then, the aspect of the eastern world ! With what a light had the history of forty years illuminated that text !

The reporter's account of the preacher's manner and personal appearance at this time may not be without interest.

" Considerably advanced in years, he has the appearance of one who has led an active, and at the same time studious life. His face cannot fail to attract attention in every educated circle, by the strong evidences it bears, of thought and mental culture. Few foreheads are loftier than his, and, if not noticeably wide, it is finely developed in the regions where phrenologists locate the best intellectual functions. Hair and whiskers almost white, give rather a venerable aspect to the face ; but beyond this there is little to denote age, for his voice is the reverse of feeble, and his movements are full of vitality. His superiority as a preacher, however, is more in matter than manner. If, which will not bear denial, the sermon he delivered yesterday morning, was, as a composition, one of the ablest ever addressed from a San Francisco pulpit, it lacked the elocutionary fire to constitute it an oration. Although easily heard, his voice lacks the force and flexibility which go to excite sympathy in an audience. Even when expressing an idea sufficiently beautiful to thrill an appreciative soul, it discovers in the intonation no consciousness of the brilliancy of the thought, or of the eloquent rounding of the language. Dr. Brown's great fault is monotony, and as he does not seem to care how far it interferes with the success of his preaching, and

trusts almost exclusively to the great merits of his sub-
ject-matter for producing effect, he cannot be regarded
as a popular minister in the conventional sense of the
term. But, monotonous as he is, and as unsympathetic
as his voice sounds, there is an intellectual pleasure in
listening to him. Teeming with information, felicitous
in language, independent in thought, vigorously combining logic and rhetoric to strengthen his points, and
connected and consistent in all the minutiæ of his discourse, he possesses abilities which render him one of
the ablest preachers whom we have heard on this coast."

The westward-bound party, including Mrs. Brown's
two little daughters, embarked on the steamer *China*,
Monday, January 6th, 1873, accompanied by Rev.
Jonathan Goble and family. The voyage occupied a
month. Early on the morning of February 7th, a sail was
descried, which proved to be that of a Japanese fishing-
boat. Soon after, eager children's voices were heard on
the guards calling out "Land in sight!" The morning
light was touching a fixed silvery cone in the horizon ; it
was Fuji, pride of Japan !

Yokohama was already a cosmopolitan port. There
was a night's delay at a hotel in the business part of the
town ; and the next day the children had their first
jinrikisha drive along Main street, which was lined
with foreign shops and gay with show-windows ; across
a canal bridge ; through a native settlement ; and up the
ascent to the Bluff, past a fox-shrine and by a steep
stairway to a house under the shadow of pines and cam-
phor trees, where they were soon sheltered in a temporary home. Mr. Brown writes in March:

"The bluff on which we live directly overlooks the
town and bay, and the prospect is one of the most
delightful I have ever beheld. [May.] All nature
is now in her bloom. The orioles warbling, trees

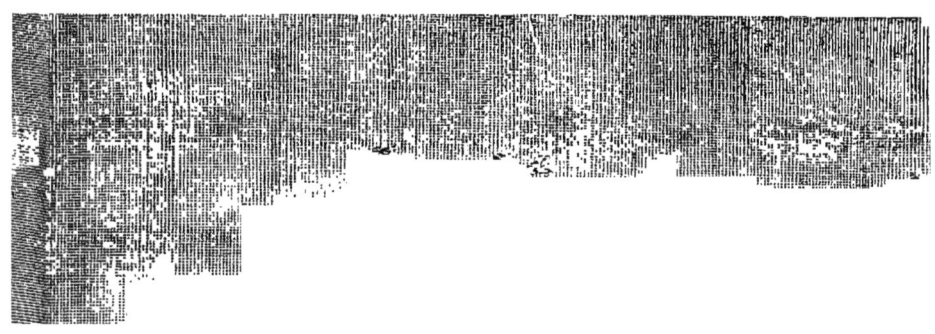

noble relic of Japanese mediæval art. A journey
of twenty miles brought them to Kamakura, once a
famous city, and still interesting with its ancient
temples and great stone gateways. Passing between
giant idols, the visitors came suddenly upon the serene
colossal face and seated figure in its grand repose. It
is itself a temple ; the dome-like head is tiled with snail-
shells in bronze, the capacious interior lighted by a window in the shoulder, contains smaller idols. Devout
Buddhist pilgrims, dressed in white, with bells on their
girdles and staves in their hands, approach with prostrations the sacred steps and mystic lotuses in bronze,
which stand in vases at its feet, with the brazier of burning incense.

Not long after landing at Yokohama, Mr. Brown had
a handshake and greeting from Assam, enjoying a fortnight's visit from an old comrade, Rev. I. J. Stoddard, looking "wasted and worn with the deadly fevers of India."
He was greatly desirous that the Japan mission should
have the benefit of Dr. Stoddard's services and experience, convinced that the invigorating sea breezes of
Yokohama would make and keep him a well man. The
request was renewed some years later, on hearing that
the Stoddards were "on the warpath again ;" had given
up their home in Iowa to sail from New York to Gauhati, and were on the eve, a third time, of undertaking
what in Mr. Brown's opinion, was "the desperate experiment of another battle with the heat and malaria
of tropical swamps." A council of physicians were of
the same opinion ; and the plucky veterans were compelled to meet "the saddest experience of their lives,"
when they "reluctantly turned back" to comfort, civilization, and the loved company of their children.

So hard is it to root out the missionary passion, strong
unto death. The life-cords are tied about the work.
Once a missionary, always a missionary. Said Dr. Bron-

son, upon his return home when nearly seventy years of age, irrecoverably ill after thirty-three years' difficult and successful service, "Oh, yes, I must go back; I wish to be buried in Assam." His last words were of the work he loved better than life.

"Dr. Nathan Brown,' said the *Missionary Magazine* of January, 1874, "is pushing on his pioneer mission work with the ardor of his younger days in Assam." Services in Japanese, and a Sunday Bible-class for the natives were already in progress three months after his arrival, and he began to "feel enough at home in the language to appreciate its beauties." Convinced that it could be shaped into metrical form, he fell into his old hymn-making habit, and in May, 1873, versified the Lord's Prayer, probably the first hymn in the Japanese language.* This he followed by others; many more were made by other missionaries, and the natives, to whom rhyme and meter were a pleasing novelty, took them up with zest, and soon learned to sing them to our own familiar tunes. He says of the language:

"It is very nearly related to the Burmese and Tartar languages; has a great many Sanscrit words, and a large Greek element. It is an *intoned* language."

---

* See page 547.

SHINTO SHRINÈ, NEAR YOKOHAMA, JAPAN, WITH WORSHIPERS, VESSEL OF HOLY WATER, ETC.

XXXVI

SHADE AND SHEEN ON THE BLUFF.

" FORTY-ONE years to-day since I left my father's house on the missionary errand. How strange, yet how kind, have been the guidings of Providence ! "

This scrap of English, dated November 7th, 1873, appears in the midst of a manuscript of Romanized Japanese, the first rough draft of a translation. It is the gospel of Mark ; chapter 6–13, had just been slowly reached, at the rate of a few verses a day. Further search discloses some other passages which do not appear in the original Greek :

"Tuesday, November 18th. To-day, —— brought in his gods or objects of worship, mostly paper, and gave them to me, saying he had no further use for them. . . . Met committee of Evangelical Alliance and organized. Saturday, January 10th, 1874, gave an address on Modern Infidelity, at the Prayer-meeting of Evangelical Alliance. January 22d. I trust I feel thankful that I have been able to complete one gospel [Mark], though there is a great deal of revision to be done before it can be printed."

Soon after Mr. Brown had finished translating Mark, his son arrived to take charge of the printing department, and they were able in the fall of 1874 to issue in Japanese a " Scripture Manual" and a small collection of hymns. A few months later they published the " Parables of Christ," " Mark's Gospel," the " Account

of the Creation,' with a few Psalms, and the Epistle
of James. In 1876, Mr. Brown's translation of
Matthew was also in the hands of the Japanese, together with the Epistles of Peter, John and Jude, and
hymn-books in Kana and Roman. A million pages of
scripture, including the first three gospels, were printed
during the three years, 1875–7, also Mr. Arthur's Catechism and several juvenile tracts, with funds from Free
Mission legacies and from the Bible Translation Society of England.

During the second year, a small, neat chapel was
erected at the foot of the compound, overlooking the
native houses just below, to be used both for religious
services and as a school-house. Here Mrs. Brown had
her school of girls from the native town. Bright, shy,
yet eager to learn, were these quaint little maids, in
their long, gaily figured, broadly-belted gowns with
wide, hanging sleeves and neat waist-folds. Later, Miss
Sands and Miss Kidder of the Woman's Board were
stationed at Yokohama and Tokio ; other day and Sabbath-schools and daily Bible classes were established,
and native Bible-women sent out into the villages. Miss
Kidder was for some time alone in the native quarter
of Tokio, teaching Japanese girls and women. She had
obtained permission to live outside the foreign conces-
sion, and established her school in the midst of the
Japanese population.

The little chapel at Yokohama was burned down on
the 6th of February, 1875, in a conflagration which
swept away the native settlement at the foot of the hill.
The flames from the burning village were driven by a
high wind directly against the front of the chapel, which
was kept for a time from igniting, by the efforts of the
family and friends, dashing on many pails of water drawn
from their well. Yokohama then had but one fire-engine,
and a very inadequate supply of water.

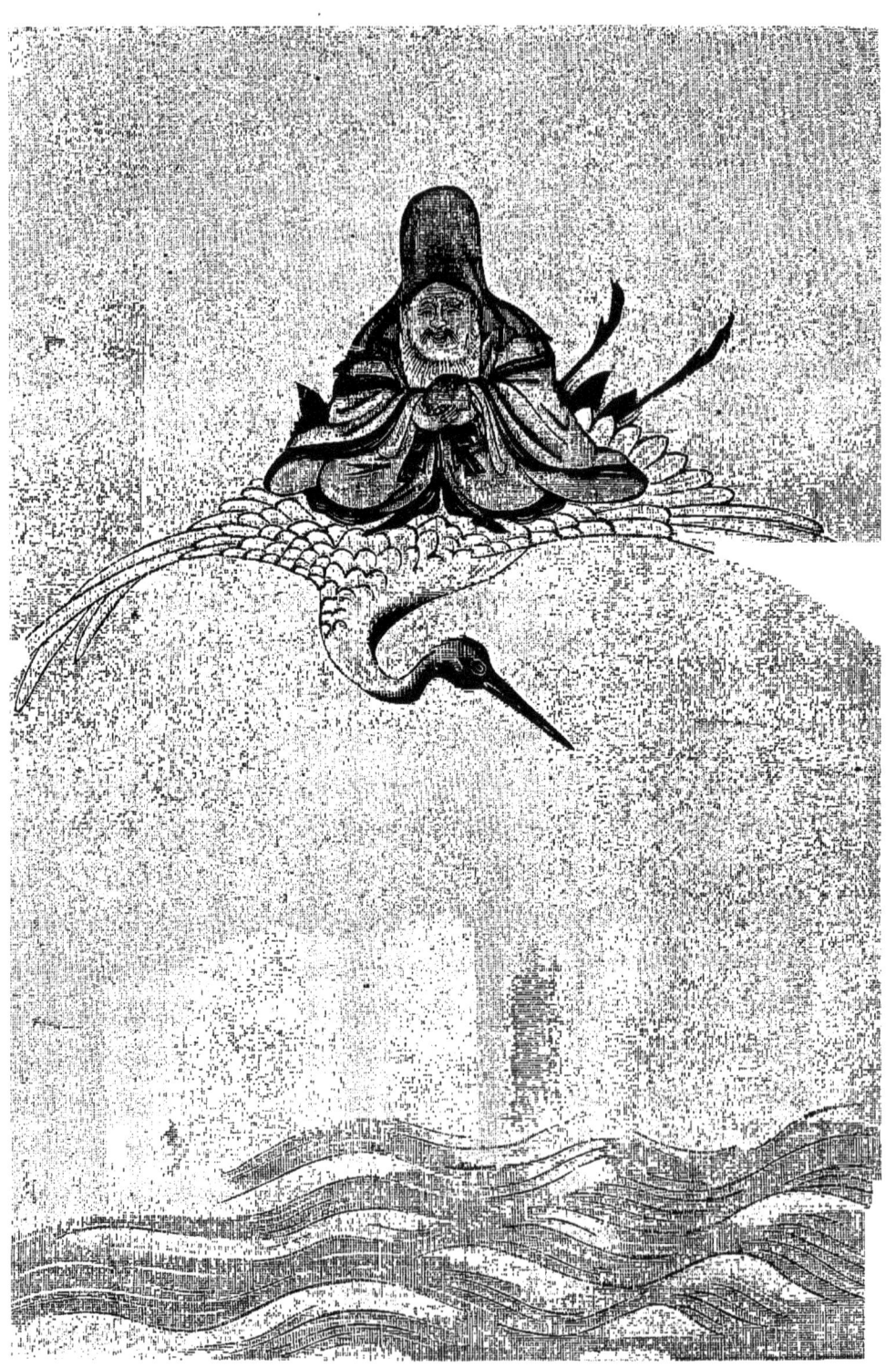

FUKORUKU JIN, THE GOD OF LONG LIFE.

" Showers of sparks and flame ignited in various parts
of the compound, and fell upon the house, the wind
driving the sparks between the upper and lower window-
sashes, and kindled the mat in several places in my study
and the bedroom. Men were outside with water to ex-
tinguish the sparks as they fell. Willie endeavored to
save the chapel, but in vain ; the beautiful building went
down."

The natives, trying to save the sliding doors from
their burning houses, had piled them up in the rear of
the chapel, where they caught fire, and enveloped the
building in a blaze. All his son could then do was to
assist in dragging away the benches, and, completely
exhausted and stifled with smoke, give up the contest
with a Yokohama fire in a typhoon.

A room was fitted up in another building for the
school and the meetings ; a new chapel was built during
the summer, and regular work resumed in it in the fall.
Conflagrations are frequent in Japan ; in November,
1883, this second chapel was burned.

That day on which the first fire occurred, Mr. and Mrs.
Brown had been in Tokio, attending the wedding of Mr.
Arinori Mori, recently returned from his American em-
bassy to fill the post of Vice-Minister of Foreign Affairs
in Japan. The ten or twelve Japanese ladies present
were very beautiful in their own national costume of
lovely crêpes and silk, costly jewels and neck-folds of
varying tints. Young Japan of the other sex, on this
occasion wore foreign dress and white gloves. Both
bride and groom were in European dress, the former in
quiet gray with pearl-looped sash, her veil drooping
from silver pins and orange flowers, the numerous
courtly neck-folds being laid aside for soft lace. The
covenant of matrimony was read in Japanese from a
long manuscript held in a double roll, in both hands of

the reader, who was one of the bridegroom's friends.
When the reading was concluded, the document was
signed by the contracting parties, the governor of Tokio,
and three other witnesses, the ceremonial being followed
by a wedding breakfast.   This simplicity was a marked
innovation upon the old form, which required half a day,
and, among the samurai, or nobility, included the changing of the bride's robes, from three to nine times, according to her rank.

The young mission proved to be no exception to the
general law that new efforts must be made under difficulties.   The enterprise, for a few years, was like a
Japanese fishing boat caught out at sea in a typhoon.
"For about two years," Mr. Brown wrote in '76, "I have
almost despaired of getting the boat righted up, and have
been quietly looking forward to the probability of ship-
wreck."   "At several periods since I came to Japan I
have thought the ship must go down, at least so far as
I was concerned, but by the interposition of a kind Providence, it is still afloat."   A complication of unforeseen
and distressing hinderances well-nigh disheartened some
of the friends of the mission at home, while Mr. Brown,
through days wherein "no small tempest lay on him,"
held on with a determined grip, recalling former years of
discouragement ; and believed it to be God's law that
success should come through suffering.   His diary says :

May 14, '75. "Repeated disappointments have almost
worn out my courage ; Lord help me to trust in Thee !"
[Sept. 30, on hearing of the appointment of a missionary,] "This is a partial relief to our great anxieties for
the fate of this mission.

> 'Oh God, my God, how good Thou art,
> How gracious to this tempted heart ;
> When tempests rage and billows roll,
> Thou art the anchor of my soul.' "

To Mrs. Julia A. Smith. " Pray for me, that I may at least live to get out the New Testament." March, '79, when the clouds had lifted : " I firmly believe there has been a Providence all through these dark trials, and I hope that some day the seed now being sown may spring up like the seed sown among the Telugoos. Let us all praise God together for what He has done for us, and trust Him more implicitly for the future. I cannot but think there is coming a glorious day for Japan, and that not very far distant."

On the 17th of December, 1875, the old pines around the mission house breathed their requiem over Mrs. Jennie Hoyt Churchill, for one year a missionary to Ningpo, China, who had during six weeks lain a patient, suffering guest under their shadow, and thence crossed the dark flood in triumph, without a fear. "Do you know," she whispered to a friend, " I am going—going very soon—perhaps to-night ?" " Is it all bright?" " Oh, so bright!—such peace! I am just bathing in God's love." Mr. Brown preached the funeral sermon from the words, " O Death, where is thy sting?" and the interment was made at Ningpo.

The year '76 closed with hope. New converts had been asking baptism, and older ones were growing daily stronger and more helpful ; Mr. and Mrs. Dobbins had arrived.

Early in the year the family had removed from under the pines to a house on the main Bluff road. This build-ing was much shaken by gales and earthquakes, and in '80, Mr. Brown put up a new one, " built as strong as he could make it," on the west side of his compound. To daughter, October 8th : " Here I sit in our new house—the neatest little place you ever saw—overlooking the beautiful bay, and with a most delightful prospect from the windows on each side. . . . You would, if you should look into my new and beautiful study, see an old man, white-haired and wrinkled, scribbling away with his pen as hard as ever."

He had passed his three-score years and ten. A poetical reminiscence of college days, dated Sept. 5, 1877, had come to him across the Pacific from his brother, W. G. Brown, who was also a loyal son of Williams. It was entitled

FIFTY YEARS AGO.

Just fifty years to-day, brother,
    Just fifty years have fled,
Since you upon Commencement day,
    Your Valedictory said.
The lights still burn in Williams' halls,
    Old Greylock stands as then,
But where are those who walked with us
    Down Hoosic's moonlit glen ?

Lo, gazing through the mist of years,
    Of sunshine and of storm,
Flits ghostlike upon memory's wall
    Full many a manly form.
Again I tread those foot-worn aisles,
    With the young, the brave, the fair,
I hear the laugh, the shout, the song,
    Ring on that haunted air.

I see the long line, arm in arm,
    With proud and martial air,
March to their annual festival,
    Up to the house of prayer :
While towering high above them all,
    A king in look and mien,
His white hair like a silver crown,
    Our Griffin's form is seen.

Ah well, if on life's stage, for truth,
  They've raised their voice as well
As when upon their ears, that day,
  His "*Tolle Vocem*" fell ;
But well or ill, their parts are played,
  They've crossed death's river o'er ;
A few, like us, of gray-haired men,
  Still linger on the shore.

My heart has followed you, brother,
  Across the stormy seas,
To where the tropic sun looks down
  On Burma's orange trees ;
Through twenty years in that dark land,
  Of tears and toil and strife,
Now lifted as on angel wings,
  Now flying for your life.

By sunny Salwen's ancient stream,
  By dark Asáma's waves,
I saw you lay your three firstborn,
  Down in their little graves ;
And when, thrice disinterred, you bore
  One through the jungles lone,
To rest where fair Sibsagar's moon
  On pagan temples shone.

On Fuji's lofty crest, brother,
  I gaze with you to-day ;
I watch the white sails come and go
  In Yokohama Bay ;
I hear the dusky Japanese
  Chant sweet the hymns you taught,
While listening children, grouped around,
  Are molded to your thought.

I visit you in dreams, brother,
   Around our father's door ;
The same green hills, the same blue skies
   Are round us evermore ;
I never have been far from you,
   Though land and sea divide,
My soul leans out to hear you sing,
   At morn and eventide.

What changes fifty years have wrought !
   Our country now is free ;
We almost fly across the land,
   We talk across the sea ;
And fifty more—the song of peace
   From every battle sod ;
Earth shouts the brotherhood of man,
   The fatherhood of God !

We're going down the hill, brother,
   The bill of life's decline ;
But though you sleep beneath the palm,
   And I beneath the pine,
The love you kindled, like a star
   In its perpetual glow,
Will burn as brightly ages hence,
   As fifty years ago.

To his brother, in reply : " I have read over and over
your beautiful lines, and not without many tears. . . .
Yes, climes and oceans cannot separate ; they can only
draw a veil between the outward forms of humanity,
but not between souls—that is, our real selves."

The new study, like its predecessors, contained "records and relics of the past." There were framed
coins upon the wall, dating many centuries back ; upon
which also was the portrait of " Osawatomie Brown,"

with a lock of his gray hair enclosed under the glass. Idols and curios, more valued for genuineness than for beauty, were here treasured; by some means the missionary found fragments of resting-time in which to copy and study the remarkable inscription on an ancient "bronze urn found at Yokohama," to trace the resemblance between Japanese, Karen and Shan traditions, and to take active interest in the investigations of the Asiatic Society of Japan, of which he was elected member on his arrival. His note-paper was ornamented with prints of coins unearthed in America and Assam, whose characters bear some resemblance to each other; and of the mystic letters on Myles Standish's sword, which still fascinated him. Chinese sword-money, ancient Japanese coinage, inscriptions from mound and cave of the old New World were objects of interest.

The quiet home-life on the Bluff was not without its occasional excitements and alarms. His journal and letter to the Magazine describe the earthquake of February 22d, 1880:

"A terrific earthquake at about one o'clock this morning. On looking around the settlement the marks of devastation are everywhere observable. Many houses are torn open, sides torn off, and roofs dislodged. More than half of the chimneys have suffered, being in most cases toppled over at the point of their emergence from the roof, and carrying with them the tiles in their course down the roof. In some cases the chimneys fell through, carrying devastation into the rooms below.

Wednesday 24th. Yesterday's paper says this earthquake is the severest experienced during the residence of foreigners in Japan. . . . The instruments used were subjected to a movement greater than they were ever intended for, the mercury in the tubes having vibrated so far that the pointers were twisted off the scale. The earthquake came from the N. N. W. . . . Brick walls came tumbling with a crash, and some houses were almost entirely demolished. Many fared much worse than we did. In the settlement, in some instances, the whole broadside of a stone building fell bodily into the street. Chimneys falling upon the roofs crushed through, endangering many lives, but happily no one was killed. We have great reason for thankfulness that the shock was of so short duration : it lasted a little less than a minute and a half. The seismometers at the Tokio College were not adapted to the recording of so high a degree of motion, but the professor in charge estimates the velocity of the shock at about eight hundred miles an hour."

The new dwelling just escaped being lost by fire in June, '81 ; "the third marvelous preservation of our house from being burned, since we arrived in Japan." The night was dark ; at sight of the flames, "neighbors and friends rushed into the compound and worked with a will," tearing down the blazing cook-house, (attached by a covered passage to the dwelling), and rapidly passing up buckets of water from the well. The dwelling-house was hurriedly emptied of its contents, and in the confusion, a thief, who was probably also the incendiary, carried away a chest which contained valuable papers and money, breaking it open and rolling it down the hill near the printing office, where it was found the next morning, strangely enough with most of the money undisturbed, having been missed in the darkness, by the robber. He had secured a small tin box containing the papers, and escaped with it. Through the efforts of the native police, the culprit was discovered and arrested in the course of a day or two, and the stolen property was promptly restored. The fire had been extinguished before it reached the dwelling.

THE SACRED MOUNTAIN, FUJI-YAMA.

During all his thirteen years' residence in Japan, Mr. Brown did not go more than twenty miles away from Yokohama. He never found time to feast his eyes on the beauty of the land he loved; to visit the ancient historic castles; to climb the mountain paths, or rest in the enchanted stillness of the inland lakes. The daily sight of Fuji, seems to have served him in place of vacations and mountain-trips. "I believe it has lengthened my life," he said. When the proximity of cholera in the town below, brought some risk, he sent his family to the beach, threw open his windows to the ocean breeze, and kept on at work. Saturday afternoons found him on his way along the beach afoot, to a ruined temple, large and clean, whose garden-steps were washed by the sea. This had been rented for a summer encampment for the family, and here might have been seen on the sands towards evening, a white-haired man with his little son, (Nathan Worth Brown, born at Yokohama, Oct. 22, 1877) gathering scallop and pecten shells, banded and shaded in tints of ˙scarlet and orange, purple, gold and pearl—each a jewel in itself—to be afterwards sent as keepsakes to friends on the other shore of that ebbing tide.

To Rev. T. P. Childs, Yokohama, Oct. 7, '82· "The cholera is nearly gone. 27,000 deaths have been reported to the government, out of 47,000 cases. Now the cold season is come, and Fujiyama,—fourteen thousand feet high—looks into my study window more beautifully than any year before since I have been here. . . . You have no idea of the influence of that mountain, looking right into my study all day—it inspires me, to see that great work of God lifting its snowy head towards the Maker! I wish you could sit in our window and see it once with us.

The crater-summit was snow-crowned from October

to June, often beaten by the storms that rocked the cities below, but itself unmoved and immovable.

The frequent severe gales of the Japan coast are in general more destructive than earthquakes. During one of these, in the fall of 1880, over twenty of the smaller craft in the harbor were dashed into fragments. In Tokio, 'many lives were lost ; large buildings were prostrated, among them the new Educational Institute of the Methodist Mission. Venerable old trees, five or six feet in circumference, snapped off in the middle like pipe-stems, all at just about the same height, twenty feet or a little below.' In the four hours' cyclone of Sept. 15th, '84, Yokohama and surrounding villages were nearly reduced to ruins. The whirlwind easily crushed the light native houses in its terrific grip, and buried the inmates under the wreck, while the flood washed dead bodies from Kawasaki down the river. Even the substantial foreign houses of the Bluff were much torn, every tiling more or less blown to pieces and interiors flooded ; the lighter roofs, verandas and glass doors carried off bodily, while house-utensils floated about outdoors. Compounds were strewn with tiles, water-pipes and limbs of trees.

From the windows facing the bay, ships were seen struggling with the storm-demon. A German vessel careened helplessly, and the crew, beaten about by the furious breakers, were rescued at last with difficulty by the launches sent out to their relief. Spray dashed high over the buildings on the bund, the wind tearing up stones and posts like straw."

XXXVII

TRANSLATION AND PRINTING.

"THE chief, almost the only object of my life now, is to complete the New Testament in the vernacular, and if possible, an edition in the Roman character," Mr. Brown wrote on New Year's day, 1877. By his seventieth birthday, Luke was finished, and several Epistles were done in the autumn; Revelation in thirty-seven working-days of February and March, '78, and Acts, "a hard pull," during the extreme heat of the following summer. On receiving an appropriation from the American and Foreign Bible Society, to print this book, he wrote to his children, "I could not help falling on my knees and weeping for joy. This will enable me to go on with the press for six months more, if not for a year." Fearing that he might be brought under the necessity of removing from his house and printing-office, he determined "to strain every nerve, and get through as soon as possible." Hebrews and John's gospel followed in the fall and winter.

Feb. 5, 1879. "To-day the translation of John is completed, and Kawakatsu * and I have knelt down and thanked the Lord for preserving our health and bringing us on thus far." The last books, the epistles to the Corinthians, were completed in July, and Mr. Brown had the gratification of seeing the whole New Testament in print August 1, 1879, the first published translation in the Japanese language.

---

* Rev. Tetsuya Kawakatsu, assistant translator and preacher.

July 31. "Now I hope to be spared to revise and make it as perfect as possible. The alterations in the manuscript of the received text which I have been obliged to follow on the testimony of the Sinaitic, Vatican and other manuscripts of earlier date than was possessed by the editors of the Received Text, are surprisingly numerous : but none of them throw any doubt on the commonly received evangelical doctrines, *i. e.*, the doctrines of the Nicene Creed." *

His love for the Bible amounted to a passion. Diagonally across a blank diary page he quotes :

" Ye may point me to its blemishes, to the wrinkles on
the rind,
But rich and ripe its manna core, my famished long-
ings find."

He believed that the pure Japanese conveyed the sense of the original with a distinctness, which terms derived from Chinese could never present to an ordinary Japanese mind. This to him was a peculiarly vital consideration in translating doctrinal terms new to the Japanese, upon the clear understanding of which the foundation truths of Christianity depend.

To daughter. " I find my having once translated the New Testament into Assamese is of incalculable benefit to me. I always have Judson's version and Yates' Bengali version at my side, and from them I often get valuable hints. They are vastly plainer than the common English version. Although I have studied the New Testament so much, it grows brighter and brighter to me every time I go over it. It has been my meat and drink since I came to Japan to see how beautifully the sense comes out in this noble tongue. The happiest

* See Appendix F.

CLASS I. STRATTIC MANUSCRIPT. (א)　　　　A.D. 325–350

j. 1. Çinaino Çahon, Gemponno dai itei Rui.

KAIOMOΛOΓOYMЄ
NOCMЄΓAЄCTIN
TOTHCЄYCЄBЄIAC
MYCTHPIONOCЄ
ΦANЄPΦΘHЄNϾAP
KIЄΔIKAIΦΘHЄN
ΠNIωΦΘHΛTЄλ-
ЄKHPYXΘHЄNЄ
ΘNЄCINЄΠICTЄY
ΘHЄNKOCMω·
ANЄΛHMΦΘHЄN
ΔOΞH
i Tim. 2:16.

Çinyakçonoçemponwa mina use-
tari. Ima aru tokorono mottomo
furuki utsuçiwaTeçindorfuçinooyo-
so ço nen maycni Çinaizanno saiçi-
ço furuki iyeni oite midapnra mono sunawaci ima biobiotoço Çinaino çahonto tonauru tokorono mono
kore nari. Kore Kristono kouseiço
oyoço 350 nenno koroni utsuçituru
daiici Ruino çahon nari. Ima Ro-
çiano Teion kono Çahonwo çojise,
çkaçe na aru touukoukuçini meşiite
sunabun tagawanu utsuçiwo borase
ruppançte korewo yoni ooyaktei
seri. Yeiçono seiçowa gençio yori
honyaku seçi tokiwa imada kono
çahonwo middessuzuriçi yuye tebike-
no utsuçiwo gemponto çburu nari.

č. Niteriano Çahon. (Irnka)

Luk 10:9, 10

The Lord's Prayer in Japanese.

1　Tenni maçimaau Ou,
　　Waarano Tçiteiyo,
　　Minawo agameto
　　Toutomase tamaye.

2　Minakwurigotowo
　　Yoni nozomaseyo,
　　Tenni naru ommune
　　Tçinimo naşaçime.

3　Nitçiyouno katewo
　　Saçiuke tamayeyo;
　　Ware lito yuruseba
　　Warewo yurusena.

4　Nidoini tameça
　　Miru koto naçini,
　　Açki yori wrarewo
　　Skuite nogaseyo.

days I spend are those when I am busy for eight hours on this enchanting work. Here I see the characteristics of each apostle, and as I study, almost feel as though they were talking with me."

"As I am translating the Scriptures, I am often surprised when the scales drop off, with which human invention has incrusted them, to see how sweet and beautiful, how accordant with reason and common-sense the teachings of the sacred writers are. Papists have foisted upon scripture the ideas of paganism. Protestants have borrowed the ideas of Papists; Baptists have followed in the wake of other Protestants, until the Bible is covered with glosses, about as thick as those of the Scribes and Pharisees, which the Savior swept away with such terrible energy! But I must stop, or you will ask me to give particulars and tell what I mean, and to do this, I should have to write a book. A sense of the shortness of life begins to press upon me, so that I want to work every minute. Last Sabbath, when I baptized the carpenter, it was the sixty-first anniversary of my own baptism. How good God has been to me!"

"I think the Bible will emerge from the dust and haze which has been thrown around it; but it will emerge a very different book, or rather *Collection of Books*, from what either Protestant or Papist makes it."

"You ask my views about future punishment. I was going to sit down and give them to you last night, but got too tired before I went to bed, and this morning the mail is off; I must defer it, therefore, till another time. I do not stand with any sect or party on these questions. I think there are mistakes in the Christian world on many of the great subjects which are the

main points in our creed.   The common-sense meaning
of the Scriptures has been so distorted as to destroy
the beauty and simplicity of revelation.   The glowing
figures of Christ and the prophets have been strained
and perverted so that the mass of Christians read their
Bibles through colored spectacles.   Hence the strifes of
the present day, most of them arising from giving a
wrong meaning to Scripture terms.   Some of the words
which are most misunderstood seem to me to be :

Faith or Belief; which is not so much an intellectual
as an emotional state, and corresponds to that with
which a little child trusts himself to his father.   *Trust*
would generally be a better word.

Salvation; now used almost solely in reference to the
future world, but in Scripture generally of the present.
' *Such as should be saved,*' in the original, ' *such as
are saved.*'   ' Save yourselves from this untoward generation.'   Jesus saves His people from their sins, prima-
rily, in this life, and, as a consequence, in the life to
come.

Heaven; probably no word is less understood than
this.   In the originals the word is almost always in the
plural—*The Heavens.*   It means the vast universe of
worlds, where God's rational creatures dwell in their
various spheres of duty and service ; viz, the stars—the
mansions where Christ has gone to prepare places for
us.   The idea commonly entertained of *two*, and only
two places, one for the righteous and one for the wicked,
is only a fraction of the truth.   The *great* division is, of
course, between the good and bad, the righteous and
wicked ; but these are subdivided into countless other
and minor divisions, all being assigned to places, positions and services, *according to their deeds* ; in other
words, according to their characters, differing "as one
star differs from another," so Paul says.   I suppose God
places everybody in just the place that is most suitable

for him, and it is a great mercy that in the future world the good will be separated from the hatred and malevolence of the bad.

God's wrath, I understand to be the most appropriate expression that can be found for the *misery* which His wise laws have inseparably connected with sin, and has no reference to His *state of mind* towards His creatures ; in this respect, He is only love. " God *is* love "—it is the very element and essence of His character. He wants that everybody should be saved. The scripture teaches this as plain as words can tell ; " He wills that all should be saved ;" " If anything more *could* have been done for his vineyard," He would have done it. "He delights *not* in the death (or the misery) of the sinner ; no, not even of Satan ; it is the necessary and inevitable connection between sin and misery that keeps the devil where he is.

As to the duration of punishment—or rather misery— it depends on character. One sin begets another. The effects of sin will be eternal. I do not expect there will ever come a time, through all the ages of eternity, when I shall look back upon any sin I have committed, without a *pang of sorrow*. If that sin is forgiven, it will alleviate the torment, and [add] to my gratitude to the Redeemer ; otherwise it will be the gnawing worm and the endless fire. I do not believe in softening down the terrible figures that Christ has given us, of the consequences of transgression ; He would not have painted it worse than it really is. And yet it pains the Heart of our loving Father, that any of His creatures should suffer.

You will see from this what my ideas of hell are. Milton, who had a wonderful insight into the workings of the mind, puts this language into the mouth of Satan ; ' *Myself am Hell !* ' Yes, there it is ; hell within, hell around, hell in this world, and hell in the world to come.

But time for sending off this letter has come, so I must stop; and I see I have in the main answered your question, which I did not expect to do when I began."

To Rev. John Stillman Brown, Oct. 21, 1883. "A man was *saved* when he was *rescued* from sin or any sinful way ; the original is the same as that for healing. . . . The more I have studied the New Testament the more I believe it is a book to be taken in a common-sense way ; and that for a common reader it is a great deal better without a commentary than with one. We give it to the Japanese people just as it is, without note or comment, and let them make up their own minds as to its doctrine."

Mr. Brown was one of the " Yokohama Translation Committee," which consisted of members of the several denominational missions, united in making a version from the Received Text. There was no danger, in their view, or his, of too much light being thrown upon the scripture, by a plurality of versions. "Now, in the tentative process of translation," he says, " the more versions there are, the more likelihood will there be of a pure version in the end—a general revision, combining the excellencies and rectifying the blemishes incident to all first attempts." Some of the most cherished and lasting friendships of his life were those formed during this co-operation. The Committee consisted of Dr. S. R. Brown of the Reformed Church ; Dr. J. C. Hepburn, Presbyterian ; Dr. D. C. Greene, Congregational ; Dr. R. S. Maclay, Methodist, and himself. On the completion, in 1880, of the Committee's version of the New Testament, (largely the work of Dr. Hepburn,) Mr. Brown was invited to continue with them upon the Old, and as one of the Revision Committee of Five, rendered some assistance in the latter work during 1880 and 1881.

He also, at their request, adapted the spelling of Scrip-ture proper names to the Japanese language, in a book of 96 pages, entitled "Rules for Transliteration and Transference of Hebrew Names," and containing 2,500 names, each carefully transliterated from Hebrew into Japanese.

While translating the Testament, he ran his presses in an adjacent building, superintending the work and correcting his proofs himself.

To Rev. Mr. Childs, October 16, '82· "I have ten hands in employ already, good, honest men, most of them Christians; always have worship with them in the morn-ing. . . . I trust that some day you may be able to come out and see them."

He believed that a Mission Press, under Christian control, was desirable, both in order the more readily to secure accuracy, and to avoid having scriptures printed on the Sabbath, in a heathen establishment. His Ja-panese compositors' work closely followed his own; once he notes that most of a chapter was in type on the evening of the day on which it was translated. But at one time unlooked-for hinderances nearly put a stop to the printing; he was obliged to dismiss hands, and days and months passed in a stress of patience, as he felt age creeping on, not without fear lest life should end before the task. Soon after, the supply of hymn-books and entire Testaments was exhausted.

The home-workers rallied to his aid. "Shall we stand still and see Brother Brown's gray hairs sink with sorrow to the grave?" said Dr. Everts at a missionary meet-ing. Encouragement had already come. "Your 'Hold-on' letter was like cold waters to a thirsty soul," the missionary wrote to a true-hearted friend. A previous " Hold-on " message had come as from the spirit-land;

"the legacy of dear Mrs. Seddinger for Bibles and Bible printing." One of the gospels was printed with a remittance from a boyhood friend of old Whitingham days, Deacon William Martin, past his fourscore years. A letter to this helper says:

"I shall never see you again in the flesh, but I hope we shall meet and take our walks again together beside the rivers of paradise, as we did in days of yore beside the Hoosac, and in the pleasant villages of Schaghticoke and Whitesboro, only it will be in a sinless world, without any sorrows or shadows."

In the fall of '81 he was "driving through the press an edition of 8000," in the new printing office which he had built the year before, on the south end of his lot. He had now issued an edition in one volume, after carefully going over doubtful and difficult points with Kawakatsu, explaining and questioning in every language understood by the latter, so as to make sure that the same idea was in the mind of both. The summer of '81 had found him studying Chinese for a Scholars' Edition (mixed Kana and Chinese), printed with funds of the American Baptist Missionary Union. This and the revised Kana were in progress during '82, his presses being continually at work. In the fall of that year two new Washington presses were received from Rev. T. P. Childs, and Mr. Brown put up a fire-proof building for them near the printing office. "I trust they will be used for mission work as long as the iron lasts," he wrote to the donor. Soon after, Kawakatsu's translation of Watts' Catechism was printed. Within the year preceding Oct., '82, two and a quarter million pages of scripture came from the presses; the next year, three millions more.

He believed in Bible Societies. A work so great as that of Scripture publication and distribution ought to be, needed, in his judgment, a separate organization that should make it a specialty, helping the heavily burdened missionary societies by printing and carrying the scriptures into outlying districts. With those individuals and societies in America and England that had forwarded this work when it was ready to fail, he felt a strong bond. His attachment to the Missionary Union and the American and Foreign Bible Society is expressed in the following letter :

"I believe and have said, that while a missionary society, whose main or sole object is evangelizing the heathen through the strictly missionary agency of preaching can also carry on the work of Scripture distribution in places where their missionaries labor, the great work of supplying the *unevangelized millions* (so far as they are anxious to be supplied) cannot be *effectually* accomplished without a separate agency, whose labors shall not be restricted to the boundaries of the preacher, but extend to evangelized and unevangelized alike, and thus saturate, so far as God's Word is allowed access, the heathen mind with Scripture truth.

We see around us in Japan the most convincing evidence of the great advantage which other denominational societies have over us in the enlargement of their work among the *heathen* by means of their *separate Bible societies*, scattering the Word far beyond the preacher's voice, and preparing rich harvests for the reapers that are crowding in where the Scriptures have prepared the way. I wish to see Baptists enjoying the same advantages. My hopes and wishes are bound up in the prosperity of our mission and Bible societies at home and abroad, especially in the Missionary Union and the American and Foreign Bible Society. My attachment to both of them is sincere, not because of any special preference for particular organizations or

(34)

boards of officers, but because I believe some such organizations are a *necessity* to the triumph of the Christian Church. I care little for names or modes of organization, but I do believe that no part of our great work should be left to languish and decay through the relinquishment of any agencies that are essential to success."*

Mr. Brown had from the first printed his translations in *hira-kana*, the cursive character used in the everyday literature of the Japanese; the familiar characters in which their dramas, songs and romances were printed. He had also omitted from his pages the intermixture of Chinese valued by literati and priests in their philosophical works, but utterly unintelligible to busy workingmen, to women and children. "We have avoided," he says, "such Chinese words as can only be understood through the hieroglyphic characters, confining ourselves to those that are in actual use in the spoken language, and therefore intelligible from the sound alone."

" Dr. Brown's translation," writes one of his associates to the *New York Examiner*, "is in pure Japanese—adapted to the needs of the common readers, while the higher classes can easily comprehend it."

Many educated and patriotic Japanese, anxious to rid their language of its foreign incubus, formed an association called the *Kanano Tomo*, for the promotion of hira-kana (called briefly *Kana*), and the abolition of Chinese hieroglyphics. This society includes some of the most accomplished native linguists, and has its adherents at court.

Mr. Brown's Kana Scriptures met with ready sale. Colporteurs carrying a supply of both the Kana and

---

* The Watch-Tower, Nov. 30, 1882.

Scholars' editions into the city and outlying villages, found an eager demand for the plain copies, and only here and there a purchaser of hieroglyphics. Of 16,000 gospels and other scriptures disposed of in 1882, 15,000 were in unmixed Kana. When his son William went to Yokohama again in 1883, as a temporary Bible missionary to organize systematic scripture distribution, desiring to test the matter for himself, he took a bundle of small books under his arm, and went out among the workmen and villagers. He found that about four-fifths of them could read. Half-a-dozen of these visits in the vicinity of Yokohama, resulted in the disposal of more than 2000 of the Kana booklets. He says:

"The tracts with illustrated covers, containing the parables of Christ, and Bible stories in their own vernacular, were usually received with gratitude and respect by the people, and they doubtless did much towards opening their hearts to the heralds of the cross. Within the temples, however, were suspicious priests, who saw their income liable to be cut off, and themselves dishonored, and these did what they could to counteract the influence of the gospel."

N. B. Jan. 1, 1884. "How was I revived yesterday by·the genial face of my little colporteur Haragútci, who had come to bring his report to my son. He reports having sold 772 gospels in pure Kana in one month (December), though only twenty of the mixed Chino-Japanese! . . . For the whole year the sales are (of both colporteurs) . . . total books or rolls in Kana, 3477; in mixed, 577.

Feb. 1. The people seemed almost wild to get them, when they found they were in their own native tongue, and in their own letters. . . . Haragútci says that at the fairs at Miso and Hatcioji, he sold and distributed hundreds of Kana gospels, while colporteurs and others with the mixtures of full Chinese could not sell any.   Datè, one of our Chogo preachers, who was at Hatcioji at the time, says he heard a great noise, some one on a stand calling to the people, and going up he found it was little Haragútci selling to the people right and left as fast as he could deal them out.

God has opened a door before us such as has never been witnessed in any unevangelized nation.   A people with a smooth, expressive and very copious tongue, and what is of greater importance, *four-fifths* of them readers."

Jan. 1, '84·   "I will give the few remaining days I have to live on earth to the cause of this beloved people —this whole people, without respect of persons—esteeming the poor as good as the rich, and equally entitled to have a language that they can read."

Superior as the Kana was, in legibility, to the mixed printing, some of the quick-witted Japanese had already discovered that the missionaries' own books were in a character clearer and simpler still.   In 1882 an old edition of the Parables in Roman Kana, that is, Kana interlined with its equivalent sounds in Roman letters, met with an unexpected sale, the whole supply being rapidly bought up, and more called for by the natives. "Their readiness to buy and pay for the Romanized Kana is remarkable," said Mr. Brown, at the close of that year.   "If we had the whole New Testament in that form it would, no doubt, meet with as large a sale as the Committee's Romanized edition."   "The Roman letter," writes Dr. Hepburn, in 1887, "is gradually taking the place of the cumbersome Chinese characters." Says Rev. C. S. Eby, the scholarly editor of the "*Chrysanthemum*:"

"This reform, (Romanization of Japanese), if successful, is, in my mind, more pregnant of good to Japan
in the way of increase in intellectual capital, and in
help on the way to western civilization, than all other
reforms put together, that have taken place in that new-
born land of the east."

As soon as the first edition of the Testament was
issued in 1879, Mr. Brown commenced revising, a work
which he carried on, when the press of other duties permitted, as long as he lived. He also translated some
portions of the Old Testament and many hymns, adding
a number of his own composition, in the enlarged Hymn
Book. The series of juvenile tracts was printed in 1878.
New editions of his Stories from the Old Testament
were called for before he could issue them.

He never reached the point at which he could stop—
the work broadened out before him, and when the pen
was at last laid aside, it was in the midst of unfinished
labors that would take another life-time to complete.
He felt that the Scriptures should be followed by a
Christian literature. Among plans jotted down in his
diary, Dec. 31, '82, was the translating of Pilgrim's
Progress, "if I can get a man of the right kind to help
me put it in colloquial ;" and a popular course on Natural
Science, adapted to counteract the inroads of European
materialism. He had begun in spare moments a " Bird
Book ; or What God has Done for the Birds ;" with
this to be associated Beasts, Fishes, Insects and Plants,
especially those of Scripture reference ; these to form
part of an " Encyclopædia of Christian Literature, by
which I mean not only Bible information, but *all Truth*
in any department of God's great book of nature." In
this connection he specifies ecclesiastical and general
history, and geological discoveries and antiquities. "This
Encyclopædia of Religious and Christian Literature

ought properly to be followed by a monthly magazine, which would in a measure supplement the work, and supply its deficiencies."

But just now, the next thing to hand was "to go on with the revised New Testament in the scholars' edition (8,000) and people's edition (small) in pure kana, it is completed."

And he was on the watch for good news from other parts of the world-field. "I feel rejoiced," (July 9, '84) "to hear of the missions to be established in Africa, and of the doings of the Publication Society for a pure Bible at home. We can afford to be a little tardy in Japan, for the sake of these other immensely important branches of the same field."

XXXVIII

" A MORE glorious mission-field the sun never shone upon," the veteran worker wrote in January, 1878, upon intimation of the possibility of abandoning the undertaking. Here, on the spot, everything is bright and cheering; converts are slowly but steadily coming in, the scriptures are scattered and are doing their work, and two lovely little charges have been gathered, whom I would as soon cut off a right hand as desert now in their infancy, with none to look after and teach them. Miss Kidder all alone at Tokio says the same; Miss Sands is equally opposed to the idea of giving up the mission."

Valued associates were gone; he alone remained to minister to the two infant churches at Yokohama and Tokio, going on at the same time with the translation and printing of the Testament. The helpers from the Woman's Board saw good fruit of their labors in converts added to the churches, some in face of stringent opposition of relatives and friends. Mr. Brown's Japanese teacher and assistant, Rev. T. Kawakatsu, preached at Tokio three Sundays out of four, to the inquirers and Christians gathered by Miss Kidder, and he himself went up once a month to preach, and administer baptism and communion. Even during this year of hinderances, twenty-one inquirers found they had "no use" for their idols, gave up the ancestral worship and found rest in a living Saviour. One of these was the wife of the preacher Kawakatsu.

Rev. James Hope Arthur had joined the mission in November, 1873. After spending the winter in the study of the language at Yokohama. Mr. and Mrs. Arthur had removed to the capital, and taken up their abode in the midst of the native population. Pupils gathered around them, converts took on the Christian name and the Baptist church was organized May 14, 1876. A year later, Mr. Arthur, compelled by declining health to relinquish these labors, sought restoration by a voyage to California. The hoped-for recovery did not result; the earnest young missionary was called home on the 9th of December, 1877, from Oakland. Devoted and enterprising, he had worked while the day lasted.

Referring to this loss and other discouraging events which had marked the history of the little mission, Mr. Brown says :

"We remember the days of darkness in Assam, when a missionary was brought to our doors a corpse, and others sickened and died ; we call to mind the severe trials that have marked the early period of almost every mission from the time of Carey down. It seems to be the order of God's providence that success must come through suffering."

To daughter, Jan. 14, '79 "Yesterday I went up to Tokio and administered the Lord's Supper. Miss Kidder says the prospects were never better there, and she does not intend to leave her post. Two more have asked for baptism. The very day that Brother Arthur died at Oakland, I was baptizing two young men in the tank he made in his compo Verily his works do follow him."

One of Mr. Arthur's last letters home says of certain Tokio converts :

MUSICIANS OF THE TEMPLE OF SHIBA, IN TOKIO.

"One of them, Miss Kidder's teacher, a woman of strong, rugged character, brought to us Saturday night a great armful of all sorts of idols as a proof of her sincerity. Sunday morning, when she told her experience to the church, she said she had worshipped the fox, the snake and the badger, as well as the idols, and when she went to her house and saw the things she had worshipped she was so ashamed, even if no one was present, that she hardly knew what to do. She had torn down the *Kami-dana*, or god-shelf, which is in every Japanese house, had torn to pieces or otherwise destroyed many of her idols, and brought the rest to us.

Another said, 'Although at first I neither believed nor understood the gospel, the wonderful story of the cross at last reached my heart ; and I believed and have put my idols into the fire.' "

Miss Kidder writes : " This people know right from wrong. They discover with ease the faults of others. They understand when one sins against the government, his neighbor, or himself, and see with wonderfully clear vision the failings of the ' Jesus Christ believers,' but are so politely indifferent, or so smilingly agree with us and go no further, that we should creep off home discouraged, were it not that we have seen that the Holy Spirit convinces some of sin and leads them to purer lives."

So identified to the Japanese mind is human government with divine, that the language recognizes no distinction between sin against God and crime against government. Hence the native Christian preacher, when he refers to his audience as sinners, feels obliged to stop and explain that he does not mean to say that they have broken the laws of the government, but have transgressed the commands of God.

The Japanese Christians evinced activity and self-reliance. Some of the young men already showed capacity and willingness to preach Christ to their country-men. Mr. Brown wrote of them :

"June 25, '76· We have now three that preach well, all having a natural gift for it, and all having become familiar with the work by practice during the past year. The hundred and twenty dollars sent annually by Brother Peter Howe,* has been of the greatest service, and if the Board could give me an appropriation of $200 in addition to that, I could keep a couple of them preaching in the villages and country nearly the whole year. . . . It has been my hope to see a native ministry raised up here, that shall go all over the land, and raise up gospel churches and gather in converts."

1879. "For the last two years we have had letters from church members residing at distances of from twenty-five to a hundred miles from this port, telling us of their efforts at preaching and exhorting, their success in awakening inquiry, and of many cases where converts are desiring baptism."

At this juncture Mr. T. P. Poate from England, for some years employed as a teacher by the Japanese government, joined the mission, and with Mrs. Poate, formerly Miss Marsh, of the Presbyterian Board, was laboring in Yokohama and neighboring villages. He was ordained at Tokio, Dec. 30, 1879, the sermon being preached by Rev. Mr. Rhees. "The charge," writes Mr. Bennett, "was given by Dr. Brown. It seemed peculiarly solemn and appropriate, and benefited others as well as the

---

* This venerable and faithful "helper in Christ," a banker in Wenona Illinois, lived to do much for the Japanese. In November, 1888, an intoxicated ruffian entered the house of Mr. and Mrs. Howe, climbed by ladder to the bedroom window, murdered the aged couple in their bed and returning home, shot himself.

one to whom it was given. Some missionary friends of other denominations, as well as a goodly number of natives, were present at this service, which was held in Miss Kidder's school-room."

The new missionary answered the letters from the northern villages in person, going with the assistant Suzúki to Morioka. Said one inquirer there, an aged woman, whose son was insane, and to whom neither physicians, priests, nor idols had proved an adequate resource in her affliction: "I don't know much; but this I do know: I have long prayed to idols, and I have gained nothing but sorrow; now I pray to the true God in heaven." The native Christian women gathered around her and told her of the compassionate Lord Jesus. "'Tis such a good thing *to trust in him*," said one, and the testimony sank into a heart all ready to respond. In May, the waters of the broad, mirror-like river received her in baptism.

Mr. Poate's lantern, bearing every evening the inscription, "*Preaching about Jesus. Entrance free*," drew increasing audiences. Subsequent missionary tours resulted in spreading the good news among the northern villages.

Meantime the little church at Yokohama was growing. The tide was never too high, nor the breakers too rough at Homoka beach, for their now aged pastor to lead Japanese converts down the wave-washed sands to their ocean baptism.

"Feb. 8, '81. It is now eight years since we landed on these shores. I have been permitted to baptize 71 persons, and the church is now in a very good state.

Dec. 24, '83. Five happy converts baptized to-day; one an old lady over seventy. Although a cold day, she shrank not from the waves, and came out of the water with a smile of joy upon her lips."

Other workers had joined the mission. Rev. Henry Rhees was preaching in the southern villages, and Rev. A. A. Bennett having arrived Nov. 30, 1879, was already reaching the young men of Yokohama. The latter says, Feb. 10, '81 :

"I want to write a few lines about last Sunday. A happier Sabbath I have not known since I reached this island empire. The weather was perfect. Mr. Poate preached at the native chapel in the morning, and after service we all went to the sea-side, a mile or so distant, where we were to have a baptism, a thing which I am thankful to say is by no means uncommon. . . . At the water's edge hymns were sung and prayer offered in Japanese ; and after Dr. Brown had addressed some solemn words to the native candidates, he spoke for a few minutes in English to the other two with such words and manner that it seemed as if he was inspired. Never on any other similar occasion have I heard the like. It was a beautiful sight as he walked far out into the water, and stood surrounded by the happy ones who were one after another, buried in that watery grave. How I wish that some or our church-members in the home-land could have stood with us there on the shore !

The afternoon with its full church and the communion service was another sight that I wish could have been witnessed. The words of Dr. Brown, as he extended the hand of fellowship, were earnest and solemn. I could not understand all of his Japanese when he spoke to the natives ; but I could understand enough to perceive their appropriateness and wisdom. He loves this people, and they love him. May God spare him to the mission for many years."

At Tokio, Miss Kidder held on with day-school, Sabbath and week-day services in the city and several out-stations, encouraged by frequent conversions. The preacher, Rev. Toriyama, was ordained pastor, January 10th, 1880, and a few months later the little church erected a building, which was dedicated July 3rd, Mr. Brown preaching the sermon.

The larger operations of other denominations were meeting with cheering success; the light was increasing against the darkness. Quietly, yet surely, each division of the army was pressing forward, and notwithstanding importations of American atheism and European Buddhism, and translations of Paine and Ingersoll, the "old, old story" won its way. Mr. Brown was able to say: "The work is getting a firmer and firmer hold, and our native strength is increasing." And Mr. Bennett: "The year 1883 was an auspicious one in the religious history of Japan. It far exceeded any previous year in its apparent good fruitage, and also, I believe, in the amount of seed sown." Miss Sands wrote: "From Kioto, Kobé and other places, we hear by telegrams of great awakenings, many conversions, and believers putting away sin, and rejoicing as never before."

In general, however, it was plodding, inch-by-inch work that the missionaries, foreign and native, had to do. Sometimes Mr. Brown took a Sunday afternoon walk for rest, which meant going about with a bundle of tracts on a missionary tramp. When the father and his two sons, the youngest six years old, went into a native village and distributed scriptures, talked with the good-natured Japanese, and found their hearts as open as their houses, it must have brought back to the older missionary, whose journeyings were now almost done, a reminiscence of Burma and Assam.

Mr. Brown frequently preached at the Union Church in Yokohama. His views on the extension and unification of the Christian Church are expressed in an address, which, as President of the Evangelical Alliance of Japan in 1880, he made at its seventh annual meeting, held with the Union Church of Tokio. Tracing the history of the church universal, from that "first alarming sign of apostacy," "the decline of Christian love," through mediæval corruptions and bondage, and the purifying but disintegrating upheavals of the Reformation, down to the nineteenth century or missionary era, he showed the tendency of missions to draw together in harmony the sects which a hundred years ago arrayed themselves against each other, in a war of fierce and bitter denunciations, "which at the present day, seem wholly unaccountable, except as we consider them a legacy from the dark and persecuting past."

"It seems as though there were something in the very principle of missions to kindle a special fraternal feeling. No sooner do the embattled hosts, each under his own banner, find themselves standing side by side on heathen soil, all bent upon a life and death struggle with a common foe, than they feel themselves drawn together by a bond of sympathy that is in no wise impaired by loyalty to their own respective colors.
. . . The Evangelical Alliance is the exponent and representative of these new and increasing aspirations after Christian love and union of action. How does it expect to promote that union? Not by any sudden ecclesiastical convulsion, hurling the great religious. organizations of Christendom into a commingled mass, and erecting a new structure on the ruins, but rather by saving and strengthening all these agencies ; leaving each branch of Christ's universal flock to correct its own errors and work its way up to the perfect gospel standard, by following its own convictions of duty, under the guidance and illumination of the Holy Spirit.
.   . This may be called a rope of sand; but it will stand the test of all time. Plans for unity and con-

formity have hitherto failed, because they were built either on the idea of force, or the idea of compromise. This alliance discards both, and strikes out boldly for soul-liberty. Give a man soul-liberty, and by God's grace he will work his way upward; put him under soul-bondage and he will either remain stationary or go downward.

. . . It is in the power of God to give His people unity of views as well as unity of action. It will come, if it come at all, in answer to prayer. And there is every evidence that it will come whenever we are prepared for the blessing."

After dwelling on the advance of the Kingdom in Japan and China, he says of India:

"At the same ratio of increase as in the last twenty years, another half century will make that vast country as really Christian as Great Britain is to-day. The last report of the Baptist Missionary Union states the number of additions to their churches in the Telugú district of Southern India to be over ten thousand baptized within the year! The missionaries of the Church of England have gathered thirty thousand converts in the district of Tinevelly. In the missions of the American Board among the Tamils of Southern India, more than seventy thousand people have thrown away their idols and accepted the God of the Bible. Simultaneously with these wonderful tidings comes the news that the dark Continent of Africa is opened; the majestic rivers that sweep through its central regions have been traversed and laid open to the civilized world; and four or five of the large missionary societies are already pushing on to occupy the countries lying around the great lakes of the interior.

How stupendous the thought when once it fully enters the mind, that the Kingdom of God is really coming, over all this globe on which we dwell. The last idol broken, the last heathen temple deserted, the last orgy of demon-worship, the last bacchanalian revelry over and gone! How the pulse quickens as we see that kingdom drawing nigh! If human calculation already begins to arrange the figures and reckon the limits of probability, we must bear in mind that when God works, the changes often come with a rapidity that confounds the wisdom of the wise. So it may be in the conversion of the world. For aúght we know, the last and crowning events of this long struggle may be crowded into the space of a hundred and twenty years. It may be that when the year two thousand shall arrive, the angel that holds the seventh trumpet will have sounded, signalling the close of the conflict, and announcing that the kingdoms of the world have become the Kingdom of our Lord and of his Christ.

Let us cherish the holy enthusiasm with which this work inspires us. We have given to it our lives, and every power we possess; our everlasting hopes are linked with the certainty of Christ's victorious coming. We do not expect to see it with these eyes. Year by year beloved comrades are falling around us, and we shall soon be with them. From the hills of glory they watch the conflict as it goes on, and we, too, will watch and wait with them, and with them share the final victory.

Let us stand side by side as brothers. If we are all pressing forward to the same kingdom, let us help and encourage each other by every means in our power. Let no unhallowed strifes mar the beauty of our onward march; no painful reminiscences of unseemly discords, unkind words or acts be left for explanation and settlement after we reach heaven. Let us be careful to avoid the occasions of alienation, not attempting to control the religious views of others, but looking well to the consistent and faithful practice of our own. Above all, let us take care how we build. Let each endeavor to plant living churches of God here upon this virgin soil, in as exact accordance with the New Testament pattern as possible, honestly aiming to follow the Master, irrespective of any human teaching. And let us have faith to believe that out of our denominational organizations God will select for the Church of the Future, all the excellencies that are to be found in each, while He purges them from every spot and stain that we in our weakness and ignorance have suffered to remain. Let us so pray, and so preach, and so live, that the proportion of hay, wood and stubble in our respective churches may be reduced to the smallest possible dimensions; and when, perhaps, some darling scheme or theory that we have cherished is swept away by the increasing light, let us be ready to say, Amen! God be thanked for this also. So shall the Saviour's prayer be fulfilled: 'Sanctify them through Thy truth; Thy word is truth. . . . That they all may be one, as Thou, Father, art in me, and I in Thee, that they also may be one in us.' Thus shall the long line of prophetic utterances arrive at completion; 'the watchmen shall lift up the voice; with the voice together shall they sing; for they shall see eye to eye when the Lord shall bring again Zion.' 'The wilderness and the solitary place shall be glad for them; and the desert shall rejoice and blossom as the rose.' Then shall the saints inherit the earth. Throughout all generations, so long as the sun and moon endure, this purified and unified Church of the Future shall fill the renewed earth with gladness and beauty; the Redeemer shall see the fruits of the travail of His soul and be satisfied; and the will of God be done on earth as it is done in heaven."

So the missionary's east window let in the coming dawn and the freshening breeze. Let who would, face

the dark, his spirit was braced by the vision of "light
fringing the far-rising slope." His Kingdom sermon,
preached at Tokio June 22d, '73' and afterwards at Yokohama, closes with a review of Japan's progress, and
a forward looking and listening.

"So far as human penetration can discern, the question
whether Japan shall be Christian, or whether it shall
plunge into an infidelity worse than the previous super-
stitions, rests with the present generation.

The world is hastening to its crisis. The human race
have been held back in the career of progress until the
fit time for them to enter upon a more elevated plane.
. . . Daily travel and intercommunication are rapidly
breaking down the division walls which superstition
has erected. Education and the printing-press are
undermining the foundations of idolatry in India.
Buddhist asceticism and Mohammedan bigotry are alike
yielding to the gradual influences of Christian light.
Old tyrannies are broken up, hoary errors exploded,
fresh fountains bursting out from arid plains and
burning sands. Freedom is in the air; we inhale the
gospel of a common brotherhood; the globe becomes
one household, and all its members are kindred. People that speak with each other every day by telegraph,
cannot long be aliens and strangers. Can we look upon
the rolling wheel of Providence and be unconscious of
the mighty movement that is sweeping the race onward
to some glorious destiny? Can we witness the dawning rays that gild the tops of these eastern mountains
and not feel the inspiration of the coming day?

God reigneth; and he has ever reigned, not only over
his Israel, but over Babylon and Egypt and Persia as
well; over India and China and Japan; they have all
been moving on to their destiny, through shade and
sheen, beneath the guardianship of his watchful eye,
until they are ripe for the great change that is now

passing over them. God reigns and shall reign, yet more gloriously. His kingdom is an everlasting kingdom, and all dominions shall serve and obey him.

> ' Hark ! the song of jubilee,
>   Loud as mighty thunders roar,
> Or the fullness of the sea
>   When it breaks upon the shore.
> Hallelujah ! for the Lord God omnipotent shall reign ;
> Hallelujah ! let the word echo round the earth and main.

*   *   *

> See Jehovah's banners furled ;
>   Sheathed his sword ; he speaks,—'tis done,
> And the kingdoms of this world
>   Are the kingdoms of his Son.
> He shall reign from pole to pole with illimitable sway ;
> He shall reign when like a scroll, yonder heavens have
>   passed away.

> Then the end.   Beneath his rod man's last enemy shall
>   fall.
> Hallelujah ! Christ in God, God in Christ, is all in all.' '

XXXIX.

THE sun, "toward heaven's descent now sloped his westering wheel," and the lingering workman, looking around, noticed that most of those who had plowed and sowed and reaped with him, were laying down their implements of labor and taking the home-path. He too, was working up toward the border.

"The only few things that now seem to have any very strong hold upon me personally are, 1st, my work; this grows more and more delightful to me every year; 2d, my little family here and in America, in which I include not only relatives but old family friends; 3d, this dear little church here, for whose prosperity my anxiety is inexpressible."

"The death of Brother Bronson [at Eaton Rapids, Mich., Nov. 10, 1883], affects me much. Many others of my old acquaintances have dropped off during the year. We shall all go soon. I begin to realize the probably near approach of the dread angel, transformed into the gracious scepter in the hand of a loving King and Father."

> "'Tis but a sigh, the band's farewell,
> The darkening of the forehead gem—
> That sleep of life's last sentinel—
> And we shall be with them!"

To daughter, on the death of his classmate and brother, Rev. Dr. James Ballard, which occurred Jan. 7, 1881:

(576)

" I was deeply interested in the extracts you gave me from Mrs. Thompson's letters respecting Uncle James' peaceful and happy death. I know how much your dear mother was attached to him. They grew up side by side, and were one in affection, thought and feeling on the great subject on which all true Christians have fixed their hearts, and for which they are ready to sacrifice their lives. He is now at rest, joined to all the sainted brotherhood and sisterhood of that large family of whom only one yet lingers on the shores of time."

April 21, '84. " The steamer to-day brought news of the death of four of my acquaintances, Rev. Norman Harris, Royal B. Hancock, Dr. J. G. Warren and Dr. Sidney A. Corey; the three former, long servants of the Missionary Union. Almost every month's mail, since I came from home, has brought tidings of the death of one or more persons of nearly my own age, with whom I have been acquainted, but this I think is the first time that the news of four old friends has reached me by the same mail. In the meantime I find my general health is failing gradually, and the time of my departure cannot be very far distant. Among my correspondents I think I have now not more than half a dozen who are older than myself: Rev. Abner Webb, Rev. William Dean (one day older), Rev. Cephas Bennett, Cousin John Stillman Brown, Brother Jonas Ballard, Dea. William Martin. May 12. To-day received a letter from Brother Bennett,* with an account of a gathering at his house on his 80th birthday!"

The final labors were pushed forward in much weakness, but without intermission, through an unusually trying hot season.

---

* Six weeks only, intervened between the death of these two old friends, Cephas Bennett in Burma, and Nathan Brown in Japan, the latter knowing not that Mr. Bennett had preceded him.

June 21, '84· "I have now completed the sixth roll of the New Testament, Scholars' edition. Have reached No. 107 of the new Hymn Book. This is a heavy work. The last six months have been chiefly given to it. Nearly half of it still remains. As soon as that is through, if life is spared, I shall be ready to hope to enter upon a Romanized edition of the Hymns and also of the New Testament. My daily prayer to my Saviour is, Lord, help me to give this people the scriptures in their own pure Kana, and also in the *Roman character.* The latter, if not so instantly pressing, is an object of wider bearings, and more pregnant with mighty results in the future. Aug. 24. . . . Went up to Tokio to visit the brethren there. All their operations are encouraging."

Among the later hymns which he put into Japanese were "There is a Fountain," "Blest be the Tie," "I love to think of Heaven," "All Hail the power of Jesus' name."

In November a physician was called; the handwriting shows muscular paralysis. He was better towards the close of the year.

"Sunday December 14. To-day I have felt much better and was able to go to the native church. The church seems to have outgrown me; I do not recognize half of the members, and when I enter the room, I feel astonished, and everything is strange to me. But not long; soon their happy voices are heard in concert, chanting the old familiar airs. Oh how lovely to see such a beautiful church congregated here to praise and worship the dear Lord, and to unite with each other in happy, harmonious devotion! Christianity wants no argument but the practical one. It is the medicine that gives happiness, love, comfort, joy in the Holy Ghost, and this being brought home as a feast to the Christian soul, all the reasoning, refinements and hair-splitting arguments of philosophers, agnostics, or whatever they may be called, are of little consequence. Now that I begin to see the gleams of recovery, my heart stretches out with new desires and prayers for the success of my special work."

His New Year's greeting of 1885, struck off at the printing-office on postal-cards, because the wearied hand could no longer keep up his general correspondence, was sent to many waiting and anxious friends :

"Yokohama, Jan. 17, 1885.

My dear Brother :—I had fully intended to write to you before the New Year, but this card is all I am equal to at present, just to wish you peace, happiness and holy joy. I have now been laid up for two months with a complication of malarial complaints which have reduced me almost to a skeleton. The skin over my hands feels like gloves, and my fingers are so numb that it is with great difficulty I can hold a pen. But the Lord has had mercy on me, and already I begin to feel the currents of a warmer blood in my veins. I hope to live a few years longer if it be God's will. We have all been astonished with this year's sale of scriptures, especially those in the pure vernacular. The returns of books and tracts disposed of will show a total of very near 30,000. Our additions [to the churches] have been about 100. Let us praise God together. The longer I live the more I realize his infinite goodness and love.

Ever yours affectionately,

N. Brown."

A greeting, years before, to one of his children, ran thus :

" A happy New Year to you, and thousands and millions more of its happy returns, for I feel more and
more, that this life is but a link that joins on to the
rest, and that we shall never forget times and seasons,
in whatever sphere of being our future may be."

As the time of his departure drew near, his human
sympathies and interests continued to increase in breadth
and strength. His heart held with a tighter clasp than
ever all who were knit to him, east and west. As long
as his band could hold a pen, each outgoing steamer
carried his punctual letters to one or both of his distant
children, though they were often dated in the small
hours of the morning.

The marriage of the two daughters who accompanied
Mrs. Brown to Japan, had narrowed the home circle,
but visits from a baby grandson added brightness to the
last months of his life.

" I am now on the verge," he wrote, May 25th; and
on July 3rd:

" I am scarcely able to sit up a moment, or scribble
with a pen, but I must, as your whole mail has poured
in upon us to-day, revised Old Testament and all.
Blessed volume! I thank the Lord for permitting me
to see it. I sympathize deeply with Brother Jonas'
family, [on the death of the mother and sister.] How
strange that the old hold out so long, and many die so
young, just budding into manhood and womanhood."

"To Mr. Jonas Ballard,* April 26, '84·

Very dear Brother: Lizzie wrote me that you were
eighty-seven years old and still moving about your busi-

---

*This brother, the last remaining member of the family of Capt. William
Ballard, died at the homestead in his ninetieth year, a few months after the
death of Nathan Brown in Yokohama.

ness. I am only seventy-seven, yet feel myself to be an old man on the borders of the grave ; have little doubt that ere I reach such an age as yours, I shall pass away.

. . . I felt more than I can express, for the present sent by A——to me from her sainted mother, and which I have received. Precious is the memory of such godly men and women as have left the ranks of our family. It is sweet to think of them as forming a lovely group of white-robed habitants of the better world. Oh, may we be so happy as to join them there. . . . I never had more strong desires for anything in my life than to see this dear people allowed the privilege of reading the scriptures in their own vernacular, which is to them like meat and drink. As Dr. Hepburn says, " It is just as delightful to a Japanese to have the Scriptures in his own tongue, as it is for ours. . . . May the Lord bless you in your declining and trying years, and bear you safely home to eternal rest.

Ever yours in the Lord,

Nathan Brown.

He was always grateful for " information about the loved ones that still remain around the old hearthstones;" each was held in lively recollection, and regarded as a member of his own family.

" Give them all my love when you write to them, and tell them their kind remembrances were very pleasant to me. Also to the dear ones at the west end,* espe-cially congratulations to——on his marriage. Long may the happy pair live to enjoy the bright sunshine, goodly fruits and social blessings of this delightfully ordered, but much maligned world. I wish I was good

---

*His sister Sophia, (Mrs. Jonathan Ballard) was then still living. A strong, gentle, sacrificing spirit, she was always, through all his wanderings, in active sympathy with her brother. A few months after his death at Yokohama, she too was called to the mansions above.

enough to stay and live upon it a hundred years longer
—but no, the divine appointment is best, and if God
was so good as to give me one life, I can trust Him to
give me another one suitable to all my wants, in some
of those resplendent orbs where Christ has gone to fit
up the many mansions."

" To Son, June 20, '85· As for me, it is impossible that
I should hold out much longer.   .   .   .   But God is
good to me.   How often I think, ' He maketh my bed
in my sickness,' and thus far He has spared me from
severe pain.   Whatever His wish is—that is my wish,
and therefore my mind is at peace."   " *I am getting ready
for my journey,*" he said to a fellow laborer, who visited
him some months later.

A favorite verse of his, which he gave as a motto to
his loved ones in the Yokohama home, was from Whit-
tier's confession of faith entitled " The Eternal Goodness," a poem which struck a true chord with his own
views of the character of God.

> " I know not where His islands lift
>   Their fronded palms in air ;
>   I only know I cannot drift
>   Beyond His love and care."

XL.

" WE had a fall of snow this morning, right in the midst of sunshine," the benumbed hand had written with difficulty on the 12th of March, 1885 ; "and again this noon we had a beautiful fall for about half an hour. Oh, if our Heavenly Father loves us so much as to provide for us such exquisite enjoyments in this life, we may be sure that he will not withdraw his goodness when we enter on a future state. I inclose the statistics of our printing—want to stay and print a few years more if it please God, not otherwise."

Last postal, August 8th. "The 5th of this month was the 69th anniversary of my baptism. I do not think I am gaining any, although I am working hard eight or ten hours every day, to get the Hymn-book finished up before the call comes. . . . All pretty well, though it is very sickly around us. Glad to get your letters, and to be remembered by friends."

The few remaining lines found in his diary, appear in Kawakatsu's handwriting :

Oct. 10, '85. " If there should be a monument erected over my grave, I enjoin it upon my executors and friends to have a very small plain stone, (costing not over twenty or twenty-five dollars,) with nothing upon it but this inscription :

In Memory of Nathan Brown, American Missionary. Born June 22, 1807; Died ——. *God bless the Japanese.*

(583)

[From last entry, Nov. 17, 1885.]   Looking into my Bible this morning without any design in reference to the place, I opened to the passage, 1st and 2nd verses of the 40th chapter of Isaiah, and with it came such a vivid impression of its application to myself, that I could not resist it as God's assurance of full pardon of all my transgressions.   It is the same feeling which I had at my conversion when a boy, and at intervals since. I now feel that God has fully reconciled me to himself, not by a partial pardon, but by a full and complete canceling of all alienation."

His last letter was written by Mrs. Brown's hand :

"Yokohama, Dec. 4, 1885.

Darling Lizzie and Willie :—I am really sorry that I cannot get up and write you a letter with my own hand, and I know you will be sadly disappointed, but our times are not in our own hands, and it is well they are not.   Although the doctors deny that I have paralysis, it is plain that I am growing a little worse every week. . . .   We are sending a fire-box, [Japanese foot-warmer] and lots of kindlers, and are glad to hear that they take, in your country.   Your donkey was the prettiest, funniest thing I ever saw.

I have got through my hymn-book, except the index, over 300 pages, which is a great relief.   I have been hard at work with an amanuensis every day. . . . I have been trying to get the lingual affinities, which I have scribbled in the margin of Hepburn's dictionary, but have not succeeded very well.   I hoped to get eight or ten pages copied."

After describing some choice bamboos of an unusually large variety, which at his request had been set out that day in the garden, he says :

"I have lain and looked at the men from my window as they have planted them ; if they live, they will be a remembrance of me.

You would think that in my precarious health, I should be withdrawing my thoughts from the things of this world, and fixing them exclusively on religious matters, but it is not so ; every beautiful flower, every bird, hill-top, valley and ocean strike me with a richer loveliness, as the work of my Father's hand, than they ever did before. I should be willing to live forever in this world, but as He has otherwise ordained, I rejoice to pass away to such other spheres as He has appointed ; and especially to obtain a nearer access and stronger love for the dear Jesus, the union of God and man.

I hope I may be able to write you many letters yet ; even if it be by another hand. Write as often as you can.

Your loving Papa."

The hymn-book index was begun ; lying in the study on his dying bed, he labored on with the faithful Kawakatsu till the task at last dropped from the hand. "I have got as far as the hymns on heaven," he had said. December 19th, was his last day's work. His beloved brother and friend, Dr. J. C. Hepburn, called often, but could find no disease. He was simply worn out. During the following week he sank perceptibly each day. Says Mr. Bennett :

"His mind had been so absorbed in his employment up to the last, that he seemed little disposed to speak to any great extent as it was supposed a Christian would, about his first glimpses of the unseen and of heaven. This was a source of regret to many of his friends. Yet, had he never gratified them, his past life left no

room for doubt with regard to the future. As Cowper
says :

> ' When one that holds communion with the skies,
> 'Has filled his urn where those pure waters rise,
> And once more mingles with us meaner things,
> 'Tis even as if an angel shook his wings.
> Immortal fragrance fills the circuit wide
> That tells us whence his treasures are supplied.
> So when a ship, well freighted with the stores
> The sun matures on India's spicy shores,
> Has dropped her anchor and her canvas furled
> In some safe haven of our western world,
> 'Twere vain inquiry to what port she went ;
> The gale informs us, laden with the scent.'

From India, from Burma, and from his western home,
the gale, scent-laden, tells us that his treasures were not
laid up here, but in that securer realm not visible to
mortal eye. To the joy of all, however, just as his sun
was sinking, the clouds that seemed to have gathered
around the horizon, dispersed. On Sunday, six days
before his death, he sang with a clear voice the hymns,
" On Jordan's stormy banks I stand," and " There is a
happy land ;" and offered up, with much feeling the
prayer here recorded, as well as it could then be written
down :—" Now, O Lord, thou hast accomplished the
work for which thou didst create this little speck of
mortality, [something lost here]. Now, O Lord, I give
again to thee this precious soul to live for eternal ages.
I pray thee, that thou wouldst take that soul and put
it in a place of safe-keeping, with the Father, Son and
Holy Ghost ; there to live through eternal ages, O Lord
my God. I pause before I have finished, [something
like, 'for I know not how to speak'] but thou, O Lord,
wilt supply the words ; forgive me my sins, sanctify my

heart; O. have mercy upon me." The conclusion of the prayer was inaudible: and God alone knows the purport of that which the lips moved to utter, but could not,*

His bodily strength ebbed away with the ebbing tide of the old year. On Friday, New Year's day, consciousness returned; he asked for his wife, who, unknown to him, was herself now lying ill in an opposite room. She disobeyed the physician's directions, rose from her bed, and sat through that long peaceful day by his side. He was restful and conscious, but too weak for many words. Noticing a change about 7 P. M., Mrs. Brown knew, when the shade was removed from the lamp, that the end was near. His low inarticulate tones were those of prayer; the spirit was conscious that it was passing to the unseen world.

Almost his last effort of speech was to ask the forgiveness of his Japanese servant, a Christian woman who had faithfully nursed and waited upon him, and to whom he feared he might have spoken too sharply in moments of suffering. When he ceased to pray, she kneeling by his bedside, with tears and sobs, prayed for a blessing upon her master, who was also her pastor; that God would take him gently "in His arms without pain, to the bosom of the Father and the Son," and at the close of the prayer he responded, *"Amen and amen."*

The family and Mr. Bennett were summoned; about 8 o'clock a faint sound came from his lips; it was the name of his little son, who was then wakened and brought for the good-night kiss. His " Good-bye, my boy," was audible; the tones of prayer continued from time to time, and in the intervals his loved familiar hymns were sung by Mr. Curtis.

Then prayer and hymn ceased; while the watchers stood weeping, the life-strings were loosed painlessly in

---

*Address at the funeral.

solemn silence; at a few minutes past ten, Jan. 1, 1886, almost imperceptibly, the last faint breath left the lips.

> " So fades a summer cloud away,
>   So sinks the gale when storms are o'er,
> So gently shuts the eye of day,
>   So dies a wave along the shore."

Here in Japan, his hopes had been more than fulfilled. He had lived thirteen years, he had been permitted to give the New Testament to the Japanese in their own vernacular; in place of one, the mission had, in 1886, eight churches, with a membership more than eight-fold what he had dared to expect.

One of the laborers hired "early in the morning," this sleeper had been strengthened to do the full measure of a day's work; the now pulseless brain and hands had been blessed with nearly fourscore years of activity; those resting feet had journeyed on many an errand of difficulty and danger. Standing by the still figure, so lifelike in all but movement, his beloved associate, Rev. A. A. Bennett said : " During his long missionary career he has literally been 'in journeyings often, in perils of waters, in perils of robbers, in perils among his own countrymen, in perils by the heathen, in perils in the city, in perils in the wilderness, in perils in the sea.' "

Friends lingered long to look at this image of sleep; the snow-crowned head, the folded hands, the venerable form, robed in white to the feet. " His face looked so peaceful," wrote one, "and the soft white woolen robe, seemed befitting the purity and serenity of that quiet rest. The Doctor did not like cut-flowers, he liked things living, free and natural, 'unhurt by art.' The family next door, however, sent in a wreath of immor-telles, which lay on the coffin, and afterwards was placed in the grave."

On Monday afternoon, January 4th, the funeral services, conducted by Rev. Mr. Bennett, commenced at
the house by the singing of the hymn, "There is an
hour of peaceful rest." The Scriptures were read by
Rev. C. H. D. Fisher, of Tokio, and prayer was offered
by Rev. J. L. Ammerman. At the request of friends,
the Missionary's Call was chanted by Dr. Hepburn, Rev.
Mr. and Mrs. Correll, and Mrs. Bennett. The able and
comprehensive biographical address of Mr. Bennett was
based on the text, 2nd Sam. iii ; 38. Its opening sentence was, " He whose embarkation to yonder country
has caused our convening here to-day, and whose ten-
antless tent lies folded before us, was one of God's
noblemen."

Dr. Cochrane followed with appropriate remarks, and
the hymn, " How Firm a Foundation," was sung. It
had been the wish of the dying missionary that Dr.
Maclay and Dr. Hepburn, the veteran workers of the
Methodist and Presbyterian missions, should also speak
at his funeral. The former was now out of the city, on
a missionary tour, and did not hear of his friend's death
till his return, on the evening of the funeral. "I cannot speak," said Dr. Hepburn ; " I feel that I have lost
a brother ; but let me sing, early, before the addresses,
lest I should be unable to do so afterward." He did
sing, and the grand bass, though at times it trembled,
bound all parts into a fine harmony.

Meantime a simultaneous service in Japanese was
held in the chapel. At the close, one of the hymns
that had been composed by their aged pastor was given
out ; but the voices of the native converts wavered and
gave way ; the hymn could not be finished. A silence,
broken by sobs, fell upon the congregation. "It was
not of a pastor only they were bereaved ; it was of a
devoted father. He had loved them, and they were
overwhelmed by the thought that they would see his

face no more." In accordance with his expressed wish, his body was borne by six Japanese Christians from the house to the mission burying-ground. Rev. T. Kawakatsu walked beside the coffin, and the other native ordained preachers followed. A brief burial-service at the grave was conducted by Rev. W. J. White. While the hymn, "Jesus Lover of my Soul" was being sung, the coffin was lowered into the grave by his fellow-laborers, Rev. Messrs. Bennett, Fisher, Thomson and White, and his sons-in-law, Messrs. McArthur and Curtis.

"A pilgrim laid to rest,' writes Mrs. McArthur, Jan. 5, "he was not, for God took him. The work He had given him to do, finished, the life here finished, the one in heaven begun; eternal rest with Christ, now his."

Kawakatsu, recalling his eleven years' association with the missionary, and instructions received from him, writes, Jan. 21, 1886:

"You know we completed the **New** Testament once, a few years ago, and soon after we began to revise it. We reached the eighth chapter of Hebrews, and he left me alone. It is his will that I complete the remaining parts of the New Testament [revision], so I am working with that all day in his study-room. I hope you will pray for me that I may revise it correctly."

Mr. Bennett took Mr. Brown's hymn-book manuscript, finished indexing, and issued the book before the close of the year. He says in the preface:

"Years ago, when it was commonly said that 'the Japanese cannot sing,' Dr. Brown commenced work on hymns for them, and his rendering of the Lord's Prayer was probably the first Christian hymn in their language. . . . On this [hymn-book] he worked till his palsied hand could no longer hold a pen. . . . Again and again has the longing asserted itself, that he had been spared to complete the work upon which he toiled so gladly. 'But,' as he himself once wrote in regard to one of his co-workers, 'all is well. The crown prepared for him he has now received, the golden harp is in his hands, and the undying music of heaven is already familiar to his enraptured ears.'"

Other dropped threads were taken up. With Mr. Bennett's assistance and direction, Kawakatsu completed the revision of the Testament, and the new edition was issued. Colporteurs went about in the country villages, and the scriptures were kept in circulation.

In the fall Mrs. Brown used the printing office for the girls' school, there establishing a Christian home, where the children could remain during the week, visiting their parents on Saturday. It was interesting, she says, to watch the development of character and change wrought by Christianity, upon these girls. Their conduct, feelings and habits were noticeably elevated. Even the expression of their countenances showed it. Soul and conscience were awakened, and as a natural consequence, their faces were illumined. The girls in many cases brought their parents and friends to the meetings, and through their own conversion were the means of converting friends and relatives.

The following occurrences of the summer of 1886 show some of the results of missionary work, and at the same time give Japan's own answer to the question sometimes asked in America: "Do the Japanese, law-abiding, intelligent and progressive as they have shown themselves to be, *need* Christianity?"

A foreign vessel lay at quarantine in Yokohama harbor. Two of the sailors were ill of cholera. "Pray for us," they said to a Japanese health officer, who had come on board. He was a deacon of the little church so dear to the aged pastor who went to his rest on New Year's day. The Japanese Christian told the European sailors of the Lord Jesus Christ, and they died, it is hoped, in the Christian faith.

The disease was spreading rapidly through the country. The government made noble efforts to relieve suffering, but men dropped dying in out-of-the-way corners, trying to hide from the police, so great was their horror of the over-crowded hospitals. It was a time of general misery and dread. At the breaking up of quarantine and removal of patients, the health officer was sent in charge of them to open a new hospital, and for two or three days was without help, the floors crowded with patients, and he obliged to hasten from dead to dying, dragging the dead in haste away from the living, and returning to do what he could for those that might be saved. "I expected to die," he said, "but I knew I must do my duty as long as I could stand." Nurses were afterwards obtained, but some of them proved incapable and brutal to the last degree. Convalescents relapsed and died, because these inhuman attendants neglected them and stole their food. No coolies could be found willing to come in and take the corpses away to the dead-house, and thence remove them by night to the cremarium. The health officer came to Mrs. Brown and asked for help. Two Christian women on the back veranda overheard the conversation and volunteered. Another who was studying and teaching in the school, came in the next morning and said:

"Sensai, [teacher] I am going to the cholera-hospital to help O Tomi, and my father is going as a nurse."

A Christian man said "I will go, and do the wash-ing;" and a Christian widow, mother of òne of the pupils, "I will go and take care of the babies;" for even infants were in the hospital, taken there with their sick mothers. Another and another came as a free-will offering, and were sent into the dreaded conta-gion, there to be confined for weeks, not knowing or asking whether they were to receive remuneration for their services.

The hospital physicians now found patients and con-valescents kindly cared for, and the death-rate de-creased. After a time, the voice of prayer and singing began to be heard in the convalescent wards. The nurses had taken their gospels and hymn-books with them. What an opening to tell the story of Him Who healed the sick in Galilee!

Meantime the physicians had brought order out of confusion. On visiting the hospital, Mrs. Brown found all its appointments admirable, and the methods system-atic. It was a large building, two or three miles out-side of the city limits, and at that time contained hun-dreds of sick persons. Each patient lay on a low pine cot, comfortably dressed and scrupulously clean. A card at the foot of each, indicated the age, date of entrance, &c., as in European hospitals. Medicines and food were kept in tubs of ice. This government hospital was un-der the supervision of the Japanese themselves, assisted by two foreign physicians.

"How do you make such men and women as these nurses of yours?" one of the native doctors asked. "I wish we could find more of them. They are very different from those we employed before."

"They have heard about Jesus Christ," was the reply, "and have learned, like Him, to care for the bodies and souls of others."

Does Japan need Christianity?

In her ferment of growth and thought; throughout her complex upreachings and developments; does she need that simple trust in the Father which its Founder enjoins, and that loyal acceptance of Him as her spiritual Leader and King, which will hold her safe amid the dangers of her present position, and safe to everlasting life?

That this crown and pearl of blessings might rest upon Japan, was the meaning of the prayer graven on the missionary's heart and on his tomb. His dust is one with that of his island home; and one with its dear people is his living spirit; praying still,

"GOD BLESS THE JAPANESE."

APPENDIX.

A.

No analysis of character has been attempted in the preceding pages; but some who knew the missionary, and were co-laborers with him in the fields of human progress, have noted his more prominent traits in correspondence and newspaper articles. "He would not equivocate, or dissemble, or compromise," wrote Dr. Patton. "To truth and duty he held an unswerving allegiance, and by no temptation or threat or sacrifice, could he be influenced to waver in any course dictated by his convictions." Dr. J. A. Smith describes him as "a genial and soulful nature, *genuine* in every way; strong in conviction and in purpose. . . Peculiarly sturdy in his convictions, he had a heart as tender as that of a child." Dr. Burlingham says: "The inscription he requested to be put upon his tombstone is like him, modest, simple, true." And an Assam missionary: "Some write much, others work more, and Dr. Brown was one of the workers."

"It was my good fortune," [wrote Bishop Harris in the Methodist *Christian Advocate*] "while in Japan, in 1873, to make the acquaintance of this devoted man, and no one received me more cordially or manifested a deeper interest in the missionary work of our own church than did he. During one of our conversations I incidentally mentioned a piece of poetry on the subject of missions, which had often touched and melted my heart as I read it, and to my great delight I learned from him that he was its author. He then gave me a copy of the poetry, as last revised by him."

"You will probably hear otherwise of the death of dear Dr. Brown," Mr. Fisher wrote from Tokio; "every one of us will mourn as a personal loss, the going from us of the father who always had, even for the youngest, a kind smile and cheerful word."

"What a solemn joy there is in thinking of the consummation of that grand and fruitful life; his calm and trustful moving on into the unseen world with the firm step of one whose eternal life began long ago, and is not to be shaken by any mere accident of presence or absence from the body."

A FRIEND, Baltimore, Feb. 8, 1886.

(597)

THE MISSIONARY'S CALL.

Words arranged from
Rev. N. BROWN, Asam, Asia.

Music by
EDWARD HOWE, Jr.

CHANT.

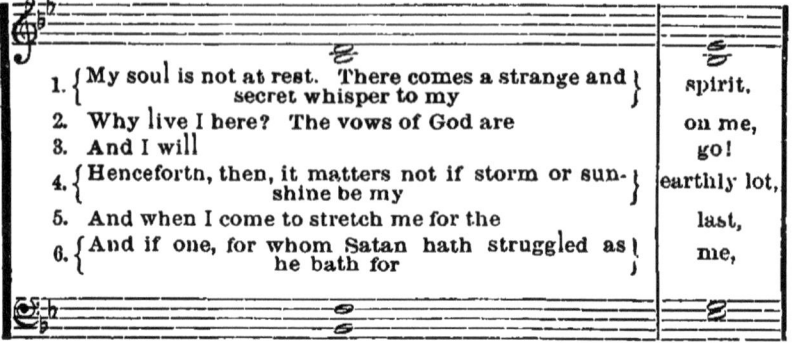

1. { My soul is not at rest. There comes a strange and secret whisper to my } spirit.
2. Why live I here? The vows of God are on me,
3. And I will go!
4. { Henceforth, then, it matters not if storm or sunshine be my } earthly lot,
5. And when I come to stretch me for the last,
6. { And if one, for whom Satan hath struggled as he hath for } me,

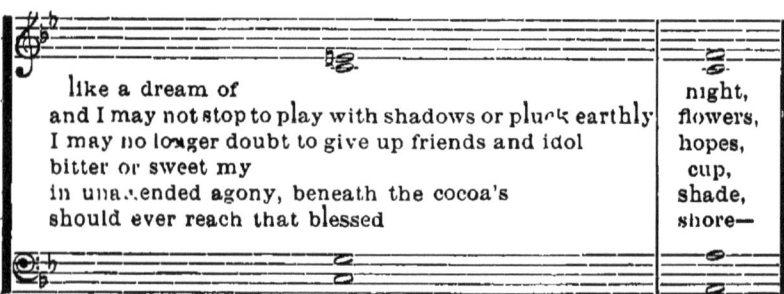

like a dream of night,
and I may not stop to play with shadows or pluck earthly flowers,
I may no longer doubt to give up friends and idol hopes,
bitter or sweet my cup,
in unattended agony, beneath the cocoa's shade,
should ever reach that blessed shore—

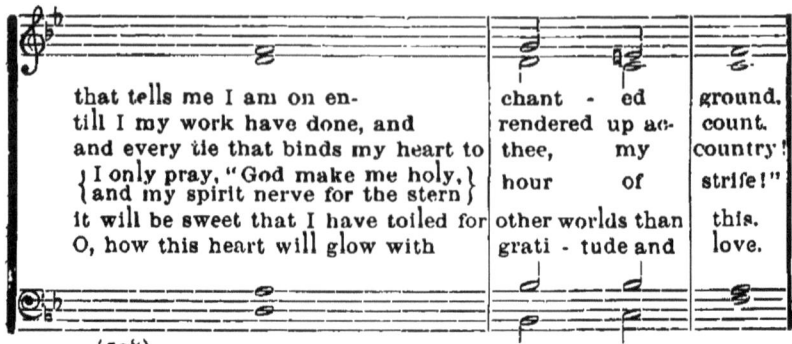

that tells me I am on enchanted ground.
till I my work have done, and rendered up account.
and every tie that binds my heart to thee, my country!
{ I only pray, "God make me holy, and my spirit nerve for the stern } hour of strife!"
it will be sweet that I have toiled for other worlds than this.
O, how this heart will glow with grati - tude and love.

(598)

Vivace.—CHORUS—after each of the first five verses.

The voice of my de‑part‑ed Lord, "Go, teach all

The voice of my de‑part‑ed Lord, "Go, teach all

nations," Comes on the night‑air, and a‑wakes mine ear.

nations," Comes on the night‑air, and a‑wakes mine ear.

CHORUS—for last verse.

Through a‑ges of e‑ter‑nal years, My spir‑it nev‑er shall re‑

Through a‑ges of e‑ter‑nal years, My spir‑it nev‑er shall re‑

pent That toil and suffering once were mine be‑low.

pent That toil and suffering once were mine be‑low.

(599)

B.

BRAHMAN SERMONS.

At one of the meetings of the American Oriental Society, of which he was a corporate member, Mr. Brown delivered, October, 1861, a Brahman sermon, in which he reproduced the style and arguments of Hindu priests as actually heard in Assam. The following is taken from the Journal of the Oriental Society :—

" Dr. Brown began with a summary exposition of the popular religion of India as distinguished from the abstruse metaphysical systems of the Hindu religious books. Its fundamental ideas are clear and simple. The universe consists of matter and spirit: the latter is God, the former the body or dress in which He is clothed. All mind is Deity: as fire may be separated and become a thousand fires, which are still all the same fire, so the original mind is divided into millions of minds, yet all are parts of the same whole. Minds pass from one body into another, and thus go on through an almost endless round of transmigration before they are again absorbed into the Deity. Two antagonistic principles are observed in constant operation—the principle of increase and preservation and the principle of destruction: these opposing powers are Vishnu, the Preserver, and Siva, the Destroyer. Preaching, of course, bears no such part in the Hindu religious services and worship as in ours, yet it was not unusual at religious festivals for learned Brahmans to harangue the assembled crowds of their countrymen on matters of religion. Their manner was very quiet, their posture a sitting one, their style of delivery, a cadenced monotone, and all gestures were eschewed; anything different from this was thought unsuited to the dignity and sacredness of the theme. Dr. Brown read in full such a harangue as is thus given ; a great part of it had been taken down connectedly as the report of a single actual address, but he had somewhat enlarged and completed it by adding a few other of the commonplaces of these discourses. It began with a lament over the degeneracy of modern times as compared with ancient, and the resulting judgments brought upon the country—in part, the domination of foreigners and the intrusion of foreign teachers. The staple of the discourse consisted thenceforward in denunciations of the missionaries, and artful and ingenious appeals to the prejudices of the auditors against them and their doctrine. Dr. Brown was himself specially denounced and threatened with misfortune for having in his profane possession a *Salgram,* or Sacred Stone, such as is revered by the Brahmans as a direct incarnation of Vishnu. The stone referred to was passed around for inspection of the members present. It was of a rounded shape, rather larger than the fist, of a very dark green color, and open on one side into a hollow within, which showed the interior cavity of some fossil shell, apparently an ammonite."

C.

LINGUAL AFFINITIES.

Mr. Brown explained some of the principles on which fair deductions as to the relationships of languages could be based, in an address on race affinities, made after his return to America :—

" Speech is the crowning glory of man, and I have a firm belief that we shall learn more from the utterances of the human voice, concerning the affinity or non-affinity of different peoples, than from any other source. If we find no analogy, there is no connection. If we find a few words identical, the connection is remote or near, according to the character of the words. If the fundamental, essential terms of any two languages, such as father, mother, head, hand, are alike, while the great bulk of words show no resemblance, it argues a remote descent from a common origin. If a large number of words connected with commerce, trade, or such as may be supposed to come from modern intercourse [correspond,] it shows no radical connection at all. If people in different parts of the earth use the same numerals, like the Hindus and Europeans, it shows a very close connection. If the numerals are widely different, like the Tartar and Hindu, it will show either that the races have no common origin, or that the separation took place in a very early age, before the use of numerals was established. If in a distant land, like Mexico or Peru, we should find very few of the fundamental terms expressive of common objects coinciding with those of the eastern continent, while the terms of religion, government, and royal names exhibited a remarkable agreement, we should not only conclude that these were conquered countries, whose original languages had maintained their ground against the foreign element, but we should also be convinced that these conquerors came from beyond the sea. We should be greatly strengthened in this conviction, if the present inhabitants had lost the meaning of these proper names, religious terms, and governmental titles, and could give no account of their origin. Philology has within her secret archives a voluminous history, and it will one day be spread before the world.

But we must not expect too much, or be discouraged, if at the first glance, we find fewer resemblances than we expected. So many exaggerated statements have been made from hasty comparisons, which further research has disproved, that careful scholars have gone to the other extreme. . . . The true discoverer doubts long ; he tries his diamond in every variety of light, and not until the evidence is positive, exhaustive and uniform does he feel willing to remit his investigations and record his verdict."

D.

Prof. Max Müller to Sir Charles Trevelyan, Oxford, Oct. 25, '54 (By permission). "I return Mr. Brown's letter with many thanks—it is a very interesting letter—it has turned a name with which I have been familiar for many years, into a real man, and what a man! I always had the greatest reverence and love for missionaries; I heard and read much about them when I was a child, and for a long time I wanted to be a missionary myself. Perha;.; I may be so still, for whenever I read their accounts and see their letters, I feel as if *there* was the proper field to work. Only, these mission-aries ought to be left much freer to act according to their own discretion. It would be quite enough if one missionary gained the intimacy, friendship and esteem of one or two natives during the whole of his life. In this way alone Christian doctrines can be expected to strike root on foreign soil; they will grow slowly, adapt themselves to the nature of the soil, assume perhaps a different shape, expression and color from what they have with us, but they will no longer be like a hot-house plant, but grow and prosper in the open air when their season comes. Numbers are nothing, but missionaries are too apt to forget that their Lord and Master was content with having gained twelve disciples, and that the growth of doctrines has never been by addition, but by multiplication.

I should like to write to Mr. Brown, and to send him my book on the Turanian Languages, where I have had to quote him so many times. He is one of the few men whose opinion I should like to have on the classifi-cation of these dialects on the borders of India and China, which I have attempted there for the first time."

E.

VERNACULAR CHRISTIAN LITERATURE FOR JAPAN.

In a paper read before the General Conference of Missionaries, at Osaka, Japan, in 1883, Mr. Brown asks:

"In what form shall a Christian literature be presented to the Japanese? The plain answer to this question would naturally be, that the books pub-lished must be in the vernacular, and in the character most widely known and most easily read by the Japanese. Such an answer will not, however, be accepted by all, probably not by a majority of the Japanese *literati* of the present day. The hieroglyphic system, introduced along with the Buddhist religion over a thousand years ago, has obtained such an entire control among the educated classes that the cultivation of the native language through the medium of its own natural resources is looked upon as an impossibility. Professors in the colleges and elsewhere have uttered their protest, warning the Japanese of the injury done to their own tongue, and the folly of attempting to make a hieroglyphic system like the Sinico-japanese, a vehicle of western learning and popular advancement; in the Japanese newspapers we have constant complaints of the inefficiency of this cumbrous macaroni writing, rendering it impossible even for government officials to read the orders addressed to them without the help of an interpreter; we have the expressed opinions of many missionaries that the corruption of Japanese through the medium of Chinese is a calamity and a barrier to all real improvement; yet these complaints generally end by saying: ' But what can we do ? How can the evil be remedied ? '

. . . The real foe with which the Christian literature of Japan has to contend is the hieroglyphic system. This system is entrenched in a citadel well-nigh impr gnable. It has a whole army of instructors depending for their livelihood on the teaching and interpreting of Chinese, together with the entire Buddhist priesthood, whose ministrations are dependent upon and interwoven with that character. All these parties would be in arms if the government should attempt to change their course of instruction from Chinese to the pure vernacular. It is difficult to find teachers who are willing to be employed in mission schools, unless the chief part of their teaching is in Chinese. They consider it to be beneath their dignity to give instruction merely in their native tongue. Such are the obstacles that stand in the way of every missionary who wishes to reach the masses of the people through a medium that all can understand.

Of the two great systems of writing that have hitherto divided the world, there can be little doubt that the hieroglyphic or ideographic is the older. In primitive times the first attempts at depicting thoughts on bark or stone must have been much the same as they still are amongst the Indians of North America and other uncivilized tribes. The earliest experiment of a savage would not be to picture a sound, or to invent a character that should be the representative of a sound. He would sooner picture a man, or a horse, a tree or a house, than seek arbitrary signs for the forms of speech by which these objects were known. That was an invention of later date, involving a much higher type of civilization than either the naming of objects or their pictorial representation. Hieroglyphic or picture-writing has two elements, the object or idea and its pictorial representative addressed to the eye. It cannot properly be called a language or tongue, because the tongue and other vocal organs have no part in this mode of communication. Speech also deals with but two elements, connecting objects and ideas with the sounds representing them, doing for the ear what hieroglyphic writing does for the eye. While it is a far superior mode of intercommunication, it still needs the written characters to make it perfect. Primitive man had, in speech, a twisted rope of two strands, idea and sound; in hieroglyphics another, of which the intertwined strands were idea and picture; but the two cords were isolated, rendering no assistance to each other, without compactness, strength or beauty, till some bright genius conceived the happy thought of making the rope of three strands instead of two, combining idea and sound, sound and picture all in one. Thus Aleph and Beth (Ox and House), each became lord of a new domain; no longer exhausting their power upon the two ideas they first represented, their respective offices were extended to the hundreds and thousands of vocables of which they formed constituent parts. Twenty other hieroglyphs were selected for similar honors, and the number of characters necessary for written language diminished from twice or thrice ten thousand to *twenty-two.* This was one of those grand discoveries from which it would be as impossible for the human race to go back, as it would be to overthrow the teachings of Galileo and Newton.

If the hieroglyphic system is good for China with its hundred different languages, it is good for Japan, England, America and all other countries, since it can as well be used with proper adaptations for one spoken language as for another. The hieroglyphics of Assyria, Babylon and Egypt sunk to oblivion in their contest with an alphabet popularizing the literature that had been hidden in mouldy temples and in the caskets of a privileged class. There was, no doubt, just as much opposition then to opening the mysteries of literature, science and religion to the common people through an easily acquired and rapidly written phonetic system as there now is to the printing of Japanese scriptures and other religious works in the native phonetic character—the ' women and children's writing,' as it is contemptuously called. But the hieroglyphics went down, never to come up again, except as curiosities for learned antiquarians to decipher. So will it be with the hieroglyphics of China, venerable and wonderful as they are, challenging universal admiration and presenting the most remarkable example of ingenuity, literary toil and patience that the world has ever seen. But no scheme of picture-writing can co-exist with modern civilization; the masses can never be chained down to a system that requires eight or ten years to obtain even a partial knowledge of the characters necessary for ordinary reading.

Can we, as missionaries, with any propriety be called on to aid in bolstering up a fallen and decayed system, which has died out in all the old nations of the earth except one, and which even there, in its own home, is tottering to its foundations ? Are we justified in spending thousands upon thousands every year for teaching Chinese in our missionary schools and seminaries, to gratify a pedantic attachment to the old relics of Buddhist literature, merely because their antiquity and sacred associations have made them venerable in the eyes of the learned? Shall we not rather anticipate whatever reformations we perceive to be inevitable and thus hasten the benefits which Christian civilization is sure to bring? Doubtless we ought to reach as many minds as possible, by whatever language or written character we may find necessary ; but it certainly is not necessary to give the preference to foreign words, foreign idioms, and to foreign hieroglyphics.''

Proceedings of the Osaka Conference, pp. 401–405.

F.

TEXT AND TRANSLATION.

Of variations in the text of ancient manuscripts, indicated in his trans. lation by interlinear notes, Mr. Brown says :

" We have availed ourselves of the small space necessarily intervening between the lines, to insert, in Roman letters, the marginal readings arising from manuscript variations, such as the Bible Union have inserted in foot. notes. We have done this chiefly for the benefit of native preachers and students who' would otherwise be at a loss to know why our translation does not conform to the English version, with which they are generally familiar. The ancient manuscripts being divided into classes, and num. bered according to their respective ages, the eye sees at a glance whether a reading is sustained by the Sinaitic, Vatican, and other copies made during the first five centuries, or whether it is a later production, dating perhaps from the ninth or tenth."

Of these and other aids to the Bible student, Dr. Griffis writes in a newspaper paragraph :

" My attention has been called, by Rev. G. T. Smith, of Akita, Japan, to the omission of an honored name and laborer in the work of Bible transla. tion in Japan. In my article, on The Complete Bible in Japanese, printed in your columns some months ago, I forgot to mention that Rev. Nathan Brown, D. D., translated the New Testament into Japanese, and published it in excellent form some months before the Union Committee's version was printed. For the first time, and no later than yesterday, I secured a copy of Dr. Brown's work from Rev. Dr. Murdock, Secretary of the Baptist Mis- sionary Union, and I have just enjoyed the pleasure of looking over it. I find that the volume is a handsome octavo, well printed in the cursive script, and thoroughly well furnished with aids to the Bible student. The Greek word *baptizo* and its grammatical variants are translated by the various forms of the Japanese word *shizumeru*, which is a remarkably close equiva- lent for the Greek.

. . . My unintentional omission of the name and work of Dr. Brown is all the more surprising to myself because I enjoyed the honor and great benefit of his personal acquaintance, as well as his respect and confidence, as several of his letters to me attest. After sixty years, and at the end of long and arduous service of his Master in Assam, this veteran missionary, scholar and translator came to Japan and gave twelve years of studious toil and personal influence to the work of propagating the gospel. Yet I had never, until yesterday, seen a copy of his work.

WILLIAM ELLIOT GRIFFIS.

Shawmut Church, Boston."

G.

ADDITIONAL POEMS OF REV. NATHAN BROWN.

TO A FRIEND:

ON THE DEATH OF HER INFANT SON

How oft the smile, beloved friend,
   That lit thy joyous brow,
Hath chased the gloom from another's breast,
   But a shade is o'er thee now !
Thou smilest yet when others smile,
   But I mark the rising sigh,
And the tear that cannot be repressed
   Comes gushing in thine eye.

Oh, did the stroke so deeply wound
   Thy soul in its bitterness,
When we bore to thee the lifeless form,
   For a mother's lips to press ?
Too rudely did we tear the dead
   From thine embrace away,
Ere yet the heart's deep cords were loosed,
   That bound thee to the clay ?

And when thou passest, lone and sad,
   Yon grassy hillock by,
Why thither turns, with a wasting grief,
   Thy fondly gazing eye ?
Thy child, the bright and beautiful,
   Is not beneath that sod ;
He is far away, he singeth songs
   In the dwelling place of God !

Then wipe thy tears and hush thy sighs ;
   Fond mother, it is well,
For him and thee, thus early called
   To bid the long farewell !
But by thy loved and absent one,
   And the solemn judgment seat,
Oh, be thou ready for the hour
   When ye again shall meet !

Lines written in an old Album:

> I often taste a bitter thing,
> Yet not for this would I that taste resign;
> I often hear unwelcome sounds, and words
> Unkind, yet not for this would I be deaf.
> The frozen lake is ruffled not by winds
> When bleak they drive, nor touched by sunbeam soft;
> The frozen heart feels not the chilling blast,
> Nor grieves nor joys; oh, let not mine be froze!

Bennington, 1830.

LINES IN AN ALBUM.

> A lone and weary way we tend
>   Through a wide, wide wilderness;
> Yet here and there we meet a friend,
>   And a word of kindliness.
>
> Anon we part, and the face we miss,
>   But the word is not forgot,
> And the radiance thrown by the kindly tone
>   Neither sorrow nor time can blot.
>
> We may meet no more in the crossings of life,
>   Where the night and the shadows illude,
> But our paths will unite when the morn grows bright,
>   And the greetings shall be renewed.

Philadelphia, 1856.

THE LORD'S PRAYER IN ENGLISH VERSE.

BY REV. N. BROWN.

I.

> Our Father in heaven, be hallowed thy name;
> Thy kingdom come and the world reclaim;
> As the angels in heaven thy pleasure fulfill,
> So here on the earth be accomplished thy will.

II.

> Give us, Father, the food on which daily we live;
> And forgive us our debts as we others forgive;
> Leave us not in the path of temptation to stray,
> But from evil deliver, and guide in thy way.

DOXOLOGY.

> For thine is the kingdom, the glory and power;
> Amen; be it so, Lord, henceforth evermore.

Lightning Source UK Ltd.
Milton Keynes UK
UKHW011428231118
332790UK00011B/1586/P